PRIESTHOOD

A History of Ordained Ministry in the Roman Catholic Church

KENAN B. OSBORNE, O.F.M.

PAULIST PRESS
New York / Mahwah

Cover art by Meinrad Craighead.
Cover design by Gloria C. Ortiz.

The Publisher gratefully acknowledges excerpts reprinted from R.M. Grant, *The Apostolic Fathers* (Thomas Nelson & Sons) used with permission; Letter of Clement, n. 42 and n. 44, 1-3 is reprinted from *Ancient Christian Writers, Letter of Clement,* trans. J.A. Kleist (Paulist Press, N.J.) used with permission; St. John Chrysostom, *On the Priesthood,* is reprinted with permission of Paulist Press. The selection appeared in *Patrology vol. 3* by Johannes Quasten; Translation of the Tridentine document on the sacrament of Order, selections from the chapter and each of the canons is from *The Church Teaches: Documents of the Church in English Translation,* trans. J.F. Clarkson, J.H. Edwards, W.J. Kelly, J.W. Welch (Herder Book Co., 1955), used by permission.

Library of Congress Cataloging-in-Publication Data

Osborne, Kenan B.
    Priesthood: a history of ordained ministry in the Roman Catholic
Church/Kenan B. Osborne.
        p.   cm.
    Bibliography: p.
    Includes index.
    ISBN 0-8091-3032-7 (pbk.): $14.95
    1. Catholic Church—Clergy—History of doctrines.   2. Clergy—
History of doctrines.   I. Title.
BX1912.076   1989   88-28171
262'.142'09—dc19   CIP

Published by Paulist Press
997 Macarthur Boulevard
Mahwah, New Jersey 07430

Printed and bound in the
United States of America

Contents

Excursus:
On the Question of the New Testament
and the Ordination of Women   86

4. Ministry in the Second Christian Century:
90 to 210 A.D.   89

5. Ministry in the High Patristic Church:
210 to 600 A.D.   130

Dedicated to
John S. Cummins, D.D.
Bishop of Oakland, California

Preface

When I first began working on this material, I had hoped to cover a history of ministry in the Roman Catholic Church, which included not only the ordained ministry but also the ministry of lay Christians as well. It was part of my hope to deal in depth with the issue of Christian women in ministry, particularly as this ministry was related to the ordained priest and deacon. The first drafting indicated clearly that this could not be done, at least by me. There was a constant moving back and forth along historical periods, which tended to complicate and obscure the flow of discussion. It became clearer and clearer that the history of the ordained ministry needed attention first. It remains my hope to write a companion volume, tracing the ministry of lay Christians throughout the centuries as also the very complex issue of women and ordained ministry.

A second issue became equally clear: the role of the episkopos and then the bishop was key. In the patristic Church, the episkopos dominates the theology and practice of ecclesial ministry. In the Middle Ages, however, theologians and canonists alike removed the episcopacy from the sacrament of Holy Order. How could this have happened? And what were its implications? These were questions which needed an answer. In answering them, one sees that an entire theology of ordained ministry is affected, often in adverse ways. Vatican II officially restored the episcopacy to the sacrament of Holy Order for the Roman Church, but such a step has created many new issues, particularly the issue of episcopal power and papal power. This remains part of the unfinished agenda.

1

A third issue clearly arose: what is the relationship between Holy Baptism and Holy Order? Often this relationship is seen as that between the priesthood of all believers and the ordained priesthood. Once more the issue is theologically excellent, but the explanation remains part of the unfinished agenda.

There is, then, an unfinished agenda to this study, or any study, on ministry in the Church. The disunity in the Christian community has found some healing in the contemporary ecumenical movement, but the lack of unity remains, affecting all parts of the Church, including its ministry. The contemporary emphasis on Jesus as the primordial sacrament seems to offer a major insight into the healing of Christian life, and it will be this presence of Jesus, the primordial minister, which will thread this volume together, and hopefully lead all Christian ministry into deeper unity.

The Ministry of Jesus

In many ways the documents of Vatican II instruct us to refocus more clearly the fundamental relationship between Christian ministry and the ministry of Jesus himself. Jesus' own ministry remains the abiding source, model and dynamism of all Christian ministry, ordained and non-ordained. It is the source, since, as Vatican II reiterates, it is Jesus himself who both calls and commissions one to Christian ministry. It is the model, since Christian ministry is gospel ministry and must reflect the true Light of the World, Jesus himself (cf. the very title of the dogmatic constitution on the Church: *Lumen Gentium*) in all that it attempts to accomplish. It is the dynamism, since only the power of Jesus' own ministry brings any power to Christian ministry. For these reasons, a book on ministry rightfully begins with Jesus.

In this present book we will look primarily at ordained ministry, but much of what is written can be applied to unordained ministry as well. For practical reasons, it seems wise to focus only on ordained ministry, leaving the issue of unordained ministry to a later date. To attempt a combination would in many ways lead only to confusion, since it would mean continually crisscrossing the same material. For the sake of clarity, then, we will confine ourselves only to the issue of the ordained minister, realizing that unordained ministry is, as well, a major ministry in the Church.

The ministry of Jesus, as we shall consider it in this first chapter, will be viewed in the following way:

1. A description of the characteristics of the ministry of Jesus himself;

2. A description of the characteristics of the message of the earthly ministry of Jesus;

3. A description of the ministry of the risen Jesus.

1. THE CHARACTERISTICS OF JESUS' OWN MINISTRY

When one reads the four gospels, one finds that the ministry of Jesus evinces several major characteristics or qualities which in many ways both describe and define his ministry. The following are, perhaps, some of the more important of these characteristics or qualities.

A. JESUS' MINISTRY IS FROM GOD

Again and again, we come across gospel passages which indicate very clearly that the Father sent Jesus. Let us consider some of the more important gospel passages, and we begin with Mark.[1]

1, 11:   You are my Son, the Beloved; my favor rests on you.

2, 1–12:   This passage deals with the cure of the paralytic and the question is raised: "How can this man talk like that? He is blaspheming. Who can forgive sins, but God?" Jesus, then, cures the paralytic, "to prove to you that the Son of Man has authority on earth to forgive sins." God is clearly presented as the source of Jesus' healing ministry.

8, 30:   "You are the Christ," is Peter's response to Jesus, that is, "you are the one sent by God."

9, 8:   This is my Son, the Beloved. Listen to him.

12, 1–12:   In the parable of the wicked husbandmen, the son who was sent last of all was also killed. The point is clearly made that Jesus has been sent, but he, too, is rejected.

14, 32–42:   In the Gethsemani scene, the prayer of Jesus reflects his dependence on the Father: "But let it be as you, not I, would have it."

In the gospel of Matthew, we find an even greater stress on the Father's sending of Jesus. Matthew repeats many of the instances in Mark which we have just mentioned, but he adds to them as well.

7, 21:   The true disciple is called: "The person who does the will of my Father in heaven." Matthew, however, presents Jesus as the true disciple of the Father.

11, 26–27:   "Yes, Father, for that is what it pleased you to do. Everything has been entrusted to me by my Father; no one knows the Son except the Father, just as no one knows the Father except the Son and those to whom the Son chooses to reveal him."

12, 15–21:   In this section Matthew cites Is 42, 1–4, which begins: "Here is my servant whom I have chosen; I will endow him with my spirit, and he will proclaim the true faith to the nations." Matthew applies this to Jesus.

12, 22–28:   In this section Jesus states that he casts out devils through the Spirit of God. In other words, God's Spirit is the empowering Spirit.

21, 11:   When Jesus enters Jerusalem in triumph, he is called: "This is the prophet, Jesus of Nazareth in Galilee."

Turning to Luke, we find once again a very clear understanding that it is God who has sent Jesus. J. Fitzmyer, in his commentary on Luke's gospel, highlights the central position that Jesus' journeying has in the gospel: "At the outset Luke notes that Jesus 'sets his face resolutely toward Jerusalem' (9:51), determined to face his destiny; that notice comes shortly after the transfiguration scene, in which Luke depicted Moses and Elijah conversing with Jesus about the *exodos,* 'departure,' that he was to complete in Jerusalem (9:31)."[2] This *exodos* is not simply his death, but his resurrection and ascension/ exaltation as well.

The *exodos* in the life and ministry of Jesus is from the Father, and Jesus is presented by Luke as fulfilling in an unswerving way this obedience to the Father's intentions. Jesus did not establish his own *exodos,* but the Father established it for Jesus. In Luke, Jesus' ministry is divinely ordained.

Luke uses many of the instances already mentioned in Mark and Matthew. There are some additional instances which are worthy to note:

2, 49:   "Did you not know that I must be about my Father's affairs?"

4, 14:   Luke notes that Jesus begins his ministry with "the power of the Spirit in him."

4, 16–30:   In this passage, Jesus in the synagogue at Nazareth reads from Is 61, 1-2: "The spirit of the Lord has been given to me, for he has anointed me. He has sent me to. . . . " Jesus then claims that this text of mission is fulfilled in him, namely, that he has been sent by the Father, just as Isaiah had foretold.

24, 13-35:   In the account of the two men on the way to Emmaus, Jesus joins them and explains: "Was it not ordained that the Christ should suffer and so enter into his glory? Then starting with Moses and going through all the prophets, he explained to them the passages throughout the scriptures that were about himself." Luke clearly says that God ordained this fate of the Christ.

The gospel of John, perhaps, is the most articulate in emphasizing the initiative of the Father in the ministry of Jesus.[3] It would be excessive to recount all the Johannine passages on this theme; a few should suffice:

1, 29-34:   John the Baptist's testimony on the Spirit descending over Jesus focuses this concern of the evangelist right from the start.

1, 40-51:   The first disciples of Jesus call him the Messiah, i.e., "the one Moses wrote about in the Law, the one about whom the prophets wrote."

3, 1-3:   Nicodemus acknowledges that Jesus is one who has come from God.

3, 16-21:   "God loved the world so much that he gave his only Son . . . For God sent his Son into the world . . . so that it may be plainly seen that what he does is done in God."

3, 29-36:   John the Baptist speaks about the one who "comes from above . . . who comes from heaven . . . whom God has sent. . . . God gives him the Spirit without reserve. The Father loves the Son and has entrusted everything to him."

4, 34:   "My food is to do the will of the one who has sent me and to complete his work."

This listing of Johannine passages could continue beyond the fourth chapter of the gospel, but by now the point has been clearly made: the evangelist sees Jesus as the one sent by the Father and as the one who does the will of the Father. Jesus' ministry is from God.

This characteristic of Jesus' ministry, attested to by all four gospels, is quite important. This ministry of Jesus is, first of all, not self-initiated; rather, it depends totally on God. There is an effacing of the human ego here and a dependence on and deference to the will of the Father.

Secondly, in all of these passages it is evident that Jesus has not been selected by a community to enter into his ministry. The Jewish community did not elect him for this, nor did his own disciples choose him. Even the Twelve did not choose Jesus. The ministry of Jesus is not community-initiated nor community-ordained. It is completely from the Father. So, too, Christian ministry is not initiated by the community nor, in its deepest sense, ordained by the community. God initiates and ordains to ministry.

This fundamental characteristic of Jesus' ministry is important for an understanding of Christian ministry. A Christian minister, like Jesus, is not self-appointed, nor even community-appointed. Naturally, the person involved plays some role in responding to God's call, and the community, too, plays some role in accepting a person for ministry. There is, indeed, a role that the community plays in the selection process of Christian ministry, but it is the role of neither calling nor sending. In Christian history communities have often played a role in the "selection process" of their ministers, e.g., the role of presbyters in selecting the episkopoi in early Egypt; the role of the people of Rome in selecting the bishop of Rome. Even today we hear voices advocating a role in the "selection process" of bishops and pastors. One must, however, read history carefully and speak in measured terms, lest the very basis of Christian ministry, namely, that Christian ministry is basically a calling and commissioning from God, be rejected. The theology of ministry, strongly voiced in the documents of Vatican II, maintains that both the call and the commission of ministry is from God, not from self and not from the community. In this respect, the documents are simply relating Christian ministry to the ministry of Jesus himself, who was sent by God.

B. JESUS' MINISTRY IS A MINISTRY OF LOVE

During his earthly life the ministry of Jesus begins and ends with love. The response of Jesus' human will to the Father's call to ministry was a loving response. Jesus readily acknowledged that the first commandment was: "Listen, Israel, the Lord our God is the one Lord, and you must love the Lord your God with all your heart, with all your soul, with all your mind and with all your strength" (Mk 12, 29–30; Mt 22, 37; Lk 10, 26–27). In his own way the fourth evangelist indicated this fullness of love when at the beginning of his account of the Lord's supper, he writes: "But now he showed how perfect his love was" (Jn 13, 1). In Greek one reads: *eis telos,* which has two meanings: (a) to the end of his life, or (b) to the end of love itself. The evangelist may have deliberately chosen this dual-meaning phrase, intending both. Jesus is the one who, in his human nature, loved God both to the end of his life and to the end of his love. In this way he fulfilled the first and the greatest of all God's commandments.

But the love of God involves the love of neighbor as well (cf. Mk 12, 31; Mt 22, 39; Lk 10, 27). 1 Jn 4, 20 says the same thing: "A man who does not love his brother that he can see cannot love God, whom he has never seen." The parable of the good Samaritan is a dim reflection of the real good Samaritan, Jesus, who healed, comforted, aided, fed—in a word, loved those whom he met as neighbor.

Jesus enlarges the term "neighbor" to include our enemies: "But I say to you: love your enemies and pray for those who persecute you; in this way you will be sons of your Father in heaven, for he causes his sun to rise on the bad men as well as the good, and his rain to fall on honest and dishonest men alike" (Mt 5, 44–45; Lk 6, 27–35). Jesus is presented as loving his own enemies even after they had condemned him and sentenced him to die: "Father," he says from the cross, "forgive them; they do not know what they are doing" (Lk 23, 34). Nor can one say that Jesus did not love Judas, even though Judas betrayed him. In fact, there is no one in all the gospels whom Jesus did not love. His hate is presented as a hate only for sin. His love, on the other hand, is presented as extending to all, friend and enemy alike.[4]

This characteristic is also an essential characteristic of Christian ministry. Whenever love is missing, neither the minister nor the ministry is Christian. This love must be seen as a forgiving love, forgiving not only seven times, but seventy times seven (Mt 19, 21–22). This forgiving love finds its model in the forgiving love of Jesus, who loved even those who persecuted him and brought on his suffering and death. In Christian ministry such actions as "anathematizing" and "excommunicating" must only be taken as the last resort, i.e., when the seventy times seven approach has already been made. In the history of the

Christian Church we find numerous occasions of such forgiving ministry. Unfortunately, we also find occasions when Christian ministry has poorly reflected this characteristic of love.

C. JESUS' MINISTRY IS A MINISTRY OF SERVICE

In the gospels we see that the ministry of Jesus was a ministry of service. After the baptism, Mark's gospel shows us Jesus in tireless activity, an activity that is not only preaching the kingdom of God, but curing those who are ill and those possessed by devils. When he appoints the Twelve, they, too, are sent out to preach and cast out devils (Mk 3, 14). Jesus' own relatives thought he was "out of his mind" (Mk 3, 21), since he did not take time to eat. Renunciation of self is the characteristic of service, as far as Jesus is concerned (Mk 8, 34–38), and when the disciples ask Jesus who is going to be the greatest in the kingdom, Jesus takes a child and says: "Anyone who welcomes one of these little children in my name, welcomes me" (Mk 9, 37). Indeed, if "anyone gives you a cup of water to drink just because you belong to Christ, then I tell you solemnly, he will most certainly not lose his reward" (Mk 9, 41).

Jesus spoke to the Twelve: "You know that among the pagans their so-called rulers lord it over them, and their great men make their authority felt. This is not to happen among you. No. Anyone who wants to become great among you must be your servant, and anyone who wants to be first among you must be slave to all. For the Son of Man did not come to be served but to serve, and to give his life as a ransom for many" (Mk 10, 42–45). In this passage Mark speaks directly of the service-model, which Jesus himself exhibits. This is the model of Christian ministry or Christian service.

In turn, the gospel of Matthew takes up the issue of discipleship with Jesus as the model for all Christian disciples. In many ways this gospel is the most "churchy" gospel, since the author is pointedly trying to build up the Christian community of his time. Matthew takes over much from Mark, but adds to the basic material and even nuances the Marcan material for his own purposes. In the sermon on the mount, the evangelist reminds his readers that an eye for an eye and a tooth for a tooth is not enough. Offer the other cheek, give someone both your tunic and your cloak, travel the extra mile. "Give to anyone who asks and if anyone wants to borrow, do not turn away" (Mt 5, 38–42). The prayer of Jesus tells us to forgive us our debts as we have forgiven those who are in debt to us (Mt 6, 12). "So always treat others as you would like them to treat you; that is the meaning of the Law and the Prophets" (Mt 7, 12). Chapters eight and nine gather together ten miracles, indicating the service that Jesus himself brings to those who are in need. The Twelve are sent out, not for themselves, but to cure and to cast out devils (Mt 10, 1). Indeed, all of chapter ten indicates that service in the name of Jesus will be neither an ego trip nor a power trip, but rather one in which there will be misunderstanding, persecution, trial and even death. The same theme appears in Mt 16, 24–26: "If anyone wants to be a follower of mine, let him renounce himself and take up his cross and follow me. For anyone who wants to save his life will lose it; but anyone who loses his life for my sake will find it. What, then, will a man gain if he wins the whole world and ruins his life? Or what has a man to offer in exchange for his life?" Matthew does not say, as Mark had done, that we must welcome children to be part of the kingdom; rather, he says that we must change and become like children (Mt 18, 3). In chapter twenty the evangelist repeats Mark's passage on leadership with service (Mt 20, 24–28).[5]

Luke pursues the identical theme. Even in the infancy-narrative section, Simeon predicts that Jesus will be a servant, one who will bring salvation yet cause the fall and rising of many in Israel (Lk 2, 34). Luke sees that Jesus goes to those who are in need, who are despised, who are the outcasts: "It is not those who are well who need the doctor, but the sick" (Lk 5, 32). In Luke, the Twelve are sent not only to preach the kingdom but also to cast out devils and to cure. The following of Jesus means losing one's own self (Lk 9, 23–26). When speaking of the child as the image of the disciple, Luke rather boldly states: "For the least among you all, that is the one who is great" (Lk 9, 48).

In Luke, the seventy (or seventy-two) are sent out just as the Twelve, for they are the laborers, not the owners, of the harvest (Lk 10, 2). Luke recounts the parable of the watchful servant who at every watch is ready for the return of the master. Peter then asks: "Do you mean this parable for us or for everyone?" Jesus' lengthy response to this question is all about service even in adverse circumstances. Jesus, in this response, does not directly answer Peter's question, but Luke is clearly stating that ministry, such as that of Peter and really of any follower of Jesus, must be a service-ministry.

At the Lord's supper, Luke pointedly includes the dispute on who is the greatest (Lk 22, 24–27). Jesus concludes by saying: "Here am I among you as one who serves." In many ways this is the theme of the arrest, trial and death of Jesus in Luke's gospel. Luke had already prefigured this kind of service by the Lord in the parable about the master who puts on an apron and serves the servants (Lk 12, 37). Fitzmyer notes that these words: "Here am I among you as one who serves," sum up in Lucan theology the entire meaning of Jesus' life and death and Luke offers this Jesus-model as the basis for all Christian service.[6]

In the gospel of John, Jesus remains, of course, the Logos become flesh, the pre-existent Lord, the mighty one. Nonetheless, Jesus is a servant throughout the gospel of John. Of special importance is the lengthy description of the good shepherd (Jn 10, 1–21) and the washing of the disciples' feet at the Lord's supper (Jn 13, 1–20). According to R. Brown[7] the washing of the feet is the symbolization in action of all that John wishes to say to describe the meaning of the arrest, trial, suffering and death of Jesus.

From all of this we can see that the four gospels indicate in no uncertain terms that Jesus was a person of service and that anyone who wishes to follow Jesus as a disciple and therefore in Christian ministry must be a servant as well. This gospel picture lies at the heart of all that Vatican II says about Christian ministry, which we will consider in depth in a later chapter. One can see how this characteristic of Jesus' ministry offers much to us as we try to understand the meaning of Christian ministry today. Service for Jesus was a commitment, to God and to neighbor. So, too, Christian service today is a commitment, and for a particularized and authorized ministry it means that a person makes a public commitment, that is, the commitment is publicly known and the minister himself or herself is in this ministerial respect no longer a private individual but a public person. *Persona publica in ecclesia,* as the well-known scholastic phrase would have it: a public person in the Church. With his commitment to public ministry from his baptism onward, Jesus was no longer a private individual, quite unknown to the wider world as had been the case prior to the baptism. From that time on he became a public figure in the Jewish world. He speaks publicly; he confronts publicly; he challenges publicly. His opponents are public officials: the priest and the highpriest, the scribes and the pharisees. It is leadership over against leadership, a confrontation which ends in Jesus' death.

Christian ministry has, over the centuries, been a service ministry, or at least has striven to be such. Indeed, the history of the Christian Church is populated by people of great service and of great public commitment. It is precisely in this area of public commitment to service that one locates the basis for Christian ordination and Christian installation into ministry. If one does not establish ordination in the area of public service, then the theology of ordination could easily be erroneous. We will, of course, come back to this; here it is only necessary to see that this is a fundamental characteristic of the ministry of Jesus and to note that it is here that one will eventually base a theology of ordination.

D. THE POLITICAL ASPECT OF JESUS' MINISTRY

When scholars begin to treat of the trial of Jesus, particularly the involvement of the high-priest and the sanhedrin in the trial of Jesus and in the communication these people had with the Roman authorities, it is clear that a sharp distinction between "church and state," religion and politics, is untenable. Jewish leaders were not only religious leaders at the time of Jesus; they were also deeply involved in the political activity of that time. At the time of Jesus Palestine was ethnically and religiously rather monolithic and a dividing line between religion and politics thereby loses meaning. The political structure of the Romans was considered an enslavement; there should have been an ethnically and religiously Jewish political structure. In the cases in which a Jew became a public figure, he became a political figure as well. He was in the public arena, and this arena was religious and political. Beyond this general publicness of such Jewish figures, there were also instances in which a Jewish person became a clearly public figure: e.g., the high-priest, the sanhedrin, certain tax collectors who openly worked for the Roman government.

N. Mitchell in his book, *Mission and Ministry,* describes the make-up of the sanhedrin at the time of Jesus. In Jerusalem, the "power of the Sanhedrin was enormous." The priests controlled a "large block of seats in the Sanhedrin. This priestly aristocracy thus combined social, political, religious and fiscal power in Jerusalem.[8]

It is well-known that Jesus refused the title "Messiah," and many scholars suggest it was the political overtones which caused Jesus to refuse the title: the Messiah was to be an outright political rebel against the Romans. This Jesus refused to be. In the 1960's and the early 1970's there were some who portrayed Jesus as the political rebel; such a portrayal was answered by a number of biblical scholars who rather conclusively indicated that such a description in no way matches the New Testament data.[9] On the other hand, Jeremias, in analyzing all three accounts of the temptations of Jesus, suggests that all three are really variants on one and the same account and are concerned with one and the same temptation: "the emergence of Jesus as a political Messiah." The early Church, Jeremias continues, was not preoccupied with a political messiah, but the pre-Easter Jewish milieu certainly was so preoccupied. Jeremias suggests that the temptation of Jesus was one that accompanied him throughout his life: namely, the temptation to "go political." This would mean, however, to become a clearly identified political figure: a political messiah. Jesus refused to be such a messiah: either as a self-appointed one or as a community-appointed one, since this was not the way he understood the will of his Father.[10]

We are evidently speaking of degrees. Jesus' ministry is indeed public, and in the milieu of Jesus' time, any and every public ministry had to be in part political. Still, Jesus will not allow himself to be coopted into a specific, political leadership role, which was the description of messiah for the most part at the time of Jesus. Perhaps the lines cannot be easily drawn, but to say that Jesus was not political in any way seems to miss the mark; and to say that he was a political messiah also seems to miss the mark.

Christian ministry, over the centuries, has wavered on this matter of politics. Quite early on Christian ministers were coopted into political structures, and these ministers used their political clout for the advancement of the gospel. In the West, the collapse of the Roman political leadership created a vacuum, which under the circumstances was filled by Christian ministers, namely, the bishops. This gave rise to the bishop as a political overlord, a situation which was general throughout the middle ages. Indeed, there were such bishops down to the nineteenth century. The bishop of Rome was a major political figure, because of the papal states, down to 1870. In our own time, political involvement by clergy has not been an unknown issue. Pope John Paul II has attempted to curtail such political involvement, but the fact remains that Christian ministry is of its very nature a public ministry, and this publicness goes beyond the inner Church structures at times.

During the Second World War, it was found that a strict separation of Church and state is impossible and dangerous. Both the Roman Catholic Church and the Lutheran Church in Germany had to face some serious political issues as the Third Reich rose in power. The theology of the two societies, stressed in *Mystici Corporis* by Pius XII, could not be taken to mean total non-interference. The political interference into the policies of the Third Reich by Cardinal Faulhaber of Munich was morally justified. So, too, the Barmen Declaration of the Lutheran community was a risky but courageous step, declaring that the Church at times cannot be politically quiet or apolitical. To see Christian ministry as totally and essentially apolitical does not seem correct; to see Christian ministry as a union of Church and state does not seem correct either. Undoubtedly, the first item on the agenda will be further study on the political aspect of Jesus' own ministry; this in itself will be of great assistance for an understanding of the political aspect of Christian ministry generally. If such a study on the political aspect of Jesus' ministry is not developed further, then any judgment on the political nature of Christian ministry cannot be validated in any conclusive way.

E. THE MINISTRY OF JESUS WAS A PREACHING MINISTRY

It is not necessary to enter into a lengthy presentation of this aspect of Jesus' ministry, but it must surely be mentioned. Jesus' ministry was that of an itinerant preacher. He journeyed throughout Galilee, preaching. This is why the Word of God is so central to the mission and ministry of Jesus. Martin Luther and John Calvin both emphasized this aspect of Christian ministry, particularly as it affects ordained ministry. In doing so, they were emphasizing a characteristic of the gospel which is almost self-evident. We will consider their position later on as also the response of the Council of Trent to this position.

Jesus did not establish a hospital ministry, taking care of the ill and the dying. He did not establish educational institutions, providing for the academic training of his followers. Rather, he preached. All those, then, who carry on the mission and ministry of Jesus must share in this preaching of the Word of God. Parents, in a real sense, preach, when they instruct their children and raise them with the values of the gospel. Christian teachers preach in the way they relay the gospel message. In a very special way, the ordained minister in the Christian Church must preach; otherwise, he would hardly be an ordained minister carrying on the mission and ministry of Jesus. Preaching is, indeed, an essential part of Christian ministry generally, and of ordained ministry in particular.

These are the main characteristics of the ministry of Jesus himself. Let us now look more carefully at the content of this ministry.

2. A DESCRIPTION OF THE MESSAGE OF THE EARTHLY MINISTRY OF JESUS

There have been many attempts to state succinctly the central message of Jesus which he himself preached during his earthly lifetime. Bonnefoy, Cullman, Bornkamm, Jeremias, Boff, Sobrino, to name only a few, have attempted to pinpoint the core of Jesus' message.[11] Perhaps such a task may never be accomplished in any satisfying way, but all of these authors, as well as many others, gravitate around several similar themes, so that at least the general perimeters of Jesus' basic message can be fairly well established. In the following pages, I am using the structure which Jeremias developed, not that his presentation does not need nuancing and clarifications, but the structure he offers is a very helpful tool through which one can catch a glimpse of the message in Jesus' own preaching.

One must, however, be clear as to the precise goal and procedure in this endeavor. First of all, the New Testament provides us with the Church community's belief in Jesus, so that the message of the New Testament in the form it now stands is an expression of the faith-commitment to Jesus which the evangelists and their communities formulated. Since the resurrection of Jesus plays a key role in this faith expression, authors, such as the ones mentioned above, attempt to go beneath the resurrection event, to the time of Jesus' own preaching in Palestine and in this preaching of Jesus himself his own resurrection was not a topic. Naturally, such an endeavor is chancy. There are no documents which directly outline Jesus' preaching as such. Rather, one only has the documents of the New Testament, which are already commentaries and statements from the standpoint of the resurrection on the meaning of Jesus, including the meaning of his own words.

During his earthly life, on the other hand, Jesus confined himself to the Jewish people. He did not engage in a universal mission, to all men and women, Jew and non-Jew alike. The message of the New Testament, however, is really a universal message, directed to Jew and non-Jew. During his earthly life, Jesus did not focus his preaching on himself, that is, that he was Lord, God, the risen One. After the resurrection, the Church community preached a Jesus who was Lord,

God and the risen One. The focus of the Church communities was centered on the Lordship of Jesus himself. These are but two of the major areas of difference which distinguish the actual preaching of Jesus during his earthly life and the message of the New Testament as such.

The schematic structure which Jeremias uses involves the following four points:

a. The return of the quenched spirit;
b. Overcoming the rule of Satan;
c. The dawn of the kingdom of God;
d. The poor have the good news preached to them.[12]

Each of these, Jeremias notes, has specific Jewish overtones which need to be appreciated if one wishes to understand the message which Jesus himself preached throughout Palestine during his earthly life. Let us consider each of them briefly.

A. THE RETURN OF THE QUENCHED SPIRIT

Through his study of the religious thought of Judaism at the time of Jesus, Jeremias finds that in the common piety of the people, there was the belief that the Spirit had been taken away from the Jewish people with the death of the final prophets.

> In the time of the patriarchs, all pious and upright men had the Spirit of God. When Israel committed sin with the golden calf, God limited the Spirit to chosen men, prophets, high priests and kings. With the death of the last writing prophets, Haggai, Zechariah and Malachai, the spirit was quenched because of the sin of Israel. After that time, it was believed, God spoke only through the echo of his voice, a poor substitute.[13]

Jeremias cites Ps 74, 1 Mac 4, 46; 9, 27; 14, 41, the apocalyptic literature, Josephus and rabbinic sources for this stance. According to this fairly prevailing view, the Spirit of God was to return at the last day, the end time. In what Jesus both said and did, he proclaimed that the Spirit of God had returned and, even more precisely, the Spirit had returned in and through himself. Therefore, the Jewish people could not help but hear that Jesus not only preached the end time, but that he was the beginning of the end time. This theme of the return of the quenched Spirit emphasizes the eschatological aspect of Jesus' preaching. When one considers how integral the Spirit of God is to the life, death and also the resurrection of Jesus, one grasps that the Spirit is clearly central to the very message of Jesus. The presence of the Spirit is seen as well in the many miracles which Jesus worked, since it is only in and through the Spirit of God that such miracles could even be done. The plentifulness of the miracles is also a sign of the end time.[14] The Spirit of God is present to Jesus at his very conception, at his birth, at his baptism, in the desert, during his prayer, at the resurrection when he sent his Spirit, and at Pentecost when the Spirit of Jesus descends on the disciples. We no longer hear an echo of God's voice, the poor substitute; we hear the very Spirit of God crying "Abba! Father!" in the depths of our being.

B. OVERCOMING THE RULE OF SATAN

The good news, or the gospel, needs to include a judgment on the power of evil. If evil would never come to an end and in the final analysis be the conclusion, then the gospel news is ultimately not good. Once more, Jeremias delves into the Jewish thinking about evil at the time of Jesus. For the majority of Jews at that time Satan was considered to be the ruler of all evil spirits. Just prior to Jesus Jewish piety thrived on angels and devils. It was in this period that the Jewish understanding of angels and devils, from which the Christian Church has derived its own understanding of angels and devils, took strong root and became a quite elaborate part of Jewish teaching. The names of the "nine choirs" of angels indicate the way in which those Jewish people understood angels: the cherubim and seraphim were basically in heaven, adoring God. Cherubim and seraphim did not have dealings with humans. On the other hand, the remaining "choirs" all had some sort of connection with the human world. The names: thrones, dominations, principalities, powers, virtues, archangels and angels, are all names of "power," names of "authority." Although these nine choirs did not become popular until the age of Pseudo-Dionysius and Gregory the Great, the thinking behind these "choirs" and the names as well went back into Jewish history. There seems to have been some influencing from Eastern religions on the Jews prior to the time of Jesus, which accounts for some of the ideas the Jews had in connection to both angels and devils. The world was divided into areas, and in these areas there were powers for good (angels) and powers for evil (devils). These were spheres of influence, a sort of territorializing of the angelic and demonic beings. For the evil spirits, Satan was the commander in chief. Destruction of Satan means, therefore, destruction of evil.[15]

Good news includes the lessening and removal of the evil which inflicts human life. If all that the good news promises is some temporal or momentary respite, but not the complete removal of pain and evil from life, then salvation is ultimately falsified. If this were the case, then Jesus would have offered only a brief panacea. But this is not what Jesus offers. In the message of Jesus, evil is never presented as the ultimate and final answer. God and God's merciful love are seen as the final answer. Jesus himself is characterized as greater than Abraham, greater than Moses, greater than Solomon; one should add that Jesus is greater than Satan.

This power over evil is evidenced in Jesus' power over sickness; the many healings are the signs of his superiority over evil. The three accounts of Jesus raising someone from the dead, namely, the raising of the daughter of Jairus, the raising of the widow's son at Naim, and the raising of Lazarus, all indicate that Jesus is greater than death and the evil of death. Again and again we read of Jesus driving out demons (Mk 3, 22, par.; Mt 9, 34; Lk 11, 15), which bespeaks his power over the underlings of Satan. Some of these accounts may not have the firm historical basis we might wish, but the impact of the message is quite clear: Satan (evil) is overcome. Satan (evil) is not the final answer. It is, of course, the death and resurrection of Jesus which is the *coup d'etat* for Satan's rule.

One might wonder, today, about the validity of a "Satan" (i.e., an actual and personal evil creature) as the source of evil, but it ought to be recalled that throughout civilized history in many of our human myths regarding the origin of evil there seems to be a pattern. The origin of evil, as we find in these myths from world cultures, is traced to two areas: (1) an original man, an original woman, an original androgynous human; (2) a power beyond that of the human framework, e.g., a demon, a devil, a god of evil. The Genesis accounts have both: there is the original human, Adam and Eve, and there is the one who is outside the human framework, the serpent, who is more cunning than all other creatures. The authors of Genesis show great wisdom in this dual presentation: tracing evil to human origins means that we as humans are in some degree personally responsible for evil. Only when we admit that we are evil, that we are sinners, can we begin to move toward the good. As in the case of alcoholics and drug addicts, only when the denial has ceased can the cure really begin, so, too, in our spiritual journey, only the acknowledgement of personal evil leads to true sanctity. To deny one's sinfulness and evil is to prefer darkness to light. Conversion from evil to good is at the very origin of spiritual growth.

Secondly, evil is also greater than any evil which one single person might do. There is a larger-than-any-one-individual power of evil, a power which moves from generation to generation. For example, the roots of war are never found exclusively in one person nor in one group of persons. In many ways wars beget wars. What remained unfinished at the conclusion of one war either through poor treaties or excessive demands for war damages returns as the cause of war in the next period of war. Today's arms build-up, the insidiousness of racism, the greed of the multi-nationals, all indicate that evil is more than the evil of a single human being. Liberation theologians today speak about personal evil and structural evil: the two sides of the origin of evil. Catholic theologians, in discussing original sin, speak about the sin of the world and about personal sin—again, the two sides of the origin of evil.[16]

The gospel announces that evil is overcome, both at the human origin and in the structural origin. Evil, totally, is overcome; it is not in any form the final answer. Only God's merciful, forgiving love is the final answer. This is indeed good news for all human beings: "Shoulder my yolk," Jesus says, "and learn from me, for I am gentle and humble in heart." The easy yolk, the light burden—these are clearly central elements of Jesus' own preaching while he lived in Palestine.

C. THE DAWN OF THE KINGDOM OF GOD

Since W. Wrede's time, at the end of the nineteenth century, the eschatological aspect of the message of Jesus has been emphasized, and this eschatological aspect has centered around the most crucial aspect of Jesus' message, namely, the kingdom of God. One might even say that the return of the quenched Spirit and the overcoming of Satan are simply facets of Jesus' preaching on the kingdom. This eschatological kingdom is one that has begun but is not yet realized: the already-but-not-yet eschatology or the realized eschatology which seems to be the more solid approach today.

The parables indicate quite often that the kingdom is at hand, even begun. The wedding has started, new garments are ready to hand, new wine skins are available, it is harvest and vinting time. A light has been lit and placed where all can see; a city has been built on the side of a mountain; the lost sheep has been found; the lost drachma has been reclaimed. There is indeed a sense of "now" in all of these images, but there is as well a sense of the "not yet." The seed is just planted and only one day will it develop into the large tree where the birds will build their nests. The elder son is still outside, unwilling to celebrate the return of his lost brother. The leaven is in the dough, causing it to rise. The sower has just sown the seed, and some has landed in good ground and has begun to germinate, but the harvest is still in the future.

Biblical scholars have dealt with the "now-but-not-yet" aspect of the kingdom of God, and with a variety of relationships between the two aspects. But what is this kingdom which Jesus preached and for which he sent out the Twelve to preach as well. The very term "kingdom of God" (quite often circumlocuted by the phrase which does not mention the name of God, the kingdom of heaven) was not a common phrase at the time of Jesus, yet Jesus used it abundantly. This kingdom is not spatial, in the sense of the kingdoms of Judah and Israel, or the kingdoms of the Amorites or Midianites. In this sense the kingdom was not a political kingdom at all. Nor is it a static kingdom which one could draw on a map, outlining frontiers which are meant to be irrevocable. Rather, the kingdom of God is a dynamic kingdom in which the presence of God himself is active. Schillebeeckx describes this kingdom as follows:

> [The kingdom of God] does not denote some area of sovereignty above and beyond this world, where God is supposed to reside and reign. What Jesus intends by it is a process, a course of events, whereby God begins to govern or act as king or Lord, an action, therefore, by which God manifests his being-God in the world for men. Thus God's lordship or dominion is the divine power itself in its saving activity within our history, but at the same time the final eschatological state of affairs that brings to

an end the evil world, dominated by the forces of calamity and of woe, and initiates the new world, in which God "appears to full advantage."[17]

W. Kasper, for his part, speaks of the kingdom of God as the main theme of Jesus' message, but reminds us that nowhere in the gospel does Jesus state clearly what the kingdom of God is. Jesus only says that it is near, and describes it through a number of parables. The kingdom of God which Jesus preaches is a "new start" in the struggle for human peace and wholeness, and only God can accomplish this.

> This thing which God alone can provide, which God ultimately himself is, is what is meant by the Kingdom of God. It involves the meaning of God's being God and Lord, which at the same time means the humanity of human beings and the salvation of the world because it means liberation from the forces of evil which are hostile to creation, and reconciliation in place of the implacable antagonism of the present world. That is the fundamental theme of Jesus' message.[18]

Kasper then goes on to describe: (a) the eschatological character of the kingdom of God; (b) its theological character; (c) its soteriological character. "We can summarize that as follows: the salvation of the Kingdom of God means the coming to power in and through human beings in the self-communicating love of God. Love reveals itself as the meaning of life. The world and man find fulfilment only in love."[19]

L. Boff, from the aspect of liberation theology, notes that the kingdom of God is not a territory but a new order:

> The kingdom of God, as is evident, implies a dynamism; it notifies us of an event and expresses the intervention of God already initiated but not yet fully completed. . . . The preaching of the kingdom is realized in two moments of time, the present and the future.[20]

For Boff, the kingdom of God is not merely spiritual, an inward kingdom, and a sort of private kingdom. Rather, it involves to some degree our total world, the spiritual and the material, the private and the social, the historical and the future, this world and the next. But it is not an unattainable utopia; for it has already begun. In Jesus we hear the words of Revelation: "Now I am making the whole of creation new. . . . It is already done" (Rev 21, 5).

The preaching of Jesus undoubtedly focused on the kingdom of God; but his life, death and resurrection—his actions, if one will—also proclaimed the kingdom of God. What Jesus did and what he said centered on the kingdom. One might note that if the kingdom was the focus of Jesus' message, then one could say that Jesus himself, as God made flesh, was not the central message of what he preached. After the resurrection, the Church began to focus on Jesus as the center of the message and Jesus as the center of the kingdom. This focus was not, it seems, part of the earthly preaching of Jesus.

D. THE POOR HAVE THE GOOD NEWS PREACHED TO THEM

The kingdom of God, central as it is to Jesus' message, cannot be understood if one does not also perceive the extent of this kingdom: it included the poor, the "anawim." Anawim are those who are materially poor, of course, but the term also, at the time of Jesus, referred to a wider group as well, namely, those who had no recourse. This included people who had means but were to some degree excommunicated from the Jewish society. In the gospels, they are called: publicans, sinners, prostitutes. They were those who notoriously failed to observe the Law. They were those who engaged in despised kinds of work: gamblers, tax collectors, money lenders, shepherds. If one sees that in the eyes of those who held religious and political power in the Palestine of Jesus' time such people were considered as rejects and were to some degree shunned, Jesus' association with them was a major affront to the religious and political structures of that period.[21]

If Jesus preached "good news" only, there would have been no reason to arrest him and kill him. One must find in this very "good news" a corresponding "bad news." What for some might be heard as good news is for others extremely bad news. As Christians, we read the gospels and find solace in the good news that is there, but news is only "good" when it is good for someone. If the news is not good for someone, then it is passed by in indifference or it is rejected as "bad news." Jesus' preaching of the return of the Spirit did not offend the leaders of the Jewish people at that time in any overwhelming way. The priests, the scribes and the pharisees would easily find the return of the quenched Spirit welcome, since as priests they were holy, as scribes they were Law-abiding, and as pharisees they were prayerfully spiritual. The same is true of the overcoming of Satan. The priests did not believe that Satan ruled them, nor did the scribes or the pharisees. If the kingdom were at hand, then the priests, the scribes and the pharisees certainly were part of that kingdom. These aspects of Jesus' preaching did not raise too much of a storm. It was this fourth issue, the poor, which caused the difficulty. The leaders of the Jewish people, the priests, the scribes and the pharisees, realized only too clearly that Jesus by associating with such anawim and publicly stating that they belonged to the kingdom was undermining their authority. It was the priests who in many ways declared such people "sinners" and thereby excommunicated them from the "pious Jews." It was the scribes, the scholars, who expounded the biblical base for calling these people "sinners." The pharisees, in their spiritual righteousness, would not even brush against such sinners, lest they become less spiritual themselves. When Jesus publicly tells his opponents that these sinners will go to heaven before they do, their authority is being publicly challenged. This was indeed for them bad news.

Jeremias rightfully notes that the major parables, for the most part, were directed to these "opponents" of Jesus (priests, scribes and pharisees). The parable of the prodigal son or good father is a clear case. The younger son who is the "sinner" is welcomed back by the father (a God-figure), but the elder son (symbolizing the priests, scribes and pharisees) could not countenance such prodigal love. The opponents of Jesus heard this parable and heard Jesus' challenge to them, and this was done in front of the masses! Only when one catches in the preaching of Jesus both the good news and the bad news will one begin to understand why Jesus ended up rejected and killed. It was this preaching of the kingdom to the poor that created the enmity. To the sinner, Zacchaeus, Jesus said: "Today salvation has come to your house." The New Testament phrase, "He ate with sinners," carries enormous meaning. These kinds of actions and words were a direct affront to the Jewish leadership of Jesus' day.[22]

These four issues were, in one way or another, central to the preaching of Jesus and central to the way he structured his life. They are part of the New Testament in no small way, and it is precisely this same message that Christian ministry must witness to today if it is to be rooted in the mission of Jesus himself. The contemporary

Christian minister must in both word and life-structure give evidence that the Spirit has returned, that evil is not the final answer, that the kingdom of God is already at hand, but above all that those who are marginated and rejected are the very ones who belong most to this kingdom of God. These are powerful themes, indeed, and yet they are the very heart of Christian ministry.

3. A DESCRIPTION OF THE MINISTRY OF THE RISEN JESUS

With the resurrection, Jesus is no longer visible to us as he once was during his earthly life. Jesus is present to us now in the sacrament of the Church, and this Church makes present to each new generation the message of Jesus. Ministry in the Church, therefore, is not self-appointed nor community-appointed; rather, the Lord calls and commissions to ministry. This ministry is a ministry of love and of service, just as the Lord's ministry on earth was. There is also some political aspect to this, which as mentioned needs to be further elaborated. The kingdom of God is not simply a spiritual, inner reality. The ministry of Jesus remains a ministry of preaching, a ministry of the word.

One of the major writings of the New Testament, namely the Letter to the Hebrews, as it is called, is a reflection on the risen ministry of Jesus. It would be far beyond the scope of this present volume to offer a complete overview of this important New Testament letter. Still, some background material is essential to understand this writing.[24] The author is unknown. It surely is not Paul. Other candidates for authorship have been proposed: Luke, Clement of Rome, Apollos, Barnabas. None of these seem to be verifiable, and the majority of scripture scholars today consider the author to be an unknown person, but still a Christian who is a leader of a community and accordingly writes with some authority. The people to whom the letter is addressed are equally mysterious. They are not in a specific way "Hebrews." This title can be verified from the end of the second century onward, but not before, and more than likely was attached to the letter by a compiler at that time. In fact many biblical scholars today consider the readership to be non-Jewish (e.g., Roeth, Julicher, Wrede, Windisch, Michel, Kasemann, Kuss). These people do not seem to be in any heresy, but they seem to be a second-generation group of Christians, somewhat tiring in their efforts to maintain the gospel standards of life. In this flagging spirit, the author attempts to rekindle their former Christian spirit. More than likely, the letter dates from 80/90 A.D., and again more than likely the community to whom it is addressed are in the neighborhood of Rome. None of these details are certain, but they seem to be the more acceptable positions.

The author, in attempting to revivify the Christian community, presents a dramatic picture of Jesus: he is the Son of God, the bearer of the final revelation, and is superior to all former messengers of God (1, 1–4, 13). Only after this magnificent portrayal of the superiority of Jesus does the author begin his presentation of the priestliness of Jesus, which covers the lengthiest part of the letter (4, 14–10, 18). Jesus is portrayed as a heavenly high priest who has entered into the holy of holies through the temptation and suffering and death of his earthly life.

Since in Jesus, the Son of God, we have the supreme high priest who has gone through to the highest heaven, we must never let go of the faith that we have professed (4, 14).

This verse sets the theme for all that follows: Jesus is such a supreme and heavenly high priest that our faith can only be strengthened. The author then goes on to describe this priestly Jesus: he is compassionate, since he has suffered in ways similar to us (5, 1–10). In this same section, we see that Jesus is presented not as one who gave himself "the glory of becoming high priest," once again, a message which rejects any self-appointment, but "he had it from the one who said to him: You are a priest of the order of Melchisedek, and for ever" (5, 5). The author immediately takes up his pastoral intent and warns against any lessening of zeal (5, 11–6, 8). In chapter seven, the author begins his most theological section: Melchisedek was a type of the priestly Jesus, and Jesus is called a "second Melchisedek" (7, 15). This second Melchisedek is of a higher order and is an unchanging or eternal priest. This priest is a heavenly priest who does not need to offer sacrifice every day, as the Aaronic priests had to do. This heavenly or risen priest has his place at the throne of the divine Majesty in the heavens: "he is the minister of the sanctuary and of the true Tent of Meeting, which the Lord and not any man set up, and so this one too must have something to offer. In fact, if he were on earth, he would not be a priest at all, since there are others who make the offerings laid down by the law" (8, 2–4).

This heavenly priest is of a far higher order and of a better covenant. Jesus has "entered into the greater, the more perfect tent"; he has "entered into the sanctuary once and for all, taking with him not the blood of goats and bull calves, but his own blood, having won an eternal redemption for us" (9, 12). Jesus has offered the perfect sacrifice: "By virtue of that one single offering, he has achieved the eternal perfection of all whom he is sanctifying" (10, 14). For the author, it is understood that the priesthood means "sacrifice," "altar," "worship." Jesus offered the perfect sacrifice and continues this once and for all offering in heaven; in many ways he himself is the altar and his suffering, death and resurrection is the cult of worship.

The picture of Jesus as priest in this letter is unique in the New Testament. Nowhere else is Jesus called "priest" (*hiereus*). Nowhere else, not even in the letters of Paul himself, is Jesus described as priest. On the other hand, the author of this "Letter to the Hebrews" in no way extends this priestliness to anyone else: ordained or unordained. The author does not present this priestly portrait of Jesus to encourage and strengthen an ordained segment of the Christian community. He is not presenting a model to a "clerical" group. Rather, he presents a portrait, and a grand one at that, of the priestly Jesus for all in his Christian community. His intention, however, is not to encourage all of them to be "priestly," but rather to present a uniquely priestly Jesus, in whom they should have unshakable faith (c. 11). If all we had were this letter, we would have no indication at all of a priestly ministry among Christians. We would have, instead, a magnificent understanding of the one priest, Jesus.

Nonetheless, this portrait of Jesus the priest helps us to understand the priestly ministry of (a) all Christians; (b) the special ordained and the special unordained ministry of Christians. All Christians, because of their baptism, share in the priestly ministry of Jesus; specially designated Christians, ordained and unordained, share in this same priestly ministry of Jesus. All must reflect the Lord: the priestly Jesus. This is a corollary of the "Letter to the Hebrews," but it is not so stated in this letter. The theme of the letter is to have unswerving faith in Jesus and not tire. To gain this renewed commitment to Jesus, the author presents us first with a picture of Jesus' superiority over angels and over Moses, and then with a picture of Jesus' superiority over the Aaronic priesthood and the priesthood of Melchisedek. The issue of a special priestly ministry within the Christian community is not at the center of this letter.

In the apostolic and sub-apostolic Church the "Letter to the Hebrews" did not have a great deal of influence. In the West, Clement of Rome in his letter to the Corinthians alludes to this writing. In the middle of the second century Hermas makes a brief allusion to it as well. In the East, there was a greater appreciation: Clement of Alexandria, Origen, Pantanus. The West began to accept this letter as canonical only in the latter part of the fourth century. In the first three hundred years of the Church, the letter did not play any noteworthy role in shaping the understanding of priestly ministry. From 400 onward it plays a stronger role.

The "Letter to the Hebrews" is very much a "Church document." The author is speaking out of and to a Church community, and the central focus of this Church remains Jesus and all that his mission and ministry were about. The priestly theme is one way of presenting Jesus. The gospels, as we have seen, concentrate on the message of Jesus, and this gospel message of Jesus remains central to the Church. The Church, continues to preach the presence of the Spirit, the overcoming of evil, the dawn of the kingdom of God and above all a kingdom which includes the marginated and the poor. If the Church, as the sacrament of Jesus, does not reflect the very message of Jesus, then it can hardly be seen as continuing the work of Christ. In this sense the Church is priestly.[25]

With the resurrection, however, Jesus is believed to be Lord, that is, God, and this becomes a centralizing part of the Church's message and therefore of the Church's ministry. The Church is basically christocentric, and this means that all ministry in the Church is christocentric as well. By christocentric one does not mean an overexaggerated mono-Christic approach, but it does mean that not only is Jesus central, but that Jesus as God or Lord is central. The New Testament term, Jesus is kyrios or Lord, cannot be set to one side in any way at all. The Spirit, the destruction of Satan, the Kingdom, the merciful love of the anawim are focused in Jesus as God made human. We will see later that this central message even means that outside Jesus there is no salvation for anyone at all.

Jesus is indeed the light of the world, and the Church's essence is to reflect that light.[23] So, too, Church ministry in all its forms is meant to reflect or sacramentalize this light of the world, Jesus. Only then is the Church truly Church and is Christian ministry truly Christian ministry. The study of the ministry of the risen Jesus is, of course, the central message of this book: namely, ministry in the Church. We will see the many ways in which the risen Jesus ministers to men and women as we trace the history of ecclesial ministry.

Before we do that however, let us first summarize the steps we have taken so far, and then turn to an important aspect in the interpretation of Church ministry, an aspect that can be rightfully called, an ecclesiological presupposition.

4. SUMMARY

Our study of Church ministry has brought us to the following summary statements:

1. Every study of Church ministry must begin with a study of the ministry of Jesus himself; this is the source, the model and the dynamism of all Church ministry.
2. The ministry of Jesus was a ministry which came from God, not a self-imposed ministry, nor a ministry which was commissioned by some group. This indicates to us that all Church ministry is due to the call and commission of the Lord; Church ministry is not a matter of self-appointment, nor even of community appointment.
3. The ministry of Jesus was a ministry of love: love of the Father and love of neighbor, but a neighbor which included the enemy as well. All Church ministry needs to reflect a love that forgives seventy times seven times.
4. The ministry of Jesus was a ministry of service. Power, self-aggrandizement, prestige and wealth are alien to this kind of ministry. This service ministry is also of a public nature, not a private or individualized situation.
5. There is some degree of political stance in Jesus' ministry, and there is some degree of political stance in Church ministry. Any attempt to make Church ministry apolitical is both dangerous and non-reflective of Jesus' own ministry.
6. The message which Jesus preached centered around the following themes: (a) the return of the quenched Spirit; (b) over-

coming the rule of Satan; (c) the dawn of the kingdom of God; (d) the poor have the good news preached to them. This continues to be the message of Church ministers.

7. With the resurrection of Jesus, however, and the development of the Christian community, belief in the risen Jesus became central to the essence of the Church and the ministry of the Church. The themes, mentioned in no. 6 above, remain valid, of course, but these must be centralized around the Lordship of the risen Jesus. The Church is christocentric; Church ministry is christocentric. This means a centrality of the risen Lord.

8. The risen Jesus continues his ministry in and through the Church's ministry, and therefore a study of Church ministry is in reality a study of the ministry of the risen Lord.

This summary is quite brief and by no means adequate for a solid basis of Christian ministry. Actually, a rather thorough course in christology is a *sine qua non* prerequisite for any study either of the Church itself or of Church ministry. However, the above outline does at least provide some of the orientation necessary to ground a study of ministry in the Church. We now turn to a major aspect of the Church which is fundamental to the study of the ministry.

2

An Ecclesiological Presupposition

There has been an extensive study of the history of Christian ministry throughout this present century. Never before in the life of the Church has there been so much historical data available to scholars on the issue of ministry in the Christian community. It seems wise, however, before taking up the thread of this history from New Testament times to the present, to consider what could be called "an ecclesiological presupposition." This ecclesiological presupposition in many ways nuances the way that one approaches the New Testament data on Christian ministry and the subsequent development of that ministry. At times, in our recent past, histories of Christian ministry have been viewed with some apprehension; certain aspects of these studies have even been seen by a few as threatening. In the Roman Catholic world, the works of Schillebeeckx and Küng come easily to mind. This apprehension, even a sense of threat, arises because a reinterpretation of the history of Christian ministry might at times call into question current ecclesiastical structures, whether in the Roman Catholic Church, in the Anglican Church, or in the Protestant Churches. The issue is quite ecumenical in scope, but in this present chapter we will consider only the Roman Catholic situation.

There seems to be two different tendencies which give rise to this ecclesiological presupposition:

1. The first approach is to see Jesus during his lifetime clearly establishing a Church, together with its basic structures and ministries. In other words, the gospels are read in such a way

as to make explicit Jesus' role in establishing a fairly detailed Church community.

2. The second approach is to see the Church, together with its structures and ministries, arising after the resurrection. In other words, the Church is a post-Easter event, and as such, under the guidance of the Holy Spirit, the early community begins to shape the details of structure and ministry.

Although one should not be overly simplistic as regards this distinction, one should, nevertheless, take into account that there actually are these two tendencies in Roman Catholic theology, and as such they form, each in its own way, an ecclesiological presupposition. If these two presuppositions are not appreciated, then the tendency seems to be that one side begins to call the other side "heretical." Rather than have this situation of "heresy-calling" continue, it would be far better if each side realized more clearly where the differences might lie. Too much argument is often spent over the particular issues of a given ministry or of a given office in the Church, whereas the root of the argument, namely, Jesus' own role in establishing the Church, is not seen as the focus. Both sides, of course, maintain that the Church is intrinsically a grace, that is, it comes from God and is not the work of human endeavor. At times, however, in the heat of the argument, this faith stance on either side is somewhat less than acknowledged.

As far back as 1932, A. Michel, writing in the *Dictionnaire de Théologie Catholique,* posed a presupposition type of question: "Did Jesus Christ," he writes, "have as regards his future work an idea which excluded or implied the institution of a new priesthood, a sacred hierarchy? The entire question of the divine institution of the sacrament of order depends on the response brought to this historical problem?"[1] Interestingly, Michel speaks of this as an historical problem, not a dogmatic one. Implied in the notion of the new priesthood and the sacred hierarchy, of course, is the institution of the Church. Rightfully, Michel says that the whole question depends on the answer; in other words, there is a presupposition, to use our terminology, an ecclesiological presupposition, which must be considered first, prior to a study of ministry in the Christian Church.

In presenting a picture of these two sides, various authors, representing each position, will be cited. These authors are merely illustrative of the two tendencies, and each cited author actually stands for a much wider group of Catholic scholars.

1. JESUS ESTABLISHED A CHURCH IN A FAIRLY DETAILED WAY

This position has been fairly traditional in the Catholic Church and therefore is considered as "standard." A. Tanquerey, whose works were widely used in Catholic seminaries throughout the world prior to Vatican II, states the position openly: "Christ established the Church as an hierarchical society by bestowing on the Apostles the threefold power of teaching, of ruling and of sanctifying the faithful."[2] Jesus, not only chose the apostles, but he trained them and sent them out to preach the kingdom of God. Peter, particularly, was singled out as the foundation of his Church, was given the keys of the kingdom, and had the right to impose or remove various obligations of the spiritual order. In turn, the apostles had the power to bind and loose, and were promised the special assistance of the Spirit to preach the gospel. It was after the resurrection that Jesus gave the power which he had promised (Mt 16, 16; 18, 18) to both Peter and the apostles (Jn 20, 23). Thus "the College of Apostles received from Jesus Christ, who was administering the offices of God, the power and authority to teach the Gospel to all peoples, to impose laws through which the divine law was preserved, and to sanctify souls through the administration of the sacraments."[3]

In this evaluation of the New Testament data, one sees that the Church was quite distinct as a hierarchical society from the synagogue, possessing special rites, such as baptism and the laying on of hands, "through which the Holy Spirit was bestowed in a special manner." Moreover, the breaking of the bread "obviously was the celebration of the eucharist."[4]

After the conversion of Cornelius, gentile-Christian communities began to grow. On the basis of an analysis, particularly of 1 Corinthians and Ephesians, Tanquerey describes the hierarchical structure of these gentile communities:

> They were subject to a holy hierarchy, that is, to the Apostles who exercised supreme authority among all the communities of the Gentiles; indeed this authority was viewed as divinely received. The Apostles oftentimes claimed it for themselves in their epistles,

in teaching, in judging, in correcting, in proposing laws or pre-
cepts, not just for the faithful, but also for the elders who took
care of the faithful. Serving under the Apostles were inferior ministers: deacons, priests or bishops, who in turn took upon themselves some authority in spiritual matters and who thus formed,
along with the Apostles, a true hierarchy.[5]

In this view, there is clearly a decisive and definite establishment
of the Church and its basic structures on the part of Christ. Indeed,
one might even say that in the passages cited above, Tanquerey goes
beyond the basic structures and maintains that a quite developed
structure of the Church was established by Jesus. The task of the
subsequent Church leadership is to maintain these structures in and
through all cultural changes. It is also clear that Tanquerey is primarily
a systematic theologian and not a biblical scholar, since he uses exegesis
in a fairly unnuanced way. One would have to test his exegesis against
solid biblical scholarship, e.g., what is the relationship of Ephesians
to the early Church? which apostles actually wrote letters which we
have today?

2. THE CHURCH DATES FROM THE RESURRECTION

A writer who represents the opposite side of the spectrum, namely,
the second approach cited above, is Hans Küng. His position was
stated early on in *Structures of the Church* and then again in *The
Church*. Basically, his position in both of these works is the same. I
am citing Küng merely as one example among many of authors who
tend toward this second approach on the establishment of the Church.

Küng expresses his approach in four statements:[6]

1. In the pre-Easter period, during his lifetime, Jesus did not
   found a Church.

Küng's argument for this is the message of Jesus, as found in the
gospels, which in no way speak of a select group, a sort of remnant.
Jesus is "aware that his mission is not to gather up the 'just,' the
'righteous,' and the 'pure,' but to gather up the whole of Israel." Indeed,
to the very last Jesus addressed himself to all the ancient people of
God. The Twelve, Küng notes, "were to represent Jesus' call to the
whole people of the twelve tribes and therefore to have the roles of

rulers and judges in the time of the eschatological consummation."[7]
Küng concludes:

> It is not surprising, then—indeed it is an argument for the au-
> thenticity of the gospel accounts, which in this respect were cer-
> tainly not inflated by the primitive Christian community—that
> the gospels do not report any public announcement by Jesus of
> his intention to found a Church or a new covenant or any pro-
> grammatic call to join a community of the elect.[8]

2. In the pre-Easter period, Jesus, by his preaching and ministry
   laid the foundations for the emergence of a post-resurrection
   Church.

The message of Jesus did divide the people of Israel, but this
was, as we saw above, over the issue of salvation. Those who followed
Jesus most intimately shared a common life experience, sharing meals
with him and developing common bonds. After the death and resurrection of Jesus this bonding continued, and these same men and
women shared their Easter faith with one another. In this wider sense,
then, a "foundation" for the eventual Church was laid during the
lifetime of Jesus.[9]

3. The Church existed from the time of faith in the resurrection.

Nowhere does Küng speak of an original "Church-less" society.
"The Church was from the first moment of faith in the resurrection
seen as something given by God. As a work of God it was regarded
as essentially different from other human groups and communities
and took on similarly a very different form." Küng states that this
community was called the "Church of God," or the "people of God,"
or the "Church of Christ." A self-identity as formed by God alone
stands at the very beginning of Church life.[10]

4. The origins of the Church do not lie solely in the intention
   and the message of Jesus in the pre-Easter period, but in the
   whole history of Jesus' life and ministry: that is, in the entire
   action of God in Jesus Christ, from Jesus' birth, his ministry
   and the calling of the disciples, through to his death and resurrection and the sending of the Spirit to the witnesses of his
   resurrection.

In this approach, the entire life, death and resurrection is seen as constitutive of the Church, which is not the case if the Church were already established prior to the death and resurrection, i.e., during the earthly lifetime of Jesus. It is the entirety of the Jesus event which gives rise to the Church; only on this integral basis can one say that "Jesus instituted a Church."[11]

Obviously, this is a long way from the approach described by Tanquerey, and between these two representative authors there are many other scholars with varying nuances on this matter of the institution of the Church. Each scholar, however, tends in one direction or the other, and this is what is meant by the ecclesiological presupposition which every scholar has on this subject of the institution of the Church and its impact on the issue of ministry in the Church. One might call these approaches "an a priori stance," or "a dogmatic stance," or "a denominational stance." Whatever the name, it is important to realize that such stances affect, in some degree, the manner in which subsequent historical data on the issue of ministry is evaluated.

One notes, however, that a number of issues are involved in both of these approaches which develop the statement that Jesus instituted the Church. First of all, the gospels speak almost exclusively about the kingdom. Only in Matthew's gospel, we realize, do we have the technical term "church" (16, 18; 18, 17). It must be seriously questioned, then, whether or not one can apply gospel passages which deal with the kingdom to the Church? And, if so, to what extent? Since "church" is mentioned frequently in the Pauline corpus, in Acts, in other New Testament epistles, to what extent do "church" and "kingdom" interrelate?

Second, Jesus seems to have preached that the end of the world was imminent. However, if the end of the world were coming soon, so it has been argued, would someone establish a Church which would be so short-lived, or, more particularly, establish a Church structure that was fairly complicated, if it was only meant to be in existence for a very short period of time?

Third, the issue of Jesus' knowledge plays a role in these discussions. In the approach which sees Jesus establishing in his lifetime a fairly structured Church, it is presupposed that Jesus knew the future of his community and was preparing it for such a future. If, on the other hand, Jesus was somewhat ignorant, humanly speaking, of the future, then questions are validly raised regarding the institution of a

Church, since Jesus could not have known how much future there really was to the existence of the world.

Finally, the very meaning and place of the resurrection of Jesus himself and its constitutive role in the institution of the Church is left to one side or even completely omitted from the discussion, if the Church had already existed in its essential structures prior to the resurrection.

Galot acknowledges this ecclesiological presupposition and the way in which it plays a major role in interpreting the data of the New Testament and the early Church. He writes:

> Nowhere does Jesus speak explicitly of successors. It has been maintained that the group of the Twelve was established to play a unique role as Jesus' own co-workers in his mission on earth. . . . By its very nature, any such task could not be passed on to others; it excluded the possibility of successors. . . . The position one takes on this issue is controlled above all by the view one entertains about the foundation of the Church. The authors who attribute to Jesus the conviction that the world would shortly come to an end and maintain that Jesus did not envision the institution of a Church, meant to develop for a long time in history, or that he had no intention of establishing any church at all, cannot admit that he willed to confer permanency to the structure he was to establish.[12]

In this ecclesiological approach one might argue that it is arbitrary to say that Jesus had an erroneous belief that the world was coming to an end quickly, and in doing so one simply denies the minor premise in a syllogistic argument. The syllogism would be constructed as follows:

MAJOR: Jesus would not establish a Church, if he thought the end of the world was quite near.

MINOR: Jesus did NOT think that the end of the world was quite near.

ERGO: Jesus did establish a Church.

The opposing position simply removes the "not" from the minor and the conclusion is quite the opposite:

ERGO: Jesus did not establish a Church.

Given the New Testament data on the issue of the end of the world and what Jesus said about it, we find very conflicting data. In some instances the end of the world is coming within the very generation to whom Jesus was speaking; at other times, it is postponed, but still coming. At times, Jesus is said to describe the end of the world as coming with cosmic signs; at other times, he is said to describe the end of the world as coming like a thief in the night. In his volume, *Jesus God and Man,* R. Brown simply lays out all the pertinent texts, and the result is not clear as to what Jesus may or may not have thought or taught about the end of the world.[13] In other words, one can hardly say that attributing to Jesus the conviction that the end of the world is coming shortly is "erroneous." The New Testament does not decide this issue of Jesus' knowledge on this matter in one way or the other.

Galot, in developing his argument mentioned above, would have been better served had he referred to Paul. In his letters to the Thessalonians, Paul indicates that the end of the world, in his view, was indeed coming soon (cf. 1 Thess 4, 13–18). Nonetheless, for Paul there was a Church, and there was ministry, and there were structures. Evidently, Paul, even though he seems to have believed in a rather imminent end of the world, had no difficulty in building up the Church, even though the interval might be of short duration.

Actually, the issue does not stand or fall on the basis of (a) what Jesus knew or did not know, which is a fairly difficult question to settle definitively, or (b) did Jesus plan for a succession in detail or not. The issue on which the dividing line between these two different ecclesiological stances rests is fundamentally the issue of the resurrection. It is the Christian belief in the risen Jesus as Kyrios or Lord that is at the very heart of the Church. The resurrection is an essential element for the very meaning and structure of the Church. Prior to the resurrection and the resurrection faith of the followers of Jesus, it appears difficult to speak about a Church, since the central focus of the Church is missing: namely, belief in the risen Jesus as Lord. This is, in my view, the area which should be discussed, not the issue of Jesus' knowledge of the future, nor even an argument over the historicity of certain passages in the gospel, such as Mt 16, 16ff, in which the author puts in the mouth of Jesus the words: "And on this rock I will build my Church." If the resurrection is an essential element of the Church, then the resurrection of Jesus must come before one can actually speak of Church in a meaningful way. To put the institution of the Church chronologically prior to the resurrection tends to relativize the importance of the resurrection of Jesus itself and the faith in the risen Lord by the disciples.

This has not been a lengthy chapter. However, the issue that it raises is of vital importance in the question of Christian ministry. Since the issue is so central, it seems to deserve more notice that a mere subtitled section of a larger unit. Rather, the issue clearly must be faced, acknowledged, and in some ways one side or the other must be explicitly preferred, if one wishes to trace the meaning of Christian ministry. If one selects the first approach, then there is less room for variance in Christian ministry; if one selects the second approach, then pastoral conditions play a much larger role in determining the details of Church structures and ministries, and as a result there is far more room for ministerial variances.

The chapter was called deliberately an ecclesiological presupposition. As a presupposition, it is not argued in depth in a study on ministry; that kind of argumentation belongs to ecclesiology and a treatise devoted exclusively to ecclesiology. In a treatise on ministry, one side or the other is simply presupposed. As an ecclesiological statement, it has to do with a theology of Church, and only in and through a theology of Church can a study on Christian ministry make any sense. Christian ministry is ecclesial ministry.

With these brief but important ideas in mind, let us now turn to the New Testament itself, in which we find the first indications of Christian ministry. From there we will continue on through the subsequent eras of Church history. Our aim is simply to look at the data and to synthesize the findings which the historical data of each era offers us. Only at the very end will we attempt to put together the material in a less historical and more theological way.

3. SUMMARY

The summary of this chapter is quite succinct:

1. The ecclesiological presupposition on Jesus' founding of the Church is crucial for an understanding of Church ministry.
2. One position holds that Jesus, during his earthly life, established in some detail the Church.
3. The second position holds that the Church really begins with

the resurrection and the belief in the Lordship of the risen Jesus.

4. Catholic scholarship ranges in a variety of ways between these two rather polar positions.

5. The resurrection of Jesus, and its significance for the very meaning of the Church, seems to be the real dividing issue between the two poles of this ecclesiological presupposition.[14]

3

Ministry: 27 to 110 A.D.

SUMMARY: During this period the extant data allows us to make the following conclusions:

1. The *naming of ministry* began to take place.
   (a) The name "The Twelve" was given by Jesus;
   (b) The name "Apostle" more than likely was given by Jesus;
   (c) All other names were given by various groups of the early Church.
2. The *functions* of these Church ministries had Jesus as the basic model, but due to pastoral needs more ministerial functions than simply those of the apostles themselves were required. Pastoral need, not Jesus' command, shaped these other ministries.
3. Both the naming and the functions of Christian ministry continued to develop during this period.
4. At the conclusion of this period, there is still no set pattern to the names for Christian ministers, and there is also no common pattern which is historically verifiable of specific functions for any of these various titles of ministry.

This chapter takes up after the death and resurrection of Jesus and covers a span of time which ends roughly at 110 A.D. This latter date has been chosen for two reasons: (a) around 110 A.D., most of the writings of the New Testament seem to have been written; not all perhaps, but the major works were completed;[1] (b) around 110 A.D., we begin to have material on the early Church from non-New Testament sources, and therefore not of canonical status. The date is, of course, somewhat arbitrary, but from a schematic viewpoint it seems to be helpful. Still, the reader should take into account that some New Testament writings may have been written after this date, and some non-New Testament writings were written prior to this date. The year 110 A.D. is simply a generalized date, not a specific one. What separates this chapter from the next chapter is more the content than the exact dating: in this chapter, the New Testament data itself is considered; in the next chapter the earliest non-New Testament data is considered.

In every interpretation of this New Testament material, it should be noted that the ecclesiological presupposition mentioned above plays a substantial role in the way in which various authors handle the same documentation. If Jesus instituted the Church during his lifetime and provided it with considerable and detailed structures, then one will indeed see in the documentation indications of this detailed institution. If, on the other hand, the Church is seen as primarily an Easter event, that is after the lifetime of Jesus, as other scholars believe, then more room is given to the pastoral needs of the early Church as far as the specific structuring of both ministry and office.

1. THE NEW TESTAMENT CHURCHES

R. Brown, in his volume *The Churches the Apostles Left Behind,* indicates that after the year 70 there seem to be seven different approaches to the Christian community. He lines them up as follows:[2]

1. The community at Antioch, in which Matthew is written;
2. The community in which I and II John are written;
3. The community in which the Fourth Gospel is written;
4. The community in which I Peter is written;
5. The community in which Luke's gospel and Acts are written;
6. The community in which the Letters to the Colossians and Ephesians are written;
7. The community in which the Pastoral Epistles are written.

These communities represent Christianity after 70, i.e., after the destruction of the temple in Jerusalem and the subsequent flight of the Jewish leadership from Jerusalem. The Christian community in Jerusalem after this time fails to play a major role in the Church.

Prior to these communities, one finds that in the years 27 to 70 there are other Churches that one can recognize and of which one has at least indirect evidence, with the exception of Paul, for whom there is, of course, direct evidence: namely:

1. The communities in which Paul was active and writing;
2. The community in which the Q source developed;
3. The community in which the substrate of Mark developed;
4. The community in which the passion narrative, together with the narrative of the Lord's Supper, developed.
5. The communities in which the material on the resurrection of Jesus developed.

These communities represent earlier strata than those which Brown describes, and since we do not have any written sources directly except those of Paul, there are at best only conjectural interpretations on the type of Christian community involved.

Below 27 is, of course, the lifetime of Jesus.

Let us use these categories which Brown (and others) have described. In doing so, I do not want to "canonize" Brown's categories. Brown's descriptions of these various Churches need, perhaps, to be nuanced and possibly, though not too probably, changed. We will use them here for schematic reasons, helping us to focus more clearly on early Church ministry as it developed in this early and non-uniform stratum of Church history. These categories at least offer us some sort of window into the Christian communal lives of those various times and places. I must add in all fairness, however, that Brown in his presentation of these early communities does not develop the following schematic breakdown as regards Christian ministry. Nonetheless, when one attaches known names of ministry, not simply passing metaphors on ministry, to each of these communities, helpful data result. Let me emphasize that in the listing below we are considering only those ministerial names which seem to have had a somewhat lasting character about them, and not simply occasional descriptive names concerning ministry.[3]

COMMUNITY	KNOWN NAMES OF MINISTRY
1. Lifetime of Jesus	The Twelve Apostle

COMMUNITY	KNOWN NAMES OF MINISTRY
2. Paul	Apostle The Twelve Prophet Teacher Deacon Deacon (for a woman; Greek is masc.) Father Servant (Hyperetes) Overseer (Proistamenos) Episkopos Leitourgos
3. Q source, Substrate of Mark Passion Narrative	The Twelve Apostle
4. Matthew	The Twelve Apostle
5. 2 and 3 John (1 John)	Presbyteros
6. Fourth Gospel	Apostle The Twelve
7. 1 Peter	Apostle Episkopos Presbyteros Neoteros (?)
8. Luke/Acts	Apostle The Twelve Episkopos Presbyteros Evangelist Teacher Prophet Servant (Hyperetes)

COMMUNITY	KNOWN NAMES OF MINISTRY
9. Colossians/Ephesians	Apostle Teacher Shepherd Prophet Evangelist
10. Pastorals	Apostle The Twelve Episkopos Presbyteros Diakonos Deacon (refers to a woman [?]) Teacher Father Preacher (Keryx) Neoteros (?) Evangelist
11. Revelation	The Twelve Presbyteros

This listing simply indicates the ecclesial spheres in which certain titles for ministry were to some degree used. It is, of course, necessary to determine the frequency of these ministerial titles, in order to understand their value. However, the benefit of this schematization is that one can see that in certain ecclesial spheres some titles stand out, while in other ecclesial spheres some titles of ministers are totally absent. In itself, the listing indicates that the naming of Church ministers is still quite in flux even at the end of this New Testament period. There is no way to claim a monolithic or standardized pattern of ministerial names and corresponding functions in the New Testament itself; these very names, rather, witness to a diversity both of title and of function. Let us now consider in detail the functions of these various names.

2. PRESBYTER AND EPISKOPOS

If we look at the Pauline material, which is the oldest written material (but not the oldest in tradition), we find that there is scant attention to either episkopos or diakonos and absolutely none to presbyter. On the other hand, Paul's letters indicate that the most esteemed minister is the apostle; after the apostle the prophet and the teacher have a major ministerial role in the Pauline corpus. In other words, in the Pauline community, as far as we can discern from textual data, the use of the titles episkopos and diakonos, much less presbyter, were not common, whereas apostle, prophet and teacher were.

In contrast to this, we have the material from Luke/Acts. In this body of material, especially in Acts, we find that apostle is indeed the highest title of Christian ministry, and it is equated in Acts with the Twelve. In other words, for the author of Acts, there are only twelve apostles. This equation of apostles and the Twelve, however, does not correspond with the Pauline material, since Paul considered himself to be an apostle, of equal status to the others, and in some way even a better apostle.

Besides apostle, we find the title presbyter of esteemed rank in Acts. Episkopos, however, is mentioned in Acts, but only in a brief way. Scholars argue as to the origin of these two titles: presbyter and episkopos. Some scholars defend the position that episkopos is of Greek-Christian origin, while presbyter is of Jewish-Christian origin. Undoubtedly, a blanket statement that episkopos comes from non-Jewish Christian communities and presbyter comes from Jewish Christian communities may not be the total answer as to their provenance. Still, there is a kernel of truth in the proposal that presbyter stems or at least is more common in Jewish Christian circles, while episkopos stems or at least is more common in Graeco-Christian circles.

> The word episkopos = overseer signifies, as a title of office, an oversight task or a management task in the service of the state, the local community, an organization, or a cultic group. In the Septuagint God who sees everything is called an episkopos (Job 20, 29; Wis 1, 6: "the episkopos of his heart"). More frequently are men called episkopos, who perform a function of oversight: governor, officer, building inspector, director, temple inspector. The Greek word episkopos (as also ephoros) is also equivalent to the Hebrew title: mebaqqer, which the leader of the reformed community of the Damascus Covenant and of the Qumran texts bore.[4]

In this observation by Ott, we see that episkopos did have Jewish rootage, so that an exclusively Greek origin of episkopos would be difficult to maintain. However, Ott goes on to state that Christian use of the leadership title, episkopos, seems to have first appeared in the Greek-speaking Christian communities with some dependence on or connection with the then common terminology for leadership positions found in the Greek speaking world.[5]

Presbyter has a different historical background. The presbyter is clearly a Jewish title for ministry, and one that goes far back in Jewish history. Bornkamm, writing in the *TWNT* on "presbyter," notes that elders are presupposed in all strata of the Old Testament tradition.

> It is generally assumed that their origin lies in the most ancient patriarchal period when Israel was made up of tribes long before the settlement and national hegemony. As heads and represen-tatives of the great families and clans the elders were leaders in the larger units which were then in the process of formation.[6]

Even in J and E, the earliest sources of Israel's history, the elders are not related to tribal constitution, but to representation of the entire people. They do not govern or initiate power, but work with and under major Jewish figures, such as Moses and Joshua. At the time of the Judges and the monarchy, the elders become influential in city structures of government and the kings often had to gain the support of the "elders of Israel" if they were to engage in successful wars with outside forces.

Deuteronomy defines some of their legal powers in an explicit way. In the exile, one finds elders both in Palestine itself and in the areas of exile. After the exile the sanhedrin developed in Jerusalem, and there were three different groups which belonged to this sanhedrin: the priests, who had clear presidency in the sanhedrin; the theological group, the scribes; and the lay group, who were the presbyters. There was also a synagogal use of the title presbyter just before the time of Jesus. This local person had a place of eminence in the synagogue, but the local presbyter did not perform any liturgical position. Both in the Jerusalem sanhedrin and in the local level, the presbyter was clearly a non-liturgical, non-priestly individual, indeed, a lay person throughout.

F. Moriarty, commenting on the use of presbyter in Isaiah 3, 2, notes: "The elders were the leading citizens of the city. As heads of the families within a clan, they settled town disputes and trials, usually at the city gate, where community affairs were handled."[7] G. Wood offers us a similar portrait of an elder in his discussion of the prophet

Joel, who speaks to the elders in 1, 2: "They were members of the municipal council. Primitively the term referred to the heads of clans within a tribe. During the monarchy, the elders managed affairs on the local level (1 Sm 30:26-31; 2 Kgs 23:1; Ez 8:1). For some of their judicial duties see Dt 19:12; 21:1-9, 18-21; 22:13-21; 25:5-10. They continued to function among the exiles (Ez 14:1; 20:1-3) and more prominently in the restored community (Ezr 5:9; 6:7; 10:8, 14)."[8]

In all of these accounts by biblical scholars, the term, presbyter, as used in the Jewish world, did not include liturgical functions. It was not "priestly" in its connotation. It was rather leadership and service to the community that marked one as an elder. A number of early Christian communities, probably more Jewish than Greek, selected this term as the name of their main leader and minister; in doing this they deliberately did not select the Jewish terms of liturgical and priestly functions. As we shall see, there was a reason for selecting presbyter as a name for Christian ministry, rather than the usual and quite available Jewish terms for liturgical, priestly ministry.

As far as episkopos is concerned there are a number of similarities with this non-liturgical aspect of presbyteros. The term was used, as we noted in passing above, in a civil and secular way, generally not in a religious way in early Greek society. Moreover, it was a term of service, but included leadership, and to that extent some sort of power. It was a term applied to lay people, not to a priestly caste, and in itself carried no priestly or ritual overtones about it.

In Acts, presbyter is used far more than episkopos to signify the main local leader of the Christian community. Fitzmyer writes:

If there is no evidence in the Pauline letters that the churches with which Paul dealt were presbyterally structured (but cf. Phil 1:1), Luke depicts Paul (not Barnabas) on Mission I (a.d. 46–49; cf. *JBC,* art. 46, n. 25-27) setting up "elders" (*presbyteroi*) "in every church" (Acts 14:23). When Paul is returning to Jerusalem from Mission III (a.d. 58), he summons the elders of Ephesus to Miletus and addresses them, telling them to be responsible "overseers" (*episkopoi*) of the church of God (20:17–28—the only place in Acts where this term appears for church officials; cf. 1:20). The "elders" appear elsewhere as functionaries or leaders in local churches (11:30; 15:2, 3, 6, 22, 23; 16:4; 20: 17; 21:18). It seems, then, that Luke attributed to Paul the structure of the community with which he was familiar in his own day. That elders were understood by him to be persons of authority can be seen from the way they are coupled with the "apostles" in Acts 15–16.[9]

Since "episkopos" is, in this Church of Luke, not the clear name for the most important local minister, but rather the title of "presbyter" holds this rank, and since the presbyters are to some degree described as appointed by apostles (e.g., Paul), it is difficult to say that there is an "episcopal succession" to the apostles as far as Acts is concerned. In Acts, there is really a "presbyteral succession" to the apostles. Put another way, one would say that the "apostolic succession" is through the presbyteroi, not the episkopoi in Acts. Brown notes that the presbyteroi in Acts (as elsewhere in the New Testament as well) do not really function as apostles, i.e., continuing the apostolic function. The apostles were itinerant; the presbyters (and episkopoi) are residential. The apostles are pictured doing many functions; only a few of these are "continued" by the presbyters/episkopoi.[10]

Titus (1, 5) was also given the task to establish presbyters in every town. In the second and third epistles of John, the one who has authority in the local community is the presbyter, who also appears to have authority over the surrounding area as well. This corresponds to the picture we have from the first epistle of John as well. The Johannine presbyters do not appear to have the same kind of authority as other New Testament presbyters, since they seem to have no authority over the false teachers (presbyters?). These Johannine letters are, of course, written at a later date than Acts and in a different Christian community. Still, the emphasis overall on presbyter, not on episkopos, cannot be set to one side. Some authors, such as Galot, speak of a presbyter-episkopos, to designate these early leaders of Christian communities.[11] In the pastorals, the term episkopos becomes somewhat more prominent than in Acts, but these pastorals are written at a later date than Acts and in a different Christian community.

Some of the early Christian communities found these two terms, presbyter and episkopos, precisely the kind of titles which they felt corresponded to the ministry of Jesus in a most special way. It must be emphasized that it was *not the origin of the titles* that determined the Christian usage, but the model of Jesus which governed both the understanding of Christian ministry and the naming of that ministry. This is why one cannot say that simply a Jewish or Greek origin lies at the root of the Christian titles presbyter and episkopos. These two titles came to be the accepted titles of the Christian leader, since they reflected the kind of ministry which Jesus himself performed. The term "hiereus" (priest) did not, in their eyes, reflect the Lord's ministry.

Schillebeeckx, in his volume, *Ministry: Leadership in the Community of Jesus Christ,* speaks often about the pneumatological origin of Christian ministry in the New Testament Churches.[12] Perhaps, there is a semantic difficulty, and no more than this, in using the term pneumatological. After all, the Spirit, to which Schillebeeckx is referring, is, indeed, the Spirit of Jesus. Nonetheless, it would appear to be more correct to emphasize the christological base for Christian ministry, rather than the pneumatological base. Throughout the New Testament, Jesus, and particularly the life of Jesus in Palestine, remains the normative aspect of Christian ministry.[13] For our present focus, it is important to remember that the titles of Christian ministry were selected on the basis of Jesus and his own modeling of ministry, and not simply because of the inspiration of the Spirit in the early Church.

Nowhere in the New Testament does it say that the apostles were episkopoi. This is important. The equation of apostles to the episkopoi or the episkopoi to the apostles was done at a later date (St. Cyprian seems to have been the first to do so), so that in the later, i.e., post-New Testament date, there was a linkage made between the "college of the apostles" and the "college of episkopoi." However, this is not something that the New Testament indicates at all. If one says that the apostles were the first "bishops," one is clearly going beyond New Testament evidence. The apostles were the first chief leaders of the Christian community, but they did not have the name "episkopos" (bishop), nor did they function in the way later episkopoi (bishops) functioned.

Moreover, one cannot claim the New Testament material in order to determine the difference between presbyter and episkopos. Both Acts and the pastoral letters, as also the Johannine letters, are not clear on the differences between presbyteroi and episkopoi. One of the most important statements on this matter is Acts 20, 17–28, in which the term episkopos appears for the first time in this document. The very same people are called, at first, "presbyteroi," and then in v. 28, "episkopoi."

From Miletus he [Paul] sent for the elders [presbyteroi] of the Church of Ephesus. When they arrived he addressed these words

to them: "You know . . . etc. [v. 28] Be on your guard for yourselves and for all the flock of which the Holy Spirit has made
you overseers [episkopoi], to feed the Church of God, which he
bought with his own blood.

It is clear that the terms presbyter and episkopos are to some
degree interchangeable. In this passage, which is so key to the Acts
presentation of what a Church missionary is all about, Paul is delivering
a sort of final discourse, a "last testament," to his fellow ministers,
whom he indiscriminately calls presbyteroi and episkopoi. R. Dillon
and J. Fitzmyer, commenting on this exact passage in Acts, say that
there is an implication of no distinction in these two titles.[14] Only
when we move into non-New Testament data do we begin to find a
clear differentiation between episkopos and presbyter. This new, non-
New Testament data indicates that there has been, in the Christian
community, a development in both the functioning and the naming
of Christian ministry.

The pastoral letters, written at a later date than Acts, present a
fairly similar approach to episkopos and presbyter. One must note,
however, that references to either episkopos or presbyter are made
only in a passing way; they are not by any means the major focus of
these letters. In 1 Tim 3, 1ff. we read:

To want to be a presiding elder [episkopos] is to want to do a
noble work. That is why the president [episkopos] must have an
impeccable character.

The letter then lists the many qualities which such a person should
have. The only reference to "managing" the Church is v. 5, which
textually might even be a later addition, since many early manuscripts
do not carry this verse at all. At any rate, the verse in no way indicates
anything precise about such Church management.

In the same chapter, vv. 8–13, we find a list of the personal
qualities for the diakonos. In v. 13 we read that those who "deacon
well" will earn a high standing for themselves. Little information is
given as to how one deacons well.

In chapter 5, v. 17ff., attention is turned to the presbyter:

The elders [presbyteroi] who do their work well while they are
in charge are to be given double consideration, especially those

who are assiduous in preaching and teaching. . . . Never accept
any accusation brought against an elder [presbyteros] unless it
is supported by two or three witnesses.

A small window is opened here as far as the functions of presbyters
are concerned: namely, they preach and teach. Still, in other New
Testament texts we find that the episkopos also preaches and teaches.

The letter to Titus, 1, 5–9, renews this interchange of presbyteros
and episkopos:

The reason I left you behind in Crete was for you to get everything
organized and appoint elders [presbyteroi] in every town in the
way that I told you.

The author then proceeds to describe the personal qualities of
such presbyteroi, and in v. 7 he notes:

Since as president [episkopos] he will be God's representative
[oikonomos], he must be irreproachable.

This free interchange of episkopos and presbyter in Acts and in
the pastoral letters cannot be set to one side. One would correctly say
that the titles of episkopos and presbyter were not yet totally differentiated, and even if we use the difference in origin of these two terms,
we could only say that what the Jewish Christian communities meant
by presbyter, their preferred title, corresponded to what the non-Jewish
Christian communities meant by episkopos, their preferred title. As
the Jewish and non-Jewish Christian groups came more and more
into contact with each other, the names came to be used in an interchangeable way. Only with the passage of time did a ranking for
these two titles begin to occur.

G. Denzer, commenting on these pastoral letters, makes the following general observations:

It is incorrect to say that the ecclesiastical organization of the
local Christian communities as reflected in the Pastorals has the
fully developed form of the second century. Rather, it agrees
with what other sources indicate for the middle of the first
century.[15]

Denzer then goes on to describe the rather developed Church organization which one finds in the letters of St. Ignatius, with each Church having a single bishop in charge, a college of presbyters beneath the bishop, and deacons beneath both of these. In the Ignatian material, there is a sharp distinction between episkopos and presbyter.

> The Pastorals, however, reflect a less developed organization. There is no single local head of the community with proper episcopal powers. In each church there is a group of presbyters (presbyteroi), who are called episkopoi.[16]

For all of these reasons, one sees that the episkopos of the second century (at least the episkopos in Ignatius of Antioch) cannot simply be equated to the episkopos mentioned in the New Testament. Nor can the presbyter of the second century be equated in an unqualified way with the presbyter mentioned in the New Testament. Both the name and the function needed to develop much further than the New Testament allows us to see, so that we are able to describe a Church organization in which an episkopos is the primary leader of the community and the presbyters are in a secondary and consultive status.

Undoubtedly, the most important items to realize as regards episkopos and presbyter are these:

1. Jesus did not establish these names; rather, they were established by the Christian community itself, i.e., only after the resurrection. Indeed, one would also have to think that these names began to be used in the Christian communities only after these early Christian groups had become somewhat more structured and complex.

2. Both episkopos and presbyter are non-liturgical, and non-priestly in origin and usage. Leadership is the primary aspect of these two titles. Applied to members of the early Church, they indicate community leadership rather than "priestly," i.e., liturgical, ministry.

3. The two names were selected at first by some of the Christian communities, though not by all in any universal or monolithic way, since they reflected the model of Jesus himself, the one

who came to serve and not be served. This connection with Jesus is essential to any appreciation of these names and functions.

4. In the New Testament, the presbyters and the episkopoi are seen as Christian leaders who preach the good news, teach the community, and in their lives model the ministry of Jesus. The presbyters in Acts and in the pastorals are somewhat different in function from the presbyters in the Johannine epistles.

5. An attempt to see in these names an understanding of the essential meaning of Christian ministry by way of "priest," or, more particularly, of "eucharist as a sacrifice," cannot be justified by the documentary evidence. Neither the name nor the function of either of these terms is derived from the eucharistic ministry. Both the name and the function are rooted in a leadership role which continues the mission of Jesus, especially the preaching of the gospel message.

6. The presbyter and the episkopos are portrayed as residential, local leaders. The apostles are not so presented in the New Testament. The presbyter and episkopos carry on only some of the activities of the apostles. In no way can they be seen or described as "second generation" apostles.

3. THE TWELVE AND THE APOSTLES

Let us consider one other important New Testament title, namely, the Twelve.[17] This title is found in many New Testament writings and at a number of different strata in these writings. It was, indeed, the most important title for a Christian minister. For many Christians the title, the Twelve, is synonomous with the apostles, so that frequently one hears that there are only twelve such men. Biblical scholars point out that this identification is not uniform in the New Testament. We have mentioned above that in the Pauline letters Paul considers himself to be an apostle of no mean stature; in fact, he ranks with the best of them. In Acts, however, Luke does not tolerate any apostle beyond the twelve (reluctantly he calls Paul an apostle, but only once).

One must be quite circumspect in ascribing to the Twelve an ecclesial function, since the New Testament itself is most reticent on this issue. The Twelve appear most often in a symbolic function, and this on two scores: first, an eschatological aspect, and, second, a universal aspect. The connection of the Twelve to the twelve patriarchs of Israel is manifest. The new Israel, the kingdom, now has its own twelve figures, just as the old Israel had. These twelve patriarchs of olden times marked the beginning of a new age; so, too, the New Testament Twelve mark the beginning of a new age, superior to all that went before, namely the beginning of a new and eschatological age. Second, just as the twelve of old symbolized the totality of Israel, so, too, do the Twelve, together with Jesus, symbolize the universality of the new age. The kingdom has come in and through Jesus, and this kingdom is for everyone. H. von Campenhausen notes:

> This much at any rate is correct, namely that there is some connection between the number of the Twelve and "Israel," the nation of the twelve tribes, and this is the reason for the choice of this particular number. The Israel in mind, however, may in fact not be the Jewish people as objects of the Christian mission, but rather the new, Christian Israel, which is to triumph at the day of Christ's return, when the kingdom of God breaks into world-history. It is this Israel which is represented by the Twelve.[18]

Rather than an ecclesial reference, the Twelve represent the kingdom, which cannot be seen as coterminous with the Church. If what von Campenhausen writes is correct, then the Twelve represent the kingdom, and only insofar as the Church reflects the kingdom would the Twelve be a part of the Church symbolization. The Twelve, either in name or in function, are not directly connected to Church structure. The early Church did indeed see itself as an eschatological community, within the Jewish religion. Since the eschaton is the coming of the kingdom, the Twelve have meaning and function in this eschatological dimension. Many of the authors of the New Testament mention the Twelve, and they are doing this after the year 70 A.D., when the Christian community and the Jewish community were clearly moving apart, so that the Christian community was developing a sense of Church separate from, in many ways, the Jewish religious community. One might think that the title, the Twelve, would have been discontinued, especially if the delay of the parousia was beginning to be accepted by the Christian groups. This is not the case. The Twelve continue to be mentioned, though not frequently, by these Christian communities, which were steadily deepening their self-identity. Nonetheless, since the Church community is itself a sign of the kingdom, though not coterminous with the kingdom, the Twelve as name and function served to recall this eschatological dimension, not simply of the Church, but of the kingdom which the Lord Jesus had preached. It is this indirect connection between the Twelve, on the one hand, and the Church, on the other, which needs to be seen clearly. To say that the Twelve have no bearing on the Church would be pressing the issue too far. To say that the Twelve are essential to the Church structure would likewise be stressing the issue too far.

Paul mentions that it was in the tradition, which he received, that the risen Jesus appeared to the Twelve (1 Cor 15, 5). This is clearly one of the links of continuity between the disciples who followed Jesus in his lifetime and the community of disciples who came to believe in Jesus as the risen Lord. This new community, the Jesus community, continues the message, mission and ministry of Jesus himself. The appearance to the Twelve, right at the beginning, indicates this christological rootage of the Church.

Luke portrays the Eleven, after the death of Judas, as needful of selecting a successor so that the number Twelve will continue (Acts 1, 26).

> Yet as the story in Acts professes and James, the son of Zebedee, one of the Twelve, is put to death by Herod Agrippa (12:2), no need is then felt to reconstitute the Twelve anew. Indeed, once it was reconstituted in chap. 1, the Twelve appear in the Lucan account only on Pentecost (2:14) and in the selection of the seven table-servers (6:2—in 6:6 they are referred to as "the apostles"). This ephemeral existence of the Twelve in the Lucan story raises problems in the understanding of the structure of the community that is recounted as stemming from Jesus himself. How does one account for the ephemeral existence of this group? Why does its influence disappear in Acts? Why is its only function, after the testimony to Israel on Pentecost, to change the community-structure by overseeing the democratic appointment of the seven table-servers?[19]

In Acts (6, 1–6) the Twelve (in v. 6 called apostles) are seen in a leadership role, regulating Church structure. The whole community is gathered together, the Twelve address them (the text does not say who does the addressing), and seven men are selected for ministry. This ministry is difficult to call "deacon ministry," since the function of these seven corresponds better with presbyters.[20] This is the last occasion in which the Twelve is mentioned in Acts.

Galot presents a somewhat different view of the Twelve, and it is evident that the ecclesial presupposition is at work in the way he structures his interpretation and approach:

> The number twelve is significant; it corresponds to the tribes of Israel and discloses the intention of establishing the foundations of a new Israel. To say it more clearly, Jesus establishes the group of the Twelve in order to establish the Church. This is his way of declaring that the role he assigns to the Twelve in the establishment of the Church is an essential one.[21]

This description does not take into account that the Twelve and the apostles are at times not synonomous with each other; consequently, he applies to the Twelve what he says about the apostles and vice versa. Nor do we find here any distinction between the kingdom and the Church, a distinction which Vatican II clearly made on the basis of excellent scriptural scholarship. What Jesus says about the Twelve, then, is transposed to a Jesus speaking about the Church. In the eschatologically minded early Christian community the Twelve had a strong eschatological aspect, which was connected to the immanent coming of the kingdom of God. This kingdom had a universal aspect, so that the Twelve represented the call of the kingdom to everyone, none excluded, unless by their own sinful choice.

When we turn to the apostles, their primary aspect comes to us through their belief in the resurrection of Jesus and also in their subsequent establishment of the Christian community. One sees a very clear ecclesial dimension to the description of the apostles, which one does not see in the Twelve. Paul himself is indeed an apostle, a believer in Jesus' resurrection, and the only personal witness to the risen Lord who writes in the New Testament. He is also one of the key founders of the Christian community. In Paul, as elsewhere, we find that apostle applies to a larger group than the Twelve, and it is this larger view of apostle which is the base for the later [much later] view that there are only twelve apostles. K. H. Schelke, for his part, concurs in this view.[22] The limited understanding of an apostle, that is, an understanding which equates apostle to twelve, is a later interpretation of the meaning of an apostle. Originally, apostle was understood by the early community in a larger way. The larger meaning was the basis for the narrower meaning.

Let us consider the gospel passages which treat of the sending of the Twelve. The first is that of Mark 6, 7:

> He made a tour around the villages, teaching. Then he summoned the Twelve and began to send them out in pairs, giving them authority over the unclean spirits. And he instructed them to take nothing for the journey except a staff—no bread, no haversack, no coppers for their purses. They were to wear sandals but, he added, "Do not take a spare tunic." And he said to them, "If you enter a house anywhere, stay there until you leave the district. And if any place does not welcome you and people refuse to listen to you, as you walk away shake off the dust from under your feet as a sign to them." So they set off to preach repentance; and they cast out many devils, and anointed many sick people with oil and cured them.

There is clearly a ministry involved in this sending out: a ministry of preaching and healing. The Twelve, then, are portrayed with a ministry; this is undeniable. Mark includes this in writing in his gospel, but not simply for some historical reason: namely, that Jesus once did this and the Twelve once did go out on such a ministry. The gospel of Mark is far more concerned with the community existing at the time of Mark's composition of this gospel. In other words, Mark includes this with an eye to his own community, somewhere between 70 and 80 A.D. What connection does Mark want to make between this historical activity of the Twelve and the actual Christian life at his own time, two generations at least after the resurrection?

It is almost a truism that discipleship is a key issue in Mark's gospel: what does it mean to be a true disciple of Jesus? Every disciple of Jesus, on this level of connection, would be, then, a person who goes out and preaches the good news and brings healing to others. Christians are called on to do this in virtue of their baptism. The Twelve, then, tell every Christian something about their baptismal dignity and commission.

If we attempt to go further than this, many uncertainties arise. The text in no way allows us to equate the Twelve with bishops or episkopoi. Such a connection is totally unverifiable by the text. Moreover, the immediate context of this section of Mark's gospel in no way allows a connection between the Twelve and their being sent out with episkopoi or bishops and their mission. Nowhere at all in the context of this passage can such a relationship be made. Even further, the wider context of Mark's gospel, and therefore Mark's Church community, does not permit a connection between the Twelve and their mission and episkopoi/bishops and their mission. We have absolutely no evidence that in the Church community of Mark the leaders were even called "episkopoi." Nor can one relate the Twelve and the sending out to presbyters, to teachers, to prophets, etc. We simply do not know what names the leaders of the Marcan Christian community used in 70–80 A.D.

There is, however, in Mark's portrayal of the Twelve, both here in 6, 7–13, and also in the selection of the Twelve, Mk 3, 13–19, a ministerial dimension, which Mark holds up as a model for ministry. In other words, the leadership positions in the Church community at the time of Mark would have seen in the Marcan portrayal of the Twelve a modeling of their leadership ministry, particularly as it focused on preaching and healing. Since we have no indication of the names of such leadership people, any more definite connection clearly goes beyond the text and context of this gospel.

In the parallel passage of Matthew 10, 1–16, we have the listing of the names (Mk 3, 13–19) and the sending out (Mk 6, 7–13) placed together. Preaching and healing remain the main objectives of this commissioning, but Matthew adds some details:

a. The Twelve are to go only to Israel, not to the gentiles.
b. They are not even to go to the Samaritans.
c. The basic theme of their preaching is not simply repentance as in Mark, but the kingdom of God and that this kingdom is close at hand, i.e., the end of the world is near.
d. The simplicity of life, as in Mark, is stressed, carrying very few personal items with them on this journey.
e. Rejection both of them personally and of their message, as in Mark, is part of the ministry, but Matthew intensifies the oppositional aspects to their preaching.

We have seen in the list of names for the Church community of Matthew, more than likely Antioch, around 70/80 A.D., that the names of Christian ministry were: the Twelve and apostle. Some would add "scribe," since the scribes in Matthew's gospel are generally treated kindly, and the author of the gospel might have been a Christian scribe himself. We saw that in the Matthew community we have no verifiable evidence for the use of such names as episkopos and presbyter. Once more, as was the case for Mark, the text does not allow us in any way to relate the Twelve to episkopos. The immediate context disallows the same. The context of the entire Matthaean gospel does not permit such a connection. To say that in Matthew's gospel we see an episcopal mission in this sending out of the Twelve is gratuitous. One could as easily say that in this sending of the Twelve one sees a presbyteral mission or a prophetic mission.

Still, Matthew includes this material, and embellishes what he has taken over from Mark, again not simply for its historical value, but for what it says to his own community for whom he was writing this gospel. The gospel of Matthew stresses discipleship, so that any and every Christian can see in the Twelve and their mission something of his or her own commission, which stems from the turning to Jesus at one's baptism.

There is, as well, a pronounced "churchiness" in Matthew's gospel. A fairly sophisticated, self-conscious group of Christians lived in Antioch at that time. There was both structure and organization. In other words, there was a ministry of leadership in this community. We do not know the names for these leadership people, but the sending of the Twelve does provide some modeling of leadership ministry for them. The eschatological element of the Twelve is emphasized more in Matthew than it is in Mark, and the Christian community in Antioch saw itself as an eschatological community. Its leadership had an eschatological aspect, so that the end of the world, the coming in fullness of the kingdom, was part of Christian life and part of Christian leadership. In this way, the Twelve, precisely as the eschatological Twelve of the final kingdom, influenced the modeling of ministry for this early Church community.

Luke's gospel follows Mark in a rather straightforward way. The selection of the Twelve is stated in a very matter-of-fact way, except that Luke mentions how Jesus spent the preceding night in prayer. This is a very striking detail, which indicates, once more, that all ministry is from God, not from oneself nor from a community.

In the sending out of the Twelve, 9, 1–6, the reliance on Mark is very clear from a textual comparison. Luke, however, improves on the Greek syntax and style in a number of small ways, which in a synoptic view of the Greek texts becomes quite evident. Contentwise, little is altered. Similar to Matthew, Luke says that the preaching is a preaching of the kingdom, but Luke does not elaborate on this.[23]

In K. Aland's *Synopsis Quattuor Evangeliorum,* at this passage of the three gospels, a very long note is added about the trials and difficulties for those who preach. Citations in Greek are made from Lk 10, 1–12; 1 Cor 9, 5–14; 1 Tim 5, 18; Jas 5, 4; Didache 11, 3–6, 11–12; 13, 1–2; the Gospel of the Egyptians; the Gospel of the Ebionites; 2 Clem. ad Cor., 5, 2; Ignatius to Poly. 2, 2; the Gospel of Thomas in Coptic, app. 1, 14; Pap. Oxy. 655. All of these passages from early Church documents indicate that the trials and persecutions were a matter of serious concern.[24] This accumulation of data indicates to us that the ministry of leadership and preaching at that early stage of the Christian Church was often a matter of actual life and death. The seriousness of such ministry had to be clearly seen and clearly accepted.

In the gospel of Luke, the texts themselves do not allow us to relate the sending of the Twelve with episkopoi. Nor does the immediate context of the various pericopes permit this. If we had only Luke's gospel, then the context of the Lucan gospel, just as the context of the Marcan and Matthaean gospels, would not allow any connection with episcopal mission. A complicating factor, however, clearly arises in the case of Luke (which is not at all the case for Mark or Matthew), since Luke wrote the Acts of the Apostles, in which the names episkopos and presbyter are quite prominent for Church ministerial leadership.

Still a second issue, only found in the Lucan material, and nowhere else in the New Testament material, is the passage which deals with the sending out of the seventy (or seventy-two), Lk 10, 1–12:

> After this the Lord appointed seventy-two others and sent them out ahead of him, in pairs, to all the towns and places he himself was to visit. He said to them, "The harvest is rich but the laborers are few, so ask the Lord of the harvest to send laborers to his harvest. Start off now, but remember, I am sending you out like lambs among wolves. Carry no purse, no haversack, no sandals. Salute no one on the road. Whatever house you go into, let your

first words be, 'Peace to this house!' And if a man of peace lives there, your peace will go and rest on him; if not, it will come back to you. Stay in the same house, taking what food and drink they have to offer, for the laborer deserves his wages; do not move from house to house. Whenever you go into a town where they make you welcome, eat what is set before you. Cure those in it who are sick, and say, 'The kingdom of God is very near to you.' But whenever you enter a town and they do not make you welcome go out into the streets and say, 'We wipe off the very dust of your town that clings to our feet, and leave it with you. Yet be sure of this: the kingdom of God is very near.' I tell you, on that day, it will not go as hard with Sodom as with that town."

A host of exegetical problems arise because of this passage. In 10, 17ff these disciples return and they express their exuberance. In both 10, 1 and 10, 17, there are manuscript discrepancies as to the number: seventy or seventy-two. The weight for either reading is about equal. The number seventy conjures up the seventy nations mentioned in Gen 10, or the seventy elders who assisted Moses (Ex 18, 21; 24, 1; Num 11, 16). There is also the Greek translation of the Hebrew scriptures, called the Septuagint (the seventy). The number seventy-two, for its part, might refer to the seventy-two nations of Gen 10, which the Septuagint reads, not the Hebrew text, or Aristeas mentions that there were seventy-two translators of the Septuagint. One can even multiply the twelve tribes of Israel by six and reach seventy-two. None of this counts for very much, and little argumentation can be made simply by the number: 70 or 72.[25]

When one compares this text on the seventy with the text on the Twelve, one sees that there are striking similarities. Many of the similarities are between the original text of Mark on the Twelve and Luke on the seventy. These similarities are, to some extent, found in Matthew's account of the Twelve as well. On the other hand, there are similarities which only relate Luke's account of the seventy to Matthew's account of the Twelve, and this indicates a Q source for such details. Luke's account of the seventy is a compilation of a Marcan source on the Twelve and a Q source, probably also on the Twelve. It is Luke who has added, for his own purposes, the number seventy.

Nothing in the text connects the seventy and Christian presbyters. Nothing in the context of the pericope connects the seventy with

Christian presbyters. Venerable Bede (d. 735) made popular the approach that the sending of the Twelve was an episcopal sending and the sending of the seventy was a presbyteral sending. However, there is nothing either in the text or the context that allows such an interpretation.

The gospel of Luke, both in the section on the Twelve and in the section on the seventy, makes no connection with either episkopos or presbyter. Acts, for its part, makes no connection between the episkopos and the Twelve, or between the presbyter and the seventy. To read such an interpretation into Acts can, therefore, only be eisegesis. Moreover, it is the clear view of biblical scholars that in Acts the names episkopos and presbyter are interchangeable. We have mentioned this above and given a number of examples both from Acts and from the Pastorals. If, on the basis of Lucan material, a connection is made between the Twelve or the seventy on the one hand, and on the other certain Christian ministerial leaders, then one could relate the Twelve with presbyters or episkopoi and the seventy with episkopoi and presbyters. There is really no way to make the following schematic view of Christian ministerial leadership based on the synoptics, but especially based on Luke:

Jesus = The Twelve = episkopoi (bishops)
Jesus = The Seventy = presbyters (priests)

Rather, the Lucan material would indicate the following schema:

Jesus = The Twelve = presbyter/episkopos
Jesus = The Seventy = presbyter/episkopos

One sees immediately the way in which this second schema nuances the entire question of episcopal succession, as it has been traditionally discussed in the Roman Catholic Church. It would seem, however, that some nuancing is inevitable. Jesus = Twelve = bishop is not sustained by the New Testament in that simplified formula. Even Galot who tends to be quite traditional sees the problem: "Judging by the intentions disclosed by Jesus, there are three degrees in the mission and power of the shepherd. These degrees do not correspond exactly to the traditional trilogy of episcopacy, presbyterate and diaconate."[26] Unfortunately, Galot does not follow through on this non-correspondence. Rather, he continues to maintain the Twelve = bishop; the Seventy = presbyter configuration.

Let me add immediately, however, that the nuancing which has to be done is not the same as a denial of the apostolic succession of bishops. All that is being said here is this: the gospel accounts on the sending of the Twelve (and the sending of the Seventy) do not allow us to connect in any simplified way either the Twelve with the episkopoi or the seventy with the presbyters. Any such connection is ruled out as far as Mark and Matthew are concerned; in the case of Luke a very nuanced connection might possibly be made. Only when we have seen a fuller picture of the early Church will we return to this issue.

Important and profound as all this is, it is also very clear that the early Church did not continue the titles: (1) the Twelve or (2) apostles. The apostles, who were so active in the founding of the Christian community, died out and there was no attempt to continue having "apostles" lead the Church. Only at a much later date in Church history did the episkopoi begin to see themselves as the successors of the apostles. When we take up ministry in the first two centuries of the Church, this will be specified in detail. We have mentioned above that nowhere in the New Testament are the apostles called "episkopoi" nor are they equated to them. Vice versa, nowhere in the New Testament are the episkopoi called apostles. As we said, when discussing the relationship to the Twelve, a simplistic schematic cannot be verified from the New Testament material, e.g.:

Jesus = Apostles = episkopoi

The same issues mentioned about the Twelve apply here. The following schema is also simplistic:

Jesus = Twelve = episkopoi

Since in Acts episkopos and presbyter are rather interchangeable, it would be as acceptable to draw the simplistic schema as follows:

Jesus = Apostles [The Twelve] = presbyter

We are confronted once again with the issue of the apostolic succession of the episcopal office, since in the above schemata the apostolic succession applies equally to the presbyteral office. On New Testament data alone, one cannot say that the episkopos is superior to the presbyter, since, again as we saw above, the two seem to be rather interchangeable titles for one and the same office.

The apostle throughout the New Testament is both a title and a figure of major consequence. Next to Jesus and next to Mary no other New Testament figures are as influential and important as the apostles. In this present context, apostle means more than the Twelve. Paul, for instance, is included under the rubric: apostle. D. Stanley and R. Brown in "Aspects of New Testament Thought" mention that J. Dupont "has argued persuasively that the disciples were not known as apostles during the ministry" of Jesus. "Therefore, the lone reference to apostles in Mk 6, 30 and Mt 10, 2 is anachronistic, as also Lk's more persistent use in five passages (6, 13; 9, 10; 17, 5; 22, 14; 24, 10). It is true that the gospels present the Twelve as being sent out during the ministry, and in this mission they were to some extent Jesus' sheluhim. But the definitive sending that constitutes the Christian apostolate came after the resurrection."[27] The ecclesiological presupposition is very much in evidence here. These two New Testament scholars, on the basis of the New Testament itself, are arguing for the post-resurrectional approach not only to Church generally, but to the naming and function of the Christian apostle.

Lightfoot over a century ago began to argue that the name and function of apostles was originally much broader than the Twelve. As noted above, in the passage from Bornkamm, this has become the more acceptable position of New Testament scholars today. Besides the Twelve, the following are called apostles in the New Testament:

James, the "brother of the Lord" (Gal 1, 9).
Paul (1 Cor 1, 1; etc.).
Barnabas (Acts 14, 14; 1 Cor 9, 6; Gal 2, 9).
Andronicus and Junius (Rom 16, 7)—probable.
False apostles (Acts 2, 2; 2 Cor 11, 13).
Perhaps even Sylvanus and Timothy (1 Thes 1, 1).
Perhaps Apollos (1 Cor 4, 6).

Even with the "perhaps" and "probable" the New Testament data (as also some post-New Testament data, e.g., the *Didache*) indicates that apostle and the Twelve are not coterminous. This wider understanding of apostle seems to be more primitive than the constricted view of apostles as referring only to the Twelve. The very extensiveness of the name and therefore function of apostles in itself indicates the reverence and respect which the earliest Church communities had for this ministerial leadership. The deliberate connection of the pastoral letters to such apostles as Peter, Paul, James and Jude, even though these men never wrote such letters, shows us how important the connection to Jesus through the apostles had become. Apostolic connection (succession) meant connection with Jesus himself.

In this sense all Church ministry must be apostolic, just as it must be christocentric. We will see, as we move into the data of the second century, that this apostolic connection to Christian ministry in its many forms (not just episcopal or even only episcopal) is part of the early view of ministry generally.

The most important aspect of the ministry of the apostle was his reflection of the ministry of Jesus. The false apostle was so named not because he did not preach nor because he did not offer the eucharist, but because he did not reflect the ministry of Jesus. In reflecting this ministry of Jesus, the apostle was clearly a leader in the Christian community. The apostle preached and taught. The apostle healed and reconciled. The apostle, on occasion, baptized. Presidency at the eucharist is a more difficult function to identify with hard data from the New Testament. By the year 60, it appears that the individual apostles were but names and memories, not personalities influencing any given community (with the exception of Rome, it seems). In the later New Testament writings only Peter, John and Paul seem to stand out in some sort of individual detail. The apostles were, however, remembered as a group or a college (to use later terminology). This collegial aspect of the apostles influenced Christian ministry from this very early Church period down to the present. Who specifically might belong to such a ministerial college or its internal structuring is quite a different question. But the collegiality of Christian ministry remains a consistent factor.

4. PROPHET AND TEACHER

It would be myopic to confine one's view of ministry and titles simply to the Twelve, apostles, episkopos, presbyter and diakonos.

Paul and his Christian communities esteemed the prophet and the teacher immediately after the apostles. These two stand out as the most important intra-ecclesial ministers after the apostles in the Pauline Churches. Neither teachers nor prophets are self-appointed, nor are they community appointed. In 1 Cor 12, 28 we read: "God has given the first place to apostles, the second to prophets, the third to teachers; after them miracles and after them the gift of healing; helpers, good leaders, those with many languages." The phrase "God has given" indicates that it is the Lord and the Spirit of the Lord who calls and commissions to Christian ministry, not the individual nor the community as a group. The prophets are those who speak in and through the Spirit. They might not have been wandering individuals at the time of Paul, but rather stable members of a community, for it cannot be ascertained clearly from his letters that they are wandering prophets. In many ways they seem quite associated with a given community and are accorded great respect by that community. It is the spiritual endowment that sets them apart and gives them a ministerial position, but this spiritual endowment is based on the way they reflect the gospel, that is, the way they reflect the mission of Jesus. False prophets are false because they distort the gospel. In this reflection of the mission of the gospel (Jesus), prophets preach and teach. In all of this they are portrayed as Christian leaders.[28]

In the third place are the teachers who again are not self-appointed nor appointed by the community. Teaching is a grace, a gift of the Lord. The teachers, like the prophets, seem to be associated with definite communities rather than forming a group of wandering instructors. It is the teaching of the gospel, of course, which is central to their function. False teachers are false not because they do not teach or preach, but because they teach and preach a false gospel. This rootage in the good news of Jesus, i.e., the christological base of their ministry, should be noted.[29]

Important as prophet and teacher were in the Pauline communities, these were not the titles which eventually gained universal acceptance in Christian communities. Prophets continued well into the next century as a definite ministry, and teachers, as well, found a place in the development of the catechumenate and eventually in the theological schools of the early Church. Still, as the leading ministries in the Church, neither the prophet nor the teacher came to be the acceptable minister in name and function for the wider Christian community. Episkopos, presbyter and diakonos prevailed. At the end of the New Testament period itself, no such settlement of either the naming of Christian ministry or the functioning of Christian ministry had been reached. Both the naming and function are still in flux.

5. DEACON

A ministry found in the New Testament which has become in name and to some degree in function an integral part of the Church is that of the deacon. In the Acts of the Apostles (6, 1–6) there is an institution of seven men with even their names clearly stated. The context for this institution is a complaint between the Hellenists and the Hebrews as regards the care of the widows. The Twelve address a "full meeting" of the disciples, and to give the Twelve undisturbed time to preach the seven are then instituted. The community makes the election and the Twelve (in this verse called the apostles) lay hands on them. Nowhere in the text are these seven called deacons, and, as mentioned previously, more and more scholars consider these seven to be more like presbyters. The connection of the seven to the eventual order of deacon has become quite tenuous.

The reasons for this change in attribution are quite complex, but the tasks of these seven men appear to be that of leadership, preaching and liturgical activity. Although the passage in Acts mentions the care of the widows and the giving out of food, it is clear that the ministry in practice was more than this. In the very next section of Acts, we find Stephen preaching, and in chapter seven, Stephen's speech is given in full. Indeed, it is the longest speech-presentation in Acts. This is followed by an account of his death. In chapter eight we find Philip preaching the gospel and baptizing.

In the Pauline corpus there are clearer indications of a Church ministry, called deacon. In Romans 16, 1, Paul writes: "I commend to you our sister Phoebe, a deaconess of the church at Cenchreae." Nothing more is said except that she deserves a welcome worthy of saints: "She has looked after a great many people, myself included," and therefore deserves help in all her own needs. Phoebe is clearly a service (diakonia) person; precisely what the ministry she had, as a deaconess, entailed is not stated.

In the introduction to the letter to the Philippians, Paul writes: "From Paul and Timothy, servants of Christ Jesus, to all the saints in Christ Jesus, together with their presiding elders (episkopoi) and deacons (diakonoi)." This is the only place in Paul's writings that mentions the words episkopos and diakonos (as titles of Church ministers). N. Flanagan notes: "Some commentators believe this is non-Pauline and speak of a later interpolation into the text. Better to accept the text as it is and recognize that the Pauline churches, too, demanded at least a minimum structure to hold them together as sociological units."[30] From this section of Paul's writings we can gain only that there were ministers called diakonoi (and episkopoi), but as to what this ministry might have involved, Paul's letters provide us with no clues whatsoever. Moreover, given the listing of ministries in the total corpus of Paul's writings, it is also clear that diakonos was not, so it seems, a major ministry. Prophet and teacher rank above deacon (and episkopos).

In 1 Tim 3, 8–12, we find a description of the ministry of deacon:

> In the same way, deacons must be respectable men, whose word can be trusted, moderate in the amount of wine they drink and with no squalid greed for money. They must be conscientious believers in the mystery of faith. They are to be examined first and only admitted as deacons if there is nothing against them. In the same way, the women must be respectable, not gossips, but sober and quite reliable. Deacons must not have been married more than once, and must be men who manage their children and families well. Those of them who carry out their duties well as deacons will earn a high standing for themselves and be rewarded with great assurance in their work for the faith in Christ Jesus.

We find a description of the kind of Christian man who should be a deacon, rather than the actual function of a deacon. The picture one is presented of a "model deacon" is clearly that of a "model Christian." The women mentioned in v. 11 might refer to their wives; there is no indication whatsoever that these women would be "deaconesses."

In his study of the question, N. Mitchell suggests that the presbyters are presented in the pastorals as a sort of "generic" title of Christian ministry. Some presbyters function ministerially as episkopoi; others as diakonoi. One might even, he says, speak of a presbyter-bishop or a presbyter/deacon. In Paul the deacon may have been a special class of teacher/preacher, and even there could be an apostle/ deacon (cf. 1 Cor 3, 5). These are all merely suggestions, of course, but once again they indicate the fluctuation both of function and naming. Even if Mitchell's suggestions are not precisely correct, the possibility that the New Testament gives rise to such a variegated picture of diaconal (as well as presbyteral and episcopal) ministry can only be allowed if the New Testament does not present a hard and fast picture of ministry.[31]

The New Testament material on deacon, sparse as it is, allows us to say that:

a. There is a Church ministry of deacon that goes back to the time of the apostles, but its exact point of origin cannot be determined.

b. This ministry is not presented as the highest ministry; it is usually mentioned after episkopos/presbyter.

c. The New Testament does not give us any precise description of the functions of a deacon. Sometimes the functions of deacons resemble those of the presbyter or episkopos.

d. In Acts, the seven are engaged in works of charity and in a preaching ministry. Many scholars do not equate the seven with deacons.

e. There is some indication of a process of installing men as deacons, but there is no indication of what this process involved. It is nowhere called an "ordination."

f. There is also mention of a ministry of deaconess, but there is no description of her function or of the process of election and installation.

g. The life of a deacon is portrayed as a truly Christian life, i.e., the model of the deacon is Jesus. Diaconate has a christological base.

This ministry was taken very seriously by the sub-apostolic Church and by the Church throughout its history. Since this early period, there has never been a time that the Church has not had a ministry of deacon. Even though there is no possible way to claim that the deacons were "instituted by Christ Jesus himself," the Church has continually seen the deacon as an integral or even essential part of its ministerial structure. Over the centuries the importance of this ministry has not always been the same, but its presence in the Church ministry-structure has never been lacking.

6. THE OTHER TITLES OF MINISTRY

In the listing of titles for ministries in the New Testament, with which this chapter began, there were many other titles beyond those mentioned above. Their presence in the literature gives evidence that the naming of ministry, in New Testament times, was somewhat in flux, and even at the end of the New Testament period not yet completely settled. The lack of a continued use of these other titles in Church history indicates that these titles as the preferred naming of Church ministry did not meet the needs of the Christian communities. In other words, these other titles, useful as they were in the apostolic communities in which they flourished, did not last as the accepted naming of ministry.

The ministerial function, which these other names involved, is not described in any detail in the New Testament. At times, the name indicates a function, e.g., keryx, would indicate preaching, but even with this the precise description of such a ministry is lacking. Cumulatively taken, however, one sees that various ministries were present, and these from the earliest stratum of Church history. Secondly, one notes that these ministries developed due to pastoral needs. No claim is made that these ministries, in name and function, originated from Jesus himself. The variety indicates that certain communities utilized names different from other communities, and the better explanation of these variances seems to be the local needs for a given ministry.

7. THE NEW TESTAMENT AND THE ISSUE OF ORDINATION

In all of the passages on New Testament ministries, we have no clear indication of any ordination rite. There are, of course, instances of a laying on of hands in the early Church, particularly in Acts and in 1 Tim 4, 14; 2 Tim 1, 6 (cf. also 2 Cor 8, 19 which speaks of an election). What this laying on of hands in each case of these New Testament passages might clearly indicate is arguable. Ordination, as we today understand this term, does not seem to be the intent of these situations, and to read an "ordination" ritual, such as one finds from the time of Hippolytus onward, would be clearly an "eisegesis."

Let us consider these passages in detail.

Acts 6, 5–6: The whole assembly approved of this proposal and elected Stephen, a man full of faith and of the Holy Spirit, together with Philip, Prochorus, Nicanor, Timon, Parmenas, and Nicolaus of Antioch, a convert to Judaism. They presented these to the apostles who prayed and laid their hands on them.

Acts 8, 17: Then they laid hands on them and they received the Holy Spirit.

Acts 13, 2–3: One day while they were offering worship to the Lord and keeping a fast, the Holy Spirit said, "I want Barnabas and Saul set apart for the work to which I have called them." So it was that after fasting and prayer they laid their hands on them and sent them off.

Acts 14, 23: In each of these churches they [Paul and Barnabas] appointed elders [presbyteroi], and with prayer and fasting they commended them to the Lord in whom they had come to believe.

Acts 19, 5: When they heard this, they were baptized in the name of the Lord Jesus, and the moment Paul had laid hands on them, the Holy Spirit came down on them, and they began to speak with tongues and to prophesy.

1 Tim 4, 14: You have in you a spiritual gift which was given to you when the prophets spoke and the body of elders (presbyterion) laid their hands on you.

1 Tim 5, 22: Do not be too quick to lay hands on any man and make yourself an accomplice in anyone else's sin.

2 Tim 1, 6: This is why I am reminding you now to fan into a flame the gift that God gave you when I laid my hands on you.

Heb 6, 2: The teaching about baptisms and the laying on of hands.

Not all these passages, dealing with the laying on of hands, are indicative of an office or ministry installation. 1 Tim 5, 22 and Heb 6, 2 might possibly be connected with some sort of a reconciliation; Acts 8, 17 and 19, 5 seem to apply to the baptismal ritual. This leaves four passages:

(1) Acts 6, 5–6 deals with the installation of the "seven."
(2) Acts 13, 2–3 deals with the commissioning of Barnabas and Saul.
(3) 1 Tim 4, 14 deals with the presbytery installing Timothy.
(4) 2 Tim 1, 6 deals with Paul laying hands on Timothy.

The two instances from Acts mention a laying on of hands, but in a passing way. In Acts 13, 1–3, Paul and Barnabas are selected for a specific task: a missionary work. They are not "ordained" to any "office." By this laying on of hands, it is not said that they are "ordained to be apostles." Through this laying on of hands, Paul and Barnabas do not receive their status in the community.

In Acts 6, 5–6, the seven are commissioned to a task and in some ways to an office in the Church. It is not clear from the text who lays hands on them: is it only the apostles or is it the gathered community? If the latter, we would have, perhaps, an instance of a community-"ordination," which is not quite consistent with the ordination rituals of the third century onward. Biblical scholars today are not of one mind on the issue of an "ordination" in this passage, with the result that we must say that there are some grounds for admitting an "ordination" in Acts 6, 5–6, but there are also grounds for denying it. A firm decision eludes us.[32] One should note, however, that there is both an election process and a commissioning process in this commissioning of the seven, and that all of this is done within a prayer context.

Since 1 and 2 Tim are not written by Paul, and even Timothy is a fictitious name, but reminiscent of a Timothy during Paul's lifetime, we cannot make any historical claim that a laying on of hands as an installation rite dates from the time of either Paul or Timothy. Consequently, we have no data whatsoever as to a ritual for the Church during the actual lifetime of Paul and Timothy. Both 1 and 2 Tim seem to date from about 110 A.D., and therefore they reflect a Christian community at that particular time, and in the particular place where these letters seem to have originated, perhaps somewhere in Asia Minor. Even with this information, one cannot generalize about Church practice beyond either the time or the locale in which these letters originated.[33]

In the context of these two passages from the letters to Timothy, it is in one case the presbyterion which lays hands on Timothy, but in the second case it is Paul himself who lays hands on him. This variance complicates the matter to some degree, so that if one wishes to emphasize that an "ordination" is described in these passages, one should note that it is the presbyters (not the episkopoi) who lay hands on Timothy. Timothy, in these letters, is pictured as a leader of the community who preaches and guides the community. No mention is made of any liturgical presidency. It would, then, be for these tasks, primarily leading, preaching, guiding, that the presbyterion or Paul lays hands on him.[34]

Ott and others see 1 Tim 5, 22 referring to an installation into an office as well, and not as an act of reconciliation.[35] In Titus 1, 5, there is no mention of a laying on of hands, but we do read: "The reason I left you behind in Crete was for you to get everything organized there and appoint elders (katasteses kata polin presbyterous) in every town, in the way that I told you." The text does not indicate the process or way in which such an appointment takes place. Some writers, of course, on the basis of the other passages, believe that the appointment takes place via a laying on of hands, but this opinion is conjectural.

This laying on of hands is a well-known ritual in the Old Testament. It is used as a rite of blessing and as part of a sacrificial ritual, but it is also used as an installation ritual. Num 8, 10 states: "When you have brought the Levites before Yahweh, the sons of Israel must lay their hands on them." This is a sort of dedication ritual, a dedication to the worship service in Judaism. In Num 27, 8, Yahweh directs Moses to lay hands on Joshua, to designate him and establish him as the leader, but in v. 23, Moses brings Joshua before the priest Eleazar as well as before the community. The P source seems to account for the emphasis of Eleazar in this ritual. In the final chapter of Deut 34, 9, Moses is described as laying hands on Joshua, but there is no mention of Eleazar the priest. It is also not stated the the Spirit of God is given to Joshua through this laying on of hands. The Spirit had come upon Joshua first; the laying on of hands by Moses was a sign of both Moses and the people that they had perceived this selection by the Spirit and acquiesced in this choice. Moreover, not all that Moses stood for, e.g., his intimacy with God, his full authority over the people, was "handed on" to Joshua.

In more recent times, authors such as Strack-Billerbeck, Coppens, and Lohse have seen a Jewish ritual of laying on of hands in the "ordination" of a scribe, thereby establishing someone as a teacher and judge. More recently, F. Hoffman in an article "L'Ordination juive a la veille du Christianisme" has shown that the extant data on such a ritual is from the second half of the first century A.D., more specifically after 70 A.D.[36] Even though there are some descriptions of these rituals which claim to go back to the very time of Moses himself, such claims have no solid historical foundation, and the Mosaic claim is made only to substantiate the use of these rituals in the eyes of the Jewish community.

Very little Old Testament data for a laying on of hands as an installation ritual is available, and this dearth of evidence does not bolster the view that a true "ordination" ritual can be found in the New Testament passages. When one realizes that between the few New Testament indications mentioned above and the ritual of Hippolytus at the beginning of the third century there is absolutely no documentary evidence for ordination, then the conjectural status of any statement on ordination prior to Hippolytus becomes even more apparent, cautioning us to avoid any apodictic approach.

In themselves, phrases which include the words "laying on of hands," do not essentially include an appointment to office or ministry. A laying on of hands, in both Old and New Testaments, can be found for blessings, healings, receiving the Spirit, reconciling. In other words, "laying on of hands" in itself is not a technical term for an "ordination." Mitchell sums up his view as follows:

> It is my conviction, then, that the laying on of hands as a "commissioning" gesture has very restricted significance in the New Testament. It seems linked to the special circumstances of people who are designated for missionary work. . . . Nowhere are bishops described as having hands laid on them for ministry in the local

church. Nor do presbyters appear to receive their status in the community through a ritual laying on of hands, though presbyters themselves may employ this gesture on some occasions (1 Tim 4:14).[37]

8. THE MINISTRY OF THE EPISKOPOS AT ROME

As stated earlier, this book is not a study of the papal ministry, and so the papal ministry will be treated only in passing. Nonetheless, it is helpful to mention here that major biblical scholars have recently focused on the issue of the role of Peter, as far as the New Testament data is concerned. These scholars were both Roman Catholic and Lutheran, and the results of their work appeared in *Peter in the New Testament*.[38] Readers should study such a volume for a detailed consideration of this matter, but their conclusions, presented at least in outline form, are helpful to contextualize the issue of ministry in the Church in its relationship to the papal ministry.

As far as Peter himself, during his own lifetime, is concerned, these scholars indicate the following:[39]

a. Simon (Peter) was one of the first to be called by Jesus.
b. He was very prominent in this group of followers.
c. It is probable that he made a confession of Jesus, not as Son of God, but as messiah.
d. It is equally probable that Peter failed at least partially to understand Jesus.

These are conclusions which one can draw with more or less probability as to the position of Peter during his lifetime, i.e., his lifetime prior to the resurrection of Jesus. In the early Church period, therefore after the resurrection, the following conclusions can be made:[40]

a. Simon came to be known as Cephas (Peter).
b. Simon (Cephas) was accorded an appearance of the risen Jesus. It would seem most probable that Jesus appeared to him first.
c. Peter had a missionary career, which included a missionary activity to the non-Jews.
d. Theologically, Peter appears to be not as stringent as James, but not as open as Paul.

The fifth Lutheran–Catholic dialogue, which took place after the preliminary study on the role of Peter in the New Testament, namely, *Papal Primacy and the Universal Church*,[41] utilized the material of the preliminary study in almost a verbatim way. The "Common Statement" reproduces the issues stated above, concluding with this observation: "Thus one may speak of a prominence that can be traced back to Peter's relationship to Jesus in his public ministry and as the risen Lord."[42] After this, the document states that there is an even greater importance which should be given to the images associated with Peter, which one finds in the New Testament. Once more, the common statement relies on the preliminary study which had listed these images, namely:[43]

a. Peter is presented as weak, failing, and sinful.
b. Peter is presented as a spiritual fisherman, a shepherd of the sheep of Christ, as a presbyter speaking to other presbyters, a proclaimer of faith in Jesus as the Son of God; as one who has received a special revelation.
c. Peter corrects those who misunderstand Paul.
d. He is the rock on which the Church is built.

Given all of this, the document then states:

When a "trajectory" of these images is traced, we find indications of a development from earlier to later images. This development of images does not constitute papacy in its later technical sense, but one can see the possibility of an orientation in that direction, when shaped by favoring factors in the subsequent church. The question whether Jesus appointed Peter the first pope has shifted in modern scholarship to the question of the extent to which the subsequent use of the images of Peter in reference to the papacy is consistent with the thrust of the New Testament.[44]

Although these conclusions of the Lutheran–Catholic dialogues cannot be taken as the "final word" on the issue of the papacy, they are included here simply to provide a framework, as far as New Testament scholarship is concerned, in which one can relate the other, more specified New Testament ministries to this Petrine ministry. In the final selection above, from the Lutheran–Roman Catholic dialogues, we see that today the emphasis is not on Jesus' selection of Peter. Rather, the emphasis is on the way in which the images used by the popes in later centuries to describe their papal ministry have or have not a New Testament ministerial basis.

9. THE EUCHARIST AND ITS RELATIONSHIP TO NEW TESTAMENT MINISTRY

In the treatment of New Testament ministry, many Roman Catholic scholars base their findings on the New Testament data on the eucharist. Naturally, a thorough study of the biblical data on the eucharist is impossible in our present context, but let us consider some of the most important aspects of the relationship between New Testament description of ministry and New Testament statements on the eucharist. We will not go beyond the New Testament data for either of these two themes.

Galot reiterates the general pattern that Catholic scholars have used to establish the basis for this relationship; he writes:

> But Luke also stresses the connection between the power conferred upon the Twelve and the commitment to sacrifice. Jesus disposes of the kingdom in favor of those who stood by him faithfully in his trials. Thus a new similarity comes to the fore. Jesus had described his pastoral power by positing a relationship between it and sacrifice. This connection perdures in the disciples.

> The power to rule is associated with the power to eat and drink at the table of Christ, that is, to celebrate the Eucharist. Luke had just quoted Jesus' words: "Do this as a memorial of me (Lk 22, 19), the words that establish the empowering of the apostles to preside at the eucharistic celebration.[45]

Galot finds a further substantiation of this relationship in the parable of the steward who is called on to supervise the estate in the master's absence. On the master's return, he must give an account of his stewardship. Galot sees an accounting by the apostles not only in the area of leadership, but also in the area of the eucharist. Moreover, both Matthew (28, 18–20) and Mark (16, 16–18) indicate the Lord's command to evangelize, and in this evangelization process baptism (another sacramental action) is mentioned. Galot goes on to cite the well-known passages dealing with reconciliation, namely, Mt 16, 19–20; 18, 18; Jn 20, 20–22; plus Lk 24, 47; and the casting out of demons mentioned in Mk 3, 14 and 16, 17. "From all these indications in the gospels," Galot concludes, "Jesus meant to impart to the Twelve the total extent of his own pastoral power. He gave them the power to rule the Church, the authority to carry out the mission of evangelization, the power to administer baptism, the power to celebrate the Eucharist and forgive sins. In today's language, Jesus transmitted to the Twelve his own priesthood, which includes leadership, the proclamation of the Word and the performance of liturgical or sacramental actions."[46]

In all of this, Galot is simply a typical voice among many, and his presentation follows a rather standard approach to the relationship of New Testament ministry and New Testament eucharist (as also the other two sacraments, baptism and reconciliation). The bulk of the New Testament material dealing with the eucharist is found in the synoptics. The bulk of the material dealing with ministry is found in the Acts of the Apostles and the various letters or epistles. In the synoptic material, other than the apostles and the Twelve, no mention is made of other ministers, such as prophets, teachers, episkopoi, presbyteroi, etc. In the Acts and epistles, in which many of the ministers are mentioned, there is little data on the eucharist. In other words, the eucharistic material rests on one set of sources for the most part; and the ministry material rests on another set of sources for the most part.

The ecclesiological presupposition, described in chapter two, plays a major role in interpreting the relationship between these sets of documents. Galot states clearly in his writings that Jesus, during his lifetime, established in a quite detailed way the ministerial structure and function of the Church. His use of the synoptics in the above passages bear witness to this. The citations that he makes are taken to be the actual words of Jesus during his lifetime or in the apparitions after the resurrection (i.e., for Jn 20, 20–22; and in the command to baptize found in Matthew and Mark). Throughout his book, the Twelve and the apostles are used interchangeably, so that apostle is seen really as only the Twelve. The eschatological dimension of the Twelve, which we discussed above, is not seen by him as primary; rather, the Twelve are seen essentially in an ecclesiological framework. A view of a Church, instituted by Jesus during his lifetime, with the eucharist in a central position of such a Church, cannot avoid making the eucharist central to an interpretation of ministry. A view of a Church, coming into being after the resurrection, with leadership, not eucharistic presidency, as the dominant ministerial activity, will shade the interpretation of ministry quite differently.[47]

Both Luke and Paul (1 Cor 11, 23–27) include the statement: "Do this as a memorial of me." Is this statement an original part of the words of institution, or is it a liturgical addition to the text? The parallel sections in Mark and Matthew do not contain this statement. Biblical scholars continue to debate the question whether the Mark/Matthew form is the earliest or the Luke/Paul form might be. Naturally, Paul's statements in 1 Cor were written down earlier than any of those found in the synoptics, but the point of the debate is on the antiquity of the tradition rather than on the antiquity of the actual writing.[48]

Jeremias attempted to see in this statement a semitic way of expressing the fact that God remembers, not an injunction to continue the celebration of the eucharist. His view has not met with strong support by biblical scholars generally, and by some it is considered to be simply unfounded.[49]

There has been a century-long interpretation that this is the first "ordination" ritual. In spite of the long tradition of this view, contemporary scholars find no basis for such an interpretation. In other words, Jesus did not ordain the apostles (disciples) at this final supper to be "priests," giving them thereby the power to celebrate the eucharist.[50]

We shall see in the next chapter that the presidency over the eucharist might not have been confined to such ministries as "presbyter" or "episkopos." Others might have presided over the eucharist in the sub-apostolic Church. Early Church ministry is far more focused on the presidency over the community, so that it is this presidency which eventually provides the basis for an exclusive presidency over the eucharist. In other words, leadership and preaching the word within a Christian community receive far more attention than liturgical or sacramental presidency. The fact that these two presidencies are not totally coterminous in the sub-apostolic Church cautions one from any over-simplistic relationship between New Testament ministry (at least in some specific name or form) and New Testament eucharist. We shall also see in a much later chapter that a theology which bases "priestly ministry" essentially and to some degree exclusively on the eucharist gave rise to some distortions, which Vatican II clearly attempted to rectify.

The view that the New Testament indicates that the total community was enjoined to celebrate the eucharist, so that in principle any baptized Christian might be the eucharistic celebrant, appears to be totally without any foundation. The reason for this rejection lies not on any one statement found in connection with the eucharist in the New Testament, e.g., "Do this in remembrance of me," as though it were spoken to all, which cannot be verified, but in the more fundamental position that from the earliest stratum of Church, a ministerial leadership is evident. The earliest Church community is not an amorphous, acephalous congregation. Ministerial leadership in general is the basis for eucharistic leadership in particular. Even in those instances in the second century which indicate that neither an episkopos nor a presbyter presided over the eucharist, but some other Christian individual, that individual had a particular status other than that of a baptized Christian.

What all of this indicates is this: an argument about New Testament ministry which starts from the eucharist to the ministry is not evident from the New Testament data itself. Rather, the argument must proceed from the ministry of leadership over the community to the liturgical or sacramental leadership. It is not because the New Testament ministers have the power to celebrate the eucharist that they are the ministers of the Christian community; rather, it is more the opposite: because they are the ministers of leadership over the Christian community do they have a presiding ministry in the eucharist. In the Acts and in the various epistles it is this ministerial leadership which is emphasized again and again, with very little mention of sacramental leadership, much less the more specific eucharistic leadership.

A strong substantiation of this non-eucharistic approach to ministry is found in the documents of Vatican II. The scholastic interpretation of priesthood based essentially on eucharist was not accepted by the bishops at Vatican II. Rather, the theology of ministry, presented in the documents of Vatican II, goes back to the New Testament understanding of ministry, which is seen as leadership and preaching, teaching and sanctifying. We will consider this in detail later in this book, but it should be indicated here that at Vatican II the bishops preferred a theology of priesthood based more on the documents of the New Testament than on the scholastic, eucharistic approach to priesthood.

10. APOSTOLIC SUCCESSION

Apostolic succession is not treated in the New Testament in the same way that we find it in the subsequent centuries. In fact "apostolic succession" as a term begins to appear only in the second century. However, the very respect and reverence which is attested to in the New Testament to the apostles indicates that an "apostolic" connection is important. Dupuy expresses well the importance of this respect for the apostles in the New Testament when he discusses the issue of ordination: "Ordination brings to expression the fact that the Church ministers, through the mediation of the apostles, stand in direct relationship to Jesus himself."[51]

The first appearance of this term "apostolic succession" arose to combat gnosticism. Certain gnostic teachers claimed that they and their followers enjoyed a special teaching which was not found in the holy writings. To counter this "special revelation" approach, the leaders of the second century Church began to emphasize a teaching which went back to the apostles, and thereby to Jesus himself. Teachings, Church structures, and theologies which were not based on Jesus himself were not considered "apostolic." This was the negative side of the term "apostolic succession." On the other hand, the claim to be "apostolic" was meant as a claim to an origin stemming from the Lord himself. Consequently, the first and most important item to state about "apostolic succession" and the New Testament is its christological rootage. Apostolic succession does not essentially mean origin from apostles, but more importantly origin from Jesus himself.

In the later New Testament writings, when the apostles were but names and memories, this apostle-connection is seen as one deserving of great reverence, since the apostle-connection was the assurance of a connection with the Lord himself.[52]

In the New Testament, it is the Church itself which is the primary focus of apostolic succession. Whenever, as in later periods of Church history, apostolic succession is reduced to one single group, e.g., the apostolic succession of "bishops," or of the "pope," New Testament data becomes more problematic than helpful for the following reasons:

a. The apostles are not called "bishops" in the New Testament, and therefore the ministry of apostles cannot be equated with episkopos and/or presbyter. The ministry of apostle and the ministry of episkopos/presbyter are not coterminous.

b. Paul, the apostle, is portrayed in the New Testament as appointing leaders (Acts 14, 23), but the presbyters whom they install in the local Churches are not equated to either Paul himself or the apostles generally. In other words they are not presented as "succeeding" to Paul or to the apostles.

c. Some aspects of the ministry of apostle are indeed carried on by the leader of the local community. In this somewhat restricted area, then, one can see a continuation or succession. However, since the name of this main local Church leader varies from document to document, one is not sure whether even this fairly restricted continuation (succession) is done by presbyter, by episkopos, by presbyter/episkopos, by presbyter/deacon, or by episkopos/deacon, or by prophet or by teacher/preacher. No specific, single group with a clear-cut title can be determined.

d. As regards Peter and the question of the "bishop of Rome," the New Testament does not indicate in any way that Peter was ever at Rome. This information comes from non-New Testament data and as data is quite respectable. However, there is no such material from the New Testament sources.

This does not mean that apostolic succession is not a major part of the New Testament. Rather, the apostolic connection or succession is predicated foundationally of the Church in its entirety. Secondly, but in a most general way, it is predicated of its ministerial leadership. The fact that the naming of this leadership is still in flux at the end of the New Testament period and really does not become stabilized until the end of the second century cautions us to avoid any simplistic approach to the apostolic succession of a definitely named Church minister at this early period, but certainly does not preclude a relationship of Church ministry under various names to the apostles. In the second century, as we shall see, various groups of Church ministers were called "successors of the apostles," a situation which was possible only if the New Testament itself had not pinpointed one group as *the* successors of the apostles.

11. SUMMARY

The following would appear to be the main points which one could find in the New Testament as regards Christian ministry:

1. Some form of ministry is evident from the earliest strata onward as far as the Church is concerned; there never seems to have been a time when the Church was without ministry. To say that this means "clergy" and "lay" might be bringing in names which only in later decades began to appear. At any rate, there are ministers and there are those to whom they ministered, and this was from the beginning.
2. The apostles are considered the ministers of highest rank. This is found in the gospels, in the Pauline letters, in Acts and in the pastorals.
3. The ministry of "apostle" as such was not continued. The Church did not employ the term apostle for its ministers beyond the founding group.
4. If there is any "college" or identifiable group of ministers in the New Testament, it is clearly the "apostles." There is also an indication, but not as clear, for a collegial structure of the presbyters.
5. The early Church did not use the liturgical or sacred title of "priest" [in Greek, *hiereus;* in Hebrew, *cohen*] for Church ministers. Even though this title was readily available, it was evidently shunned by the early Church for designation of its ministers. In the New Testament only the Jewish priests, Jesus [and only in Hebrews], and all the baptized are called: *hiereus.*
6. The names for Christian ministers varied. There does not seem to be any standard pattern or universal preference for one title over the other, even at the end of the New Testament period. The naming of the Christian minister during the New Testament period was still in flux. Jesus certainly did not give any names for ministry (other than the Twelve and perhaps apostle) to the community.

7. In Paul, after the apostle, we find the prophet and the teacher of highest rank. In Paul presbyters are not mentioned at all, and only once, and quite in passing, do we find episkopos and diakonos.

8. In Acts and in the pastorals, we find episkopos/presbyteros the titles which seem to be preferred. These two titles appear to be interchangeable. They appear to be titles for the chief leadership position in a local Church. Besides administrative duties, they seem to be preachers and teachers. Liturgical leadership is minimally alluded to.

9. Christian ministers of all ranks are not self-appointed nor community appointed; rather ministry is a gift, a grace, coming from the Lord. The community, on occasion, is portrayed as having some role is the selection process.

10. The model for all ministry in the New Testament, and the dominant or defining aspect for all ministry, is Jesus himself. Christian ministry is radically Christocentric.

11. The ministry of deacons is attested to in the New Testament. Their functions, at times, seem to parallel those of episkopos/presbyter. The seven, mentioned in Acts, do not seem to be the first "deacons."

12. Many titles or names of Church ministers, found in the New Testament, did not survive historically as the preferred titles of Church ministry. Still, these names and titles did refer to legitimate Church ministers at the time of the New Testament writings, and must be seen as such.

13. Any statement on ordination, based on New Testament data alone, is conjectural. Most New Testament references to a laying on of hands cannot be interpreted as an ordination ritual. The one or two passages which remain are highly debated.

14. The essential aspect of ministry, based on New Testament sources, cannot be seen in the "power to celebrate the eucharist." This scholastic approach does not adequately do justice to the New Testament. The theology of ministry in Vatican II reflects New Testament data in a much more comprehensive way.

15. The position of Peter, or a Petrine ministry, in the New Testament would seem to follow the schematization presented by the ecumenical studies mentioned above.

16. Apostolic succession primarily means a connection with Jesus himself. The fundamental "successor" is the Church itself. Only in a most general way can one speak of a ministerial "apostolic succession" in the New Testament. The term itself is not a scriptural term, and it appears only in the second century to counter the private revelations of certain gnostic groups.

With this New Testament data in front of us, let us go to the next stage in Church history, which in some respects overlaps the writing of the New Testament, but also must be seen as moving beyond the New Testament as the Christian community grows in numbers and strength, and the pastoral situation begins to call for a more complex approach to Christian ministry.

Excursus on the Question
of the New Testament
and the Ordination of Women

Within the past few decades the issue of the ordination of women not only as regards the New Testament data, but also as regards the data from Christian tradition, has become of keen interest and importance. The importance of the issue is indicated by the fact that the Sacred Congregation for the Doctrine of the Faith issued a Declaration on the question of the admission of women to the ministerial priesthood. This Declaration was promulgated at Rome on October 15, 1976. Prior to this Declaration the Pontifical Biblical Commission was asked to study the role of women in the biblical material and the priesthood, the celebrant of the eucharist and the leader of the local Christian community.[1] It is not the scope of this present volume to present all the material relating to these questions, but some positional statement seems needed. We will consider here only the New Testament and the data which it offers, not the data from the Christian tradition. Before one focuses on the issue of ordination and women in the New Testament, the first theme would be:

A. WOMEN AND MINISTRY IN THE NEW TESTAMENT

Are women portrayed in active ministerial roles in the New Testament? The Pontifical Biblical Commission concludes on this matter:

> According to the witness of the New Testament, especially the Pauline epistles, women are associated with the different charismatic ministries (diaconies) of the Church (1 Cor 12, 4; 1 Tim

86

3, 11, cf. 8): prophecy, service, probably even apostolate . . .
without, nevertheless, being of the Twelve. They have a place in
the liturgy at least as prophetesses (1 Cor 11, 4).[2]

Robert Karris emphasizes Gal 3, 28: "And there are no more
distinctions between Jew and Greek, slave and free, male and female,
but all of you are one in Christ Jesus." This seems to be part of a
baptismal formula, i.e., a theological formula dealing with baptism.[3]
It was not, apparently, created by Paul, but Paul incorporated it into
his thinking. One can say, then, that at least in the Pauline Churches,
the New Testament data clearly indicates a role of women in ministry.
1 Tim 3, 11 also appears to indicate a feminine role in ministry.

After the era of the Pauline communities, a reaction apparently
set in, due either to an anti-gnostic defense of the gospel, or to a
victory of the dominant patriarchal model of the culture. Perhaps
both factors played a role, but as one moves into the last decade of
the first century and the beginning of the second century, women's
roles in ministry are curtailed. Karris links this with "early catholicism"
and such writings as Luke-Acts, Colossians, Ephesians, 1 and 2 Timothy, Titus, 1 and 2 Peter and Jude.

B. THE ISSUE OF ORDINATION

Before one discusses the question of the ordination of women,
some consideration should be given to the question of ordination generally. As we have seen in the previous chapter, ordination, in the
sense that one finds it in the third century onward, is not at all visible
in the New Testament. This does not mean that the later, elaborate
ordination rituals run counter to the New Testament data, but it does
mean that ordination, whether for men or for women, is not clearly
attested to in the New Testament itself. There were ministers, and
there had to be some sort of installation into these ministries. We
have considered all the texts relative to the laying on of hands, and
we have seen the difficulties in each of them. The manner in which
one is established in the ministry, as far as the data of the New Testament is concerned, remains unclear; any position one takes on the
matter is fraught with conjecture.

C. THE ORDINATION OF WOMEN IN THE NEW TESTAMENT

On the basis of the above, one must say that the particular question on the ordination of women in the New Testament is somewhat

unanswerable. The Pontifical Biblical Commission concluded: "It does not seem that the New Testament by itself alone will permit us to settle in a clear way and once and for all the problem of the possible accession of women to the presbyterate."[4] This is a fair but cautious statement on the matter. It does not say that women, on the basis of the New Testament, could not possibly be ordained (a negative conclusion); nor does it say that they must be ordained (a positive conclusion). Rather, the Commission, in this statement, indicates that as far as the New Testament is concerned, the issue is open-ended and not settled.

There is much that can and should be said on the issue of women and ordination. These few words on the New Testament basis on this matter in no way complete this complex issue. However, this volume, unfortunately, cannot enter into the various aspects of the topic; accordingly, only here and there will the topic be treated in the chapters which follow. This should not be construed, however, as if the issue is unimportant.

4

Ministry in the Second Christian Century: 90 to 210 A.D.

In this chapter we will focus on the historical data, outside that of the New Testament, dating from the end of the first century down to the beginning of the third century, roughly from about 90 A.D. to 210 A.D. Some of the documentation seems to be coterminous with the last writings of the New Testament itself. These non-New Testament documents offer valuable insight into Church life at this early period. Prior to 90 A.D. there is little extant material. On the other end of the period, somewhere around 210 or at least before the Decian persecution, we see that a sort of plateau has been reached as regards the names and functions of ministry. By this latter time, we have extant documentation on an ordination ritual, fairly established nomenclature for ministry, and even some extended theological discussion on Christian ministry.

In one sense, this period is the most difficult of all to appraise. The New Testament material enjoys "canonicity." It is a fairly "closed" set of documents, which remain normative for the entire Christian community. Difficult as the New Testament data is to interpret at times, it is, nonetheless, a fairly stabilized unit. This cannot be said of the non-New Testament literature which begins to appear about 90 A.D. and continues into the beginning of the third century. From the third century onward, there is an abundance of Christian literature to deal with, and the picture of early Church life then becomes fuller and theologically more nuanced. It is the in-between period, 90 to

89

210, which seems to offer considerable hermeneutical controversy as regards ministry, and this for various reasons:

1. The documentation is extremely limited, both in the number of documents themselves and in their topical discussion on Christian ministry. Ministry, as a theme, is for the most part treated in a secondary or occasional way.
2. The titles for Christian ministers at the beginning of this period are still not fully set, and do not become set until late in the second century. This diversity prolongs the unclarity of the situation.
3. There are no clear statements as to a ritual for ordination. Dupuy comments: "How someone in the early Church is called to ecclesial ministry is not described in the New Testament, so that theories relative to ordination have in part a hypothetical quality about them."[1] This hypothetical quality remains throughout this period, and only at the end of the period with Hippolytus do we have the first extant ordination ritual.
4. Many commentators in dealing with this period simply translate episkopos as bishop and presbyteros as priest, but what a later Church community means by bishop and priest cannot be readily identified, without many qualifications, to this early documentary use of episkopos and presbyteros. In what follows, I will generally use the Greek terms, episkopos and presbyteros, rather than the terms: bishop and priest.
5. These episkopoi and presbyteroi, and also the diakonoi, are, in this period's documention, described strongly in terms of presiding over the community; secondly there are also occasions when the qualities of Christian ministers are enumerated; in a third place we find mention of liturgical activity. On the basis of this period's documentation, then, presidency over the community ranks first, not liturgical leadership as regards the manner in which Christian ministry is presented.
6. The qualities of Christian ministers recounted in this period's documentation might be seen as the beginning of a "priestly spirituality." When one looks at the material more deeply, one sees, rather, that the description is that of a Christian spirituality in general, not that of a distinctive "priestly spirituality."

Other factors might also be listed, which give rise to the hermeneutical difficulty of this period's documentation, but these are singled out to indicate at least some of the major reasons for interpretative problems. It must also be stated again that the ecclesiological presupposition, described above, plays no little role in each author's interpretation of the data. At times, the presupposition rather than the text seems to dictate the interpretation.

Cognizant of the problems, let us now look carefully at the documentation. For the sake of clarity, the chapter is divided into two sections:

1. The naming and function of Christian ministry.
2. Ordination to Christian ministry.

There is much more data on the first topic than on the second, so that the sections are of noticeably unequal length, but since the two issues are so important, we will want to consider each of them in detail.

1. THE NAMING AND FUNCTION OF CHRISTIAN MINISTRY

In this section we will consider, document by document and in chronological order, the various statements on the name and the function of Christian ministry.

A. THE DIDACHE

Dating the *Didache* is not an easy matter, since it is a compilation of documents, some of which stem from a Jewish background coterminous, it seems, with Jesus' own life. Audet would like to date the document quite early; others would prefer a date somewhere around 150 A.D. It seems to have come in its present format from a Christian community in Syria.[2]

Mention of ministry is not extensive in the *Didache:* the following passage is, however, important:

> Accordingly, elect for yourselves bishops [episkopoi] and deacons [diakonoi], men who are an honor to the Lord, of gentle disposition, not attached to money, honest and well-tried; for they, too, render you the sacred service of the prophets and teachers.

Do not, then, despise them; for they are your dignitaries together
with the prophets and teachers.[3]

The quality of the ministerial person stands in the forefront, not
the function of the ministry. J. Quasten notes: "There are no indications whatever in the *Didache* which would warrant the assumption
of a monarchical episcopate. The heads of the communities are called
episkopoi and diakonoi; but whether these episkopoi were simple
priests or bishops is not clear. Nowhere is mention made of presbyters."[4]

In the *Didache,* great attention is give to the prophets: in 13, 3
they are called high priests; in 10, 7, they are to celebrate the eucharist;
they are not to be judged (11, 11); nor are they to be criticized since
that would be sinful (11, 7). Since so much attention is given to the
prophet, it seems evident that the ministry of prophet was, for whatever
reason, quite under the limelight at this time in the Syriac Church.

H.-M. Legrand, agreeing with Audet that the document should
be dated prior to 100 A.D., concludes that the prophets in the *Didache*
celebrated the eucharist along with the apostles (taken in the sense of
messengers) as also the episkopoi, who are, in the *Didache,* not seen
as successors of the apostles. Legrand then notes, regarding all three
groups: "Their denominations are quite other than sacerdotal."[5] In
other words, presiding over the community, not liturgical action, is
the basis for the name and function of these ministries.

Grant states that "in the Didache the real successors of the apostles
are the prophets and teachers."[6] Actually, there is no mention of
"succession" at all; only if one is looking for a succession will one
make a judgment. Grant also mentions that the apostles (apostle taken
in a very broad sense) seem to have moved from community to community, and the *Didache,* according to some scholars, indicates a development away from this itinerant ministry to a stable, even appointed
ministry within a community (cf. 13, 1; 15, 1–2). However, Grant
nuances this judgment by saying that this may be the case in some
instance, but in others it is not.

The *Didache,* written perhaps alongside New Testament writings,
gives us another insight into early ministry which parallels much of
the New Testament data: names are still in a flux; episkopos is certainly
not yet the main minister in the *Didache* community; apostle and
prophet are by far the superior ministries. Kraft notes that the mention

of episkopoi and diakonoi (15, 1) is, perhaps, one of the more recently composed parts of the *Didache*.[7] These episkopoi and diakonoi are not appointed by apostles, but by the more general "you." Nor is the episkopos in any way a monarchical episkopos.

B. THE FIRST LETTER OF CLEMENT

Irenaeus tells us in *Adversus Haereses* (3, 3, 3) that Clement was the third successor of Peter in the Christian community at Rome. Eusebius mentions the same thing (*His. eccl.* 3, 15, 34). This letter of Clement seems to date from 90 to 100 A.D., written at Rome, and sent to the Christian community in Corinth. The occasion for the letter is the rebellion against the Church leadership at Corinth, which had driven the presbyters from their office. A critical situation regarding ministry and presidency had arisen in the Christian community at Corinth.

There seems to be no clear evidence that the Corinthian community had appealed to Rome on this matter, a view espoused some decades ago in an attempt to strengthen the Roman Church's position in the Christian world of that age. Rather, scholars today emphasize the relationship between Rome and Corinth, the capital city and the Roman colony, together with all its trade and athletic competition. Ideas, news, people flowed from Rome to Corinth, from Corinth to Rome. In the letter there is no mention whatsoever of jurisdiction or primacy of Roman Christian leadership over the Corinthian community. Almost at this identical time, Ignatius of Antioch did not hesitate to write to many communities in the cities of Asia Minor, and this in a fairly authoritative way; so, too, Clement writes to Corinth. Neither in the letters of Ignatius nor in the letter of Clement, however, does one find jurisdiction and primacy. This theme, however, is a matter of ecclesiology and needs to be considered in a study of the Church, rather than in a study of ministry.

As far as ministry and presidency is concerned, Clement is clearly christological. Minister and presiders are not self-appointed, nor are they appointed by the community. They have been commissioned by the Lord. We read:

> The Apostles preached to us the Gospel received from Jesus Christ, and Jesus Christ was God's ambassador. Christ, in other words, comes with a message from God and the Apostles with

a message from Christ. Both these orderly arrangements, therefore, originate from the will of God. And so, after receiving their instructions and being fully assured through the Resurrection of our Lord Jesus Christ, as well as confirmed in faith by the word of God, they went forth, equipped with the fullness of the Holy Spirit, to preach the good news that the Kingdom of God was close at hand. From land to land, accordingly, and from city to city they preached, and from among their earliest converts appointed men whom they had tested by the Spirit to act as bishops [episkopoi] and deacons for the future believers. And this was no innovation, for, a long time before the Scripture had spoken about bishops [episkopoi] and deacons, somewhere it says: "I will establish their overseers in observance of the law and their ministers in fidelity."[8]

Clement in a later passage reiterates these ideas:

Our Apostles, too, were given to understand by our Lord Jesus Christ that the office of bishop [episkopos] would give rise to intrigues. For this reason, equipped as they were with perfect foreknowledge, they appointed the men mentioned before, and afterwards laid down a rule once for all to this effect: when these men die, other approved men shall succeed to their sacred ministry. Consequently, we deem it an injustice to eject from the sacred ministry the persons who were appointed either by them, or later, with the consent of the whole Church, by other men in high repute and have ministered to the flock of Christ faultlessly, humbly, quietly and unselfishly, and have moreover, over a long period of time, earned the esteem of all. Indeed, it will be no small sin for us if we oust men who have irreproachably and piously offered the sacrifices proper to the episcopate. Happy the presbyters who have before now completed life's journey and taken their departure in mature age and laden with fruit! They, surely, do not have to fear that anyone will dislodge them from the place built for them. Yes, we see that you removed some, their good conduct notwithstanding, from the sacred ministry on which their faultless discharge had shed lustre.[9]

This is a very interesting section of Clement's letter, long though both passages are. The theme is clearly Church ministry and more precisely, it should be noted, the theme of succession in Church ministry. Clement calls these ministers "episkopoi," but in 44 he also calls them "presbyteroi." Once again we see a sort of equivalency to the titles, which Grant calls to our attention.[10] The naming of Christian ministers at the time of this letter is still in flux.

Clement emphasizes that the ministry is one of preaching. Just as Jesus came with a message from God, so, too, the apostles come with a message from Christ (cf. 42, 1). This preaching is a message of the kingdom. In the places which they visited, the apostles then appointed episkopoi and diakonoi (cf. 42, 4). It seems that Clement is basing himself on the Acts of the Apostles for this data. In fact, throughout his letter, Acts plays a major role, while the letters of Paul hardly exert any influence. At any rate, a stabilized presidency of the community and a local ministry of preaching has taken place: this is the ministry of episkopos/presbyter and to some degree deacon. Besides preaching, mention is indeed made of a liturgical ministry: in 44, 4 these ministers are to "offer the gifts." Liturgical ministry is also seen in 40, 1-5, in which reference is made to "order" or "appointment" (six times), to "decrees" (twice) and to "services" (twice). The text in 40 is as follows:

> Since, therefore, this is evident to all of us, and we have explored the depths of the divine knowledge, we are obliged to carry out in fullest detail what the Master has commanded us to do at stated times. He has ordered the sacrifices to be offered and the services to be held, and this not in a random and irregular fashion, but at definite times and seasons. He has, moreover, Himself, by His sovereign will determined where and by whom He wants them to be carried out. Thus, all things are done religiously, acceptable to His good pleasure, dependent on His will. Those, therefore, that make their offerings at the prescribed times are acceptable and blessed; for, since they comply with the ordinances of the Master, they do not sin. Special functions are assigned to the high priest; a special office is imposed upon the priests; and special ministrations fall to the Levites. The layman is bound by the rules laid down for the laity.[11]

Throughout these passages from Clement, the christocentric aspect of ministry is clearly evident: references to Jesus are abundant. It would, however, stretch the evidence to say apodictically that in Clement the episkopoi/presbyteroi are "sacerdotal" figures. Based on the material of the letter presented in 40, in which the author takes up the question of the Aaronite priesthood, some comparison is made with these Old Testament priestly figures. It is also true that Clement uses the Greek term "hiereus" [priest] for the Christian minister. This seems to be the first extant occurrence of this usage. In spite of this brief mention of hiereus, Legrand can remark: "Clement contents himself with a comparison which by the deliberate choice of certain non-ritual terms precludes the assimilation of the ministers of the New Testament to those of the Old Covenant."[12] In other words, the ministry of presiding over the eucharist was associated with the ministry of presiding over the community and is a part of the latter, rather than vice versa. It is not a special ordination to "priesthood" which is the root for presiding over the community; rather, it is the commission to preside over the community which allows for a presiding over the eucharist.

Legrand's comments do not detract from Grant's analysis of this letter of Clement. For Grant, "it seems hard to deny that for Clement the episcopate is analogous to the office of the high priest. But if this is so, we should expect to find presbyters the equivalent of priests, and deacons the equivalent of Levites."[13] These analogies are not to be found. Moreover, presbyters and episkopoi, Grant notes, are interchangeable. The emphasis is not on the sacerdotality of the ministers, but on order.

In the last passage from Clement, cited above, there is a clear difference between those who preside and the lay person. This *laikos* is someone who has a function distinct from and lower than the episkopos/presbyteros and deacon. As remarked above, the basic structure for Clement is one of community-presidency, rather than ordination-presidency, so that the distinction between *laikos* and *episkopos/presbyter* is also to be seen in the framework of presiding within the community.[14] Clement's letter offers us insight into the following issues:

1. Ministry is radically christocentric. The Lord appoints Church ministers; there is no question of either self-appointment to such office nor even community appointment. The community, however, is involved to some degree in the process of appointment.

2. Episkopos and presbyteros are still fairly equivalent names.

3. Presidency over the community is the basis for presidency over the liturgy, not vice versa. Ordination is not mentioned; appointment is.

4. Preaching and teaching is central to this presidency. There is, however, no office of "teacher."

5. Ministers seems to have been appointed for life; death seems to be the reason for cessation of such ministers. Deposition is not an acceptable route.

6. The qualities of ministers are, to some degree, stated.

7. The Christian ministers do have liturgical functions: the eucharist is referred to.

8. A distinction is made between laikos and episkopos/presbyteros, deacon.

9. The intervention of the Church at Rome into the Christian community at Corinth does not seem to be made on the basis of a "Roman jurisdiction."

C. IGNATIUS OF ANTIOCH

Ignatius, the episkopos of Antioch, was sentenced to die at Rome during the reign of Trajan (98–117). Ignatius' writings, therefore, are representative of the first decade of the second century and tell us something of the Church's life in Asia Minor. On his way to Rome, Ignatius wrote to the Christian communities of Ephesus, Magnesia, Tralles, Philadelphia and Smyrna. He also sent a personal letter to Polycarp of Smyrna, and a general letter to the Christian community at Rome. The textual discussion on these letters has been quite complex. It is our present interest to focus on the material in these letters dealing with ministry.

H. Lietzmann has written: "In Ignatius we already find that the monarchical episcopate is an accomplished fact and is applicable to both Syria and Western Asia Minor."[15] The following map indicates the area in which those ancient cities to which Ignatius sent his letters can be found.

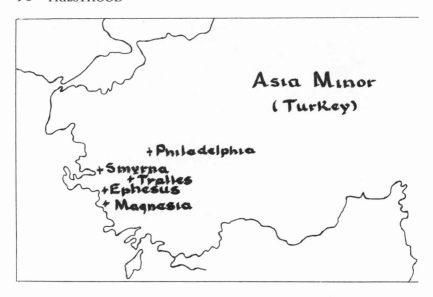

One sees that the area is rather small, in comparison with the Roman world of that time. As a result, one cannot make sweeping judgments about conditions beyond the area under discussion. In other words, at this time we know nothing about the situation in Rome, Carthage, Alexandria, etc., as far as a monarchical episcopacy is concerned. On the other hand, it is abundantly clear, in the Ignatian letters, that there is, to some degree, a monarchical episcopacy in the Christian communities which receive these letters.[16] The episkopos has become the name for the main minister in the local Churches of Asia Minor, to which these letters are written. Beneath the episkopos is the presbyter and then the deacon. Last of all are the lay people. We see in these letters a model of episcopal structure which will eventually become the standard model throughout most of the Christian world, but this does not occur until the end of the third century. At the time of Ignatius we can only determine what is happening in this area of Western Asia Minor.

In the letters, Ignatius clearly sees ministry as christocentric. Jesus is the foundation for all ministry in the Church. For instance in the letter to the Magnesians we read:

As, then, the Lord did nothing apart from the Father, either by himself or through the apostles, since he was united with him, so you must do nothing apart from the bishop and the presbyters. Do not try to make anything appear praiseworthy by yourselves, but let there be in common one prayer, one petition, one mind, one hope in love, in blameless joy—which is Jesus Christ, than whom nothing is better. All of you must run together as one temple of God, as to one sanctuary, to one Jesus Christ, who proceeded from one Father and is with the one and departed to the one.[17]

Jesus is, then, the source, the model and the goal of all Christian ministry. Christian ministry does not come about by self-appointment, nor by community-appointment. In the same letter, Ignatius develops his thought on this even further:

Since, then, in the persons already mentioned I have beheld the whole congregation in faith and have loved it, I exhort you: be eager to do everything in God's harmony, with the bishop presiding in the place of God and the presbytery in the place of the council of apostles and the deacons, most sweet to me, entrusted with the service of Jesus Christ—who before the ages was with the Father and was made manifest at the end.[18]

In his letter to the Trallians, Ignatius resumes this thought:

For when you subject yourselves to the bishop as to Jesus Christ, you appear to me to be living not in human fashion but like Jesus Christ, who died for us so that by believing in his death you might escape dying. Therefore it is necessary that, as is actually the case, you do nothing apart from the bishop, but be subject also to the presbytery as to the apostles of Jesus Christ our hope; for if we live in him we shall be found in him. Those who are deacons of the mysteries of Jesus Christ, must please all men in every way. For they are not ministers of food and drink but servants of the Church of God; therefore, they must guard themselves from accusations as from fire.[19]

In both of the above passages we see that for Ignatius it is the presbytery which is the "successor" to the apostles. The episkopos presides in the place of God or in the place of Jesus. The ministry of deacons is presented as one of the more prominent ministries. In all of these the emphasis is clearly on presidency over the community, not on liturgical presidency. In the letter to the Trallians we read further:

> Similarly all are to respect the deacons as Jesus Christ and the bishop as a copy of the Father and the presbyters as the council of God and the band of the apostles. For apart from these no group can be called a church.[20]

In the letter to the Ephesians, Ignatius returns to this theme of the variety of ministries and yet their interdependence:

> Therefore it is fitting for you to run your race together with the bishop's purpose—as you do. For presbytery—worthy of fame, worthy of God—is attuned to the bishop like strings to a lyre. Therefore by your unity and harmonious love Jesus Christ is sung.[21]

In Ignatius' letters we see that the episkopos is the presider of the community and the presider of the liturgy as well. He teaches and he preaches. On the other hand, the presbyters, generally referred to in the plural, act as counselors to the episkopos. This is a detail of no small significance, and, as we shall see, this idea returns in the earliest ordination ritual which we have, that of Hippolytus' *Traditio Apostolica* around 210. The deacons are beneath both episkopos and presbyters. W. Bauer, who is somewhat critical about the extent of Ignatius' monarchical episcopacy, nonetheless sees that in the letters, if not in fact, a monarchical episcopacy is indeed stressed: "The first and foremost figure is the bishop, who is like God or Christ, in whose place he stands. And just as there can be no second, even approximately similar position beside them, neither can there be such beside the bishop. At a suitably respectable distance behind him come the presbyters and the deacons, attentive to his beck and call and obliged to render him due reverence. The administration of the particular community should rest completely in the hands of this one bishop who sets in motion and supervises all its activities, without whom no ecclesiastical function has validity and who, by virtue of this office, is immune to any criticism no matter how young in years or deficient in character he might be."[22] These are indeed strong words to describe the episcopal position in the Christian communities of Western Asia Minor.

Bauer and with him Bultmann claim that Ignatius really represents a minority opinion under strong monarchical leadership over against a majority group which has a congregational leadership. Bauer believes that Ignatius is stressing an ideal situation, rather than a real one. There is no doubt that the letters present only the "perfect picture," whereas reality is always less than perfect. In this sense, the letters do inculcate an ideal, but this ideal presents the guidelines for the actual situations. As we know from subsequent history, this ideal clearly influenced the course of Christian leadership to an enormous degree.

In the gospel of Matthew, seemingly of Antiochene origin, there is no mention of a Church leader beyond the Twelve and the apostles. This gospel was written after 70 A.D. Ignatius is writing but thirty years or so later. A development of ministry in that short time does raise questions. The book of Revelation also addresses "letters" to Churches in Asia Minor, but again there does not seem to be an established Church structure as we find in the Ignatian letters. Many of the issues which Bauer mentions do raise questions about the Church of Ignatius in Antioch and the surrounding Churches in Asia Minor to whom he writes his letters. These issues at least caution us to qualify our statements, to some degree, regarding the ecclesiastical structure which Ignatius presents.

Ignatius speaks only of Old Testament prophets, and for him there is only one teacher, Jesus Christ (Eph 15, 1). Evidently, the ministries of prophet and teacher did not play a role in the Churches under consideration. In contrast, the role of the episkopos is quite well delineated. For Ignatius there is no Church without an episkopos, and the episkopoi have, in his mind, been appointed throughout the entire Christian world. Some have noted that in his letter to the Church at Rome, there is no mention of episkopos, and, so they argue, the Church at Rome did not, at that time, have an episkopos. But Ignatius does not mention presbyter or deacon either in these letters. One can only say that the lack of mention really is no argument against such kinds of leadership roles in the Roman Christian Church.[23]

Deacons play a prominent role in the Ignatian structure. They serve in a sort of ambassadorial status, or missionary status, preaching and teaching, but above all in leadership roles. They also have a liturgical role. This importance of the deacon to the episkopos will remain strong in the patristic period. Both Elchin[24] and Mitchell[25] emphasize this diaconal role in the letters of Ignatius.

The Ignatian letters have been rightfully called "jewels" of early patristic literature, and because there is something special about these letters, they have influenced strongly the structuring of Christian ministry in the decades following Ignatius' death. As Grant remarks: "It was generally believed that the order achieved in Ignatius' time deserved preference . . . it [the order] became established in the second century."[26]

The presentation of ministry in Ignatius of Antioch might be summarized as follows:

1. The christocentrism of the entire Church, including ministry is key to Ignatius' view.

2. Jesus is to be seen, in one way or another, behind every ministry. It is Jesus who is the real minister.

3. The episkopos is the presider over the community par excellence. Above all, he is the Christian leader of the community. Because he is the leader over the community, he is also the leader over the liturgical worship. In other words, his leadership is not attributed to an "ordination."

4. Presbyters are of second rank. They form a sort of "college," and are meant to offer advice to the episkopos.

5. The deacons are in the third place of ministry, but often receive from Ignatius more encomia than the presbyters do.

D. POLYCARP'S LETTER TO THE PHILIPPIANS

Polycarp was the episkopos of Smyrna, also in Western Asia Minor, who suffered a martyr's death around 156. Irenaeus tells us that Polycarp wrote many letters to various Christian communities. The only one that we have extant is that to the Philippians, which might actually be a conflation of two letters, one written about 110 and the other about 130. At any rate, what we have in this letter is a window into the Christian Church both at Smyrna and at Philippi during the first half of the second century.

In the letter Polycarp does not mention episkopos, but speaks only about presbyters:

The presbyters must be tenderhearted, merciful toward all, turning back [the sheep] that have gone astray, visiting the sick, not neglecting widow or orphan or poor man, but always taking thought for that which is honorable in the sight of God and of man, abstaining from all anger, respect of persons, unrighteous judgement, being far from all love of money, not hastily believing [anything] against anyone, not stern in judgement, knowing that we are all debtors because of sin.[27]

The focus of this passage is clearly on pastoral care and the qualities of a Christian minister. In W. R. Shoedel's translation, the translator pinpoints the many New Testament references in this brief paragraph, and by so doing we see once more that the standard for Christian ministry is christological.[28] Jesus, the center of the New Testament, is the model of Christian ministry. Polycarp makes no mention of an episkopos at Philippi, but only of presbyters and deacons. Because of this omission of episkopos, Quasten says that "one might be justified in concluding that the Christian community of Philippi was governed by a committee of presbyters."[29] Such a presbyteral leadership committee does reappear elsewhere at times in the early Church as the center of local Church administration. If this presbyteral leadership for Philippi is historically accurate, then we have another indication that the monarchical episcopacy, found in Ignatius' letters, cannot be seen as a universal phenomenon at the beginning of the second century.

The qualities of a presbyter, presented by Polycarp, are similar to the qualities of a deacon (cf. 6, 1), and the themes which are mentioned are found abundantly in the Old and New Testaments, particularly the latter.

Deacons are also mentioned in Polycarp's letter: "Likewise must deacons be blameless before his righteousness as ministers of God and Christ and not of men; not slanderers, not insincere, not lovers of money, temperate in everything, compassionate, attentive, walking according to the truth of the Lord, who was minister of all."[30] The pastoral care of diaconal ministry is emphasized, and the deacon is described as a very Christlike individual. Indeed, the description of the deacon reminds one of the description of the deacon in 1 Tim 3, 8-13. The community is to be deferential to the deacon as they would be to Jesus himself (5, 3). Since the deacons are especially singled out in this letter, one could say that their ministry had become prominent in the Christian community at Philippi and important in the eyes of Polycarp. This corresponds well with Ignatius' letters and with Clement (although in Clement the deacon is not very prominent).

Polycarp makes no mention whatsoever of an ordination. In chapter 11, Polycarp, discussing Valens, says that Valens "was formerly made an elder [presbyteros] among you." In what way this took place is not mentioned, but by becoming a presbyter Valens was indeed given an office (11, 1), which he had made unrecognizable because of his bad conduct. Nonetheless, Polycarp urges the Philippians to reinstate Valens and not deal harshly either with him or his wife.

From this letter of Polycarp we can gather the following data:

1. Polycarp is an episkopos, but he does not mention an episkopos for the Church at Philippi.

2. Presbyters are an administrative or leadership group in the Christian community at Philippi. They are to reflect gospel traits.

3. Deacons are especially singled out. They, too, are in a leadership role, and must reflect Jesus.

E. THE LETTER OF BARNABAS

The letter of Barnabas has engendered a great deal of dispute among patristic scholars. Today, no one really claims that the author is indeed the Barnabas, of whom we read in the New Testament. Even the text of the letter no way indicates that the author's name is Barnabas. The attribution to Barnabas is quite ancient, and the letter was extremely popular throughout the East, so much so that the Codex Sinaiticus ranks this letter with the canonical books of the New Testament. In the West, however, the letter was for all practical purposes unknown. As a result, the letter offers us an insight only into a Christian community of the Eastern Church. The dating of this letter varies with the patristic scholars, going from 70 to 138 A.D. More than likely, it dates more from the end of this spectrum rather than from the earlier part of it.

R. Kraft remarks: "There is nothing in the epistle that enables us to determine how the community was organized, or how its worship was conducted. Apart from the references to the ministry of "teachers" (see 4, 3; 9, 3—"prophetic" figures? [cf. 16, 9]), there are only vague allusions to 'those in authority' (or perhaps, 'those economically prosperous'? [21, 2]), and to those 'who proclaim the Lord's word' (19, 9b [=Did. 4, 11]; cf 10, 11c; 16, 10)."[31]

Since the ministry of "teacher" and of "prophet" came to be overshadowed by the ministry of episkopos and presbyter, we have in this letter an indication that in the East these ministries of prophet and teacher were still quite active. Since the letter probably dates from the second and third decades of the second century, we have another indication that the naming and function of Christian ministers is still in flux at that particular time.

F. THE SHEPHERD OF HERMAS

This work, called the *Shepherd of Hermas,* is of great importance for the sacrament of reconciliation. In this work there is much said about the Church, and this in a quite mystical way, but there is no detailed description of ministry. Since there is an allusion to Hermas' brother, Pius, who was episkopos of Rome, one dates this book somewhere around the time of the reign of Pius I, 140–150 A.D. It is also an account which reflects the Western Church at that time, especially the Christian Church at Rome.

In the section on reconciliation (4, 3, 1–6) the author speaks of "certain teachers" who had discussed baptism with the neophytes. In the section on baptism (Similitude 9, 16), the author notes that the apostles and teachers "who preached in the name of the Son of God, and died in the power and faith of the Son of God, preached also to those who had died before them and they gave to them the seal of the preaching." On this section Quasten notes that so thoroughly did Hermas believe that baptism was necessary for salvation that "the Apostles and teachers descended into limbo after death to baptize the righteous departed of pre-Christian times."[32] It is clear that teachers still played a major role in Christian ministry.

The document speaks of episkopoi, presbyteroi and deacons. The presbyters are presented as the leaders of the community (*proistamenoi* of the Church), directors of the group (*proegoumenoi*), presiders (*protokathedritai*) and shepherds (*poimenes*). The author speaks about the tasks of the episkopoi: providing for the needy and the widows. The deacons, too, must take care of the widows and needy, under the supervision of the episkopoi. Grant writes:

In general, we should assume, the apostles and teachers are dead, while the bishops and deacons are alive. Of the bishops we learn little, except that they, or some of them, are hospitable and help the destitute and the widows of the community. . . .

We know, therefore, that there are bishops and deacons, but we know little about them. On the other hand, there is a key passage (Vis. 2, 4, 3) in which Hermas explicitly speaks of "the elders who are in charge of the Church." This must show that bishops and presbyters, as in Clement's letter, are practically identical; it also suggests that no one presbyter was to be called *the* bishop.[33]

In all of this one sees that there is still flux in the naming and the function of these various ministries, and the documentation stems particularly from the West and even from Rome in the second quarter of the second century.

G. ST. JUSTIN, THE APOLOGIST

St. Justin, a prolific writer and a highly educated Christian, came to Rome during the reign of Antoninus Pius (138–161). Originally, he was from Flavia Neapolis and had attended stoic, peripatetic and pythagorean schools. Shortly after this broad education, he converted to Christianity and moved to Rome. He was martyred about 165. He represents, therefore, in his writings basically the Western Church, and more specifically the Roman Christian community, but due to his Eastern background he also offers some insight into Eastern aspects of Church life as well.

Nowhere does Justin treat directly of ministry. We are indebted to him for his invaluable sketches of the ritual of baptism and eucharist, and in these writings he refers to the presider as the *proestos* (65); the same term is used in his description of the Sunday eucharistic liturgy (67). He also mentions deacons (67). This is, indeed, rather scant material, but it still helps us see that at this early period in Rome, there was indeed a minister of the Christian community, recognized as the liturgical presider. Besides this main presider, there are also other ministers of lesser importance: the deacon and the lector. This latter read the memoirs of the apostles and the writings of the prophets, and after this public reading, the presider instructed the community. We see once more that the main minister of the Christian community has the task of preaching or teaching, as well as liturgical presidency.

Although the material on ministry in Justin is referred to in a most tangential way, it nonetheless opens a small window in the Christian world at Rome around the middle of the second century.

H. ST. IRENAEUS OF LYONS

More than likely, Irenaeus was born in Smyrna, Asia Minor, somewhere between 140 and 160. In either 177 or 178 he became a presbyter at the Christian Church in Lyons. As a presbyter he was sent to Bishops Eleutherius at Rome to discuss the vexing issue of montanism. When he returned to Lyons, he found that the aged bishop, Photinus, had died; Irenaeus was then made episkopos of Lyons. The time of his death is unknown, nor are we even sure that he was martyred, although he is venerated as a martyr. He left to us a highly important work, which we call in its Latin (therefore, a later and translated work) *Adversus Haereses.* In the original Greek it is entitled: *The Detection and Overthrow of the Pretended but False Gnosis.*

There are valuable statements on ministry in this volume, which give us some picture of Christian ministry in certain parts of the West in the last two decades of the second century. For Irenaeus the episkopos is the highest and chief leader of the Christian community, not only in Lyons but, as he believes, throughout the Christian world. He writes:

> Anyone who wishes to discern the truth may see in every church
> in the whole world the Apostolic tradition clear and manifest.
> We can enumerate those who were appointed as bishops in the
> churches by the Apostles and their successors to our own day,
> who never knew and never taught anything resembling their (the
> Gnostics') foolish doctrine.[34]

Apostolic tradition is, for Irenaeus, the touchstone of the true Church. More than any author we have studied so far, Irenaeus emphasizes this apostolic tradition, and he means this in a quite historical way, but above all in a theological or spiritual way. One must trace one's faith back to the apostles. The anti-gnostic overtones of this emphasis are quite clear. Private revelations are not to be tolerated. To insure this connection with Jesus, Irenaeus presumes that there are actually episkopoi all over the Christian world, and these have been so appointed by the apostles themselves, or by successors of these apostles.

This ecclesiology is the foundation of Irenaeus' understanding of ministry, and as we see it is not at all confined to the episkopos at Rome, but it is meant to validate all the episkopoi in the Christian communities and in consequence to validate all true Christian communities. He goes on to say:

> But it would be very long in a book of this kind, to enumerate the episcopal lists in all the churches, but by pointing out the apostolic tradition and creed which has been brought down to us by a succession of bishops in the greatest, most ancient, and well known Church, founded by the two most glorious Apostles, Peter and Paul at Rome, we can confute all those who in any other way, either for self-pleasing or for vainglory or blindness or badness, hold unauthorized meetings.[35]

There then follows a statement which has been the focus of much attention over the years:

> For with this Church [Rome], because of its more efficient leadership, all Churches must agree, that is to say, the faithful of all places, because in it the apostolic tradition has been always preserved by the (faithful) in all places.[36]

Apostolicity of ministry is indeed the touchstone; all episkopoi who are in the true Church are therefore apostolic. This apostolic foundation for ministry is most evident in the Church of Rome, (a) because this Church [in Irenaeus' understanding] was founded by the two great apostles, Peter and Paul. Irenaeus evidently believes that there are more than twelve apostles, since Paul is clearly and most highly placed in that august group; (b) because the Church at Rome enjoys a distinction, *propter potentiorem principalitatem,* as the Latin translation has it. What is the Greek original, since Irenaeus wrote in Greek? This is a crucial question. A number of Greek words have been suggested: *authentia, exousia, katholikos, hegemenikos, proegouemnos, proteuein, arche, archaion, archaiotes.* A. Ehrhard and J. Quasten prefer the English: more efficient leadership; Van den Eynde and Bardy would prefer the term: superior origin.[37] Irenaeus does not seem to be talking about the ecclesial constitution with a primacy of the episkopos at Rome. When he writes that all "must agree" with the Roman Church, Quasten notes that this is more by way of fact than of obligation. Since it is a fact that the Roman Church is teaching apostolic doctrine, we must all agree.[38] Without any doubt this passage "is of great importance for the history of the primacy, because Irenaeus attributes to the Church of Rome, a 'more efficient leadership' than to any other Church."[39] At the time of Irenaeus it would be difficult to assert that Irenaeus had the idea of Roman primacy when penning this passage.

Irenaeus employs his same argument, apostolic succession, to the presbyters; he writes:

> Wherefore it is incumbent to obey the presbyters who are in the Church, those who as I have shown possess the succession from the Apostles; those who, together with the succession of the epis-copate, have received the certain gift of truth, according to the good pleasure of the Father.[40]

Ott comments on Irenaeus' approach to the presbyters: "[Presbyter] is a title of honor by means of which he [Irenaeus] describes the followers of the apostles, e.g., Polycarp, or the followers of the followers of the apostles, who are the bearers and protectors of the apostolic tradition, but he also joins them to the ruling bishops of his own time, who are the successors of the apostles and who have received the certain charism of truth in this succession into the office of epi-skopos."[41]

It is important to note in the passage from Irenaeus, which deals with the episkopos of Rome, that the counting does not begin with Peter. Peter is not the first. The first is Linus, then Anaclete, then (trito topo) in the third place Clement, etc. (Adv. Haer. 3, 3, 2–3). In later enumerations, the first on the list will be Peter, and then secondly, Linus, etc. In the enumeration of Irenaeus, the founder is quite special and different. Linus is given simply leitourgia, an official capacity which is not totally the same as the official status of Peter, the founder. Nonetheless, for Irenaeus, the "blessed apostles" on the command of the Lord Jesus founded the Church, and it was these same "blessed apostles" who provided for the continuation of the Lord's Church.[42]

With Irenaeus, roughly around 180 A.D., we come to a sort of closure and opening as regards Christian ministry. By 180 or thereabouts, the naming of Christian ministry had become fairly stabilized. The name "episkopos" was the accepted name for the highest and chief leader of the local Christian community; next to him were the presbyters, quite often spoken of in the plural form; then the deacons. This does not mean that only at this time of Irenaeus do we have a "chief leader" of the community. Such chief leaders had been in the Christian communities from the beginning, e.g., the apostles. The name of the main leader, however, varied. Around the time of Irenaeus, the name of this main leader had become rather universally the episkopos.

The description of apostolic succession is also varied. From the data we have considered, the following emerges:

1. In the *Didache* the prophets are the successors of the apostles;

2. In Ignatius the presbyters are the successors of the apostles;

3. In Irenaeus both the episkopoi and the presbyters are the successors of the apostles.

This variance indicates rather clearly that at this early time, the second century, the issue of apostolic succession had not been uniformly determined. Only in a later Church period do we have the more universally accepted position of the apostolic succession of the "bishops." Even more than the names of the successors of the apostles, however, is the realization that the Church itself is fundamentally apostolic, and false Church communities, false doctrines, false teachings, etc., are false because they are not apostolic.

In this period of Church history up to Irenaeus, the *function* of the various ministries was by no means as uniform as the naming. In certain Churches the relationship of episkopos and presbyters was different from that of other Churches. In terms of function, nonetheless, it is correct to say that the emphasis is still far more on the leadership of the community than on the leadership of the liturgy. At this particular era of Church history, as Legrand has pointed out, structurally it is because someone is the leader of the community that he is also thereby the leader at the liturgy, not the other way around: namely, because one is structurally the leader of the liturgy (namely, through ordination) is he, therefore, the leader of the community as well.

As one moves into the end of the second century and the beginning of the third century, Christian writing expands geometrically, and there is an abundance of material on almost all facets of Christian life and theology. It would be a gigantic task to recount all that these Christian authors after Irenaeus have written on the subject of ministry, in the same way that we have done with the few authors treated above. The above authors spoke in only a brief and often tangential way about ministry; the authors after Irenaeus wrote at length and quite often in a focused way on ministry. Still, there are four authors in particular who reflect in a striking way the picture of Christian ministry at the end of the second and the beginning of the third century. Even though we will consider each of them in a rather summary way, the main ideas on ministry which they offer us are invaluable.

I. ORIGEN, TERTULLIAN, HIPPOLYTUS AND THE AUTHOR OF THE DIDASCALIA APOSTOLORUM

These four authors reflect four different Church areas: Origen that at Alexandria; Tertullian that at Carthage; Hippolytus that at Rome; the unknown author of the *Didascalia Apostolorum* most probably the Church in Syria or perhaps Palestine. Origen was born around 185 and died about 253. Tertullian was born in Carthage about 155 and died sometime after 220. Hippolytus died in 235 and was quite active in Rome around 212, when Origen first heard him. The unknown author of the *Didascalia Apostolorum* seems to have written in the third century, more particularly, according to solid scholarship, the early part of the third century. These four men, then, are, more or less, all contemporaries and present us with a picture of the wide Christian Church at that time.

In Alexandria, where Origen taught, the episkopos was the most important Christian leader. Origen's predecessor at the school, Clement of Alexandria, had written: "According to my opinion the grades here in the Church of episkopoi, presbyteroi, and diakonoi, are imitations of the angelic glory."[42] Although Clement's attempt to relate the ecclesiastical hierarchy to the angelic hierarchy was not taken up by later writers in any substantial degree, it is, nonetheless, indicative of an attempt to theologize the ranking of these groups, and, as we shall see, this theologizing of ministerial rank will continue. For Clement the episkopos was the highest Church leader, and Origen does not dispute this at all. He presumes this tri-partite hierarchy for a Christian

community and never calls it into question, but Origen does go on
to theologize this hierarchy. For instance he writes:

> There are some, who, I know not how, arrogate to themselves
> a power exceeding that of the priests [hieratiche taxis], presumably
> because they know nothing of sacerdotal science.[44]

Whereas prior to this the words ordinarily used had been episkopos and presbyteros and diakonos (although Clement had used the
word *hiereus*), we now begin—but only begin—to hear the Greek
form of priest, *hiereus,* used more and more in connection with the
other titles. Origen, no doubt, did not start this, but due to his influence, this usage, which is not substantiated by the New Testament,
begins to take over in the Christian communities. Origen himself had
had a difficult time getting ordained, but he seems to have obtained
ordination to the presbyterate outside of Alexandria, yet after ordination he returns to Alexandria.[45] Even though he had many difficulties
with the episkopos at Alexandria, Demetrios, Origen is found very
much in the priestly world: he preaches regularly, he attends synods,
he argues with heretics. Since he had been well known as a scholar
and theologian prior to his ordination, and since he was so intellectually
trained and gifted, he did manage to be somewhat apart from the run-
of-the-mill presbyter. However, we do not find in his writings any
anti-episcopacy, anti-presbytery (what we today might term anti-clericalism); Origen is very much an ecclesial individual. He sees the
Church primarily from a spiritual or faith dimension, not a structural
or constitutional dimension. For Origen it is only natural that the
presbyter be a teacher, for the presbyter is active with the catechumens,
with the mature Christians, with the very learned. The episkopos for
his part is to be active in every aspect of Church life: he is the community leader. Presbyter or episkopos, for Origen, means a deeply
spiritual person. It is the spirituality of the office that attracts the
attention and study of Origen. This holiness is, of course, seen in the
very term *hiereus.*[46] Much of what Origen writes on the episkopos
has to do with the episkopos' failure to measure up to the high spiritual
ideal which belongs to his office.

> Most of the bishops, says Origen, are completely lacking in un-
> derstanding of their proper vocation. Instead of acting as religious

examples and sympathetic physicians of the soul to their congregations, they are worldly-minded, pursue earthly occupations
and affairs, long for wealth and land, are haughty, quarrelsome,
and self-assertive, allow themselves to be flattered and corrupted,
and are often less particular in the conduct of their business than
secular officials. . . .

As things are, the most sordid methods of intrigue and demagogy
are brought into play as soon as there is a chance of snatching
an office, especially the highest and most lucrative office, that of
bishop. Clergy brag about their seniority, and try to ensure that
their children or relatives will succeed them. Such clergy are, in
fact, Pharaoh rather than God. These 'tyrants' will not take advice
even from equals, much less from a layman or a pagan. The
only thing they take seriously are their advantages and privileges,
just like the Pharisees of old.[47]

These are rather indicting and gloomy words, but beneath the
problems we see that a "clergy class" had begun to develop as a normal
part of Church life. Origen does not contest that aspect; he urges,
rather, that each take his vocation seriously. In Origen we also see,
once more, the christocentric aspect of ministry: the Lord has called
and appointed, so one should live up to that lofty vocation. Hierarchy,
for Origen, is a sacred thing, not to be rejected in any way; it is meant
to reflect the Lord. To underline the spirituality of the ministry, Origen,
exegete that he is, delves into the Old Testament and compares the
episkopoi, presbyters and deacons to the Levites, i.e., to the Old Testament priest. Again, this is not to be found in the New Testament
which shied away from both the Greek and the Hebrew terms for
"priest" as far as leadership in the community was concerned. In Origen, however, the functioning of the Christian minister is being theologized along the lines of the Old Testament priests. This is the fairly
new step or at least an emphasis which Origen gives both to his work
and to the subsequent generation of Christians.

Pelikan notes that the Old Testament gradually contributed to
the development of the Christian concept of ministry, as authors began
to use the Old Testament to show that Christian ministry stood in
continuity with the Levitical priesthood. "Origen," Pelikan notes,
"combined the apostolic and the priestly definitions of the Christian
ministry."[48]

Three important aspects regarding Christian ministry can, then, be found in the writings of Origen:

1. Origen witnesses to the historical fact that the hierarchy of episkopos, presbyter and deacon had become standard in the East at his time. The naming and function of Christian ministry had reached a stabilized situation.

2. More than any other writer before him, Origen has presented a strong "theology of ministry." Even when Origen recounts negative aspects of episcopal and priestly ministry, he is offering a theological picture of ministry to his contemporaries. In Origen, this theology of ministry can also be seen as a spirituality of ministry, which is clearly Christocentric.

3. Origen, more than anyone before him, methodically employs Old Testament descriptions of the priest (hiereus) to the Christian minister. In many ways, Origen is a key figure in the renaming of the Christian minister: namely, calling the Christian ministry (episkopos and presbyter) a "priest."

Even though there is a mention of lector in Tertullian, it is not all that conclusive that he sees the clerical ministry beyond episkopos, presbyter and deacon. Like Origen, Tertullian, in his early period, accepted clerical leadership in the Church as a given. In his Montanist period, this acceptance does, of course, change. We are indebted to Tertullian for the terms *ordinatio* and *ordinare.*[49]

> With the emergence of Christian Latin in Tertullian we see that the analogy of the *ordo* and the people of the city of Rome was taken up to describe the relationship of the clergy to the people of God.[50]

In Latin culture, at the time of Tertullian, the people (*plebs*) were one group, and the *ordo* or *ordines* were another. Thus, we find in the Latin literature of that time the expression *ordo et populus* or *ordo et plebs*. In North Africa of that period plebs was preferred over populus. In the Roman world, there was the *ordo* of the senate; there was also, at least from the time of the Gracci onward, an *ordo* of the *equites.* As such these *ordines* betokened a specific class or group, and membership in these various orders was highly restricted, either as in the case of the senate because of birth, or as in the case of the equites because of imperial selection. The senate was called often the *ordo amplissimus;* the two orders were called *ordo uterque.* Only at a much later date than that of the late second and third century do we find the populus (or *plebs*) called an *ordo.* Those who belonged in these *ordines* were the people who could be placed in leadership offices within the empire.[51]

Tertullian (and others) began to speak of the clergy as an *ordo* in the Church distinct from the people (i.e., the lay). This manner of speaking became commonplace in the West. In the liturgy of the eucharist we find this very ancient prayer statement: *nos* (i.e., those in order) *et plebs tua sancta* (we [i.e., those in order] and your holy people). From Constantine on we find that this manner of speaking has become official. In itself, the word ordo does not have a sacramental overtone; rather, it is an honor or dignity, but one which carries with it leadership responsibilities. Dupuy notes: "One notices how much the structure of the Church has been influenced by the structure of the political society."[52]

The influence of Tertullian went in another direction as well. In his *De Pudicitia* he states very clearly the Montanist position, which in his later life he had espoused. He is speaking of the Church and the forgiveness of sins in the Church; he writes:

> And accordingly, 'the Church,' it is true, will forgive sins: but [it will be] the Church of the Spirit, by means of a spiritual man; not the Church which consists of a number of bishops.[53]

Instead of apostolic succession, as the touchstone for orthodoxy, Tertullian, and with him the Montanists, place sanctity. This begins so to spiritualize the Church that any evident ministry is invalid unless that ministry is itself spiritual. This kind of thinking—and Tertullian is only one, but an important one, who espoused it—led to the century-long problem in the Church on the re-ordination question as also the re-baptism question. If a minister is not "spiritual," then how can he impart the Spirit, either at baptism or at ordination. In an indirect way, then, Tertullian by his opposite opinion helps us, today, to see the value of the criterion of apostolic succession, rather than the criterion of personal sanctity. This latter is extremely difficult to verify, whereas the apostolic succession, though difficult, too, is at least somewhat more objective.

Earlier in his career, Tertullian had defended the apostolic succession of the Church against its enemies, and Tertullian notes that the episkopoi are the original "heirs" "who received the apostolic teaching and who can therefore still testify to it today not only in those churches which are of apostolic foundation but also in all of the others which developed from them and agree with them."[54] One finds in this account of Tertullian's ideas something which dominated the North African Church down to its collapse, when North Africa was run over by the Islamic nation, namely, a network of agreement with other Churches on both doctrine and practice. It was this collegiality of Churches, in doctrine and in practice, which was the sign of apostolic succession in the faith. Carthage and the North African Christian Churches were leaders in developing episcopal councils; this North African Church took episcopal collegiality very seriously, and did so because this was one of the main ways in which apostolic succession could be tested and verified.[55]

One could study more deeply the works of Tertullian, particularly in his orthodox period, and see that for him episkopoi were indeed leaders and presiders, ranking above the lay people in a permanent way. They were preachers and teachers. They were presiders at liturgy. Their positions are not presented in any tentative way, and so it is accurate to conclude that at the time of Tertullian, in North Africa, the episkopoi were without any doubt the main leaders of the Christian community, and that this leadership put them in an *ordo*. Beneath the episkopos, but part of ordo, were the presbyters and the deacons. Nowhere, however, does Tertullian describe the process or ceremony whereby one is brought into the clerical *ordo*.

We might enumerate the contributions which Tertullian has given to the history of ministry in the following way:

1. Tertullian bears witness to the stabilization of the names and functions of episkopos, presbyter and deacon.

2. Tertullian's influence brought about the use of the terms *ordo* and *ordinare* within the context of Christian ministry.

3. Tertullian's use of *ordo* allows one to speak of cleric/lay. Up to Tertullian such usage had not been widespread.

4. Tertullian is the first to mention another grade: that of lector, but it is not clear whether Tertullian considered the lector to be part of the clerical order.

5. Tertullian helps one see the need for "apostolic succession," since a spiritual ministry alone has little verification. The Catholic description of apostolic succession, which Tertullian early on promoted, strongly influenced the collegial framework of the North African Church.

Hippolytus, for his part, who was such a major intellectual figure at Rome in his day, has left us a book of immense importance: *The Apostolic Tradition.*[56] In this book we have the oldest known ordination ritual for episkopos, presbyter and deacon. Since Hippolytus was highly traditional, his work would not be innovative, but conservative. What he offers us is the tradition which he knew about and which had been going on in Rome for some time. Since the focus of our attention will be on the ordination ritual of Hippolytus, we will return to him in a lengthy way in the next section. However, in Hippolytus one finds, again, the stabilized naming and function of episkopos, presbyter and deacon. Hippolytus, thus, witnesses to this hierarchy at Rome at the end of the second century and the beginning of the third century.

The *Didascalia Apostolorum* was originally written in Greek, but we have only an early Syriac translation and extensive fragments of a Latin translation. It purports to be compiled by the apostles immediately after the "council at Jerusalem" (cf. Acts 15), and although this is surely fiction, the desire to root Church teaching and practice in apostolic foundations should not be overlooked.[57] The picture it affords us of the Church at the end of the third century, and in particular the picture of the episkopos, is very helpful. In fact, the main part of the book deals with the episkopos: eight chapters, namely, cc. 4 to 11. The episkopos is clearly the highest leader of the Christian community, and the description that the author presents is, first of all, one that deals with his moral character. Like Origen he mentions many possible failings of an episkopos, but by and large the material is morally persuasive toward a gospel man of service. Again and again the author returns to the theme of the gospel life of the bishop, and in this way he indicates that Jesus is the model of all ministry. His lengthy citations from Ezekiel and the book of Kings and the book of Numbers are really secondary to his gospel orientation, although they do indicate the tendency to use the Old Testament in some way to describe and define the Christian minister.[58]

Secondly, the bishop is portrayed in his leadership and his teaching or preaching capacity. Indeed, much of the material stays on these themes. Only in a rather passing way does the author mention the liturgical or sacramental functions of the episkopos. In this volume, the text clearly makes community leadership the basis for liturgical leadership, not vice versa. The episkopos is to be fifty years old, as a general rule, and the husband of one wife. Maturity is required of the episkopos; celibacy is by no means even suggested.[59]

The episkopos stands in reference to God: "This is your chief and your leader, and he is your mighty king. He rules in the place of the Almighty; but let him be honoured by you as God, for the bishop sits for you in the place of God Almighty. But the deacon stands in the place of Christ; and do you love him. And the deaconess shall be honoured by you in the place of the Holy Spirit; and the presbyters shall be to you in the likeness of the Apostles."[60] In a way that is reminiscent of Ignatius. The author relates the episkopos to God, and the presbyters to the apostles. This will not become the ordinary way of considering the successors to the apostles in the ensuing centuries.

The presbyters are mentioned only in a passing manner, but they are appointed by the episkopos, and their function is to be the counselors of the episkopos. At liturgical functions, they have their places around the chair of the episkopos in the eastern part of the building. These details about the presbyter confirm the picture that in this early period the presbyter did not, unless in some few, exceptional instances, play much of a liturgical role. In other words he was "ordained" (if we can yet speak of this) but he never celebrated the eucharist nor was the main presider at baptism nor preached nor did any of those things which we generally associate with the priest of today.[61]

On the other hand the deacon is a very prominent minister and handles most of the pastoral situations of the community. He is the "hearing of the bishop, and his mouth and his heart and his soul."

Since he holds the place of Christ in the community, the relationship to the episkopos is modeled on that of Christ and his heavenly Father. Lay people should approach the deacon first, if they have any matter which the episkopos should consider. Deacons are appointed by the bishop (again, as in the case of the presbyters, there is no mention of an "ordination"). One deacon should assist at the altar during the Eucharist; another should stand at the door and moderate the attendance, i.e., disallow those who should not be present, make sure that the catechumens and penitents leave at the proper time, etc. In all, the deacon is prominently pastoral.[62]

There is no sense of "experimental ministry" in this volume: the naming and functions of the episkopos, the presbyter and the deacon are taken for granted and are described as entrenched. All in all, the picture we receive from the *Didascalia Apostolorum* is consistent with the picture we find in most of the other material for the third century. Let us now go to Hippolytus and his contribution which is that of our first extant ordination ritual.

2. ORDINATION TO MINISTRY

During this same period, i.e., from the time of the resurrection to the beginning of the third century, we have hardly anything at all on the issue of ordination. The issue is, however, quite complex, even though there is practically no documentation at all during the first two centuries. Part of the problem lies with the development of the episkopos in East and West. Dupuy mentions that in the West a collegial presbyterium for both the episkopos and presbyter was dominant, while in the East a monarchical form of episkopos dominated. There is, he suggests, a difference between East and West in the approach to episkope. "In the East one viewed the episkopos as the leader of the local community; the battle against gnostic excesses had favored the high-positioning of the episkopos. In Rome and in the West, one made reference to the migration of Peter [to Rome] and ascribed to him the desire to transfer the universal episkope of Jerusalem, which for a long time had also been associated with Antioch, to the capital of the Roman empire. This ecclesiological difference between East and West has so influenced the theology of ecclesiological office that it is even clearly perceptible today."[62] Dupuy may, however, be stretching the documentation too far.

However, in both East and West, some form of monarchical epi-skopos had become standard at the end of the second century. By then, both the presbyter and the deacon were beneath the episkopos. But how were any of these invested, enthroned, ordained, established? It seems that there were two forms of installation: there was (a) an "enthroning" rite, and the early references to such things as the "chair" at Antioch reflect this ritual.[63] There was also (b) an "ordination" rite, generally with the laying on of hands.

The New Testament, as we saw, offers nothing unquestioned on the issue of the laying on of hands. Each pericope, in which this laying on of hands was mentioned, has been seriously challenged as far as any ordination ritual is concerned.

Clement does indeed say that the apostles and their successors installed episkopoi and diakonoi, but he does not mention the way in which this installation took place. His use of the term *kathistanai* implies an "enthroning" ritual, rather than a laying on of hands ritual. In its turn, the *Didache* speaks of an election of episkopoi and diakonoi which is done by the community, but the form of this election is not described. Even Tertullian, who uses the terms *ordinatio* and *ordinare,* nowhere describes what ritual activity these words refer to.

It is only in the *Apostolic Tradition* of Hippolytus that we have a clear ordination ritual, and as one can see, it is far from being prim-itive. Let us look first at the text of Hippolytus. In this text, Hippolytus recounts the prayer to be said for the ordinand plus some of the rubrics (and even at times some explanation of the rubrics), but it is precisely in the prayers that we find the import or meaning of each ordination. Hippolytus gives us such prayers for the ordination of the episkopos, the presbyter and the deacon. Let us look at each of these in turn.

A. ORDINATION OF AN EPISKOPOS

Let the bishop [episkopos] be ordained after he has been chosen by all the people. When he has been named and shall please all, let him, with the presbytery and such bishops as may be present, assemble with the people on a Sunday. While all give their con-sent, the bishops shall lay their hands upon him, and the pres-bytery shall stand by in silence. All indeed shall keep silent, praying in their heart for the descent of the Spirit. Then one of the bishops who are present shall, at the request of all, lay his hand on him who is ordained bishop and shall pray as follows, saying:

God and Father of our Lord Jesus Christ, Father of mercies and God of all comfort, who dwellest on high yet has respect to the lowly, who knowest all things before they come to pass: Thou hast appointed the borders of thy church by the word of thy grace, predestinating from the beginning the righteous race of Abraham. And making them princes and priests, and leaving not thy sanctuary without a ministry, thou hast from the beginning of the world been well pleased to be glorified among those whom thou hast chosen. Pour forth now that power, which is thine, of thy royal spirit, which thou gavest to thy beloved Servant Jesus Christ, which he bestowed on his holy apostles, who established the church in every place, the church which thou hast sanctified unto unceasing glory and praise of thy name. Thou who knowest the hearts of all, grant to this thy servant, whom thou hast chosen to be bishop, [to feed thy holy flock] and to serve as thy high priest without blame, ministering night and day, to propitiate thy countenance without ceasing and to offer thee the gifts of thy holy church. And by the Spirit of high-priesthood to have authority to remit sins according to thy commandments, to assign the lots according to thy precept, to loose every bond according to the authority which thou gavest to thy apostles, and to please thee in meekness and purity of heart, offering to thee an odour of sweet savour. Through the Servant Jesus Christ our Lord, through whom be to thee glory, might, honour, with the Holy Spirit in the holy church now and always and world without end. Amen[64]

After this the kiss of peace is given to the newly ordained epi-skopos by all, and then the eucharist follows. In the text for the eu-charistic prayer there are also prayers of blessing for those who offer oil or cheese and olives.

This earliest ordination prayer reveals much to us. First of all, since Hippolytus is by no means an innovator, what he presents here cannot be understood as a new ordination prayer, but rather one that had been in use in the Church at Rome for some time. This would place the ordination rite more than likely back into the last decade or even decades of the second century. Moreover, the prayers are well put together, which indicates that they have probably been in liturgical use for some time.

Since the church is not simply a local church, the ministry of other episkopoi is important, for their presence at the ceremony symbolizes this wider, universal Church. However, the document notes that the selection of the local bishop is made by the people. No exact procedures are detailed, but the voice of the people on this matter is clearly stated.

Laying on of hands by the other episkopoi is a central part of the liturgy. The attending presbyters, however, do not lay hands on the episkopos. There is no mention of any anointing. One episkopos (there is no indication of precisely who this one episkopos might be) then lays hands on the man to be ordained and recites the lengthy prayer. It is precisely in this prayer that we see the theological depths of the ordination. Certain issues should be underscored:

1. Even though the people have elected the episkopos-to-be, the prayer states unequivocally that God has chosen this man for the ministry of episkopos. This, as we saw above, reflects the characteristics of the very ministry of Jesus himself. There is basically neither a self-appointment nor a community appointment to Christian ministry.

2. Jesus is the source of ministry. Through the apostles Jesus has established the Church in every place, and the ordination of this new episkopos assures the local community that the Church of Jesus is in their midst as well. The ecclesiological dimension of this ministry is made very evident.

3. The Spirit is asked to come upon this episkopos-to-be so that he might (a) feed the flock, i.e., lead the community; (b) serve as priest, i.e., liturgical presidency; (c) reconcile. This latter makes an indirect mention to Mt 16, 16; 18, 18; Jn 20, 22. In these duties the episkopos gives evidence of a ministry of service and love, two characteristics of Jesus' own ministry which we described in the first chapter.

4. The episkopos is clearly a public figure in the Church. His leadership of the community is not a private matter, and he

is described within the framework of a lengthy series of such public figures: Abraham, Jesus himself, the apostles, and now this new episkopos.

B. ORDINATION OF A PRESBYTER

In n. 8. Hippolytus gives us the first ordination of a presbyter which we have. Again the text includes some brief rubrical material and then a consecratory prayer.

> But when a presbyter is ordained, the bishop shall lay his hand upon his head, while the presbyters touch him, and he shall say according to those things that were said above, as we have prescribed above concerning the bishop, praying and saying:

> God and Father of our Lord Jesus Christ, look upon this thy servant, and grant him the Spirit of grace and counsel of a presbyter, that he may sustain and govern thy people with a pure heart; as thou didst look upon thy chosen people and didst command Moses that he should choose presbyters, whom thou didst fill with thy Spirit, which thou gavest to thy servant. And now, O Lord, grant that there may be unfailingly preserved amongst us the Spirit of thy grace and make us worthy that, believing, we may minister to thee in simplicity of heart, praising thee. Through the Servant Jesus Christ, through whom be to thee glory and honour, with [the] Holy Spirit in the holy church, both now and always and world without end. Amen.[65]

An episkopos, and only one, ordains a presbyter. The presbyter is seen more as a minister within a local church, whereas the episkopos is seen both as the local minister, but collegially related to the other episkopoi. In the ordination, his fellow presbyters place their hands on the man to be ordained, indicating the collegiality of the presbyters themselves. The ritual is one of laying on of hands; there is no mention of any anointing.

The prayer which the episkopos says asks that the new presbyter be given "the Spirit of grace and counsel" to "sustain and govern" the people. There is no mention at all of any sacramental function. As we know from other sources at this time and in the two centuries ahead, the presbyters were primarily, though at times not exclusively, a council for the episkopos. They were neither sacramental ministers, nor ministers of the Word, as we understand these ministries today. Nor does it seem that they were in every instance full-time in the ministry, such as the episkopos was and the deacons were. It seems that during the week, they continued to work at their own tasks and careers, and only on Sundays take part in the liturgy and provide counsel to the episkopos as needed. But these items are not stated in the prayer. They are simply mentioned to indicate that the prayer, which asks for the grace of counsel, fits in well with the picture of a presbyter in the third, fourth and fifth centuries.

The ministry of the presbyter is a grace, i.e., God calls the presbyter and endows him with the needed graces. Since the task of the presbyter is basically counsel, not active pastoral and sacramental ministry, the characteristics of service and love are not stressed. There is a certain public aspect to the presbyter, but not at all the same as that of the episkopos. One sees that the portrait of the presbyter in Hippolytus, which must be judged as traditional and common, is quite different from that of the "priest" which we begin to see after 400 A.D. down to our own day. After 400 A.D. the sacramental and pastoral ministry begins to dominate the life and function of a priest, and the function of counseling the episkopos becomes secondary or even non-operative.

I do not want to move too quickly ahead of our historical narrative, but Hippolytus' ordination ritual, indeed the entire *Apostolic Tradition,* received its major import into scholarship with Hauler's publication of the Latin text in 1900. In 1848 Tattum had published a Bohairic text and in 1883 Lagarde published a Sahidic text. Still, it has only been from 1900 on that Hippolytus' *Apostolic Tradition* has really been part of the early data, influencing the contemporary study of the history of the sacraments. Since in this ordination no mention is made that a presbyter should preach, Luther's position on presbyteral ordination is somewhat challenged, since for Luther the preaching of the Word is essential for priestly ministry. On the other hand, the Roman Catholic official condemnation of Anglican Orders, based on the changes in the Edwardian ordinal, which made no mention of a priest offering sacrifice, is likewise challenged by this early ordination ritual of a presbyter, since this early ritual, too, has no mention of offering a sacrifice. Neither Lutheran scholars nor Roman Catholic scholars, however, deny that in this document of Hippolytus there is not a true ordination to the presbyterate. However, if they are validly ordained, then the questions arise: Is preaching the Word essential to presbyteral ordination? Is the power to celebrate the eucharist essential to presbyteral ordination? If Hippolytus' portrait of a presbyter were unique, one might answer yes to these questions and simply declare invalid the ordinations of Hippolytus, but the portrait of the presbyter in Hippolytus perdures for the next two centuries: namely, a presbyter as a counselor of the episkopos and not a man either preaching the Word or presiding at the eucharist.

C. ORDINATION OF A DEACON

In the *Apostolic Tradition* the deacon is a major minister in the Church, and his ordination is described in n. 9. Much more detail is given to the ordination of a deacon than to that of a presbyter.

But the deacon, when he is ordained, is chosen according to those things that were said above, the bishop alone in like manner laying his hands upon him, as we have prescribed. When the deacon is ordained, this is the reason why the bishop alone shall lay his hands upon him: he is not ordained to the priesthood but to serve the bishop and to carry out the bishop's commands. He does not take part in the council of the clergy; he is to attend to his own duties and to make known to the bishop such things as are needful. He does not receive the Spirit that is possessed by the presbytery, in which the presbyters share; he receives only what is confided in him under the bishop's authority.

For this cause the bishop alone shall make him a deacon. But on a presbyter, however, the presbyters shall lay their hands because of the common and like Spirit of the clergy. Yet the presbyter has only the power to receive; but he has no power to give. For this reason a presbyter does not ordain the clergy; but at the ordination of a presbyter he seals while the bishop ordains.

Over a deacon, then, he [the episkopos] shall say as follows:

O God, who hast created all things and hast ordered them by thy Word, the Father of our Lord Jesus Christ, whom thou didst send to minister thy will and to manifest to us thy desire: grant [the] Holy Spirit of grace and care and diligence to this thy servant, whom thou hast chosen to serve the church and to offer in thy holy sanctuary the gifts that are offered to thee by thine appointed priests, so that serving without blame and with a pure heart he may be counted worthy of this exalted office, by thy goodwill, praising thee continually. Through thy Servant Jesus Christ, through whom be to thee glory and honour, with [the] Holy Spirit, in the holy church, both now and always and world without end. Amen.[66]

The distinctions which are made in the first part between deacon and presbyter appear to have been placed in the text to preclude diaconal encroachment into presbyteral tasks, as also to clarify the distinctive rites. As one knows, the *Apostolic Tradition* has many textual variants, added at different times in its textual history. As new issues surfaced, clarifications were made.

Once more, in the prayer, we see that God has chosen the deacon: the ministry is not self-appointed, not community appointed, and not even an episcopal appointment. Mention is made of the deacon's bringing the gifts to the altar of the eucharist, indicating a clear liturgical ministry. The deacon is to serve and minister, but as the introduction states, he is at the beck and call of the episkopos. The picture of the deacon in Hippolytus corresponds rather accurately with that picture which we saw in the *Didascalia Apostolorum.*

The deacon's office is called an exalted office—in some texts even a "high and exalted office," or in one of the Ethipoic manuscripts (Horner's) an "exalted priesthood." From the earliest times, the deacon has been seen as a high office or ministry in the Church. Later, it will be called a major order in the Church. The vicissitudes of the diaconate in the Christian Church cannot be denied, but from the early Church onward there has never been a time when the Church had no deacons. This unbroken history alone indicates that no discussion of Church ministry is possible without a discussion of the deacon and his "exalted office."

This has been a lengthy overview, but one that is most important to tread again and again. On the basis of the material which we have considered it seems that such statements as the following one from Galot would need better nuancing:

With regard to this development, it is important to remember that ranks existed in the authority of priests from the beginning, namely, the ranks instituted by Jesus himself when he appointed the Twelve under the primacy of Peter and entrusted the seventy-two disciples a similar mission. In the early Church the Twelve exercised the highest authority and were assisted by ministers of lower rank. The later development duplicates these two ranks within the framework of the local church: a bishop and a group of presbyters.[67]

D. TEACHERS AND PROPHETS

Von Campenhausen, for weighty and substantial reasons, devotes an entire chapter of his book on ministry to: "Prophets and Teachers in the Second Century."[68] He does this not to bring out the difference between the official and charismatic ministries (which he calls a contemporary distinction) but to indicate the role that prophets and teachers played throughout the second century. Early in the second century, the Ebionites developed a cadre of teachers, trained for six years, and in their teaching the Ebionite followers found the correct teaching. In the second half of the second century, the Montanists thrived with their sense of a "new prophecy." Justin and Hermas both speak of prophets in their communities. Gnostic teachers proclaimed a core of knowledge which did not come from the "official Church." Justin after becoming a Christian retained his insignia of a "philosopher's cloak," and Tertullian did likewise. Barnabas speaks reverently of teachers and Polycarp was an "apostolic and prophetic teacher." Clement of Alexandria, the precursor of Origen in many ways, was a lay teacher. Neither prophet nor teacher became part of *ordo*. Both ministries perdured during the centuries, but they generally came to be outside the naming of official ecclesiastical ministry.

Many of these prophets and teachers were, of course, lay people (i.e., those not called episkopos, presbyter, deacon), and this alone indicates that lay ministry was active. Since the distinction cleric/lay was still in the developing stages, this very terminology might be somewhat anachronistic. Still, Church ministry from the beginning was broader than simply the ministries of episkopos, presbyter and deacon. Tertullian, we said, did not seem to include lector into the clerical ordo. If this is correct, then we have the first indication of the (later so to be called) minor orders performed by a "lay person."

Women in ministry is far more difficult to determine in this second century. Clearly the Montanists had women ministers. In *De Baptismo* Tertullian writes against a woman teacher. Tertullian even seems to deny women the right to teach at all. *The Acts of Paul and Thecla* are from the second century. Thecla is portrayed as a helper in the ministry of Paul. The historical accuracy of this work is, even today, still not settled, but from what we know of the Pauline Churches, women in ministry would be quite acceptable. Origen writes in an adamant way against women teaching. He seems to be writing against the Montanists and their inclusion of women in a ministry of preaching and prophecy. All in all, one would have to say that the second century offers some, but very little, indication of women in ministry. There is absolutely no data from this century on women in the so-called "ordained" ministries.

Perhaps one might summarize the data which we find from 90 to 210 A.D. as follows:

1. By the end of this period, but not at the beginning, the episkopos has become the major leader in the local Christian community.

2. On the other hand, the presbyter had moved into a minister and leader of second rank. One can speak quite often, at the end of this period, of a "college of presbyters," whose primary task was not liturgical, but rather the giving of advice to the episkopos in the area of community leadership.

3. The naming of ministry, episkopos, presbyter and deacon, has lasted in a standard way and a ranked way from 200 to the present.

4. Only at the end of this period do we begin to hear the connection of episkopos and presbyter to hiereus, sacerdos, pontifex. In other words a priestly interpretation, i.e., priestly in the sense of the Jewish and Greek world, began to become more dominant. Liturgy began to be the basis for Church leadership, rather than Church leadership be the basis for liturgical leadership.

5. All ministry is seen consistently as a call and commission from the Lord. Nowhere is there mention of self-appointment or even community appointment to ministry.

6. The community plays a role, acknowledging what the Lord has done. This acknowledgement is a realization of apostolic succession, as Irenaeus emphasizes.

7. Only around 200 do we have an ordination ritual which can be verified. Installation from 90 to Hippolytus remains a matter of hypothesis, with no historical data for verification.

8. In the ordination ritual of Hippolytus, the episkopos is ordained for pastoral leadership and exemplarity of Christian life. Liturgical leadership is not the primary focus of the ordination rite.

9. In the ordination of presbyter in the ritual of Hippolytus, providing pastoral advice to the episkopos is the central focus. No mention is made of liturgical leadership.

10. Deacons played an important role in the pastoral ministry of the Church. In many ways they were more visible to the Christian community than the presbyters.

11. There is a continued ministry of prophecy and teaching. Some of this ministry is performed by lay people. The data, therefore, does indicate that Church ministry is more than simply that of episkopos, presbyter and deacon.

12. Only a few details in the data of the second century indicate that women might have been part of ministry. There is some, but it is difficult to interpret and so thin that solid conclusions cannot be drawn out. There is no indication of women in "ordained ministry."

5

Ministry in the
High Patristic Church
210 to 600 A.D.

Often in discussing the early Church, authors will divide the material from the Council of Nicaea, 325 A.D., forward and backward, but in the case of ministry, it seems better to mark a break at the end of the second and beginning of the third centuries, for the reasons which we have seen in the last chapter. In many ways Hippolytus, Origen, Tertullian, and the *Didascalia Apostolorum* could have as easily begun this period, but in many ways they are also the closure of the first two centuries. At this turning point, the episkopos, now quite clearly and universally named, and therefore the bishop, had become the center of ministry. In discussing the *Didascalia Apostolorum,* H. Connolly writes that, at least in the Church which the *Didascalia* considers, the bishop "is indeed the centre and pivot of the whole community. He holds the place of God in relation to his people; he is their father after God, their mediator with God, their high priest, their leader and king."[1] These are strong words to describe the episkopos, but in the ecclesial life of that time the episkopos had become the pivot and focus of leadership and ministry. The *Didascalia* speaks of this situation as quite normal for an episkopos, in the sense that it had become the ordinary way that a Christian community perceived its leadership and ministry. Tertullian, Origen, Hippolytus, plus many other lesser writers at that time, concur in this presentation.

At the other end of our period is a figure who represents in his own way both a closure and a beginning: Pope Gregory the Great. In many ways he summarizes what has preceded him, and yet Gregory opens up new approaches to the theology of ministry. Somewhere in the area of 600 A.D., then, seems to be an excellent transition point. J. Pelikan, in his series on *Christian Tradition,* also uses the year 600 to move, in both the East and the West, into a new phase of Church history.[2] Actually, we will go only to the time of Gregory in this chapter, leaving a consideration of this important churchman to the next chapter, since his influential stance as a beginning phase of ministry tends to outweigh his importance as a closing phase of Church ministry. Thus, 600 A.D. is a quite generalized date, for Gregory himself lived prior to 600 and died only in 604.

Because the writings on ministry of this golden age of patristic literature are too vast to cover in detail, we will consider, consequently, only certain processes which moved both at a fairly rapid pace and with strong influence during the period 210 to 600 A.D. These processes could be described as follows:

1. A process of theological development of apostolic succession as a guarantee of orthodox Church ministry.
2. A process of increased clericalization, in which the ordained ministry in the Church became more and more separated from the laity.
3. A process of increased theologizing on ministry in the Church in which the notion of "priest" (hiereus) becomes dominant.
4. A process of diversification in the pastoral ministries occasioned by the pastoral needs of a growing Church.

These four processes are, of course, inter-dependent, so that each is only understood in its relationship to the others. For the sake of clarity, however, we will consider each of them separately, realizing full well that this separate treatment does not do full justice to the processes involved.

1. THEOLOGICAL DEVELOPMENT OF APOSTOLIC SUCCESSION

Tracing material back to important ancestral figures was a part of the Jewish scene, even before the time of Jesus. We have, for instance, the apocryphal books of *III and IV Esdras,* the Enoch cycle, the *Apocalypse of Baruch,* and the *Testaments of the Twelve Patriarchs.* None of these works come from the authors mentioned in the titles, but the titles clearly enhance the work. We find a similar pattern in the canonical works of the New Testament. The gospels of Matthew and of John, according to Papias, are attributed to the two apostles of these names. The letters 1 and 2 Peter are ascribed to the apostle Peter. James is the name of another author of a New Testament letter, and often in Church tradition this James has been considered to be another apostle. In the Pauline material we have those letters which are genuine, and then others which in very ancient Church tradition have been attributed to him, e.g., 1 and 2 Timothy, Titus, even Hebrews.

Outside the canonical New Testament, we have a host of apocryphal material, dating primarily from 100 to 200 A.D. There are gospels:

> *Gospel according to the Hebrews*
> *Gospel of the Twelve Apostles*
> *Gospel according to Peter*
> *Protoevangelium of James*
> *Gospel of Thomas*
> *Gospel of Philip*
> *Gospel of Matthias*
> *Gospel of Barnabas*
> *Gospel of Bartholomew*
> *Gospel of Andrew*
> *Gospel of Thaddeus*
> Even a *Gospel of Judas Iscariot* and a *Gospel of Eve.*

We also have, besides the canonical *Acts of the Apostles, the Acts of Paul, the Acts of Peter, the Acts of Peter and Paul, the Acts of John, the Acts of Andrew, the Acts of Thomas, the Acts of Thaddeus.*

In the New Testament we have the book of Revelation, or the Apocalypse, but there are others:

> *The Apocalypse of Peter*
> *The Apocalypse of Paul*
> *The Apocalypse of Stephen*
> *The Apocalypse of Thomas*

The Apocalypse of John
Even an *Apocalypse of the Blessed Virgin Mary.*

There are letters or epistles: the *Epistola Apostolorum,* and three others ascribed to Paul: namely, a letter to the Laodiceans, one to the Alexandrians, and a third letter to the Corinthians.

Today we might look askance at this widespread use of an author's name, who in reality had no connection with the volume being written and published. However, this widespread use indicates to us very clearly that in the years 100 to 200 A.D., within the Christian community, a tendency to base positions on the apostles was common. This phenomenon of writing under a famous pseudonym is part of the background for the theme of apostolic succession, since such writings reflect the tendency to root one's teachings in the time of the apostles. Clement, as we saw, utilizes this apostolic importance when he disallows the Corinthians from debarring the presbyters from office. Irenaeus likewise utilizes the concept of apostolicity in dealing with the gnostics. Tertullian also refers to apostolicity in his writings.[3] The reality of an "apostolic succession" or "apostolicity" is present in the Church even before it is systematically theologized.

In the early creeds, the Church was reverently called "apostolic" and therefore true. "We believe in one, holy, catholic, and apostolic Church." This is not found, to be sure, in the Nicene Creed, but does appear in other creeds around the same time (c. 325).[4] It does appear in Epiphanius, and in the creeds attributed to the councils of Constantinople (381) and Chalcedon (451). The so-called "Apostles' Creed" does not have the term "apostolic," and since many expositions of the creed in the middle ages were expositions of the "Apostles' Creed," a discussion on "apostolic" is lacking. This lack is also seen, and for the same reason, in discussions on the "Creed" at the time of the Reformation, in both Protestant and Catholic writings. After the publication of the Tridentine Catechism, in which "apostolic" is mentioned, the discussions on the issue among theologians intensified. In this counter-reformation period, authors often developed their positions around three categories:

a. The apostolicity of origin;
b. The apostolicity of teaching;
c. The apostolicity of Church hierarchy.

As time went on, it was the third "apostolicity" which received the lion's share of attention, so that in many instances "apostolic succession" means simply a succession of hierarchical ministry, and not primarily either of origin or of teaching. This brief overview of the history of apostolicity helps us locate the many strands of apostolic succession in the early Church, which was not burdened with the apologetic concerns one finds in the post-reformation Churches.[4]

The early tracing to an apostolic origin has been considered by some scholars, in recent times, as part of the Greek inheritance of the Church, particularly due to a gnostic influence. It is true that only in 165 A.D. do we find in the letter of Ptolomaeus to Flora the words, "tradition of the apostles," and "in the way of the apostles."[5] Still, the number of gospels, acts, apocalypses, etc., enumerated above, plus the respective statements in Clement, Irenaeus, and Tertullian, indicate that this endeavor to trace one's position back to major leading figures of the past was equally Jewish and non-Jewish.

Let us utilize the threefold distinction as an organizational tool, to see in what ways this period of Church history developed the theology of apostolic succession.

A. APOSTOLIC ORIGIN

Irenaeus mentioned that the origin of various episcopal centers was due to a foundation by an apostle. This produced in the patristic period a ranking of these episcopal sees. The bishops of Jerusalem claimed that James, after Jesus, had been the founder of that Church community; the bishops of Antioch claimed Peter; the bishops of Alexandria claimed Mark; the bishops of Rome claimed both Peter and Paul.

Bauer begins his book on *Orthodoxy and Heresy in Earliest Christianity* with a story recounted in Eusebius' *Ecclesiastical History.* It seems that King Abgar V Ukkama of Edessa (9–46 A.D.) heard about Jesus and his miraculous healings. Since the Jews were opposed to Jesus, Abgar offers Jesus a home in Edessa. Jesus answers by letter, blessing Abgar, but refusing the invitation on the grounds that he still has a mission to accomplish in Palestine. The story, of course, does not end here, for after the ascension, Thomas sends Thaddeus to Edessa, where he heals Abgar and many others. Thaddeus tells all the citizens of Edessa about Jesus. Eusebius notes that he is translating the actual letters and documents from the Syriac. A later account, the

Doctrina Addai, recounts all these events, but in greater detail. Indeed, there are many early references to the "holy" king Abgar. From the fourth century the remains of the apostle Thomas were to be found in Edessa. These apostolic connections, which brought about the very origin of the faith in Edessa, were referred to again and again by many writers to "confirm" the truth of the Edessan community which claimed to be in succession with this origin.

Not only the Church of Edessa, but other Churches as well claimed an apostolic origin. J. N. D. Kelly reminds us:

> The fourth and fifth centuries were the epoch of the self-conscious emergence of the great patriarchates: the position of Rome, Alexandria and Antioch was recognized at Nicaea (325), while Constantinople and Jerusalem were later accorded the rank of patriarchates at the councils of Constantinople (381) and Chalcedon (451) respectively.[6]

Such acknowledgement was not accomplished without a great deal of argument, even animosity, since each of these patriarchates had jurisdiction over surrounding areas. With the exception of Constantinople, the capital, the other patriarchates all made claims of apostolic origin.

Rome, of course, especially from Siricius (384–399) onward, began to develop the implications of this apostolic origin. Innocent I, particularly, focused on a passage from Cyprian: Petrus initium episcopatus (Peter is the beginning of episcopacy). Cyprian was treating of the unity of the episcopacy, but Innocent used this to mean that all the bishops in the West owe their origin to Peter and his followers. Whether Innocent correctly cited Cyprian is not the main point; the main point is to see that apostolic origin is the basis for truth and orthodoxy. Leo the Great systematized this thinking of Cyprian and Innocent in the following way: Peter, who confessed the Lord, is always present in the Roman cathedra: he is, therein, the sure foundation, the keeper of the keys of heaven, the shepherd of the entire flock.[7] In a very developed way, we have here continued evidence for this theology of apostolic origin.

B. APOSTOLIC TEACHING

To teach what the apostles taught: this is the touchstone of true faith and true orthodoxy. Any other gospel is anathema. When the bishops were gathered at Chalcedon, we find a most traditional and conservative introduction to their statements: "Following therefore the holy fathers." In his analysis, Ortíz de Urbina writes:

> The study of the inner structure of the chalcedonian symbol places us before a surprising fact. The formula is not an original creation, but it is similar to a mosaic, almost entirely constructed from tesserae which are already available.[8]

He goes on to say that the opening sentence, "following the holy fathers," is a confession of theological tradition. The bishops at Chalcedon did not see themselves as new constructors of dogma, but as custodians of a faith that has come from the ancient past.[9]

Pelikan, in discussing the criteria of apostolic continuity of teaching, notes that Marcion had severed the Old from the New Testament and isolated Paul from the rest of the apostolic community. The gnostics radicalized the division between creation and salvation and made a sort of ontological principle out of this disunity. Even the apostles, in their view, had accommodated their teaching to the "erroneous" views of their own times. As a result, apostolic teaching could not, in itself, be totally justified; a new teaching was needed as a corrective of these "apostolic errors." The montanists thought the Church had fallen from its apostolic purity and had compromised its ancient teachings. New apostles, or new spiritual successors to the apostles, were the real Church.[10]

These errors needed a corrective, and this corrective was that the Church was truly teaching the doctrine of the apostles. As Clement of Rome had said: "Christ comes with a message from God; the apostles with a message from Christ."[11] According to Tertullian, even the Old Testament can be read in a way that refers not only to Jesus, but also to the apostles and their successors. The first criterion of apostolic teaching, then, is, according to Pelikan: there is one God who has arranged all things: the God of the apostles and of the Old and the New Testament.[12]

The second criterion is that the apostles agree with each other. There could be no preferring Paul over John, Luke over Mark, etc. The development of the canon of the New Testament in this period of patristic times is evidence of this homogenous apostolic continuity in teaching. All the canonical books were accepted as the word of God. John Knox states:

Canonicity and apostolicity became almost synonymous terms.
. . . The argument moved both ways: II Peter, since it was pre-
sumably written by an apostle, must be accorded canonical status;
Hebrews, because it obviously deserved canonical status, must
have been written by an apostle.[13]

Although the listing of these canonical books fluctuated for many
centuries, the principle, namely, that in these canonical books one
heard the voices of the very apostles of Jesus Christ, remained stable.[14]
The development of the creeds were also voices of the apostolic teaching. In all these cases, the "doctrine of the Church" was transmitted
"in orderly succession from the apostles" and remains "in the Churches
to the present day," as Origen wrote.[15]

The apostolic tradition was a public tradition: the apostles had
not taught one set of doctrines in secret and another in the open,
suppressing a portion of their tradition to be transmitted through
a special succession to the Gnostic elite. So palpable was this
apostolic tradition that even if the apostles had not left behind
their doctrine, the church would still be in a position to follow
"the structure of the tradition which they handed on to those
to whom they committed the churches" (Irenaeus, *Adv. Haer.* 3,
4, 1).[16]

C. APOSTOLIC HIERARCHICAL SUCCESSION

But who are the successors of the apostles? In the preceding chapter, we have seen that in the *Didache,* the prophet and teacher succeeded the apostles; in Ignatius it was the presbyters who succeeded
the apostles; in Irenaeus it was the episkopoi and the presbyters; in
the *Didascalia Apostolorum* it was again the presbyters, but not the
episkopoi. There seems to have been no set pattern in all of this, since
apostolicity was not focused exclusively on a particular ministry, but
rather on all facets of the teaching and the origin of the Church.
Teachings, writings, rituals, practices, and also leadership people in
the Church, all had to have apostolic succession, and the apostolic
succession of a given ministry would have meant nothing if the Church
were itself not of apostolic succession. It is today necessary to stress
this total apostolicity, since in many areas of discussion, particularly
from the reformation time on, "apostolic succession" has been focused
too exclusively on episcopal or papal succession, with the impression
that in this area alone one finds apostolicity. Diaconate as a ministry

is of apostolic succession; presbyters are of apostolic succession; even lay ministry is of apostolic succession. In a word, all ministry in the Church is of apostolic succession, in one way or another.

In the third century and onward, we find that the episkopos has become not only the main leader of the Christian community, but also, in many ways, the sole leader. The episkopos alone preached; he alone celebrated the eucharist; he was the main liturgical person in the ritual of baptism; he was the main liturgical person in the ritual of public penance. Liturgy centered around the episkopos and the leadership of the community did likewise. This liturgical focus, with the growing importance and solemnity of the ordination ritual, began to move the source of ministerial centrality away from Church leadership to Church ordination. If, in the century before, one could say: "Because the episkopos was a leader of the Christian community, therefore he was also the leader at the liturgy," one would, in the second half of the third and from the fourth century onward, say: "Because the episkopos is the ordained liturgist, therefore he is also the leader of the ecclesial community." In the West, through the influence of Tertullian, there were technical terms for this ritual of enthronement: *ordination.* The higher the ordo the more leadership one possessed, but the basis for such leadership was *ordo.* In the East, a different terminology arose; it was the laying on of hands which engendered the technical terms: *cheirotonein, cheirotethein, cheirotenia, cheirothesis.* This was a more biblical term than ordination, and in this laying on of hands, it might be noted, there was at first no chrismation or anointing.

Regardless of the terms: ordination or laying on of hands, or regardless of the different rituals for this conferral of office, both East and West began to solemnize the ceremony more and more. The episkopos, through this sacred ritual, was portrayed as one being taken into a succession to the apostles themselves. One must be cautious about generalizations. Botte notes, wisely, that "we have to wait several centuries from the time of the apostolic tradition [Hippolytus] before we meet fresh liturgical documents on ordination."[17] After the *Traditio Apostolica,* Bligh reminds us:

> Next come the three famous "Sacramentaries" of the Roman Church, called the Leonine, the Gelasian, and the Gregorian, after the three Popes—St. Leo (d. a.d. 461), St. Gelasius (d. 496)

and St. Gregory the Great (d. 604)—to whom they have been ascribed. The Sacramentaries are not, as their name suggests to modern ears, collections of prayers and rubrics for the administration of the seven sacraments. They were compiled long before the word "sacrament" acquired the precise technical meaning we give it today, and long before the period (about a.d. 1150) when the doctrine that there are seven sacraments became fully explicit. They include, therefore, many other rites of blessings and consecrations, such as the rite of coronation.[18]

Later, those parts of the Sacramentaries which included the prayers for the eucharist were separated into "Missals." However, we do have a manuscript for the Leonine Sacramentary, dating probably from the seventh century (the end of our present period), for the Gelasian Sacramentary, dating from the seventh or eighth centuries (later than our period of investigation), and texts for the Gregorian Sacramentary, dating probably from the end of the sixth century (and so within our period of investigation). The material for all of these Sacramentaries clearly antedates the respective texts and so would be indicative of the theology and ritual of the period we are considering. Whether or not any part of these Sacramentaries goes back to the three popes is a highly controverted issue among scholars. In the Leonine and Gregorian Sacramentaries there is a lengthy tracing of God's provident work in giving ministers first to the chosen people of the Old Testament and then to the people of God in the New Testament and subsequent Church history (cf. the Preface). In this way the succession to the apostles is clearly stated.

After the *Didascalia Apostolorum,* which is one of the last major documents not to call the episkopoi the successors of the apostles, one really finds that the episkopos is almost unanimously hailed as the successor of the apostles, not the presbyter nor the prophet. This was not merely a personal honor, for it had social effects:

a. The ordained episkopos was seen as the successor of the apostles and therefore the major symbol of apostolic orthodoxy in the local community. Between the episkopos and the local community a sort of marriage took place that was to be unbreakable, and this "marriage" was an assurance of the apostolicity of the local Church.

b. The ordained episkopos was there by divine commission, not by his own endeavor, nor by the will of the community, nor even by the selection of fellow episkopoi. Just as the Lord had called and commissioned his apostles, so, too, the Lord was calling and commissioning this man to be the "apostle" for this local community.

c. There was only one episkopos for each local area. For instance, at the time of Augustine, in 411, a meeting was held in Carthage, consisting of 268 catholic episkopoi and 279 donatist episkopoi—a large number of episkopoi for the small region of North Africa. Other examples could be cited, but the picture we have would be something like this: where today we would have a priest-pastor, at this early time, in the East and West, there would have been an episkopos-pastor. Each one would be a regional episkopos.

d. In each of these areas, the various episkopoi at times gradually began to come under the metropolitan, especially in the East. We see this, for instance, in Athanasius, Cyril of Alexandria, John of Antioch; and the episkopos of Rome treasured the name of metropolitan of the West. In all of this we see a "collegium."

e. Bishops individually, and bishops within an area (e.g., North Africa) began to correspond with each other or meet together in regional synods. This collegial networking assured each area of apostolic succession.[19]

f. At the Council of Nicaea something new occurred. Instead of each geographical group meeting on its own, debating and determining issues, and then relaying such local decisions to some of the other Churches, the emperor called all the main episkopoi to Nicaea for a general meeting in 325. At the end of this meeting, Athanasius is quoted to remark: "The Holy Spirit has spoken through us!" This was a step forward in collegiality, and also in an understanding of apostolic succession.

g. In all of this, the collegium is of the episkopoi. The understanding of bishop was three-pronged: (1) from the Lord; (2)
to the local Church; (3) with one's fellow episkopoi.

One of the ways in which this apostolic succession, not only of
the episkopoi themselves, but of orthodox teaching as well, can be
seen is in the number of councils which took place. These councils
were localized in nature and were called at the behest of the episkopos.
Even though we do not have complete historical details on many of
these councils, and even though we do not even have the exact dates
for them, one could say that there was intense conciliar activity during
this period of Church history. J. Guademet notes:

> More than seventy-five councils met during the fourth century,
> at least ten of which were at Rome, and most of them took place
> in the last quarter of the century; in the fifth century about twenty
> councils were held at Rome. But the African series hold first
> place; it began with the Council of Carthage in 348–349, and
> after 394 others followed in quick succession. From 394 to 426
> at least twenty-four councils met in the African capital.[20]

In the fourth and fifth centuries there was no centralized Church,
and even the councils which were held at Rome were local councils.
These numerous councils stand as tremendous historical witnesses to
the "college of episkopoi." The collegiality of episkopoi was the way
in which individual episkopoi and a local group of episkopoi could
maintain their touch with the apostolic succession. There was networking among local groups, that is, the results of one council would
be sent to another area, not with the need for ratification, but for the
purpose of dissemination. At times there were questions, such as we
find in the case of the African bishops, under Augustine, and the
Roman handling of Pelagius and Coelestius. In leadership, in discipline,
in liturgy, in almost every phase of Christian life, the patristic Church
was an episcopal Church, and it was this "sacrament of episkope"
which was one of the surest signs of apostolicity.

The relationship between episkopos and apostle, met with here
and there in the first two centuries, took on a systematic precision
from 200 onward, which more and more involved an identification.

Cyprian in many of his writings indicates this: "the apostles, i.e., the bishops"; "Christ, who speaks to the apostles, and because of this to all the leaders [bishops] who succeed to the apostles by a vicarious ordination"; he calls bishops "successors" to the apostles, and they are this by an "ordination of succession."[21] In a way differing from that of Irenaeus, Cyprian counted the apostles as "first." They were the first bishops, and subsequent bishops, therefore, are apostolic. In 256, at a council of Carthage, one of the bishops said: [The apostles] "to whom we succeed, governing the Church of God with identical power."[22] What Cyprian had developed becomes the normal theologizing of episcopal power in the Church: the episkopos succeeds to the apostles, not simply through a succession of one leader after the other, but in the succession of an identity of function and power. It is this kind of theologizing which moves strongly from 200 to 600. Basil, John Chrysostom, Ambrose, Augustine, Jerome, Peter Chrysologus, Paulinus of Nola, and many others are all witnesses of this kind of theologizing.[23]

Congar notes that the apostles had two functions. First, they were the eye-witnesses to the Lord himself, and especially recipients of the appearances of the risen Lord. In this respect, the episkopoi are not the successors of the apostles. Second, Congar notes, the apostles were the teachers and leaders of the Christian community.[24] It is only in this respect that the episkopoi can be seen as the successors of the apostles. However, as we saw in the preceding chapter the naming, at first, was not uniform. It would be better to say that the chief leaders of the community (whatever name they might have had) were the successors to the apostles. Around 200 these chief leaders came to be called "episkopoi" in a fairly uniform way throughout the Christian world, and so, at that time, the phrase "the episkopoi (bishops) are the successors of the apostles" begins to make sense. This does not mean that there was no apostolic succession; it simply means that the apostolic succession which is part of the ecclesial dimension of the Christian community existed in a more varied way early on, but as the episkopoi, both in name and in function, came to be universally accepted as the chief leaders and teachers of the community, then it also became clear that in and through the episkopoi apostolic succession came to continue. Indeed, the episkopos in many ways from 200 on was not only the main but also the only liturgical leader: leadership became a mono-episkope.

Congar also notes that there are some differences even in this second function between apostle on the one side and episkopos on the other. The apostles were part of normative establishment of tradition; the episkopoi have no authority to constitute any normative tradition or revelation. The apostles, secondly, acted as individuals as well as a group; the bishops do not succeed individually to any one apostle, but as a collegium the bishops succeed to the collegium of the apostles.[25]

It is also important to remember that apostolic succession does *not* mean some things:

a. Apostolic succession does not mean that apostle and episkopos are identical in function or authority. Congar's words above bring out this distinction.

b. Apostolic succession is not simply the unbroken relationship between an episkopos and an apostle. Even if one were able to verify historically that the bishop of a given see today can trace his lineage, in an unbroken fashion, down to one of the apostles, this, in itself, would not be apostolic succession.

c. Apostolic succession is not a matter of the validity of the sacraments. The tractarians of the Oxford Movement seemed to have espoused this direction. The validity of the sacraments presupposes apostolic succession; not, apostolic succession presupposes the validity of the sacraments. The apostolic Church is the foundation for any and every apostolic sacrament, not vice versa.

Apostolic succession, moreover, needs to be considered christologically. Jesus is at the very heart of apostolic succession. Although this process is called "apostolic" succession, the apostles are not the main actors. Jesus is the main actor. Jesus comes with a message from God; the apostles come with a message from Jesus. The very Word of God is the hidden reality in the sacrament of the apostle; to perceive only the sign would be to miss the reality. Jesus is, in contemporary theological language, the primordial sacrament in each and every ministerial sacrament.

It is noteworthy, that in the earliest lists of episcopal succession, e.g., in Irenaeus, the founding apostle is not the "first episkopos." After Peter, Irenaeus tells us, we have Linus, Anacletus, and in third place, Clement. In Tertullian, on the other hand, as well as in Hippolytus, and then Cyprian, we have the first apostle included in the lists. They do this since they are concerned about the position and authority of the contemporary episkopoi, but this is clearly a new accentuation of the issue.[26]

Episcopal succession to the apostles becomes a commonplace during this period of Church history. It is never questioned. The bishops in their writings (and they were the main theologians from 100 to 600) again and again mention this apostolic succession of Church hierarchy. But, for an understanding of ministry, certain aspects of this apostolicity need to be considered calmly but frankly.

1. Episcopal collegiality, which was, perhaps, at its strongest during this period, found an expression in the many forms of communication between the bishops themselves. As these forms of communication (letter, synods, regional councils, etc.) multiplied, the collegiality of the bishops reached both a spiritual and ecclesial depth. In this way, the meaning of episcopal ministry—what is a bishop—also developed. The college of bishops is not simply the sum of individual bishops. On the other hand, it is fundamentally the college of bishops which is the successor of the "college of apostles." Individual bishops do not succeed to individual apostles.

   We find in this particular period of Church history (235–600) a strong expression of such episcopal collegiality, and therefore we find in this particular period of Church history essential characteristics of what the ministry of bishop really involves.

2. On the other hand, in this same period of time, we find a different, though vital, dynamic in Church ministry gaining in ascendancy: namely, the role of the bishop of Rome. In this dynamic, each bishop individually is more and more bonded to the pope, so that the monarchical or papal aspect of episcopacy is highlighted. Only in relationship to the head, the pope, is a bishop theologically understandable, either as an individual bishop or as part of the college of bishops.

The more that the first aspect is stressed, so it seems, the less the second aspect is stressed, and vice versa. The Eastern bishops in many ways tended to resist the intrusion of the bishop of Rome into their regions. The Western bishops manifest some, but less resistance to this. Likewise, some popes rather pointedly pushed the papal privilege, while other popes were not so strong.

Botte, in his analysis of collegiality, mentions that the Church shaped its constitution in many ways after the pattern of the Roman Empire. In doing this, the Church acquired a juridical structure, which with the growth and development of metropolitans and patriarchs tended to become somewhat rigid. Even regionality of bishops (local synods, councils, etc.) raised issues which local Churches might not have found necessary to deal with, and in this way, regulations for regions began to take place. At times, there were even conflicts in these regulations (e.g., the date for celebrating Easter), and the interventions of the Roman See became more and more frequent.

> So from the fourth century the political influence of the Empire, together with Roman legalism, transformed the Church by firmly securing the little primitive autonomous communities in the iron collar of a gigantic juridical machine. It is quite certain that the juridical structure of the Church developed in stages, and it was only gradually that the autonomy of the bishop found itself reduced.[27]

These are fairly harsh words, but the idea is solid. There is, indeed, a conflicting dynamism between the local bishop and his ministry, or the bishops as a college, on the one hand, and the papacy on the other. If the bishops minister without the pope, then their own collegiality is not clear; if the pope ministers with the bishops, then his own ministry is not clear. The collegiality of the bishops cuts against local autonomy in many ways; an isolation of the bishop of Rome from his fellow-bishops makes the ministry of the Roman See unintelligible. This jockeying for the right balance grows during this period of Church history, but reaches a critical point in the centuries following 600, as we shall see.

Let us move to the other processes, since one process cannot be fully understood without the others.

2. A PROCESS OF INCREASED CLERICALIZATION

It would be totally misreading the evidence to think that only at the beginning of the third century does one find the first appearance of the clerical state. From the earliest sources, even without the name "cleric" we have the distinction between the ministerial leaders and the lay people. The letter of Clement to the Corinthians already indicated this and Ignatius in his letters reiterates this position as far as Asia Minor is concerned. A clericalization process is already in full swing at the beginning of the third century. Any suggestion that originally there was a completely democratic or congregational Christian community cannot be authenticated. The fact that in the earlier literature we find less of a distinction than we find, say, in 500 or 600 is equally true. There clearly is a process in these early centuries which tended to differentiate more and more the clerical area from the lay area. It is to this process that we now turn our attention.

If we consider the style of life, i.e., the sociological and cultural elements which characterize the cleric, we see from history how time-conditioned most of this style really is. In the early Church, for instance, presbyteroi and even some episkopoi continued to live as ordinary working men, tending their farms or other businesses. Only in the case of need did the local episkopos subsidize the presbyter. In most respects, sociologically, the presbyter was not differentiated from the lay person. As time went by, this changed.

Only from the fifth century onward did the presbyteros begin to wear special clothing, outside the liturgy, thus separating himself symbolically from the lay person.[28] About this same time, 400, we find that the tonsure was being prescribed somewhat generally for the clergy.[29] Tonsure, which was a part of early Egyptian spirituality, based to some degree on 1 Cor 11, 44ff, was first part of a monk's life. Gradually, it was taken over by the clergy (as also by penitents) from the fourth century onward. The style of hair also distinguished cleric from lay.

Only from the sixth century onward did celibacy begin to be required in a general way. Until then, it had been proposed, legislated, and resisted; indeed, celibacy of the clergy was far from universal in practice, even in post-tridentine times. There can be no doubt that the early Church and the Church of this patristic period had a high esteem for celibacy. It is also difficult to say exactly when an unmarried clergy, in the West became both mandatory and realized in actuality.[30] The celibate life style, however, did slowly take hold, and it, too, began to separate the cleric from the lay. One should add, however, that throughout the historical material on the celibate clergy, the Church has never officially declared that celibacy is an essential element of deacon, priest or bishop. In other words, marriage is not per se an invalidating impediment to ordination.

In the East (as in the West) bishops were celibate, but in the fourth century the custom began in which the episcopacy was conferred on monks alone. Because these men were monks, they were celibate—not because they were bishops. Still, it had also been the case for those chosen to be bishops to abstain from marriage, and if married to dismiss their wives. It was easier, however, to select someone from the monasteries for the episcopacy.[31] At first, the monks opposed the ordination of one of their own, for in the monasticism of the desert (and still substantially so in Eastern monasticism) priests were excluded.

In the West, clergy were admitted into the monastic life, and it was the example of Augustine which facilitated this situation. Naturally, the clerical monk was quite differentiated from the layperson.[32]

We find that certain councils, e.g., the Council of Saragosa (381), the Council of Chalcedon (451), the Council of Angers (453), and the Council of Tours (461), declared that orders were irrevocable and forbade clerics to return to lay life.[33] Councils do not enact such legislation if the contrary custom is not going on; evidently, then, clerics had ceased to function as special ministers and in the Church had joined the lay people. This irrevocability of order, based to some degree on Augustine's teaching, was another step in this process of clericalization.

B. Cooke, in his analysis of early ministry, writes:

> The distinction of the clergy from the laity was greatly abetted, sociologically and psychologically, by the treatment given to the clergy by the civil power. As part of his support of the church, Constantine granted to the clergy (at least those directly and professionally concerned with worship) exemption from civil and military service, from subjection to civil courts, and from taxation. This grant, which was honored for the most part by Constantine's successors, passed in substance into the Theodosian and Justinian codes, which in turn had their effect in passing on this clerical exemption to the feudal legislation of the Merovingian and Carolingian periods.[34]

The exemption from civil courts for clergy helped to develop ecclesiastical courts, but there were other factors as well: namely, the care the episkopos had for widows and orphans. Basil, in his struggle with the emperor Valens, clearly pushed for ecclesiastical jurisdiction rather than civil jurisdiction in such cases.[35]

Living apart from the general run of people, wearing identifying clothing, remaining unmarried, acceptance into a group which had only lifelong commitment allowable to it, tonsured, exempt from civil and military service, untouched by civil taxation, and out of the reach of civil courts—all this clearly led to a "group apart," a separated caste, which is endorsed by the very etymology of the word "kleros."

Distinction between cleric and lay is one thing: the degree of such a distinction is quite another. As the degree of distinction, sociologically, psychologically, culturally, widened, so, too, did the theological base for such a distinction widen. The process of clericalization influenced, in no small measure, the process of theologizing on the clergy.

3. A PROCESS OF THEOLOGIZING

The two aspects which we have mentioned above, namely, the increasing use of the Greek word *hiereus* (Latin: *sacerdos* and *pontifex*), and the clericalization process, both influenced the way in which the fathers of the Church spoke about the ordained ministry. Both aspects also influenced the way in which apostolic succession was used.

Theology of ministry focused on the person of the priest. More and more the priesthood was seen in terms of the Aaronic and Levitical priesthood of the Old Testament. St. Gregory of Nazianz, who was ordained against his will around 362, but urged or even forced to do so by his own father, also named Gregory, who was the bishop of Nazianz, wrote some years after the event his *Apologeticus de fuga*. In this work he described at great length the priestly office and tried to justify his own initial reaction to ordination, namely, his flight from the city of Nazianz. The *Apologeticus de fuga* was used in an extensive way by John Chrysostom for his even more famous treatise on the priesthood.

Theodore of Mopsuestia (d. 428), more or less a contemporary of Gregory of Nazianz, also wrote a treatise on the priesthood, *De Sacerdotio*. But it was John Chrysostom (d. 407) who wrote the most influential book on the priesthood for that particular time: *Peri Hierosyne* (*De Sacerdotio*). Quasten notes: "No work of Chrysostom is better known and none has been more frequently translated and printed more often than his six books *On the Priesthood*."[36] Isidore of Pelusium, only a few years after Chrysostom's death, speaks of this work. Jerome read it with appreciation. Suidas extolled it. Basil clearly studied it since it is in a form of dialogue between Basil and John Chrysostom, who were close friends. In this dialogue, a defense of Basil is made by Chrysostom.

Here is how Chrysostom describes the priest:

> The Priest's relations with his people involve much difficulty. But if any inquire about his relations with God, he will find the others to be as nothing, since these require a greater and more thorough earnestness. For he who acts as an ambassador on behalf of the whole city—but why do I say the city? on behalf of the whole world indeed—prays that God would be merciful to the sins of all, not only of the living, but also of the departed. What manner of man ought he to be? For my part I think that the boldness of speech of Moses and Elias is insufficient for such supplication. For as though he were entrusted with the whole world and were himself the father of all men, he draws near to God, beseeching that wars may be quelled; asking for peace and plenty, and a swift deliverance from all the ills that beset each one, publicly and privately; and he ought as much to excel in every respect all those on whose behalf he prays, as rulers their subjects.[37]

For Chrysostom the priest's dimensions are worldwide; Moses, Elias, temporal rulers—all cannot hold a candle to the priest. But he continues:

> And whenever he invokes the Holy Spirit and offers the most dread sacrifice, and constantly handles the common Lord of all, tell me what rank shall we give him? What great purity? and what real piety must we demand of him? For consider what manner of hands they ought to be which minister in these things, and of what kind his tongue which utters such words, and ought not the soul which receives so great a spirit be purer and holier than anything in the world? At such a time angels stand by the Priest; and their whole sanctuary and the space around the altars is filled with the powers of heaven, in honor of him who lieth thereon. For this, indeed, is capable of being proved from the very rites which are being then celebrated. I myself, moreover, have heard some one once relate, that a certain aged, venerable

man, accustomed to see revelations, used to tell him, that he, being thought worthy of this kind, at such a time, saw, on a sudden, so far as was possible for him, a multitude of angels, clothed in shining robes, and encircling the altar, and bending down, as one might see soldiers in the presence of their King, and for my part I believe it.[38]

Even though at times Chrysostom speaks of the human side of the priest, it is clear that he places the priest at a very high level. Such a theology of the priest could not help but divide the clergy and lay even more. The dignity of the priest was greater than angels, and it was the closeness to the Eucharist which both demanded and bestowed holiness and purity. Since Chrysostom's work was an immediate "best seller," its influence on the theology and spirituality of the priesthood remained dominant for centuries.

One finds this same approach to ministry in the development of the ordination ritual. The *Centre de Pastorale Liturgique* in 1955 hosted a discussion on this theme of ordination, which was subsequently published as a book. B. Botte, P. M. Gy, J. Lecuyer, and A. G. Martimort were among the contributors who addressed the issue of the Old Testament influence on the early ordination prayers. The typology of Aaron and the sons of Aaron seems to have been utilized strongly in Rome, but used only for the bishop. The addition of this typology is an accretion to already existing prayers. In the Byzantine and Syrian Churches, the Aaronic typology is found only in a most insignificant way. Botte comments: "The typology of the Old Testament is only an imperfect analogy, and has never been the means of an adequate definition of Christian priesthood."[39] Nonetheless, the ordination of Aaron involved two rites: he was clothed with rich vestments and, secondly, he was anointed. In the early middle ages the imposition of vestments and the anointing became part of episcopal ordination (and later presbyteral ordination) in conformity with this Aaronic typology. The rites are, clearly, an addition to an already existing ritual of ordination.

In the ordination prayers of Hippolytus, the anointing was taken in a spiritual sense only, but, as Botte notes, it progresses "to material unction." i.e., an actual anointing.[40] Martimort, for his part, remarks that the typology of Aaron leads to a function which "will be especially of ritual character." The typology of Moses, on the other hand, leads to a "picture of a leader of the people much more than of a ritual function."[41] This has particular significance for the *Apostolic Tradition*'s prayer for the presbyters which emphasizes Moses, not Aaron. At the time of Hippolytus, the presbyter was ordained primarily to offer counsel to the episkopos, a function of leadership; at that time the episkopos was alone the liturgical leader.

It is interesting to note that these scholars did not find in the early ordination prayers which they studied any allusion to a missionary function, i.e., preaching to the non-Christians.[42] Again, we see in this that ministry is intra-ecclesial, i.e., it is meant for the Christian community, not the non-Christian world.

At the end of the fourth century and the beginning of the fifth century we begin to have evidential data from the Eastern Churches. The first is that of the *Apostolic Constitutions.* The ordination ritual found in this book is basically the same as that of Hippolytus' *Apostolic Tradition,* but we find an addition: the imposition of the book of the gospels in the consecration of the bishop. No formula is attached to this, nor is any specific meaning given to it. The Church of Antioch knew of this rite, for both John Chrysostom and pseudo-Dionysius allude to it. It is also found in all the rites of the Syrian group.

The prayers which one finds in the West Syrian/Byzantine groups of ordinals is typical of the East generally: "Divine grace which heals all that is infirm and supplies what is wanting chooses N. as bishop of N." In this prayer there is an unambiguous statement that God chooses someone for the ministry of bishop—not the community, nor the person himself. In a corresponding Byzantine ritual, the imposition of the book of the gospels receives an interpretation; it is called a "yoke," but one that is placed on the head and not on the shoulders. The interpretation is of a later date than the actual rite of imposition. Botte thinks that there might have been an earlier interpretation than "yoke," namely, that the gospels should fill the elected bishop who is being ordained.[43]

Botte and the other authors pay special interest to the *Euchologium Baraberini* 336, which though ancient is difficult to date precisely. In this volume the prayers for the ordination of a bishop are of great value:

O sovereign Lord and our God, who by thine apostle Paul didst set up the hierarchy of degrees and orders for the service of thy most pure mysteries at thy holy altar—first apostles, then prophets, then doctors; do thou strengthen, O sovereign of the universe, by the coming, power and grace of thy Holy Spirit, him whom thou has judged worthy to receive the yoke of the gospel and the dignity of the high priesthood by the hand of me, a sinner, and of those who celebrate with me, as thou didst strengthen the apostles and prophets, as thou didst anoint kings and sanctify high priests. Make him to be a high priest without reproach and adorned with all dignity; make him to be holy so that he may be worthy to intercede for the salvation of the people and to be heard by thee.[44]

A second prayer from the same volume, *Euchologium Barberini,* reads as follows:

O Lord our God, who, since the nature of man cannot sustain the essence of thy divinity, didst by thy dispensation raise up doctors subject to the same passions as ourselves who approach thy throne to offer the sacrifice and the oblation for thy people; do thou, O Lord, thou, the true Pastor who didst give thy life for the flock, make him who has been appointed a dispenser of the grace of the sovereign priesthood to be thine imitator, a guide to the blind, a light in the darkness, a teacher of the foolish, a tutor of little ones, a lamp shining in the world, so that after he has formed the souls who have been entrusted to him in this life, he may stand before thy tribunal without shame and may receive the great reward which thou hast prepared for those who have striven to preach thy gospel.[45]

In these early prayers, the episkopoi are seen as mediators of divine grace. They are set apart and chosen precisely as episkopoi for these purposes. God's grace is implored to make them perfect and holy and consecrated for ministry. The only liturgical actions mentioned are: the healing of the sick by laying hands on them, and the power to bind and loose. Additional prayers list: to stand at the altar, to proclaim the gospel, to preach, to offer spiritual gifts and sacrifices, to renew the people through baptism. In another East Syrian prayer we find such sacerdotal functions attributed to the episkopos as: laying hands on the sick, offering spiritual oblations, consecrating the baptismal water, adorning the sons of the Holy Church with the works of justice.

In his analysis of the early ordination texts, Botte discusses the accounts we find in Jacobite and Maronite texts, but in his judgment the two rites which have the best guarantee of antiquity are the Byzantine and the Nestorian.[46] These two rituals are found in material which has been attributed to Serapion and therefore connected to Alexandria, and both are based on Hippolytus and the *Apostolic Tradition.*

In early Eastern ordination rituals, references to the Old Testament are almost nil. Jesus, on the other hand, is seen as the source of ministry and this ministry has come down from Jesus through the apostles to the episkopoi who are seen as presiding over a community (the pastoral and the leadership aspect of episcopacy) and, in a secondary but important way, as presiding over the liturgy. Community leadership still prevails over liturgical leadership, or, as one might say, the ministry of Jesus as seen in the gospels is the center of ministry, not exclusively the eucharistic ministry.

In the Eastern Church the early ordination prayers for the presbyter focus on counseling and on wisdom, not on liturgical functions. For the deacon one hears that he is the minister of the episkopos not of the presbyter. The deacon, too, is to shine with the spirit of discernment and knowledge and to serve the community in purity and without reproach.

In these discussions on priesthood and in these ordination rituals, we clearly see a hierarchy of ministry: episkopos on top, presbyter, and then deacon. In the year 200 we hear for the first time the titles subdeacon and lector, but without any indication of either their roles or their relationship to episkopos, presbyter and deacon. During the period 200 to 600 we do see the rise of the so-called minor orders. We will come back to these later, but one notices that throughout this development of minor order, the hierarchy of episkopos, presbyter and deacon is never challenged.

Can we, in the period 200 to 400, equate the episkopos with our present bishop? the presbyter with our present priest? and the deacon with our present deacon? The answer must be mixed: to some degree, yes, and to some degree, no. From 200 to 400 the emphasis on the episkopos falls on his community leadership. The ordination rituals pray for this in a most eminent way. Liturgical leadership flows from community leadership, and in this period it is the episkopos who so dominates the liturgy that in an almost total way no sacramental liturgy was celebrated without him. He was a mono-episcopal liturgical president. This is one of the differences between the episkopos of this period and the bishop today, since today the presbyter is the most common liturgical leader of the sacramental rituals, not the bishop.

Secondly, the number of episkopoi at this period of time in a rather small area indicates, as we noted above, that where in later ages one would find a presbyter-pastor, at this juncture of Church history the episkopos is the pastor. This is a second difference between the role of the episkopos at that time, 200 to 400, and the later bishop.

Around 400, as we shall see momentarily, this structure of functions begins to change, and the presbyter begins to take on more liturgical leadership. Also as one moves into the Merovingian period, we find that the ritual also changes, with the addition of such ceremonies as the handing on of liturgical instruments (chalice, paten, etc.), anointings, vestings. All of these additional rites focus ministry from leadership of the community to liturgical leadership, with special emphasis on the eucharist. As Botte reminds us, the typology of the Old Testament (i.e., that of Aaron and Levi), in the West, heavily influenced the Roman rituals in the direction of liturgical priestly activities.[47]

Nonetheless, in all of these early rituals, the hierarchy is clearly portrayed as willed by God. Episcopal consecration, in which three episkopoi performed the ritual, was never seen as a purely personal act by which one individual communicates the powers he possesses to another individual. Rather, it is the collective act of the leaders of the Church communities incorporating a new individual into the *ordo episkoporum*. The same is true of the presbyter who is incorporated into a *presbyterium*. God does the calling and God does the empowering. The individual episkopoi and the community acknowledge this working of God's grace in a solemn and liturgical way: ordination.

In these early rituals, the mention of apostles is frequent, and the episkopoi are seen as the successors of the apostles. Presbyters, in these rituals, are not seen as successors of the apostles. The rituals evidence the theological position of apostolic succession of the episkopoi, which from the time of Cyprian on became so strong that there was a sort of identification between episkopos and apostle.

Undoubtedly due to the influence of John Chrysostom's work on the priesthood, the Eastern rituals in particular emphasize both for the episkopos and for the presbyter the role of mediator. This is a new emphasis. In 1 Tim 2, 5–6, we read: "There is only one mediator between God and mankind, himself a man, Christ Jesus, who sacrificed himself as a ransom for them all." Whether this passage played a role in the relationship of episkopos and presbyter on the one hand and mediator on the other is still a moot question. It is clear, however, that mediation was not generally mentioned as a priestly function until the time of Chrysostom, not that he himself started this, but rather that it was in his period of time that mediation became associated with priestly ministry. Chrysostom furthered this approach, of course, by incorporating it into his treatise on the priesthood. With the entry of this idea into the normal discussion on priesthood, a step is clearly made in the direction which the scholastic theological world will use: namely, that priesthood is a spiritual power. Coupled with the emphasis on the eucharist as the centering for priestly ministry, this power will in the scholastic framework be seen as a spiritual eucharistic power par excellence.

Another item that is of interest in this early period and the rituals of ordination which were then in vogue is the lack of any transmission of juridical powers. Ordination was not seen in a juridical way; rather, it was seen as a conferral of divine grace. This grace is not given for one's own personal sanctification, but for the community. The prayers are for pastoral leadership, good shepherding, true teaching, liturgical presidency and generous healing, just as Jesus was and in line with Jesus' instructions to his apostles. Jesus remains in all of these rituals the basis for Christian ministry: faithful to God's call, serving, loving, healing, bringing faith and peace in the Spirit.

4. A PROCESS OF INCREASED MINISTERIAL DIVERSIFICATION

Around the end of the fourth century and the beginning of the fifth century, we find a process of diversification as regards pastoral ministry. From the beginning Christianity had been an urban phenomenon, rather than a rural phenomenon. The major centers of early Christianity are all important cities for that time: Jerusalem, Antioch, Rome, Corinth, Philippi, Smyrna, Ephesus, Nicaea, Constantinople, etc. In all these cities episkopoi are the leaders of the Christian community. With the validation of Christianity for the Roman empire and the growth of the Christian population, new pastoral problems appear, particularly the pastoral care of the rural areas, which understandably were sparsely populated. Until the end of 400, more or less, rural Christians and those who were neophytes had to trek into the main city, to the Christian center, for instruction in the catechumenate, for the eucharist, and for reconciliation. In short, almost all their Christian needs were met only in the cities.

A solution, particularly widespread in the West, less so in the East, was the establishment of the chore-episkopos: the episkopos in the field. Cooke notes:

> For a time, the somewhat ill-defined office of chorepiskopos (roughly like an auxiliary bishop) was utilized, with these "assistant bishops" functioning in the rural areas; but by the end of the tenth century this institution had been abandoned.[48]

A chore-episkopos was not quite an auxiliary bishop; in the major cities the primary episkopos was often called the metropolitan, and a large number of episkopoi were to some degree under him. It was the positioning of an episkopos in the rural areas that gave rise to this nomenclature of chore-episkopos.

As this office of chore-episkopos was not too attractive, the presbyter was given the task of providing pastoral care for the rural Christians. At first this meant the eucharistic liturgy on the ordinary Sundays, together with the task of preaching. Both the celebration of the Sunday eucharist and the office of preaching had been restricted to the episkopos. With the presbyter moving out of a counseling role into a liturgical and leadership role, we see clearly a process of diversification. The training of catechumens, which had been done in the episcopal Church, was also transferred to the rural community under the leadership of the presbyter. The actual baptism remained in the urban episcopal church, at least for a while, but as time went by the presbyter in the East and West began to baptize as well in his rural Church community. In the East, the laying on of hands by the episkopos was also transferred to the presbyter, but in the West this was generally retained by the episkopos, and we have the beginning of the separation of the sacrament of baptism into the water bath (baptism) and the laying on of hands and at times anointing (eventually to be seen as confirmation).

This new role of the presbyter grew in importance, and in time it is the presbyter who is seen as the normal liturgical presider over almost all the sacraments, and he is the normal person who preaches at Sunday liturgies, and he is the normal pastoral minister for a given community. In this way, the presbyter becomes the normal pastor of the parish community, and the number of episkopoi decreases.

The urban episcopal Church, in 300 to 400 is, in many ways, the golden age of the diaconate. The episkopos as the central leader is by and large not too accessible; the presbyters are the counselors and not really that involved in pastoral ministry. The deacons, on the other hand, during this time, were the most evident pastoral ministers in the community: visiting the sick, caring for the dying, providing for the needy, etc., all tasks which today we associate strongly with the parish priest. As we know from Jerome, this positioning of the deacons to the detriment of the presbyter was not without critic. Jerome writes:

> I am told that someone has been mad enough to put deacons before presbyters, that is, before bishops. For when the apostle clearly teaches that presbyters are the same as bishops must not a mere server of tables and of widows be insane to set himself up arrogantly over men through whose prayers the body and blood of Christ are made present?[49]

Again:

> But you will say how comes it then that at Rome a presbyter is only ordained on the recommendation of a deacon? To which I reply as follows. Why do you bring forward a custom that exists in one city only? Why do you oppose to the laws of the church a paltry exception which has given rise to arrogance and pride?[50]

Again:

> Their fewness makes deacons persons of consequence while presbyters are less thought of owing to their great numbers. But even in the church of Rome, the deacons stand while the presbyters seat themselves, although bad habits have by degrees so far crept in that I have seen a deacon, in the absence of a bishop, seat

himself among the presbyters and at social gatherings give his blessing to them.[51]

The situation which Jerome describes was not actually found only in Rome. Deacons were in the fifth century at their zenith of power. The increased pastoral activity of the presbyters slowly eroded this prominence of the deacon.

> During the long and eventful centuries from Nicea to the reformation the permanent diaconate at first flourished and then declined. The seeds of diaconal decline were already planted with the rise of sacerdotalism in the third century and the restrictive legislation of the early fourth century. A confusion of roles between deacons and "priests" and a struggle for identity continued into the Middle Ages. Gradually, the diaconate receded in importance until the diaconal order became merely a preliminary and ceremonial step to the sacralized priesthood.[52]

After this process of diversification has taken hold, we begin to see in the presbyter of that age the priest that the middle ages and beyond has known so well, both in name and function. With the decrease, consequently, of the number of episkopoi, who had been almost local pastors, we also see in the episkopos of that emerging time (400 onward), both in name and function, the bishop that the middle ages and beyond knew so well. It is at this juncture, roughly around 400, that bishop and priest, in the senses that we understand these terms, truly begin to operate within the Christian community. This was due of course to the Holy Spirit, but through the pastoral needs of a growing and diversifying Christian community.

During this period of the Church the woman minister also reached a certain plateau, especially the deaconesses. Echlin writes:

> Deaconesses were usually considered subordinate to deacons. At the Eucharist, for example, they received only one piece of bread while the deacon received two (Apostolic Constitutions, 8:30). Deaconesses communicated the needs and desires of women to the presiding bishop (2:26), guarded the door through which women entered the church and escorted women worshippers to their proper place (2:57).[52]

Widows, too, seemed to have been considered a special group or ordo in the Church. Their ministry was that of prayer and pastoral service. The deaconess, at least in the Eastern Churches, was more clearly a ministry. The ritual for a deaconess was similar to that of the deacon. As the baptismal ritual unfolded, deaconesses took an active role both in the instruction of the catechumens and in the baptismal ritual itself, as far as women were concerned. In the *Apostolic Constitutions,* the deaconess is mentioned (19–20) behind that of deacon and before that of subdeacon. Osiek analyzes the data from the *Apostolic Constitutions,* and concludes to the possibility that in this period a deaconess was truly ordained.[53] The material might be read differently, but it cannot be read from a dogmatic or a priori standpoint that ordination of women is in principle impossible. The historical data do not lead to such an a priori stance.

Lay ministry continued throughout this period as well, but with the ever-increasing number of "minor orders," many of these lay ministries were "clericalized." From 235 to 600 clerical ministry dominates over non-clerical ministry. The lay monk, however, rose to enormous prominence in this same period.

5. THE INTERRELATIONSHIP OF THESE VARIOUS PROCESSES

As mentioned earlier, one cannot see these four processes in isolation. They are quite interrelated. The process of apostolicity focused more and more on the episkopos, to some degree individually, but more and more as a college of bishops. This collegiality of bishops is quite strong at the end of our period, 600, but we begin to see in Gregory a strong positioning of the apostolic succession of the pope alongside this collegial episcopacy. As the episkopos, however, became more and more a liturgical leader and a leader with apostolic succession, a setting apart, or clericalization process, moved rapidly forward. This episcopal clericalization included the clericalization of the presbyter and the deacon, and those in minor orders to some degree, as well. Cleric and lay divided the Church, not only sociologically but theologically also. More and more attention was given to the theologizing of the cleric: at all levels, episkopos, presbyter, deacon and minor orders. This theologizing was enhanced by the use of the term "hiereus" and by an extensive use of Old Testament priestly references. Jesus still remains the center of Christian ministry, but his position as "hiereus" is emphasized and his priesthood is likewise described in Old Testament terminology. This use of the Old Testament is particularly evident in the West in the ordination rituals. As the presbyter took on more and more the liturgical functions which at any earlier period had been fairly much the exclusive prerogative of the episkopos, the presbyter's clericalization and theologizing processes also moved forward. Gy helps us understand this development; he summarizes the use of sacerdos in the early Church as it applied to episkopos and presbyter in the following chronological schema:

1. Around 200, for the first time, sacerdos is applied to episkopos. Cyprian, in an indirect way, loosely extends sacerdotal to the presbyter as well, but even for Cyprian the episkopos is sacerdos.
2. From roughly 350 to 500 sacerdos normally refers to the episkopos. The diversification process in which the presbyter takes on some of the liturgical functions which the episkopoi had been doing only begins in earnest between 400 and 500.
3. In the Carolingian period sacerdos refers as much to priest as to bishop, but most frequently to priest.
4. In the eleventh century, sacerdos refers normally to priest.[54]

We are going to see that in this process of development, during the Carolingian period and the early scholastic period, the focus of sacerdos is no longer episkopos as it is during 210–600, but rather the presbyter, to the extent that episkopos in the scholastic period is placed outside the sphere of sacred order. But this is getting us ahead of ourselves to some degree.

6

Ministry in the
Early Medieval Church
600 to 1000 A.D.

It is well known that the theology of priesthood developed by the major scholastics (Alexander of Hales, Thomas Aquinas, Bonaventure, Albert the Great and John Duns Scotus) remained, in the Latin Church, the standard approach to the theology of Holy Order from the thirteenth century to the middle of the twentieth century, a total of seven hundred years. This scholastic theology of the priesthood, which proved to be so strong and almost immovable, did not simply begin in the thirteenth century, nor even in the important century prior to high scholasticism. It had its roots primarily in the early medieval period: 600 to 1000, a period which we want to consider at some detail in this chapter. Indeed, without an appreciation of what occurred in the Western World during this period (600–1000), the scholastic approach to priesthood is *contextually* unintelligible.

These four hundred years, however, span a large section of Church history, and many events and tendencies developed during these transformative and often turbulent centuries. Naturally, we cannot present here a full picture of Church history during this epoch; as a result, we will concentrate on three specific situations, which in a fundamental way affected the Western approach to the issue of priesthood and ordained ministry generally. These three issues are:

1. The separation of the Western and Eastern Christian Churches. In the ninth century, this split came to be known as the "Pho-

tian Schism," but the division involves much more than the election and installation of Photius at Constantinople.

2. The Frankish structuring of the Church, which is called the proprietary church structure. This structuring all but made the parish priest (presbyter) independent of the bishop. This separation of bishop from presbyter is key to both the early medieval development of priesthood and to the scholastic definition of priesthood.

3. The increased involvement of the papacy in the local, episcopal Church. Papal intrusion into local Church life further reduced the position of the college of bishops and thus contributed enormously to the scholastic understanding of Holy Order.

These three issues, as one notices immediately, were not theoretical issues. Indeed, there was no "theologizing" on priesthood, from which a form of Church structure and practice then evolved. Rather, the practical or actual development of Church structure eventually led to a way of "theologizing" on Church ministry. Accordingly, in this chapter we are not dealing with a history of ideas on ordained ministry, but rather with a history of events, which laid the foundation for the scholastic theological approach to priesthood. In this instance, *praxis* preceded *theoria.*

A second observation might also be in order, namely, that the focus of this chapter will often be on the bishop. Indeed, the role of the bishop in all of the above is decisive. In the early Church, as we have seen, the naming of "episkopos" as the central and dominant local leader and the establishment of his functions dominated the way one pieced together the data of the early Church. The "episkopos" was and is the key figure in the study of ministry in the early Church. The bishop (episkopos) is also the key figure in this period as well, but not under the rubric of "naming and function." Rather, it is the position of episcopacy within the framework of Christian priesthood itself which centralizes the ministerial development of this era. All three of the issues mentioned above affect in one way or another the positioning of the bishop within the Church in a fundamental way. Perhaps we might schematize the situation as follows, comparing the Church situation in 600 A.D. with that of the Church in 1000 A.D.:

600 A.D.

East and West are still one as far as the Church is concerned.

The bishop/episkopos is the main "priestly" figure in the local churches.

The bishop of Rome, the pope, remains by and large a Roman figure. The pope's involvement in local or regional matters is infrequent. Episcopal collegiality in both East and West is the major form of local or regional Church government.

1000 A.D.

East and West are separate and develop their respective Church ministerial structures.

In the West, the presbyter is the main "priestly" figure; the bishop will soon be theologically considered outside the sacrament of Order. In the East the episkopos remains the central priestly figure.

In the West, the pope has become a dominant figure in local or regional Church matters. In the East the bishop of Rome has no regional influence. The collegiality of the bishops has almost disappeared in the West; in the East, episcopal collegiality has begun to take on ethnic traits.

In each of these comparisons, the bishop plays a key role, as is evident. Let us now consider these issues singly and in more detail, but only from the standpoint of their connection to the theme of ordained ministry. After treating each of these particular issues, we will in section four turn our attention to some additional factors which also influenced the structuring of Church ministry in the West, in such a way as to help lay the foundations for the scholastic theology of priesthood.

1. THE DIVISION OF THE EASTERN AND WESTERN CHRISTIAN CHURCHES

Even though there is an eventual split between the East and the West, there is still a basic Christian unity between East and West, so much so that when one looks at Church history from the peak of the patristic period down to the peak of the scholastic period, one cannot but see a certain uniformity about the Church, both in the East and the West. Pelikan writes:

> During the fifth and sixth centuries, christology and mystagogy in the East, and anthropology and ecclesiology in the West, brought together much of the dogmatic development of the preceding centuries and laid the foundations for later constructions of Christian dogma.[1]

Even though Pelikan has in mind specifically such doctrines as christology, ecclesiology and liturgical forms of worship, his ideas can easily be extended to include an understanding of Church ministry. This bringing together Pelikan calls the "orthodox consensus," and he cites Vincent of Lerin's famous dictum as a sort of catchword for the movement: "everywhere, always and by all" ("Id teneamus quod ubique, quod semper, quod ab omnibus creditum est" *Commonit.* c. 2). In this movement toward an orthodox consensus, authority and tradition in Pelikan's view are of the highest importance. He cites a passage from *On the Catholic Faith,* at one time attributed to Boethius, but more likely written at a later date than the time of Boethius:

> This catholic church, then, spread throughout the world, is known by three particular marks: whatever is believed or taught in it has the authority of the Scriptures or of universal tradition or at least of its own proper usage.[2]

As a criterion, universality meant that the Church doctrine was in no way to be understood as a series of private views, but rather as the long-standing, i.e., since apostolic times, teaching of the "catholic" Church. Catholicity was "the mark both of the true Church and of true doctrine, for these were inseparable."[3] This catholicity went beyond Eastern or Western Churches, beyond Greek or Latin Churches, for it was truly a universality of the entire Church and of doctrine, a "catholic" approach in the sense of the Greek: *kat' holos.*

In this respect, then, the Church came to be seen as the "repository of truth, the dispenser of grace, the guarantee of salvation, and the matrix of acceptable worship."[4] Congar, in his lengthy study *Tradition and Traditions,* mentions that the very term "tradition" (*paradosis*) was not used very much by the apostolic Fathers; nonetheless, the idea was, even in that early time, beginning to be shaped. Congar states that this tradition involved three elements: "a deposit handed on, a living teaching authority, a transmission by succession."[5] In the ante-Nicene period the terms *regula fidei* and *regula veritatis* (rule of faith or rule of truth) were employed to describe this Catholic tradition. Irenaeus, Hippolytus, Tertullian, Novatian, Clement of Alexandria and Origen all used these terms. In the post-Nicene period, the Fathers continued this manner of describing tradition, but since none of these later Fathers could claim to have been a student of one who had known an apostle (a claim made by Irenaeus), there developed in the post-Nicene period a respect for and a reference to the "Fathers" of the faith. This appeal to early Christian authority, beyond the scriptures, was made by Athanasius; during the Nestorian crisis the appeal was raised again and again by many bishops; the argument over the famous *Tria Capitula* rested strongly on the appeal to the "Fathers." These "Fathers" were at first only bishops, but by the time of Vincent of Lerins the term included all orthodox teachers of the faith. "They were seen as following in the line of Christ and the apostles as transmitters of the truth. When a documented and critical argument was sought in their writings, the fact that they were bishops, i.e., the value of succession in the Irenaean sense, took second place to the fact that they were theologians."[6]

The locus of catholicity was in ecclesiology, i.e., in the total Church. Nonetheless, specialized or ordained Church authority had taken on a very embracing role. The four early councils: Nicaea (325), Constantinople (381), Ephesus (431), and Chalcedon (451), attended by key bishops and some imperial lay delegates, tended to become highly normative both in the East and in the West. These four councils not only claimed the authority of the Fathers of the past, but as time went by they were also seen as authoritative statements of the very bishops who had attended these synods. Just as there were four gospels which were normative, so, too, there were four councils which were normative. Gregory the Great at the end of the sixth century was particularly fond of using this comparison of gospel and council, and this parallel comparison has lasted down to the present day, although with some modifications. Congar has gathered together the salient points of this "quaternity," noting first "La valeur de 'quaternite' " and only then discussing the high estimation of these four early councils.[7] Congar notes:

> La raison pour laquelle les quatre premiers conciles sont privilègies et représentent une sorte de critère ou de référence normative pour tous les autres, c'est qu'ils ont defini LA FOI. Ils sont, vecué et formuleé par l'Église dans la suite des apôtres et de l'Évangile, l'expression même de la foi, dans la profession de laquelle le chrétien est baptise, uni a Dieu, sauve.[8]

Universality at the beginning of our time period was also seen as spatial: the later East/West splitting of the Christian world had not yet occurred in such force as to break this consensus of spatial universality. The "Fathers" of the Church were both Eastern and Western, and conformity to the ancient doctrines, as we read again and again, was conformity to the "Fathers of the Church." Notice the plural of "Fathers," but the singular of the "Church." Heretics were those who destroyed these patristic teachings, and therefore destroyed the Church as well. It was, of course, commonly understood that the true Fathers were quite in conformity with scripture. Augustine was one of these true Fathers; Origen, however, was only controversially seen as a true Father, since he had apparently deviated from the faith. Eusebius, the famous early Church historian, used the terms orthodox, ancient and ecclesiatical in a rather interchangeable way. This spatial universality, therefore, was "historical," since each age and space of Church existence shared in the orthodox, the ancient and the ecclesiastical.

But spatial universality was also to be found in a contemporary way. In the early middle ages, given the lack of communication, what was experienced in one ecclesial area was often considered, if it were something basic, to be uniform throughout the Christian world. This spatial universality, both in the sense of its antecedent spatial life and in the sense of its contemporary spatial life, needs to be appreciated in a study of this particular period of Church history, not only at the beginning of the seventh century but throughout the medieval period itself. An example of this spatial universality in a contemporary way might be seen in the Merovingian notion of an apostolic see. The early Church had enjoyed apostolic sees, and likewise in Gaul the Merovingian Church had its own apostolic sees, not because of any specific apostle, but because of the bishop himself. O. M. Dalton, in his volumes *The History of the Franks,* illustrates this:

> The phrase is used in a letter of Clovis, written 507–511: *Dominis sanctis at apostolica sede dignissimis episcopis.* . . . The same words are used in Radegund's letter . . . and in the letter of the bishops written in 589. Fortunatus addresses his letter to Syagrius, bishop of Autun: *Domino Sancto et apostolica sede dignissimo domino Syagrio papae,* the title *papa* being also applied to bishops who were not even metropolitans. The phrase *apostolica sedes* was, therefore, commonly applied to ordinary sees.[9]

Today, we might be somewhat amused at this usage of "apostolic see." But its use in these Merovingian times indicates an ecclesiology which is universal and catholic. The Church of the apostles was the very Church in which the Gallic people were leading their lives. Though spatially separated from one another and from the sees of the East and of Italy and North Africa, etc., their Churches were one because of the apostolic base. Their bishops were as apostolic as those in other Christian areas. Once again, there is no sense of division along an East/West bias.

Still, as Pelikan reminds us, the consensus was not simply a clerical matter, for the lay person had ways of expressing Church doctrine as well.[10] Christian devotion was highly valued, as one can see in the devotion to Mary, particularly in the East as the *Theotokos* (mother of God). The interest and enthusiasm of the lay people in such devotions clearly influenced Church doctrine on such matters. Prosper of Aquitaine (d. cir. 455) formulated the doctrine in a way which would remain a by-word in the Church down to the present time: "Lex orandi, lex credendi." (The rule of prayer expresses the rule of belief.) The Church, throughout the centuries, had prayed, so it was firmly believed, in conformity with apostolic tradition. True prayer in the Church is also part of apostolic succession and consequently could only reflect Christian truth. An instance of this situation might be seen in the prayerful devotion to the mother of God: at this early period, the prayer of the Christian folk regarding Mary far outstripped the written theology on Mary.

In the East, as in the West, this orthodox consensus was overwhelmingly central to both Christian practice and Christian belief. In the East Justinian oversaw a theology which was eminently traditional. In the West, the respect for Ambrose and especially Augustine was based both on their theological acumen and on their strongly traditional approach to the Christian life. Dionysius the Areopagite, who influenced both East and West in an enormous degree, described the Church hierarchy he experienced: bishop, priest, deacon. For Dionysius, this earthly hierarchy was modeled after the celestial hierarchy. To oppose the hierarchical structure of the Church, therefore, was, in Dionysian thought, to oppose God's very own hierarchical structure. Likewise, for Dionysius, the goal of our Christian life is deification, but this deification comes only after a passage from purification through illumination to ultimate union. As one sees, this process became almost synonomous with Christian spirituality. However, in Dionysius' writings one makes this spiritual passage *only* through the Church: namely, through the Church's sacraments and its hierarchical ministry. Ministry and Church hierarchy are therefore quite central both to theology and to spirituality in this Dionysian framework, and, as we know, the Areopagite's writings eventually became fairly standard in both East and West.[11]

H. Marot in his essay, "Conciles antenicéens et conciles oecumeniques," describes the collegial character of the bishops in early ecclesiology: "Les évêques, qui ne sont pas des individus isolés et dont les Églises sont en communion, forment un collège, et ce collège est un, comme l'église ellemême."[12] T.-P. Camelot in his analysis of the ecumenical councils of the fourth and fifth centuries mirrors this same ecclesiology: the gathered bishops represent the universal Church, both East and West. They are fully conscious of their role as continuing the college of the apostles. Their unanimity expresses the very faith of the Church.[13]

In 600 A.D., both in the East and in the West, the bishops were clearly seen as the successors of the apostles and, more importantly for our investigation, as the major priestly figures in the Church. This hierarchical ministry was of a piece. In the course of Church history which followed, down to Michael Caerularius, the patriarch of Constantinople (1043–1058), the Christian East and the Christian West parted company, and part of this separation is manifest in distinctive ministerial structures. The issue of ministry was not the central issue, although the issue of papal ministry did play a centralizing role. The position of bishops was not the central issue, and yet in the West a different approach to bishops gradually took place.

In spite of the emphasis on this "orthodox consensus" doctrinally between East and West, it is astounding that, when the major scholastics began to develop their theology of priesthood, the bishop was gradually viewed as an "outsider" to Holy Order. This scholastic exclusion of episcopacy from Holy Order can only be judged as a remarkable theological step, quite "out of step" with patristic thought and early medieval thought. Such a step, however, remained unthinkable in the Eastern Churches, in which the episkopos continued to retain the position of ministerial or priestly centrality. When one reflects on the scholastic exclusion of the bishop from a theology of Holy Order, and, at the same time, reflects on this "orthodox consensus" of the patristic and early medieval Church, the question immediately arises: How could the Latin Church in the twelfth and thirteenth centuries break so strongly with that orthodox consensus? The division or schism of East and West alone cannot account for this remarkable Western position on Church ministry.[14] Other factors need to be involved, as we shall see, but it must be stressed here that the position of the episkopos in the Eastern Churches after the division and the position of the bishop in the Western Church after the division is a major rending of this "orthodox consensus." In many ways, this positioning of the bishop/episkopos in a theology of Holy Order creates a different theology of ministry in the East and in the West. Later, we will return to this East/West division, but let us consider now the additional factors which brought on this re-positioning of the bishop in the Western theology of Holy Order.

2. THE FRANKISH STRUCTURING OF MINISTRY

Let us consider, in the second place, the Frankish influence on the structuring of the Church, for this Frankish re-structuring also played a role in the re-positioning of episkopos/presbyter in the theology of priesthood. In the eighth century, the Frankish kingdoms started to establish themselves in the West, and it was the resultant marriage of the Frankish kingdom and Western Christianity which gave rise to the Carolingian, Holy Roman Empire. Since the establishment of this Western Holy Roman Empire, however, further estranged the East/West relationships, we will focus the development of the theology of priesthood and episcopacy primarily from the standpoint of the Western theological world.

This entry of the Franks into the mainstream of Christian life, it must be admitted, brought some new and significant factors into the shaping of Christian ministry. In this Frankish world, however, two tendencies as regards ministry began to co-exist:

1. On the one hand, the rural Churches of the West in the Frankish empire had their own rights of ownership, their own juridical structures, and their own form for appointment of presbyteral leadership. This localized autonomy was a strongly Frankish approach, which affected the relationship of bishop and priest. This form of local Church structure was called the "proprietary Church."

2. On the other hand, the urban Church had its more Roman style, with episcopal leadership, episcopal juridical structures, and set patterns for appointment of bishops, priests connected to the urban Church, and deacons. This episcopal structure was rooted in the patristic Church, at least from 200 A.D. onward.

The rural situation of the Frankish kingdom was not at all the same as that of the chore-episkopoi treated above. The chore-episkopoi and the rural Churches, which they at first (and subsequently the presbyters) served, were extended arms of the central urban baptismal church, which was episcopally centered. Frankish procedure was much more localized, so that the rural churches were centered on the local scene, with little or no tie, at times, to the episcopal, urban church. The tie of the local Church and its leader, the priest, was with the lord of the land, rather than with the bishop. This centering of loyalty must be understood if one wishes to grasp the meaning of ministry in this early medieval period.

At the turn of the seventh to eighth centuries, ecclesiastical properties were secularized on a large scale throughout the West. This meant that many ecclesiastical Churches came under the control of the lords, moving them away from episcopal control. Moreover, even the urban, baptismal churches, which remained ecclesiastically under the bishop, were often administered by lay people. To prevent this from happening in a total way, the bishops themselves began to utilize the structure of the Frankish proprietary church, which they did not perceive clearly as also a Church structure, and which had in it the seeds of alienating the priest from episcopal jurisdiction. Moreover, many monasteries in Europe did exactly the same thing, placing the monastery under the sovereignty of the local lord. Eventually, there was scarcely a church in the Frankish kingdom which did not have a lay or religious (acting in the capacity of a local lord) proprietor. Such popes as Eugene II and Leo IV protested, as also some bishops, but we find documented the increasing success of the Frankish proprietary Church structure, e.g. in the ecclesiastical capitularies of Louis the Pious (818–819).

> The filling of prelacies by the ruler had been an essential element in the administration of the Frankish Church since the sixth century. Most sees formally possessed the right to elect their bishops, whereas the abbots of the monasteries were in most cases determined by the founder or lord of the proprietary church. But the discrepancy between practice and law was here especially strong. In 818–819 Louis the Pious granted the right of election to all sees and to imperial monasteries of the ordo regularis, but he retained the right to confirm and invest, which involved a review of the election.[15]

A proprietary church was a product of property law. "It [the church building] was reduced to juridical form by virtue of the stone altar firmly connected with the earth. For the church building and its equipment, rectory and cemetery, the landed property donated to the church with its peasants, the income from the tithe, offerings and stole fees, in short whatever the altar attracted around itself belonged to it as its appurtenances and was, like the altar itself, the property of the landlord."[16] Charles the Great decreed that such property must stay within the Church's sphere, and of course, such property was meant to serve the Christian community. This was its primary function. Still, there was at times surplus income generated from such properties, and the danger of exploiting these properties was all too real.

To carry out the function of the property, a priest was needed, just as a mill needed a miller, but it was no longer the bishop who appointed the priest, but the proprietor, the lay person. The priest selected would naturally be in favor of the proprietor, and often the man was selected from among the proprietor's serfs themselves, and conditions for his tenure as priest were laid down by the proprietor, so that the maximum amount of income could be generated from the estate. Clearly, such conditions were often made to the abasement of the priest. These proprietary rights could be sold, willed as part of an inheritance, and even rights over certain aspects could be separated from rights over other aspects and given, in some way or another, to various owners.[17] From the beginning, the proprietary Church was doomed for problems, and it eventually did require a major reform to change the situation. But in the seventh century down to the eleventh and twelfth centuries (when the major reforms were in progress), the situation of the proprietary church was quite general throughout the Frankish kingdom and affected the structuring of Western Church ministry in a dramatic way.

As one can see, the presbyter was really beholden to the lay proprietor, not to the bishop. In this way, the bishops lost a great deal of control over these various churches, and since they, too, went along with this Frankish proprietary law, they also willingly gave up their control over such churches. Removed to some degree from the bishop, the priest liturgically, administratively, educationally became for all practical purposes the major spiritual leader of the local community. The local parish became the real focus of Church life, not the diocese, nor the urban baptismal Church with its station churches or satellite rural churches. Already in the Merovingian period, parishes were a normal part of Church life, but even at that early date, parish priests became independent of bishops. Lay owners began to establish rural parishes and determine who would be the local priest. Dalton notes: "The position of the country parson with regard to the parish somewhat resembled that of the bishop to the diocese."[18]

In the Frankish world, the priest's appointment was made not through the bishop but through the proprietor. Naturally, ordination came through the bishop, but not the appointment. The spiritual activity of the parish rose and fell, depending on the quality of the appointed priest. Since the proprietor, for monetary reasons, had a vested interest in this church property, he was not interested in appointing incapable caretakers, but in many instances it was not the spiritual caretaking which was of prime importance. Moreover, the proprietor could count on the loyalty of the priest, whom he had appointed, and who also, therefore, lived in economic dependence on the proprietor, and this, too, helped to insure the fidelity of the people to whom the priest ministered. Such a localization of church life created a climate of liturgical pluralism and at times theological pluralism as well, but it gave a prominence to the presbyter in the structuring of Church ministry, which the ordinary priest had not had prior to this.

We find at the end of the ninth century several books which deal with the duties and qualifications of such priests: *De synodalibus causis* by Regino of Pruem; *Admonitio synodalis,* also called *Homilia Leonis.* These offer us an insight into the kind of person who was, at that time, ordained to the priestly ministry, and who therefore represented the Church to the local Christian community. Jungmann summarizes the duties of the priests at that time as follows:

> Duties to which the priests were referred concerned the integrity of the parish property, the condition of the buildings, and the cleanliness of the church, which was not to be used as a granary, the neatness and care of vestments and vessels, the atrium of the church had to be inclosed, and women's dances were not permitted there. The pyx, with the Blessed Sacrament, lay on the table-shaped altar for the communion of the sick. Otherwise, only the four Gospels and, in contrast to the custom of previous centuries, relics of saints in a worthy setting were also on the altar.[19]

The priest rose early to celebrate Lauds, but one also begins to hear of Prime, Terce, Sext and None, in some of the sources. At Terce the priest celebrated Mass, and hopefully there was a cleric at hand to respond and read the epistle. The priest fasted until noon, and then again celebrated Mass, this time for pilgrims. On Sundays, the parishioners were required to attend Lauds, Sunday Mass and Vespers.

Books which the priest should have were: the sacramentary (missal), the lectionary, the antiphonary, the homiliary, a correct explanation of the creed and the Lord's prayer, a martyrology, and perhaps the forty homilies of Gregory the Great. The priest's homilies, given the fact that he had access to such a small library, were obviously most simple. The sacrament of reconciliation was increasingly that of the Celtic form, not the Roman form. Tarrif penance began to come in vogue, so that the possibility of "bribery" was also lurking in the wings.

The priest's personal life of holiness was important. He was not to have a woman live with him; he was not to bear arms; he was not to engage in falcon hunting or hunting with dogs; he was not to visit taverns; he should avoid attending wedding celebrations; he should wear clerical dress at all times. Interestingly, one of the motives for wearing such clerical dress was this: were he to die without his stole, only the customary *Wergeld* was to be paid for him, but if he died with his stole on, he would receive the normal, triple *Wergeld.*

The books, from which we gather this kind of material, outlined the form of priestly ministry which was presented as the "ideal," not the actual. Practice undoubtedly lagged behind. Nonetheless, it is evident that the priestly ministry centered around the Mass and the sacraments. In these books the priest was primarily a liturgical person, and both the Church and the state were behind this structure of ministry. This centering of priesthood on the liturgy, especially the eucharist, will play a major role in the theologizing on priestly ministry in the scholastic period. In this ministerial framework, it was the presbyter who acted as the main priestly figure for the Christian community, and it was more specifically the presbyter at the eucharist who was seen as the priestly one.

From our knowledge of what will transpire in the high scholastic period, we can see that many steps have been taken:

1. The priest has become in many ways independent of the bishop.
2. The priest and the parish have become the focus of Church life.
3. In this Church life, it is the Mass above all, but also the other sacraments, which have become paramount.

It is no wonder, then, that in the high scholastic period, the priest, not the bishop, will be seen as *sacerdos,* indeed, as the highest order in Holy Orders. Moreover, it will be the priest's role with the eucharist that centers the theology of ministry in the scholastic period and from then on in the Western Church until Vatican II. The rootage of this scholastic theology on priestly ministry goes back to this Frankish structuring of Church ministry, and once this practice was theologized by the scholastic theologians, it became the main approach to priestly practice and theology for about seven hundred years.

Let us turn, for the moment, to the bishop during this same period. In the Italian-influenced world, episcopal structures, which had developed in the patristic period, were still very much in force. In this world, the bishop played a continuing role, since he was in charge of the baptismal church and all those satellite churches under him. Cathedral chapters gradually came to the fore, and eventually those priests who belonged to these chapters were called "canons." On the other hand, however, priests who were administering pro-prietary churches were not called canons, while all those priests on the bishop's list (canon) were called canons, since these latter belonged under his jurisdiction. But as time went on, the term canon was re-served only for those priests who were connected to the cathedral chapters.[20] This distinction between those on the bishop's list (canon) and those not on the list is still another indication of the Frankish structuring of ministry.

Canons had a great deal of influence over the administration of a diocese, and a variety of positions began to unfold: the archdeacon was the most important, then the praepositus, and finally the dean of the cathedral. In time, the dean assumed almost all the responsibilities for the administration of the cathedral, and the archdeacon rose in power so that he rivaled the bishop himself. A canon, called *cantor,* took care of the liturgy, but he was aided by the *thesaurarius* and the *sacrista.* The praepositus was assisted by the *camerarius* and the *cellararius.* In many instances, these canons led a sort of collegial life. Support for them came from the cathedral, with a portion of the cathedral income going directly to the bishop (*mensa episcopalis*), and a portion going directly to the chapter. Sometimes a portion was set aside for the royal service. The chapter portion used its share partly for the group of canons as a group, and partly for each of the individual canons, allotting an amount according to rank.[21] Because of all of this, the position of a canon was sought after.

The nobility found the structure of the chapter and its canons of great value, and many a noble son was to be found among the canons. This insured both a place for the son, and some control over the Church as well. The upward mobility of the canons also meant that sons of nobility might become bishops themselves. In all of this, the bishops lost a certain share of direct control in the dispensing of churches and clergy, for the state had its own voices in these matters as well. Many canons from noble families enjoyed their own private income besides that of the cathedral income, and the bishop was again somewhat excluded from control over them. Such canons were in large degree economically independent of the bishop. Liturgically, bishops continued to ordain, confirm and, on special occasions, baptize. Bishops prepared the holy oils and consecrated churches, altars and sacred vessels. Besides these liturgical tasks, bishops were charged with clergy-education, a rather formidable task for that day and age. Bishops established holy days, the times for fasting, tithing responsibilities, and other such administrative tasks. The poor, the orphans, the widows fell under the bishop's care, although on many occasions these were tasks he delegated to someone else. Of great significance for a number of issues in Church life, the bishops began to take on the duties of an ecclesiastical judge. Synods were to be held on a regular basis, with the bishop overseeing many aspects of the larger diocesan church. In all of this, the earlier model of the monarchical bishop is evident: the bishop, in his diocese, was fairly autonomous and supreme, even though, through the intrusion of the state, an erosion of his jurisdiction can be seen. However, it is also clear that as the bishop became more and more an administrative person, he was not the dominant liturgical person, except on major occasions. This preoccupation with administration contributed to the significance of the priest as the major liturgical person in Church ministry.[22]

The Gallican bishops from Merovingian times on had not been too open to Roman or papal claims of power. These bishops handled affairs of the Church quite by themselves, at least for the most part. In 833, for instance, when Pope Gregory IV appeared in Gaul itself just prior to the deposition of Louis the Pious, the Gallican bishops notified Gregory that he had no right to interfere in their dioceses, and "that if he came to excommunicate, he should return excommunicated himself."[23] In the aftermath of Louis the Pious' deposition, his restoration, and the division of his empire between Lothar and Charles, kings deposed bishops and archbishops and they gained support from bishops and archbishops. The influence of the crown in Church ministry was not stopped, but rather increased. Louis' son, Charles, had himself anointed emperor at Orleans in 848 by the archbishop of Sens and in 869 there was a second anointing at Metz by the archbishop of Riez. The Carolingian notion of Empire and State acquired a profound expression in the rich symbolism of the coronation ritual. Hincmar of Reims drew up this ritual and give it its definitive form in the coronation ordo of 877. According to Schramm, "The King was thereafter a christus Domini, separated from the laity, anointed like a priest."[24] This commingling of the Church and the crown went from emperor to bishop to priest, and it was precisely this kind of commingling, with all its undesirable wake, that eventually demanded reform.

It is evident that at this same period of time (700–900) there had developed really two opposite forms of priestly ministry: one under the monarchical bishop, which followed the traditional pattern rather strongly; the other in which the priest was quite independent of the bishop, but not independent of the proprietor. Inevitably a clash of such two diverse ministerial models had to occur. In this struggle for some sort of supremacy between these two models, the Frankish structure won out and became the standard approach for priestly ministry. Even the Roman form of Church structure became involved in this Frankish proprietary form. In the ninth century the situation of many cathedral churches and many monasteries showed such signs of this proprietary structure that a reform was needed. Kempf lists four causes for this ninth century malaise: secularizing usurpation by rulers, squandering of the property by lay abbots, lack of protection because of a growing weakness in the royal power, and the devastation wrought by the Vikings.[25] The influence of rulers and royalty is quite clear in this assessment. It is, of course, the reform of Cluny and the Gregorian reforms which put an end to many of these problems.

Unfortunately, an overarching term has gained great favor in historical writings which covers this Frankish structuring together with its many implications: namely, "lay investiture." This term, lay investiture, with all its own implications seems to say that the problem is to be found with the involvement of the lay person in hierarchical matters. The lay person in the Church is thereby seen as the villain, which is certainly not the case. Lay involvement in selection of local bishops had been commonplace long before the Frankish Church structuring movement took place, and often with very beneficial results. It is by no means the "lay" involvement per se which caused the problems; rather, it is the involvement of such factors as greed, political power, and self-interest which caused the problems. Even if there had not been this so-called lay-investiture movement, the hierarchy itself was not immune to greed, political power and self-interest. Moreover, the involvement of the "lay" person was limited to a minute group: namely, a few nobility who found feudal appointment either to the local parish Church or to the cathedral chapter an opportunity to enrich themselves (greed), to enhance their prestige (political power), or to move upward personally (self-interest). It would seem that the term "lay investiture" is not the most felicitous nor the most perceptive.

The cluniac reform attempted to gain exemption from local bishops and from local lords, placing monasteries directly under the pope. This desire for exemption as a major part of reform was not part of the Lotharingian or German monastic reform movements. Exemption alone cannot be seen as a guaranteed preservation from decadence. Of more importance was the priory system developed by Cluny, which brought sundry monasteries under an abbatial dependence. The cluniac reform, however, did lay the foundation for the subsequent Gregorian reform: namely, by the insistence from Abbot Odo onward of a papal connection.

Gregory and his reform (1073–1085) mark the real end of the Frankish structuring of ministry, at least in any overwhelming way. For Gregory there were the two orders: regnum et sacerdotium, but sacerdotium was higher than regnum. Hincmar's approach was certainly not that of Gregory. Nor was there any doubt in Gregory's mind who ought to decide the areas of distinction in these two realms:

> One alone could, in his view, claim to be the proper interpreter of the divine will—Peter's vicar in Rome. For Christ, who gave Peter supreme authority and bade him establish the Roman Church, prayed for Peter's faith so that the Roman Church cannot err, and Peter lives on by entering, as Gregory firmly believed, into a sort of personal union with every successor and elevating him, by virtue of his own merits, to a better and holier being. Hence all Christians must obey the Pope, who is responsible for their salvation, and under his leadership fight for the Kingdom of God, not only priests and monks who are subject to his superepiscopal authority, but also secular rulers.[26]

This is a forceful statement of Gregory's vision. It clearly is not that of the Frankish empire. This leads us, of course, to our third consideration.

3. THE PAPAL STRUCTURING OF MINISTRY

From the time of Gregory the Great (d. 604) the hegemony of the Pope became more and more important. Indeed, Gregory is called the last of the Fathers of the Church and in many ways the first of the popes. In some degree there is a truth to this statement. As the Church had become more and more a part of the Roman society in the early and high patristic period, the local episkopos began to take on more and more a strengthened social position. Then, as the Roman leadership, throughout many areas of the empire, lost its foothold, the total regional leadership was often picked up, for all practical purposes, by the local episkopos, once again strengthening the social position of the bishop. In each of these two instances, the strengthening of the episkopos was a strengthening of the Church structure. So, too, in the case of the papacy, the strengthening of papal power was a strengthening of a practical system of Church government, and in the West this strengthening of the papal power took place at the very time when the Byzantine emperor was losing a foothold in the West.

As the episkopos became more and more the leader of the Church, and in some instances the political leader as well, so, too, did theologians develop a basis or rationale for such leadership. We saw this tendency to provide a theological base for some given Church situation in Cyprian, who called the apostles "episkopoi"—a stance which no one prior to Cyprian had done. This, of course, heightened the theological importance of the episkopos of Cyprian's time. Moreover, we saw this same tendency in the *Didascalia Apostolorum,* whose author calls the episkopos one who stands in the very place of God. This theologizing clearly enhanced the position of the episkopos. We now see this theologizing tendency in the case of the pope. Although Leo I had done much to establish the contours of the papal office in practice and in an administrative way, it was really Gregory who gave it a "doctrinal base." Gregory writes:

> To all who know the Gospel it is obvious that by the voice of the Lord the care of the entire church was committed to the holy apostle and prince of all the apostles, Peter. . . . Behold, he received the keys of the kingdom of heaven, the power to bind and loose was given to him, and the care and principality of the entire church was committed to him. . . . Am I defending my

own cause in this matter? Am I vindicating some special injury
of my own? Is it not rather the cause of Almighty God, the cause
of the universal church? . . . And we certainly know that many
priests of the church of Constantinople have fallen into the whirl-
pool of heresy and have become not only heretics but heresiarchs.
. . . Certainly, in honor of Peter, the prince of the apostles, [the
title "universal"] was offered to the Roman pontiff by the venerable Council of Chalcedon.[27]

These and many other texts from the writings of Gregory do not
intend to say that Gregory was trying to exalt Peter among the twelve,
so much as to say that Gregory wanted to exalt the bishop of Rome
among all other bishops at the end of the sixth century. For Gregory,
Rome was the focus for truth and orthodoxy. *Rome* was the great
defender of tradition. *Rome* was the central agency to resolve disputed
ecclesiastical matters. In all of this, *Rome,* therefore, was the very
touchstone for obedience to God himself.

As Pelikan comes to end his first volume on Christian tradition,
in which he draws his historical research at the end of the sixth century
around the issue of catholic orthodoxy, he notes that after Gregory
"the fundamental assumption underlying almost all the doctrinal treatises and biblical commentaries of Western theologians was the teaching authority of the bishop of Rome."[28] How one limited this authority
was often debated; but the fact of the authority was not debated.

Nonetheless, all scholars agree that this Roman issue was at that
time a very complex situation. The seventh century, 600–700, was a
veritable turning point for the Church, both East and West, for it was
during this time that the Arab nations advanced into the West. E.
Ewig notes, however, that during this seventh century the Church was
really not yet an East/West dichotomy. Conceptually, the Church and
the empire were still united and politically there was still much validity
to the term "one empire."[29] Even though there had been conflicts and
language barriers, the union of the Church and the empire was still
a spiritual reality. The popes, indeed, did become the spokesmen of
Italy, but at the same time they spoke for a religious and ecclesiastical
group which "still saw the Empire as a unity." Greek influence was
perhaps at its highest, when there was a restoration of peace in the
Church in 681, and between 678 and 752 eleven of the thirteen popes
were Sicilians, Greeks or Syrians. Eastern influence brought into the

universal Church the feasts of the Exaltation of the Holy Cross and the Marian feasts of purification, annunciation, assumption, and birth. The *Monasteria Diaconiae* involved Greek and oriental liturgical practices and became centers of advice for many popes.

Still, a breakdown of East/West relations was in the air. Pope Constantine, in 710, went to Constantinople to converse with Justinian II, but it was the last of such visits of a pope to an emperor. Subsequently, the West defied an imperial edict, attempting to arrest Martin I, and Philippicus Bardanes (711–713) was not recognized as the emperor by the West due to the influence of the Pope. This breakdown, internally, between East and West came at the very end of the seventh century and the beginning of the eighth century. By then, Latin Africa had come to a virtual end as a Christian area. Whatever Christian remnants lived on in North Africa lost all historical importance. On the heels of the fall of Christian North Africa, Spain became the target for Musa, the Muslim governor of Arab Africa, and it was not until 733 that Charles Martel finally turned the tide. Gregory II, writing to the emperor, Leo III, observed that the center of gravity of the Christian world is beginning to shift to the "inner West." This "inner West," bastion of the once wide-flung Christian world, will play an influential role in the way that the popes and the clergy generally come to think of Christianity, at least in the West.

There is no doubt that historically the strengthening of papal power, which made revolutionary strides in this early medieval Church period, affected the structuring of Church ministry in the West. The bishops in the latter part of our historical period were more and more centered around the pope, whereas in the preceding centuries, when the papal power was not so geographically strong, the bishops were more centered in a collegial way with one another. As the pope became a more dominant force in the Western Church and in the Western world, this collegiality of the bishops lost its importance, an importance which we noted at the time of Cyprian, of Augustine, of Basil and of Cyril of Alexandria. This restructuring of episcopal ministry, due to the influence of the pope in local dioceses and regions, leads directly to the theological position in the scholastic period that the bishops were not the apex of the priesthood, but only a position of jurisdiction and dignity.

However, this new situation came about gradually. In the West, between 600 and 1000, the papacy began to exert more and more a *universal* jurisdiction, which practically it had not exercised before. Nonetheless, one must also recall that it was during this same time that the papacy reached its lowest mark ever, both morally and politically. In some respects, then, it is not surprising that in an effort to regain moral and political stature, after the low point of papal power, there would be an increasing jurisdictional activity on the part of the papacy, not only in Rome and Italy, but also throughout the West.

The Western episcopal structure eased this growth of papal power, for although the East had developed a "metropolitan" form of administration within the Church, so that one bishop was the metropolitan bishop over a number of other bishops, this form had not developed to any great degree in the West. At best, the metropolitan bishop was, in the West, simply a chairman of the meeting. Metropolitan synods did establish new dioceses, did institute new bishops and depose unworthy ones, but as time went by recourse to Rome in all these cases—i.e., establishing a new diocese, creating a new bishop, deposing an unworthy one—became more frequent, and this recourse to Rome eventually undermined any authority these metropolitan synods might have had. One also finds that Rome encouraged this recourse to itself, so that one cannot say that this was simply a matter of regular legal procedure. This encouragement was in many respects designed to enhance the papal position.[30]

The state, however, found metropolitan synods and imperial synods, at times, very beneficial as a means to enhance the unity of the empire, and gradually the state began to play more and more a role in the election of new bishops, and even at times the local people played a role in such elections. The distinction between election on the one hand and ordination on the other remained constant. Only the bishop ordained, but the state gained a great deal of control in the election process, i.e., in selecting those whom the bishop would consequently ordain. Provincial synods, as one can well imagine, came to have little or no influence at all in this process and were gradually eliminated from the ecclesiastical scene.

Rome also came into the local dioceses by way of the pallium. The pallium was offered to an archbishop (the Western successor to metropolitans) by the pope. It was, at first, a liturgical gesture, having its origins in the Byzantine court ceremonials. The pope, in imitation of this Byzantine court ceremonial, presented the pallium as a special mark of favor; originally, there was no jurisdictional connection with

it. As time went by, however, Rome began to require the newly consecrated archbishop to ask for the pallium within three months of his
consecration. Thus, a new step was taken: the pallium was now a
confirmation by Rome both of the episcopal consecration and of the
appointment. Jungmann states the case quite concisely: The new
bishop "was neither to officiate at the consecration of suffragans nor
to occupy the throne" until he had received the pallium.[31]

Later on, other jurisdictional privileges and rights were attached
to the giving of the pallium: one could have the cross carried ahead
of him; one could ride a horse adorned in red; one could decide urgent
cases which otherwise should have been decided by Rome. The pallium
made the archbishop more and more into an agent of the pope. Indeed,
the archbishop shared to some degree in the primacy of the pope.

The pope, too, was developing his position. In spite of all the
vicissitudes of the bishop of Rome, it was precisely his position in the
papal states which helped in many ways to keep his jurisdiction alive.
From the Byzantine empire the bishop of Rome had gained a certain
status as the Western representative of the empire. As East and West
separated, the bishop of Rome retained this political prestige, which
in fact he really never abandoned. Separated from Constantinople
politically, the bishop of Rome became "autonomous," and one of
the major symbols of this autonomy is the tiara. Sergius III (d. 911)
is portrayed wearing the tiara, but he is clearly not the first pope to
do so. But what is so important about the tiara? It must be remembered
that the emperor of the Byzantine empire had worn a tiara, signifying
that he was autonomous; in the West, the papal states became the
remnant of that autonomous Byzantine rule, and the ruler of the papal
states was the surviving ruler in the West of this Byzantine remnant.
The wearing of the tiara, of course, signified imperial power, an imperial power over the papal states and more importantly an imperial
power over the spiritual realm of the Church.

On the issue of appeal from a diocese to Rome, we find during
this period of Church history many instances when an appeal was
made from the bishop's court to the papal court—even in the middle
of the proceedings. Again, Rome did not refuse such appeals, even
though bishops again and again, but vainly, attempted to curtail such
appeals or at least not to allow them until the case had run its course
in the episcopal courts themselves. Nonetheless, cleric and lay alike
jettisoned episcopal procedures and powers by going directly to Rome.

Such an openness on the Roman side could not help but curtail episcopal prestige and jurisdiction, but even more it allowed papal authority to penetrate more and more, in a direct way, into the local spheres, and this penetration was, at a later age, interpreted officially as a matter of jurisdiction.

It is difficult to generalize on the issue of papal power over the lengthy period of four hundred years: 600 to 1000. Gregory I (590–604) was a dominant figure. His two immediate successors, Sabinian and Boniface III, were popes for too short a time to have any lasting influence. Boniface IV (608–615) became entangled in the *Tria Capitalia* dispute and due to poor information mishandled the Roman side of the issue. Boniface V (619–625) corresponded with Bishop Laurentius, the successor of St. Augustine of Canterbury, and also with Bishkop Mellitus of London. King Eadbald himself even wrote to Boniface.[32] This indicates some extension of papal power into England but it was not in any way overbearing. Vitalian (657–672) had the longest reign of any pope in the seventh century, but he fought with the emperor, Constans II, over the Church at Ravenna, and struggled with the succession at Canterbury after the Synod of Whitby. Vitalian agreed on Theodore of Tarsus, a monk who had studied at Athens, but he was sent with the pope's instruction that Theodore "introduce no Greek customs contrary to the true Faith."

As mentioned previously, from 678 to 752, eleven of the thirteen popes were Sicilians, Greeks or Syrians, a detail which indicates the Eastern influence on the Roman see. Still, it was in this eighth century that we have the beginnings of the so-called papal states: a geographical area which involved Rome, Ravenna, Spoleto and Benevento.[34] Eventually, the rise or decline of the papal states, threatened by the Lombard "sword of Damocles," required the intervention of Pepin, Charles and Carloman, as well as the emperor in Constantinople. This political Western base gave a decided edge to papal power in the centuries which followed. Stephen III (768–772) tried to assuage the Lombard king, Desiderius, but his pontificate ended in dismal failure. Carloman died in 771, and Charles became the sole leader of the Frankish kingdom. Hadrian I (772–795) opted for Charles against the Lombards. With Charles the Great in the West and a strong pope, Hadrian, in Rome, one sees that the West, with the Frankish kingdom and the papal states, truly becomes "the inner West." With the arrival of Charles at Rome, his baptism, the *promissio* of the papal states, a new era began. No longer did the emperor's name and regnal years appear on documents and coins; from now on it was the papal name and image. With Charles' backing, from 774 onward, the papal states had seceded from the empire, and the pope became a sovereign ruler. The tie of the papacy with the East has been politically severed; a political and economic base has been established in the West for the papacy; mutual allegiancies and dependencies have been established between the pope and the Frankish king. A geographical, economical, political sub-structure for papal power in the West has been formed. This basis, as well as the spiritual base, provides the pope with access into the regional areas of the Church which he had not had before.

The fusion of Western empire and the Church reached a major peak in the Synod of Paris convoked at Paris in 829 by Louis the Pious. Jonas of Orleans drew up the acts, and in this synod an inclusion of the Church into the empire and the empire into the Church was documented.[35] For the papacy the climax occurred in the ninth century under Nicholas I (858–867), Hadrian II (867–872) and John VIII (872–882), but even under John the papacy began to enter a time of severe degradation. The popes who followed John were weak, greedy, ineffectual. Formosus, above all, made a mockery of papal spiritual power. In the first half of the tenth century the papacy was under the control of the lay leaders in Rome: Theophylact and then Marozia, his daughter, followed Alberic of Spoleto. The German emperors, the Ottos, strengthened both their position and that of the papacy. In fact, Otto III made his home in Rome. Remarkably, around 1000, the emperor and the pope enjoyed an exalted position in the Christian West, but it rested on a fragile foundation.[36] In spite of the ups and downs of the various popes, the intervention of the papacy in the world of politics and in regional matters, even at the instigation of the state, had continued throughout this period. Emperors and other lords found often that a papal connection enhanced their own positions. Similar in many ways to other Western bishops, the bishop of Rome himself came under the dominance of the feudal lords. This had two effects: first, it gave, on many occasions, a wider political, economic and spiritual base to the pope, and, second, this very extension of papal presence tended to lessen the prestige of regional episcopal collegiality. Bishops were important, of course, but often because of their connections with the pope or with the Western emperor; they were not important because of their collegial nature.

The state contributed its share in the changes of episcopal ministry. More and more bishops were from families of the nobility and related to the state by blood. They were in many cases, because of these ties, civil leaders as well as Church leaders, possessing a fiefdom of their own. In a given area they might even be the highest ecclesiastical and at the same time political leader. State officials were not reluctant to call on bishops to act as judges in civil matters, since, after all, the bishops were, for that age, some of the most learned people about. Of particular concern were complex marriage cases, which involved nobility (and which therefore involved landed estates, wealth, rights of succession, etc.). The bishops were not reluctant to enter into these judicial matters. A study of the history of the sacrament of marriage would, of course, be the locus where this is spelled out in detail; but let us simply mention this involvement into the marriage situation as one of the juridical concerns which took up a bishop's time and energy. In doing so, however, the bishop had to delegate more and more his local or regional spiritual and pastoral tasks to others, namely to priests. The bishop was still needed for ordinations and, as time went on, for confirmation, as well as for the blessing of oil and other episcopal tasks, but the daily pastoral care and spiritual education of the people were left to the priest. Once more, we find a reason why high scholasticism will find the apex of sacerdos in the priest, not in the bishop. Nor, one might add, did scholastic theology of the priesthood claim that the pope was the highest priest. In fact, many of the scholastic theologians said that the pope as a priest was at the very same level as the ordinary presbyter. *Qua* priest, pope and presbyter were the same.

Let us pause a moment and gather together the various steps which our argument has taken, regarding the historical basis for the eventual Western theology of ministry. These various steps might be formulated as follows:

1. An orthodox consensus had developed both in the East and in the West, and this consensus was by its very nature traditional.

2. Part of this tradition was the acceptance of the Church of the true Fathers. Such a Church had a definite hierarchical form: the bishop was the highest in this hierarchy, then the priest, then the deacon, and then sundry other minor orders. There was, at this period of Church history, no dispute about either the naming or the functions of these ministers.

3. Since the heritage of the great Fathers was considered to be of apostolic origin, hierarchical orders were also considered "apostolic" in origin. The theologians of this time, of course, did not have the historical data regarding the rise of the naming and function of Christian ministers which we have today. For them the kind of ministry which had taken root in the universal Church was simply considered, by and large, to be the way it was *ab initio* (from the beginning).

4. The functions of the bishop, priest and deacon had been fairly well defined. This included the sacramental functions of the presbyters in which the presbyters from the fifth century onward had begun to engage due to the growth of the rural areas of the Christian community.

5. There was as well a "theology of ministry" which had gained almost universal acceptance. This theology of ministry was influenced in great part by three important figures: Gregory of Nazianz, John Chrysostom and Dionysius the Areopagite.

6. The Christian world was still coterminous with the empire, and the Church and the empire were spiritually, and in many ways politically, one. Only in the late seventh and first half of the eighth century did this spiritual and political unity begin to fall apart.

7. At the end of the seventh century, with the loss of the Christian world in North Africa as well as major parts of Spain, together with areas around Constantinople, a shift in the center of gravity took place, namely, toward the inner West. However, one can not yet speak even at this date of a clear division in the Church between East and West.

8. The central figure in the East, the emperor, beleaguered by the iconoclastic strife internally and by the threat of Islam externally, lost a great deal of his power, and consequently the central figure in the West, the pope, became more and more important, not only in Rome and Italy, but also in a wider geographical sphere. He became in many ways the universal bishop. Moreover, the political situation of that period greatly enhanced his growing position of hegemony and strength.

9. One finds, however, another side of this picture: namely, that with the growth of the papal hegemony, episcopal collegial leadership in the West declined. The mounting papal monopoly in the West diminished, not only practically but also theologically, episcopal collegiality.

10. In the East, on the contrary, episcopal collegiality continued to be the model of Church leadership at its highest level, but as national

linguistic groupings became more and more prominent, the episcopal collegiality formed itself along these linguistic and ethnic lines and a breakup of Eastern episcopal collegiality also took place.

4. OTHER FACTORS BEARING ON THE ISSUE OF ORDAINED MINISTRY

Lest the three issues mentioned above appear exclusive, let us consider a few other factors which eventually led to the scholastic theological position on the priesthood. These additional factors did not play as powerful a role in the exclusion of the bishop from a theology of holy order, but they were still highly influential.

The *lex orandi, lex credendi* (the rule of prayer establishes the rule of faith) continued to play a major role in the theologizing on ministry and especially on priesthood. With the rise of monasticism in this period of the early middle ages, devotional piety of the people took on a monastic structure. The full canonical hours went from the monasteries into the local Churches. In the Byzantine period, diocesan priests were held to Lauds and Vespers, to be celebrated with the people. But in 747, for instance, at the Synod of Cloveshoe in England, influenced by St. Boniface, all churches were required to celebrate all the hours. In 816, the Synod of Aachen reiterated the same procedure.[37] The priest was clearly to be a man of prayer, but a prayer life that was typically monastic.

Prayer books begin to make their appearance in the ninth century, and devotion to the holy cross, to the Trinity, to each of the Three Persons, to saints, can be found in these books. Jesus is still the Lord, of course, and the crucifix is portrayed with angels and other symbols of victory and glory. His humanity, however, is not stressed; his divinity, his otherness, is stressed. Otherness of religion becomes dominant, and heaven will be a magnificent monastery in which all will be perfect monks and nuns. Jesus, too, is seen as the "perfect monk." The priest is encouraged to imitate Jesus and himself be a "perfect monk."

With this kind of devotional material, it was inevitable that clergy and lay became more and more separated. Clerical life moves even further away from the borders of ordinary lay life. The liturgy of the eucharist indicates this: for the first time we find incensations, a procession with the gospel book, intricate chants which only trained clergy could sing. The eucharistic canon was prayed totally in silence, theologically justified by allusions to the Old Testament in which the priest entered alone into the Holy of Holies. At first the kiss of peace had been highly encouraged and given to all; gradually, it was restricted only to communicants, so that the image might be one of gift from the altar (clergy) to the people. When one notes that a number of ninth century synods attempted to require communion by all Christians at least on Christmas, Easter and Pentecost, it is evident that lay people did not receive communion even this infrequently. If this was so, then the kiss of peace was rarely given as well.

From Germanic tradition, people prayed with their hands folded, whereas the Byzantine stance of prayer was the lifting up of the hands. Interestingly, then, the lay people fold their hands to pray, while the priest lifts his in the style of the Byzantine *orans,* another symbolic different:ation of lay and cleric. From Germanic custom comes the custom of the newly-ordained placing his hands into those of the bishop and promising obedience just as the vassal had done to the liege lord. Latin became incomprehensible to the lay people, and the liturgy gradually lost its ability to "speak" to them. In the East, on the other hand, Cyril and Methodius had made abundant use of vernacular languages, but in the West the eucharist was to be celebrated only in the three languages in the inscription on the cross of Jesus: Greek, Latin and Hebrew. The altar, too, was at this time moved from the area of the people to the back wall of the church, where formerly the bishop's cathedra had been placed.

In the ninth century, the pure white bread came to be used for eucharist, and as this white bread became popular, communion was no longer given in the hand but on the tongue. Shortly after this, the consecrated cup was not given to the lay people at all. The mass itself was considered a synopsis of all salvation, with the Old Testament readings and antiphons in the first stage; then the gloria of the angels indicating the incarnation, and, in the eucharist proper, the death and resurrection of Jesus. But in all of this, the mass became the exclusive domain of the priest and clergy. Before, during and after mass, certain private prayers were enjoined on him, which gradually became part of the actual liturgy itself, such as the recitation of psalm 42 at the beginning of Mass, the prayer at the washing of the hands, the prayer at communion.

Monasteries became increasingly clerical, with a large number of priests celebrating votive masses for the special intentions of the people. This multiplicity of masses, above all private masses, affected the diocesan priest as well. Not until the Synod of Seligenstadt do we have a synodal decision to limit the number of masses to three per day, and only with Alexander II (d. 1073) do we have the limit of one mass per day for the rule. Such rules would not be part of synodal or papal statements, unless the opposite were occurring. Celebration of mass was the focus of priestly ministry.

The first eucharistic controversies in the Church, which took place at this time of Church history, played a role in an understanding of the priest. Officially, the Church backed the realist approach to the eucharist, the so-called Ambrosian approach, over the symbolical approach, the so-called Augustinian approach. That the priest touched the very body of Jesus when he touched the host was one of the issues stressed, particularly in the pious and popular discussions which emanated from the theological dialogues. Priestly hands and priestly words were, therefore, most sacred, and a priestly life must be closer to that of angels than to other men and women.

With this material, one has all the components for the scholastic theological synthesis on the sacrament of Holy Order: spiritually, the eucharist will dominate, but since the eucharist is the highest privilege and power of the presbyter, therefore the priest, not the bishop, is at the apex of priesthood. The bishop, therefore, qua bishop, can only be understood as an additional dignity, involving jurisdiction. Since it is seen only as a dignity or jurisdictional position, what is the source of that dignity or jurisdiction? The answer is clear: the pope. He confers the dignity (and therefore can take it away) and the jurisdiction (and therefore can revoke it). The bishop, *qua* bishop, is totally dependent on the papacy; he is, in all respects, except for his priesthood, an agent of the pope. As bishop, he has not received "episcopal power" from the apostles; "priestly power and grace" are conferred by Christ through the sacrament of ordination, and therefore there is an apostolic succession to priesthood, but not to "episcopacy," except through the successor of the prince of the apostles, the pope. The transformation of the episcopacy in the West is enormous, and the scholastics merely theorized on the practical situation of their day, in which the priest was supreme from the standpoint of ordination, the bishop from the standpoint of jurisdiction.

However, there remain some issues which do not fit well into this theological framework. With the separation of the East from the West, the West continued to honor the Eastern theological position on ministry. By and large, Eastern bishops were considered bishops in the fullest degree by the West, except for an allegiance to the pope. This means, however, that the Eastern bishops, and the theology of ministry which they evidence, is one in which the apex of the sacrament of Holy Order is not the priest, but the episkopos; that the bishop is fully bishop, without any connection to the pope. The West and the East do not completely mesh on theology of priesthood:

THE WEST	THE EAST
Priest is the highest priestly figure.	Bishop is the highest priestly figure.
Episcopacy is a dignity and a position of jurisdiction.	Episcopacy is a part of sacred order.
The bishop depends on the approval of Rome for both selection and consecration.	The episkopos does not depend on the pope.
The collegiality of the bishops is compromised by the papal supremacy.	The collegiality of the bishops remains strong, though split by ethnic division.

These two approaches are not totally unifiable, and it is noteworthy that the Roman Church has never spoken out against the Eastern approach, in spite of the fact that the Roman Church had, at least to some degree, a rather different approach to priestly ministry than the Eastern Churches. The fact that the bishops of the East in no way needed papal approval, and yet were and are fully bishops in the Christian community, offers some powerful insights into our contemporary understanding of episcopal ministry and the possible ramifications this East/West situation has for Western ecumenical discussion not only on episcopacy but also on priesthood. But we will look at this ecumenical aspect in a later chapter.

In all of this, the stage is set for the medieval or scholastic synthesis on priesthood which will subsequently dominate Western Church thinking down to Vatican II. Let us first, however, summarize our data-gathering:

5. SUMMARY

1. Prior to 450, the episkopos was considered, theologically and practically, as the fullness of priestly ministry, even though the exact phrase "fullness of priestly ministry" might not be the term used. Liturgically and administratively the episkopos was the central and dominant figure in the Church. By 1100 the presbyter was considered the fullness of the priesthood. This holds true only in the West, and theologically as a more or less common approach only from 1100.

2. Although the episkopos had been seen in the sacerdotium or Holy Order, by 1100 he is no longer, *qua* bishop, in Holy Order; from this time on the episcopacy is simply a title of honor and of jurisdiction in the thinking of most theologians and canonists. This holds true only in the West, and theologically as a more or less common approach only from 1100.

3. In the East, episkopos continued to be seen as the "fullness of the priesthood," and his connection to the sacrament of Order was never lost.

4. In the West, the priest, due to the Frankish rural situation, tended to become more and more independent of the bishop and more and more dependent on the proprietor. Ordination, however, by the bishop was never disputed nor lost sight of, but the election of the candidate for such priestly ordination was increasingly under the control of the lay proprietor.

5. The eucharist focused the priestly ministry in an ever-increasing way all through this early medieval period. The priest was different from all others in the Church, even including the deacon, because of his sacred "power" particularly as regards the celebration of the eucharist.

6. By 1100 the Celtic form of the sacrament of reconciliation had for all practical purposes supplanted the Roman system of reconciliation. In the Roman system, the bishop had been the prime liturgical figure; in the Celtic system, it was the priest. The usual minister of the sacrament of reconciliation, by 1100, was the priest.

7. In the patristic period, it was the episkopos who presided over the baptismal church. Early rural Churches were sat-

ellites of this central baptismal Church. Gradually, in the West, the rural Church was administered by the priest, and the priest became the usual minister of the sacrament of baptism.

8. Prior to 751, the beginning of the Carolingian reformation, anointing of the sick was administered by lay and clergy alike, with a clear preponderance for lay administration of this sacrament. By 1100 anointing was reserved to the priest (not even the deacon was allowed to anoint), since anointing involved the forgiveness of sins, which was a distinctive mark of the sacrament of Order: the power to forgive sin. Once more we see the clericalization of the sacraments during this period.

9. Similarly, prior to 751, marriage did not involve clergy, unless lay people asked for clergy participation. Marriage of clergy, prior to 751, did involve clerical participation. However, at the end of this period, by 1000, the ministry of the priest was necessary for the validity of marriage, at least in the majority of cases.

10. The ministry of confirmation and of Holy Orders was around 1000 considered the domain of the bishops, but both theologians and Church lawyers considered the priest as a minister of confirmation, if he were so delegated by the pope or at times by the bishop. In the East, the "confirmation" ritual remained as part of the baptismal ritual, and the priest was seen as the ordinary minister of confirmation.

11. A debate arose among the theologians and Church lawyers on the "power to ordain." It became quite an open question, and one finds in the fourteenth and fifteenth centuries priests ordaining to priesthood. This could only happen if the presbyter was seen as the apex of the priesthood.

12. In the latter part of this period of Church history the pope is seen to be more and more omni-competent, both theologically and jurisdictionally, on the diocesan and even local level. The pope could delegate powers directly: e.g., the power to confirm; the power to ordain to bishops other than the local bishop; the power to adjudicate cases; the power to intervene in diocesan cases. This intervention by the pope into the diocesan structures was not readily accepted. In other

words, in the West there was at this time no prevailing doctrine that the pope had supreme ordinary authority or supreme ordinary jurisdiction in local dioceses. The reform of Gregory VII will alter this prevailing doctrine in a decisive way.

13. Hand in hand with these developments is the movement which sees bishops and archbishops as an outreach of the bishop of Rome. In the patristic and early medieval periods there was a collegiality of bishops. The lateral relation to fellow bishops diminishes, however, as the vertical relation of the individual bishop to the pope takes on greater emphasis. In the East the collegiality of the bishops, at least within a linguistic and ethnic framework, continued to flourish.

Excursus on Minor Orders: An Historical Survey

Christian ministries, which have come to be known as minor orders, seem to have come into existence around 200 A.D. The early data for these minor orders is sketchy at best. However, in a very short time, these Christian ministries began to take on a very organized form.

In *De Praescriptione haereticorum* (41, 6), Tertullian mentions lectors: "Therefore, someone [among your heretical group] is an episkopos today and tomorrow another person is; today one is a deacon, and tomorrow he is a lector; today someone is a presbyter and tomorrow he is a lay person." In this passage, Tertullian is not advocating a mix-up of duties; rather, he is taking to task the heretics for creating this kind of a ministerial situation. In all other places, Tertullian mentions only: episkopos, presbyter, and deacon. Consequently, it seems unlikely that Tertullian considers the lector part of the "clerical state."

In almost the same period as that of Tertullian, Hippolytus in the *Apostolic Tradition* mentions lector and subdeacon, but this mention might be due to some later reworking of the text, to accommodate the *Apostolic Tradition* to the situation at the time of the re-editing.

The *Liber Pontificalis XXI,* which, of course, is a medieval document, notes that the order of subdeacon was begun by Pope Fabian, who was the episkopos of Rome from 236 to 250. There is no evidence for this at all.

The *Didascalia Apostolorum* mentions subdeacon and lector, but each is mentioned in only a single passing statement. "But if there be also a lector, let him too receive with the presbyters."[25] For the subdeacon we read: "So now the bishop also takes for himself from the people those whom he accounts and knows to be worthy of him and of his office, and appoints him presbyters as counsellors and assessors, and deacons and subdeacons, as many as he has need of in proportion to the ministry of the house."[27] Connolly states that it seems the subdeacon is no more than a servant of the deacon. The passage on the lector is disputed; Achelis believes that it is an addition of later date, while Connolly leans to an original statement. At any rate, the passages tell us little on the subject of these minor orders.

Pope Cornelius (251–253) in his letter to the episkopos, Fabius of Antioch, assembles a list of the ministers at Rome: there are one episkopos, forty-six presbyters, seven deacons, seven subdeacons, forty-two acolytes, fifty-two exorcists, lectors and porters. This listing is the oldest extant data on these various ministries.

Cyprian in his letters mentions subdeacons, acolytes, exorcists and lectors. The *Gesta apud Zenophilum,* a text from North Africa, mentions subdeacons, lectors, and fossores (those who bury the dead). Eusebius, in his *History of the Church,* mentions lectors and exorcists.

It is evident that minor orders began to appear in a variety of ways around the end of the third century and the beginning of the fourth century. No straightforward pattern is evident in these minor orders, and one might even question our titling of them as "orders." They were lesser ministries in the Church, that is true, but whether they might be designated at this early date as "orders" is not clearly evident.

Nonetheless, pastoral ministry was developing in a more complex fashion, and this complexity necessitated the proliferation of various, auxiliary ministries. The point that should be noted here is this: the pastoral needs of the local Churches were the bases for the development of such ministries. There was no established, centralized program for this kind of ministerial development: each local or regional Church provided for its own needs. This responding to local needs seems the better way to account for the diversity of these lesser ministries in this early Church period.

As one moves into the fourth and fifth centuries, a clearer picture of these minor ministries begins to take shape. Ott remarks that during this period there was still a great deal of difference, depending on locale. In many ways, these minor ministries, which in their beginnings seemed to shoot up with a great deal of strength, gradually lost their very meaning. The task of porters was frequently turned over to lay people from the fifth century onward. Even at an earlier date, namely from the fourth century onward, the office of lector was given to lay people, provided they could read publicly. Little by little, the presbyters took over the tasks of the exorcists.

At times, a child was already designated a lector, and only when he reached the age of thirty was he entrusted with the task of acolyte or subdeacon. After this, he became eligible for deacon or even presbyter. If one began as an adult, the first ministry often was that of lector or exorcist. After two years in such ministry, he was eligible to be an acolyte or subdeacon. Five years later he could become a deacon, and only then a presbyter or episkopos. It seems that Pope Liberius was, from youth onward, a lector, then deacon, then episkopos. Pope Damasus (366–384) and Pope Siricius (384–399) seem to have moved in the same way.

Pope Innocent I (402–417) refers to only four stages: lector, acolyte, deacon and sacerdos (presbyter and/or episkopos). Other references, but to a variety of stages, are found in the writings of Pope Zosimus (417–418) and Pope Gelasius I (492–496).

Set intervals, i.e., a movement from one ministry to the next, do not seem to have followed any established pattern. To go from deacon to pope (therefore episkopos) was frequent, with no ordination to presbyter. Ott mentions the following popes in this category: Liberius, Felix II, Damasus, Siricius, Eulalius, Leo I, Hilary, Felix II, Anastasius II, Symmachus, Hormisdas, Boniface, Agapitus, Vigilius, Gregory I, Sabinian, probably both Boniface III and Boniface IV as also John IV and John V. This listing of such popes spans a period of several hundred years, namely, from 352 to 686, and therefore must be seen as a fairly acceptable practice and not merely as an historical "quirk." This situation, also, indicates the prominence of the deacon, since only someone with a great deal of experience and visibility (in the cases above, a deacon) would be selected as pope (episkopos). It likewise indicates, at least in Rome, that the presbyter was not that visible and prominent a minister, at least in many cases. Nor is there any historical evidence that in this early period there was a "theology" of intervals, i.e., one did not have to move up a ladder of ministries.

In the Eastern Church, we find similarly a variety of such lesser ministries and again no set pattern of intervals or stages. Lectors, subdeacons, exorcists are referred to again and again, but we also find such lesser ministries as: singer (psaltes), hermeneut (translator), deaconess, kopiates (one who buries the dead). At the cathedral in Constantinople at the time of Justinian (527–565) a list indicates the following: sixty presbyters, one hundred deacons, forty deaconesses, ninety subdeacons, one hundred and ten lectors, twenty-five singers. These were part of the clerical state. There were also one hundred porters, but they were not considered part of the clerical state. The *Apostolic Constitutions* speaks of an ordination for the following ministries: bishop, priest, deacon, deaconess, subdeacon and lector.

At the end of the fifth century, the *Statuta Ecclesiae Antiqua,* which was a compilation of a number of more or less canonical documents of that time, offers a ranking of ministries, a description which eventually influenced the Western Church's program of intervals. We find in this document the following ministries which are clearly ranked in an ascending order: psalmist, porter, lector, exorcist, acolyte, subdeacon, deacon, presbyter, and finally bishop. One cannot, however, conclude that this ranking and naming was common throughout southern Gaul, the place of origin for this document. Other documents from the same time and place indicate variations. Still, in time, this listing, with the exception of psalmist, became the standard ranking and naming for the minor orders in the Western Church.

Isidore of Seville (d. 636), influenced by the *Statuta Ecclesiae Antiqua,* mentioned the following minor orders: porter, psalmist, lector, exorcist, acolyte, subdeacon, deacon, presbyter, bishop. Gratian utilized this list of Isidore in his *Decretals.* Hrabanus Maurus (d. 856) mentions eight ministries, as also Amalar of Metz (d. 850). Ivo of Chartres (d. 1072) mentions only seven: psalmist and bishop are omitted. Peter Damian, Hugh of St. Victor, and then Peter Lombard enumerate only seven. By the time of Peter Lombard, only seven orders are mentioned. Besides these theologians, the canonists also enumerate only seven orders: e.g., Rufinus and Sicard of Cremona. By 1150 one can say, then, that the clerical state begins with tonsure, followed by porter, lector, exorcist, acolyte, subdeacon, deacon and priest. These were the minor and major orders. Bishop, at this juncture of theological history, was not considered part of holy orders.

This brief overview on the issue of the minor ministries leads us to the following conclusions:

1. Minor ministries begin to show up in the Church, both in the East and the West from the latter part of the third century onward. At first, we have only the mention of certain minor

ministries; in the fourth century, the number of such ministries grows.

2. Not simply on an East/West basis, but in the East as well as in the West, there is no set pattern for such ministries. Local Churches exhibit variety. Nor is there any set pattern of intervals for such ministries, even as prerequisites for the major ministries of deacon, presbyter and episkopos.

3. Pastoral need, more than any other factor, contributed to the rise of such minor ministries. No central Church, e.g., Rome or Constantinople, regulated the naming or ranking of these ministries.

4. The rite of entry into some of these ministries was called an ordination; at least this is clear from documents in the Eastern Churches. In these ordination rituals, deaconesses were clearly included. The question whether women were ever ordained in the early Church seems be answered in the affirmative, as far as this evidence indicates, i.e., to the order of deaconess.

5. In the West, but only gradually, a set pattern for the names of the minor orders, and a set pattern for stages of the minor and major orders, were established: tonsure, as the first step, then porter, lector, exorcist, acolyte, subdeacon, deacon, priest. By 1150 there were, in the West, seven orders to holy order.

6. By 1150 the bishop was not considered, theologically, to be a part of holy order; still, one must go through the stages of the orders and eventually be ordained a priest to be eligible for the "dignity" of bishop.

7. In time, these minor orders became more or less formalized stages to ordination to the priesthood. Even the order of deacon was seen as merely one step in the passage to priestly ordination.

8. Only in the renewal after Vatican II were the minor orders dropped from the Western Church, and in their place a series of ministries, open to both those who were intending to be ordained and those not intending to be ordained. In this same renewal, the order of deacon was opened to those who did not wish to be ordained priest.

Further consideration of these minor orders will be taken up in the chapter which deals with the Council of Trent and the sacrament of Order, as well as in the chapter on Vatican II's theology of ministry.

7

Ministry in the
Scholastic Period: 1000 to 1400 A.D.

This chapter will consider the issue of Christian ministry in the scholastic period, i.e., from 1000 to 1400. For the Western Church this was a time of theological development which shaped most of the theology of the Western Church for the succeeding centuries. In spite of the scholastic use of Aristotelian categories, the theology of these centuries was, in many ways, traditional, and this is clearly the case in the matter of Christian ministry. There is nothing radically new in what the scholastic theologians developed by way of ordained ministry. What they inherited in the practice of the Church is precisely the area to which they brought their theological acumen. In the brief study on the minor orders, recounted above, we have seen that by 1150 most of the theologians and a number of canonists enumerated only seven: namely, porter, lector, exorcist, acolyte, subdeacon, deacon and priest. Ivo of Chartres (d. 1116) and Peter Damian (d. 1072) were influential on this issue. More influential, however, were Hugh of St. Victor and Peter Lombard, who both taught that there were only these seven, which meant, as one sees, that the bishop is not enumerated in the list of holy orders. By 1150, both in theology and to some extent in canon law, episcopacy was not seen as part of order. There were, of course, a few who continued to maintain eight orders, sometimes even nine, but they were a clear minority in scholastic theology, and had little influence on the Church.

Anselm of Bec, who later became the archbishop of Canterbury (1033–1109), has rightfully been called the "Father of Scholasticism."

Prior to Anselm, other theologians, particularly those who were involved with the first eucharistic controversies, men such as Paschasius Radbertus, Ratramnus, Rathier of Verona, Heriger of Lobbes, Fulbert of Chartres, Berengarius himself, and Guitmund of Aversa, had begun to use dialectics and Aristotelian categories. However, it was Anselm "who, boldly and undismayed, showed his contemporaries how dialectics and metaphysical speculation could be applied to theological questions without violating the reverence due to mysteries of faith by rationalistic arrogance."[1] In many ways, all the scholastic theologians who followed Anselm, including the major or high scholastic theologians, are indebted to Anselm to an enormous degree.

However, even Anselm would not have made such an intellectual mark on Western theology had not previous scholars developed a school system of no mean caliber. In the early medieval period there were the palace schools and the monastery schools. Anselm himself comes from a monastery school system. These monastic schools were followed by the cathedral schools, which in turn gave way to the universities. This medieval concentration of scholarly exchange, both from the standpoint of scholars themselves assembling together in one locale, and from the standpoint of assembling library resources, provided a needed base so that a scholastic renewal of theology on such a grand scale might take place. Western theology, as well as Western intellectual life generally, owes much to the rise and development of these various school systems.[2]

Anselm and other scholars, some of whom are mentioned above, as well as the strengthened school system of the medieval period, flourish in the period 1000 to 1100. They are, therefore, the linkage between the early medieval period and the period of high scholasticism. In that same century, an issue, germane to our subject, also arose: the relationship of holy order on the one hand and jurisdiction on the other. At first, the concepts of order and jurisdiction were not clearly distinguished, but at least a beginning was made. The question of simony, more particularly simoniacal ordinations, resurrected the whole discussion on reordination, which had plagued the early Church. In the patristic material, available to the early medieval scholar, passages from St. Cyprian denied validity to orders administered by heretics; but there were also available passages from St. Augustine, who held a view contrary to that of Cyprian. Pope Formosus had likewise been involved in this issue of simoniacal ordinations, and therefore the question of priesthood and ordination was, to some degree, quite current for the scholastic investigations. The writings of Auxilius from the tenth century, namely *In defensionem sacrae ordinationis papae Formosi* and *Infensor et defensor,* had some influence on Peter Damian and Humbert of Silva Candida in the eleventh century (at least the latter work of Auxilius seems to have been known to Peter Damian and Humbert). Only as the scholastic theologians clarified such theological concepts as sacrament and sacramental character, *res sacramenti* and *sacramentum tantum,* did some resolution to this newly resurrected question of reordination take place.[3] In all of this, one notes that the study of Christian priesthood in the scholastic period really begins with the period of Church history, starting around 1000 A.D. However, the major theological work was done from 1100 onward.

1. THE NUMBER OF SACRED ORDERS

Some of the theologians of the twelfth century who maintained the sevenfold number of holy orders attempted to base this number of the *Ordines Christi.* They taught that Jesus, before his suffering and death, exercised the first five orders, and, with his suffering and death, the last two orders. Although this may appear somewhat naive today, one should nevertheless see that these theologians were at least attempting to give a christological foundation for Church ministry. Holy order reflected the very ministry of Jesus himself.[4] This theological foundation for ministry, namely in the ministry of Jesus himself, was, as we have seen, firmly rooted in the Church's long tradition. The way in which this christological foundation was approached by these twelfth century scholars might be questioned, but the thrust of their approach is clearly consonant with the best of theology.

It was clear to the theologians and canonists of this time that only the deacon and priest went back to the time of the apostles; all the other orders, they noted, had been established by the Church over the course of history. For Peter Lombard, as for others, tonsure was not an order, nor was cantor; the fact that Peter Lombard addressed both these topics indicates that he knew that they had existed in the Church for a long time and deserved the name of tradition. Still, for Peter Lombard as for most of the other twelfth century theologians, they were not part of the sacrament of order.[5] Subdiaconate, in this century, had been connected with the promise of celibacy, and this was seen as the traditional usage in the Church. This connection of subdiaconate with celibacy was the reason why theologians and canonists referred to the subdiaconate as one of the major orders in contrast to the minor orders. One must realize that the medieval scholar did not have access to the historical data to which we today are privy. These medieval scholars had some sense of history, but for the most part what they experienced as the practice of the Church in their day, especially the more important practices, was the way the Church had always been. One might even speak, although this is clearly an anachronistic way of speaking, of a scholastic theologizing on the praxis of the Church of their day. This is particularly true in the matter of the sacraments, including that of order.

In the eighth century Bede the Venerable (d. 735) had commented on the difference between bishop and priest, and had compared Jesus' sending out of the twelve to the bishops, and the sending out of the seventy [or seventy-two] to the priests. The bishops, then, took the place of the apostles, and the priests that of the seventy disciples. This exegesis of Bede was repeated again and again during the early and high middle ages by such scholars as Theodolph of Orleans, Peter Damian, Ivo of Chartres, Hugh of St. Victor, Gratian, Peter Lombard, Sikard of Cremona—to mention only a few. Basing themselves on Bede's approach, authors began to describe the difference between bishop and priest. Sikard, for instance, thought that in the administration of the Christian community, the bishop was above the priest, just as the apostles were above the seventy, but in the administration of the sacraments they were equal. Every priest could administer all the sacraments in the same way that Peter himself had done.[6] This line of thought became rather standard throughout the scholastic period. The bishop's role was that of Church administration, the priest's role that of sacramental administration.

Scholastic theologians did not spend the majority of their efforts and time discussing the relationship between bishop and priest. Rather, it was the meaning and value of holy orders which focused their attention. Perhaps Hugh of St. Victor tried the hardest to bring together bishop and priest within the sacrament of Order. It was his teaching that within one order there might be several degrees. At the time of Hugh there were deacons and archdeacons, but both belonged to the *Order of Deacon,* with, nonetheless, degrees within that order to allow the archdeacon to be higher than the mere deacon. So, too, the bishop and priest. There is only one *Order of Priesthood,* but there are two degrees: sacerdotal and episcopal.[7] Hugh was not followed in this to any great extent. For his part, Peter Lombard in chapters 14–16 discusses the office of the bishop, and he says right at the start: "There are other names, not of orders, but of dignities and offices. Bishop is the name both of dignity and office."[8] It is clear that Peter Lombard does not see bishop as a degree in the order of priesthood. Episcopacy is only an office and a dignity. He bases himself on a very respected sacred writer of the past, namely, Isidore of Seville. From Isidore Lombard provides us with the etymology of the word episkopos: namely to oversee and administer (c. 15), which in Peter Lombard's view has nothing per se to do with the administration of the sacraments, but only with the administration of the Church community. Then, following the lead of Hugh, Peter Lombard goes on to discuss the grades of this office and dignity: patriarchs, archbishops, metropolitans and lastly bishop (c. 17), applying Hugh's teaching on different grades, not to order, but to office and dignity. This teaching of Peter Lombard dominated scholastic thought.

One can rightfully say, however, that first Peter Lombard and, following him, the majority of scholastic theologians and also not a few scholastic canonists, such as Rufinus and Sikard of Cremona, as well as the author of the *Summa Parisiensis,* maintained that the sacrament of order (a) did not include the bishop, (b) considered only priest and deacon to be from Jesus and the apostles, and (c) regarded the other five orders as instituted by the Church. It was this view that held sway in Western thought on the sacrament of order from the twelfth century down to the twentieth century, when the number of orders was radically changed.

2. THE DEFINITION OF THE SACRAMENT OF ORDER

But what is "order"? Again it is Peter Lombard who provides the medieval leadership, since he is seemingly the first to have given a definition of order:

> Si autem quaeritur, quid sit quod hic vocatur ordo, sane, dici potest, signaculum quoddam esse, id est sacrum quiddam, quo spiritualis potestas traditur ordinato et officium.[9]

If, however, one asks: what is that which is here called order, it
can indeed be said to be a certain sign, that is, something sacred,
by which a spiritual power and office is given to the one ordained.

Ott notes that the Latin term "signaculum," which has Augustinian rootage, indicates the external ritual, which is the sacrament of
the internal gift of the spiritual power and office.[10] Peter Lombard,
in a section which precedes his chapter on the definition of order,
had already used the phrase "promotio potestatis." In the history of
the Church, those who were ordained had an office, and with that
office there was a spiritual power. Peter Lombard in no way made
up this understanding of *Holy Order;* rather, on the basis of tradition,
he was rather identifying it in his definition. We have already seen
that in the Frankish structure, the priest was indeed put into a position
of power by the proprietor over the local church. Besides administrative
powers over the land, the crops, etc., there was also the spiritual power
of the priest: the administration of the sacraments. In the cathedral
churches, the priests also had positions of power. We saw this in the
way that the canons of a cathedral were stratified. There was administrative power as regards certain tasks, but there was the administration
of the sacraments as well. In this first definition of order, then, we
have the term "power," and this definition will continue to influence
Western theology for centuries. Bandinus, Gandulphus of Bologna,
and Rufinus all cited this definition, and, at times, verbatim.

Other theologians, however, altered Peter Lombard's meaning of
"signaculum." Rather than have this "signaculum" refer to the ritual,
they referred it to that spiritual sign, which remained with the ordained
person throughout his life. Sikard of Cremona and the author of the
volume, *Magister Praepositinus,* led the way on this matter. This, of
course, was eventually compared to the "character" at baptism, which
stays with the baptized Christian throughout his or her life. Finally,
the "signaculum" came to be seen theologically and technically as the
"character" of order. At least some scholastic theologians went in this
direction. Peter Lombard, of course, did not in any way equate *signaculum* with a sacramental character.

When one leaves the twelfth century, and moves into the high
scholastic period, we find that the great scholastic theologians, Alexander of Hales, Albert the Great, St. Thomas Aquinas, St. Bonaventure, John Duns Scotus, all followed this pattern, equating

signaculum with sacramental character. Indeed, all the traditional lines of thought, that is, those which had been worked out in the twelfth century, were continued and systematized in the thirteenth century.

For all of these major scholastic theologians of the thirteenth century, the issue of the sacramentality of order was not a question at all: in holy order, there were external signs, there was a conferral of grace, and—for priesthood and diaconate—one could claim New Testament origin. Holy order was, indeed, a sacrament. Some of these same theologians used the occasion at the Lord's Supper, when Jesus said: "Do this in remembrance of me," as the scriptural base for the institution of the sacrament of order, but this was by no means a unanimous or even common opinion of thirteenth century theologians.

The connection of order with the eucharist is, however, common and almost unanimous. It seems that Alexander of Hales (d. 1245) was the first to highlight this. In his definition of order, Alexander presents the definition of Peter Lombard, cited above, and then goes on to give a second definition:

> Ordo est sacramentum spiritualis potestatis ad aliquod officium ordinatum in Ecclesia ad sacramentum communionis.[11]

> Order is a sacrament of spiritual power for some office established in the Church for the sacrament of communion.

"Power," "Church" and "Eucharist"—these three ideas will galvanize the high scholastic approach to the sacrament of order. After Alexander, Philip the Chancellor (d. 1236) uses this approach, and Albert the Great (d. 1280) does so as well in his *Commentary on the Sentences,* although he had not used this eucharistic connection in a work which he had written earlier, namely his *Tractatus de Sacramentis* (1246). Ott notes in this regard: "The thought of the relationship of the power, which is given in the sacrament of order to the eucharist, becomes the common inheritance of the theologians who follow [Alexander]. This opinion served as the major argument for excluding the episcopacy from the sacrament of order."[12]

It would be redundant to cite all the major scholastic theologians who wrote in this vein regarding the relationship of priesthood and episcopacy. Let me include here simply a number of passages from

St. Thomas, since in many ways Thomas has had such a major influence on the centuries which followed him. In the *Summa* he writes:

> Since the consecration conferred in the sacrament of orders is directed to the sacrament of the eucharist, as stated above, the principal act of each order is that whereby it is most nearly directed to the sacrament of the eucharist. In this respect, too, one order ranks above another, in so far as one act is more nearly directed to that same sacrament.[13]

Again:

> Just as a temple, an altar, vessels and vestments, so too ministers, who are ordained for the eucharist, need a consecration; and this consecration is the sacrament of order. And therefore a distinction of orders is to be made on the basis of their relationship to the eucharist.[14]

Again:

> A priest has two acts: the first is the principal one, namely to consecrate the body of Christ; the second is of lesser importance, namely to prepare the people of God to receive this sacrament. . . . As regards the first act, the power of the priest does not depend on any higher power except divine power.[15]

Other passages could be cited as well, but the point is clear: priesthood is centered in the eucharist. All the other orders, deacon, subdeacon, etc., are defined and valued only insofar as they relate to the eucharist. This theory of a eucharistic priesthood dominated Western theology of priesthood down to Vatican II. The use of the word "theory" is deliberate here, although in the centuries between high scholasticism and Vatican II, many theologians would have called this "the ordinary teaching of the Church." From our vantage point of Vatican II, we can look back and see that it can only be a theological theory, since the bishops at Vatican II moved deliberately beyond this eucharistic approach to priesthood, making a broader understanding of priest the "ordinary magisterium of the Church" for our day. We will, of course, consider this in a later chapter. The citations from St.

Thomas, on this matter, could be, as mentioned, multiplied, not only from the works of St. Thomas himself, but also from the works of all the other major scholastic theologians. This approach to the sacrament of order was commonly held by all the major scholastic theologians, both Dominican and Franciscan. Three essential elements of this scholastic definition of priesthood are as follows:

1. Priesthood is focused on the eucharist.

2. Priesthood is seen as a power.

3. Priesthood culminates not in the bishop but in the priest.

Let us consider each of these in some detail. First of all, the notion that the priesthood focused essentially and principally on the eucharist created a liturgical or sacramental understanding of priest. It is evident that one can hardly say that this is not a christocentric approach, since Jesus is truly present in the eucharist. But the christological base of an understanding of ordained ministry is somewhat narrowed by this approach, and Vatican II will officially widen this christological base. Priesthood, in the conciliar documents of Vatican II, is based on the total and comprehensive mission of Jesus, and not exclusively on the eucharist. The priesthood is more than a sacramental priesthood; it is a priesthood which reflects the threefold mission of Jesus: to teach, to sanctify and to lead. Vatican II in no way implied that the scholastic approach was erroneous, only that it was too narrow, and to bring out the Church's full understanding of priesthood, the council teaches that the priesthood must be seen in the light of the full mission of Jesus himself. Vatican II, of course, and its pronouncements on the sacrament of order will be taken up in detail at a later stage of this volume, but it is important to note in the study of the scholastic theology of the sacrament of order both the solid theological issues in it as well as the clear limitations of its presentation. The exclusive centralization of priesthood to eucharist is one of these limitations.

The second element of the scholastic definition of priesthood is that it is essentially a power, *potestas*. That the definition of priesthood focused on power tended to move theological thought away from the New Testament understanding of ministry as service. Power can, indeed, be seen as service, but it can, unfortunately, also be seen as domination, and the danger to move away from the humble service of Jesus to an "arrogance of power" remained a constant factor in the history of ordained ministry. Again, Vatican II, in its many documents, did not say that the "power" approach was erroneous, but it did attempt to place the theology and practice of ordained ministry on the basis of service, rather than power. The scholastic theologians did not, of course, consider the power of order as a power of arrogance. For them, this was a sacred power, that is, a sharing in the very power of Jesus to bring holiness, through the sacraments, to sinful men and women. Jesus had come in power: the power of grace, the power of reconciliation, the power of salvation, the power of the gospel. It was the sacredness of the power, rather than power as such, which these theologians emphasized. In their writings on the subject of order, however, service, *diakonia,* is not central; rather, it is the power to consecrate the bread and wine into the Body and Blood of Christ, and the power to forgive sins, which are their normal ways of expressing this power. Service, diakonia, might be theologically a more biblically refined way to speak of ministry, and especially ordained ministry, but for the scholastic theologian, *potestas* was the normal way of describing the essence of the sacrament of order. This power must be seen as focused essentially and principally on the eucharist, and it is from this eucharistic power that any and all other priestly powers derive.

This brings us to the third issue: the exclusion of the episcopacy from the sacrament of holy order. The episcopacy was seen as a dignity and office, and not as the "fullness of the priesthood." This separation of episcopacy from priesthood, of necessity, re-established the basis for episcopal collegiality. No scholastic theologian, of course, denied that the college of bishops succeeded to the college of apostles. That was never an issue in scholastic theology. With the theological and systematic exclusion of episcopacy from the sacrament of order, however, the basis of this collegiality was no longer associated with ordination. The early Church, the patristic Church, the early medieval Church, had seen the bishop as the chief ecclesial minister, and, at least from Hippolytus' time on, the chief ordained ecclesial minister. The priesthood of Jesus and the priesthood of the apostles and the priesthood of the episkopoi/bishops were all interconnected. With the exclusion of the episcopacy from priesthood, the collegial connection to Jesus and his apostles had to be found elsewhere, namely, in a dignity and an office, i.e., in administration or jurisdiction. We saw above that St. Thomas had said that as far as the power of the priest was concerned, namely, to consecrate the bread and wine, only divine power was above him. There is a directness between Jesus and each priest; in the case of the episcopacy, the bishop as priest was, of course, in similar directness to Jesus; but as bishop his office and dignity were not that clearly direct, and this opened the way to a different approach to collegiality, namely, one through jurisdiction which was conferred by the pope. Scholastic theologians did not clearly see this displacement of the basis of collegiality, but from our present standpoint with the advantage of historical data in front of us, we are able to see that there was a clear connection between the exclusion of episcopacy from the sacrament of order and a decline in the appreciation of the collegiality of bishops. From the scholastic period onward the exclusion of episcopacy from the sacrament of order had a theological explanation. In the twentieth century this theological explanation is seen as misleading.

We have noted in the preceding chapter that the papacy had more and more directly intervened in diocesan and inter-diocesan matters. The so-called *Dictatus of Pope Gregory VII,* a sort of private memorandum written around 1075, is a listing of ideas which in many ways influenced the papacy and the way it operated. Although this is a disputed document, in many ways it nonetheless witnesses directly to the loss of episcopal importance as regards the sacrament of order and the subsequent loss of importance as regards episcopal collegiality. Only those items in the *Dictatus* pertaining to the episcopal issue are cited below:

1. That the Roman church was founded by the Lord alone.
2. That only the Roman pontiff is rightly called universal.
3. That he alone can depose or re-establish bishops.
4. That his legate, even if of inferior rank, is above all bishops in council; and he can give sentence of deposition against them.
7. That it is permitted to him alone to establish new laws for the necessity of the time, to make new peoples into congregations, to make an abbacy of canonical establishment and vice versa, to divide a rich bishopric and combine poor ones.
8. That he alone can use imperial insignia.

9. That all princes kiss the feet of the pope alone.
10. That his name alone is recited in the churches.
13. That it is permitted to him to transfer bishops, under pressure of necessity, from one see to another.
14. That throughout the church, wherever he wishes, he can ordain a cleric.
18. That his decision ought to be reviewed by no one and that he alone can review the decisions of everyone.
21. That the greater cases of every church ought to be referred to him.
25. That he can depose and re-establish bishops without a meeting of the synod.[16]

This *Dictatus* never became law, of course, but its tenor indicates a movement which severely limited the collegiality of the bishops. In the patristic period, bishops gathered in councils and determined many issues;[17] in the Carolingian period we have many Gallic councils;[18] but as the papacy begins to assert itself from Gregory the Great onward, the collegial aspect of the bishops is more and more restricted, until only the great general councils of the Church, under the supervision of the pope, really have any merit. It is interesting to look through a book such as that of Denzinger and note that as one moves toward the pontificate of Innocent III (1198–1216), the number of local councils cited diminishes, and from the time of Innocent III on, which is part of the high scholastic period, the papal statements and the "ecumencial" councils alone are cited. From this period onward, the bishops, when gathered into an ecumencial council, are clearly collegial. Outside of these great councils, the bishops have generally acted more on an individual basis than on a collegial basis. An assembly of bishops in a region was looked upon with some fear, and the battle over conciliarism, which began to arise shortly after the thirteenth century, in many ways was a battle over episcopal collegiality. This tension has never been fully resolved, since the issue of episcopal collegiality has never been adequately settled. A major step was taken, however, at Vatican II, when the bishop was reinstated, as it were, into the ordained ministry, and the collegiality of the bishops was stressed. There is strong theological basis for seeing these two steps: the re-inclusion of the episcopacy into the sacrament of order and the renewal of episcopal collegiality as essentially interrelated.

Prior to this scholastic theological definition of the sacrament of order, the relationship of the papacy to the bishop had been one in which the individual bishop became increasingly dependent on the pope. We saw this in the examples mentioned on pallium and judicial matters. At that earlier time, however, the bishop was still the major priest in a diocese, and the relationship of the papacy to the bishop was to him as *sacerdos*. With the exclusion of the episcopacy from sacred order, the relationship begins to take on a different structure, namely, one that is based on dignity and office alone. Little by little, the distinction of *potestas ordinis* and *potestas iurisdictionis* was elaborated, and the relationship of papacy to bishop was theologically elaborated in the structure of jurisdiction, not order.

The three issues: eucharist, power, episcopacy, were the major aspects of the scholastic approach to ordained ministry, and each of them was good in itself, but too narrow to last. The theology of priestly ministry as developed by the scholastics necessarily needed a revision, but that revision was long in coming, due to the reformation period and the subsequent, rather defensive counter-reformation theology which followed in the Roman Church.

This section on the definition of the sacrament of order has been lengthy and more analytical than merely expository. However, this definition of the sacrament of order is the very essence of the scholastic theology on the sacrament of order, and therefore certainly deserves not only an exposition, but also a careful analysis. Let us now consider some of the secondary elements in their theology of the sacrament of order.

3. THE SACRAMENT OF ORDER AND ECCLESIOLOGY

St. Thomas in the *Summa* divides his material into five sections: (1) order in general; (2) the distinction of orders; (3) the conferral of orders; (4) the impediments to orders; (5) issues connected with orders. The very first question, in the section dealing with order in general, starts with the Church. In other words, Thomas begins his discussion of order with the Church; he asks whether there should be order in the Church. To answer this, he begins with the way in which God acts generally: namely, creation and all of God's works *ad extra* reflect God himself. This means beauty and therefore order.

> Consequently, in order that this beauty might not be lacking in
> the Church, God established order in it, in such a way that certain

ones minister the sacraments to others, and in this way they are similar to God, as it were, working along with God, just as in our natural body, certain members influence the others.[19]

Only if one understands the Church as an ordered society, reflecting an orderly God, will one understand the meaning of the sacrament of order in the Church. This has a contemporary ring to it, since, in contemporary theology, the Church is seen as the basic sacrament, from which all the other sacraments derive their meaning. St. Thomas, of course, does not use the term "sacrament" for Church, but the flow of his thought, namely, from the Church to the individual sacrament, mirrors the contemporary approach of the Church as a basic sacrament.

St. Bonaventure follows a different pattern from that of Thomas. He discusses the element of external sign first and does this through the subject of tonsure. Tonsure, of course, was the first stage—but by no means an order—into clerical life. The cutting of one's hair was itself a sign, but a sign on the most important part of the human body, the head. It was also a sign of learning, since vanity and excess over trivial matters is discarded for wisdom. Third, it is a sign of circularity, the corona, which indicates the goal of our spiritual life: simplicity of mind and heart with the God of all simplicity. There is something spiritual and mystical in the way Bonaventure proceeds, but tonsure, as a sign, was a sign of position in the Church, and a disposition for the sacrament of order. Bonaventure, after this, proceeds in a sort of "chronological way," following the pattern, then in practice, of someone who eventually would be ordained priest. In this process within the Church structure, a young man began with tonsure, thereby becoming a cleric. The next stage, of course, is the reception of the first minor order; consequently, Bonaventure turns his attention to order and asks whether there is order in the Church.

Along with Thomas, he bases his answer, which is affirmative, on the issue of beauty. Disarray is a lack of beauty; orderliness is a sign of beauty. But Bonaventure gives a second reason, namely, rectitude. For Bonaventure, as for all of the scholastic theologians, the sacraments were instituted primarily to help sinful people. Had there been no sin, there would have been no need of sacraments.

Since the majority of the Church is in a state, in which deviation is possible, the Church needs a leader and regulator, and since one [leader or regulator] cannot be adequate for everyone and for all situations, it is necessary to distribute, according to a more or less degree, the offices and powers, so that the Church might be ruled and directed without error.[21]

Once again, the ecclesiological base for the sacrament of order is stressed; it is because of the nature of the Church itself that the sacrament of order both should be and is. Theologically stated in line with our contemporary approach, one would say that the Church as basic sacrament establishes the meaning and validity of the individual sacraments, in this case, the sacrament of order.

John Duns Scotus begins with a more pointed kind of question: whether there are seven orders in the Church, in such a way that order or ordination is a sacrament. From this question he goes on to take issue with Bonaventure's definition of order, although he does not replicate it word for word: "The sacrament of order is a spiritual power to perform some act in the Church's hierarchy."[22] Scotus feels that such a definition (a) would include the episcopacy and (b) and would not include the two powers in the priesthood, namely the power to celebrate the eucharist and the power to forgive sins. Scotus therefore moves to Augustine's approach in the *De Civitate Dei,* in which order is seen as the orderliness of the universe: "Order is the fitting arrangement of similar and dissimilar things, providing a place for each."[23] One also, Scotus notes, sees this orderliness in the political sphere, in which some hold a preeminent place over others. In this political sphere, those in more prominent places are said to be in an "order."

Both of these meanings, orderliness in the cosmos and a preeminence in a political structure, have a bearing within the Church. The Church is a *politia ordinata,* and as such evidences this twofold meaning: the entire Church is structured in an orderly way, providing a place for similar and dissimilar parts, with each part in its proper place. Moreover, there are members in the Church who have a preeminent place. The preeminence of certain people in the Church is based on the performance or better the disposition to perform such ecclesial acts. On this basis Scotus presents his definition of order:

Sic possit Ordo, ut hic loquimur de Ordine, dici gradus praeeminens in Ecclesia disponens ad actum aliquem Ecclesiasticum eminentem.[24]

> In this way it can be said that order, as we are speaking of order here, is a preeminent role in the Church, disposing someone for an eminent ecclesial act.

The eminent ecclesial acts are, for Scotus, the celebration of the eucharist and the forgiveness of sins, and other sacramental acts. At the end of this section, he states that, as far as priesthood is concerned, order "is that eminent grade in the Church, disposing someone *de congruo* to perform an act belonging to the consecration or dispensation of the eucharist."[25] We see, once more, that the eucharist is the essential focus of the sacrament of order. Scotus speaks of this disposition as *de congruo,* which means that the one ordained has no real aptitude *de condigno,* but that the disposition is really a grace of God, dependent on God's generosity and superabundance of love and mercy. In other words, ordination gives no "right" to perform an act; the disposition remains a grace of God through and through. *De congruo* indicates in a strong way this incongruity on our part, but a generous congruity on the part of God.[26]

Scotus, with Thomas and Bonaventure, sees the sacrament of order against the framework of the Church. Only in and through the Church does the sacrament of order have any meaning or value. This ecclesiological basis is fundamental to Scotus' position. It is interesting to note that the position of Scotus, which emphasized the two powers of the priest: (1) that of consecrating the eucharistic bread and wine and (2) that of forgiving sins, rather than simply the single power of consecration, became, after the reformation, the more common opinion among Roman Catholic theologians.

All of these men, and they are but the major spokesmen for this period, speak of the sacrament of order. However, in Gregory of Nazianz, in John Chrysostom, in Ignatius of Antioch and Irenaeus, in the entire patristic period and to some degree in the first part of the Carolingian period, the referent was rarely to "order" but rather to "priest." On the other hand, the scholastics speak primarily about order, and their arguments stem, as we have just seen, from an understanding of what order means in the universe, in a society, in the human body. The patristic discussion flowed from the understanding of priesthood and ministry; the scholastic discussion flowed from the understanding of order. The ecclesiological foundation for the scholastics is itself based on the wider concept of order, since the Church is an orderly and ordered sacred society. As we have mentioned frequently, this ecclesiological base is a plus for the theology of the scholastics on this matter of the sacrament of order. It could easily be said that this ecclesiological framework remains one of the most significant aspects of the scholastic theology of order. Advantageous as it may be, it has as well a narrowness and limitation about it. When ministry and priesthood centered the discussion, as we found in the patristic period, Jesus was far more central. This centrality of Jesus, for an understanding of ministry and priesthood, is exactly what Vatican II picks up and stresses in its documentation. More profound than the Church is the role of Jesus in understanding ordained ministry as well as unordained ministry. An ecclesiological basis is indeed necessary in the matter of the sacrament of order, but this ecclesiological basis itself is not intelligible, unless there is a christological base. The stress on order and ordination tends to emphasize the Church, but not Jesus, and this is another major limitation to the scholastic approach.

Let us consider, however, the role that Jesus played in the presentation of this sacrament by these great scholastic theologians.

4. JESUS AND THE SACRAMENT OF ORDER

When one studies the section in the *Summa* of Thomas which deals with the sacrament of order, one finds that the christological element is not very strong. This section comprises questions 34 to 40 inclusive of the *tertia pars.* There are, in all, thirty-five articles in these questions. Thomas speaks, of course, about the eucharist, *corpus Christi,* and about *plebs Christi* and *corpus Christi mysticum,* these latter two only four or five times. In question 36 he treats of the qualities which those who receive the sacrament of order should have. Other than a mention of the mystical body of Christ (art. 2) there is no mention of Jesus as model for those who receive the sacrament. In question 37, article 2 he mentions the "sacraments of Christ." In article 5 of the same question, in the response to the second objection, he mentions that Jesus gave the primary priestly power to his disciples at the Lord's supper, when he said: "Take and eat. . . . Do this in memory of me" (Lk 22, 19), and the secondary power of forgiving sins after the resurrection. In question 38, art. 2, he mentions that the sacraments continue the effectiveness of the passion of Christ. In discussing whether someone who has committed murder should be ordained (art. 4), he speaks about those who shed the blood of Jesus. A murderer reflects those who killed Jesus, whereas the ministers of the eucharist reflect the reconciliation and peace which the death of Jesus brought about. Only once, in question 40, art. 4, does he speak about the ministry of Jesus:

> To the third objection it should be said that the perfections of all natural things preexist exemplarily in God, and thus Christ is the exemplar of all ecclesial offices. Hence, every minister of the Church, in some way or another, bears a typology to Christ. . . . Nevertheless, he is higher who represents Christ according to a greater perfection. A priest represents Christ in this that through himself he performs certain ministry, but a bishop [represents Christ] in this, that he institutes other ministers and founds a Church.[27]

This is strongly christological: Jesus is the exemplar of all ministries, especially ordained ministries, in the Church. Thomas singles out the priest and the bishop. Thomas even goes on to say that the bishop is a "spouse of the Church, just as Christ is" (cf. also art. 7 where he repeats this idea). Thomas in a brief way connects this with the sacramental character which configures one to Christ (art. 5). It is unfortunate that in this entire section on the sacrament of order, this idea of Jesus as exemplar of all ministry plays no operative role. This single mention, cited above, stands out in its solitude.

In Bonaventure's *Commentary on the Sentences,* distinctions twenty-four and twenty-five deal with the sacrament of order. We find the sacrament of the eucharist stressed, of course, and this is the body of Christ. Bonaventure speaks about Melchisedek as the type of the priesthood of Jesus and that the sacramental character configures us to Jesus (Pars 2, art. 1, q. 1). The deacon reflects the full light of the gospel message, namely the *doctrina Christi* (q. 4). In the same place he speaks of the mystical body of Christ, which is, of course, the Church. In treating of the question whether a woman might be ordained, Bonaventure likens the one ordained to the mediator, Jesus, who is male (D. 25, art. 2, q. 1). In dealing with the issue of priestly celibacy, and above all the question of a bigamist being ordained, Bonaventure writes that the primary signification of order is that the ordained signifies Christ as the spouse of the Church. Since Christ has only one spouse, the Church, how could a bigamist signify the Lord through ordination (q. 3)?

Again, we see in this writing of Bonaventure that Jesus and his ministry is not an operative factor. The instances in which he mentions

Jesus are to a certain degree tangential to his main argument. As has been said, the eucharist is not tangential; but the ministry of Jesus, his example of service that one finds in the gospels, the washing of the feet of his disciples, etc.—all these hardly play a role in Bonaventure's theological analysis of the sacrament of order.

Scotus speaks again and again about the eucharist, the body of Christ, but throughout his analysis the ministry of Jesus, the exemplarity of Jesus for ministry, and Jesus' own statements on ministry are lacking. Whereas the Church, for Scotus, plays a great role, Jesus is not presented as the exemplar of Christian priestly ministry.

Perhaps if these authors had asked the question about Jesus as priest and the sacrament of priestly ministry, the emphases would have been different. But instead they asked about order and ordination, and this led them into an ecclesial framework, but not a christological one. This in no way implies that they did not see Jesus himself as a priest, but only that they did not approach the sacrament via the priestliness of Jesus. This in no way implies, again, that they did not see the ordained person as a special representative of Jesus' priestliness, but, again, this was not the way that they approached the sacrament. They approached it via order: order in the Church and specific orders for individuals in that Church.

A final word should be added about the scholastic approach to bishop. Although these theologians did not include the bishop in the sacrament of order, still there was expressed an enormous regard for episcopacy. The dignity of a bishop shared in the dignity of the apostles. The Church was, of course, a Church of sacraments, but it was more than that. The Church was both eucharistically the Body of Christ and mystically the Body of Christ. In this mystical Body of Christ, the bishops played a most eminent role. Moreover, the pope played an even superior role in this mystical Body of Christ, although as priest he was to that extent on the same level as any priest in the Church. None of this eminence and pre-eminence, however, was seen as part of the sacrament of holy order.

The main elements of the sacrament of order were theologically systematized by these scholastic men, and their approach remained the standard approach of the Roman Church during the fourteenth and fifteenth centuries. This leads us, of course, to the Reformation period, and the rejection of order as a sacrament in the Christian Church by the Reformers.

8

Ministry in the
Theology of the Reformers

The question of ministry within the Christian Church was not the main focus of such reformation theologians as Luther and Calvin. There were other theological issues which were far deeper and more divisive: the relationship of grace and good works; the question of justification; the place of the Word in both Christian theology and Christian practice; the authority of the pope. However, since a theology of Christian ministry involves in some way or another all of these basic issues, the theology of Christian ministry, as far as the Reformers saw it, could not but be affected by the way one theologized on the issues of grace and good works, justification, the eminent place of the Word in the Christian Church, and the role of the papacy. It is clear, therefore, that a study of ministry in the Church at the time of the Reformation must include as well some consideration of these more profound and more divisive issues. A comprehensive study of these issues is beyond the scope of this chapter. We will, however, touch on these deeper themes throughout this study of the Reformation's approach to ordained ministry.

Besides these theological issues, internal to the Reformation of the sixteenth century, one must likewise take into account that there were a host of issues, both practical and theoretical, which had been plaguing the Church for some centuries and which needed to be remedied. The Reformation of the sixteenth century did not occur suddenly in the Western Church. S. Harrison Thomson notes:

It is a commonplace to assert that the Protestant Reformation did not come unheralded onto the European historical scene. It had a long preparation. Every failure to remove the abuses that had crept into the Church only made it more certain that the effort would have to be repeated in a more forceful manner. If any of the reform endeavors—for example, those of the councils, the mystics, certain progressive popes or cardinals, the reformers within the older orders, the reform-minded laymen, or the humanist reformers—had succeeded, the Protestant Reformation would probably not have occurred, or at least it would have been postponed for a long time.[1]

None of these earlier reform movements, not even the powerful Gregorian reform, had occasioned adequate healing within the Church. Reform was still in the air in the sixteenth century, and it began to move into the Church with the power of a hurricane. These new reform efforts were led, in great part, by highly trained and insightful men. In time, on the Roman side, equally highly trained and insightful men also rose up in defense of the Roman Church. One of the most powerful inner-Church struggles began to take place. It ended, as we know so well, in a shattered Western Christianity, and the force of this sixteenth-century clash still, even in the twentieth century, causes aftershock upon after-shock. The Reformation was and remains a major reshaping of the Western Christian world, and because of this overwhelming change, the Reformation remains a most difficult, because most complex, issue to analyze. This complexity and comprehensiveness of the Reformation protest and the Roman Catholic response make the study of Christian ministry during the Reformation period no mean or easy task. What follows, then, is but a survey of some of the major aspects of this complex and comprehensive event. This survey is fairly lengthy, but no study of the history of the ordained ministry in the Roman Catholic Church can by-pass the charges raised by the Reformation theologians.

The two major Reformers were, of course, Martin Luther and John Calvin, although there were many other influential figures as well. However, in this chapter, we will consider only these two, since the Roman Catholic response on ordained ministry, formulated at the Council of Trent, focused primarily on the writings of these two writers.

1. MARTIN LUTHER AND THE LUTHERAN THEOLOGY OF MINISTRY

The documentation for the Lutheran approach to ministry is found, in its most authoritative way, in *Die Bekenntnisschriften der evangelischlutherischen Kirche,* a volume which gathers together the major documents of the Lutheran tradition.[2] An English edition is that edited by Theodore Tappert, called *The Book of Concord.*[3] In these volumes the following Lutheran documents are gathered together:

The Augsburg Confession
The Apology of the Augsburg Confession
The Smalkald Articles
The Tractatus on the Power and Primacy of the Pope
The Large Catechism
The Epitome of the Formula of Concord
The Solid Declaration of the Formula of Concord

Most of these documents were originally composed both in Latin and in German, so that either text has its authoritative position. Besides these official documents, one must also utilize the writings of Luther himself. This, however, is not an easy task. John Reumann cautions us, however, by reminding us that "the doctrine of ministry cannot be called a major item in Reformation controversy with Rome. There is in the Lutheran confessions, for example, 'surprisingly little about the office of the ministry'; it is 'incidental and secondary to the real controversy'."[4]

In a very detailed and highly documented article by Peter Manns, "Amt und Eucharistie in der Theologie Martin Luthers," the author tells us that the issue of ministry in Luther's own writings has been a serious topic of discussion in the German world during the past two centuries. He refers to H. Fagerberg's *Bekenntnis, Kirche und Amt in der deutschen konfessionellen Theologie des 19. Jahrhunderts*[5] both for detailed bibliographical material of the nineteenth century and for a history of the controverted areas on this issue. Manns also draws up a solid bibliography of twentieth-century German authors, who have dealt with this subject.[6]

In the North American scene, the Lutheran position on official ministry has also been a topic of controversy. George Lindbeck, for instance, notes, in opposition to the position held by Rudolph Sohm, that the *Confessio Augustana* refers to specific ministries in its use of *ministerium,* and not to a general ministerial office which every Christian by virtue of the common priesthood of all believers has and uses whenever he or she as a Christian proclaims or witnesses to the Word of God. Rather, Lindbeck states, the documents "think of a public office involving particular rights and duties to be exercised only or chiefly by the limited number of individuals who are formally inducted into it."[7]

A. C. Piepkorn, in his own analysis of the confessional statements, "The Sacred Ministry and Holy Ordination in the Symbolical Books of the Lutheran Tradition," concurs with Lindbeck's approach: from the *Large Catechism* Piepkorn can state that the Church consists of "preachers and Christians" [*Decalog,* 262]; God himself "instituted the sacred ministry (*ministerium ecclesiasticum:* Predigtamt) of teaching the gospel and of administering the sacraments."[8]

> To give the sacred ministry an exclusively functional character and to eliminate distinctions between "lay people" and "ordained persons," some theologians argue that the Lutheran view of the sacred ministry sees it only as a function or office that exists only in its actual discharge, but never as an order in the church. But the symbolical books see the sacred ministry both as an office (*ministerium; Amt*) and as an order or estate (*ordo; Stand*) within the Church.[9]

Piepkorn cites the *Apology of the Augsburg Confession:* 13, 11–12; 22, 13; 28, 13; the *Smalkald Articles,* III, 11, 1. Further, he writes: "The symbolical books nowhere attempt to derive the sacred ministry from the universal priesthood of the faithful."[10] The Wittenburg ordination ritual (H), drawn up after 1530, speaks of two sanctifications: the first sanctification is through the Word and the sacrament of baptism; the second is the vocation into the ministry. This comes from God, not from the people. In this, the Lutheran approach is totally in keeping with the gospels.

The *Apology of the Augsburg Confession* distinguishes between a power of order and a power of jurisdiction, and they are presented not as tasks for the Church totally, but rather for specific ministers: bishops and priests, as public persons within the Church [*Apol.* 28, 13, 9; 12, 28]. In all of this material, we see that much of traditional theological terminology and concepts are truly part of the Lutheran approach as well as they were part of the Roman Catholic approach. (a) In the Church there is a ministry which is not identical with the general ministry of all baptized. (b) This specialized ministry is exercised by a few and in a public way. (c) These few have been designated for that purpose by God and by the Church.

Luther, however, appears not to be totally consistent in his discussions on official Church ministry. In *The Babylonian Captivity of the Church* we read:

> We are all priests, as many of us are Christians. But the priests, we call them, are ministers chosen from among us, who do all they do in our name.[11]

But we likewise find other statements in Luther's writings which take a different approach. In his *Exposition of Psalm 82,* written around 1530, we read:

> It is true that all Christians are priests, but they are not all pastors. Over and above that he is a Christian and priest, he must also have an office and a field of work that has been committed to his charge.[12]

Von den Schleichern und Winkelpredigern tells us that "a distinction is given between preacher and laymen."[13] Contemporary Lutheran scholars have attempted in varying ways to harmonize these apparently different approaches. B. Gerrish speaks of a tension with the prominence being given, in Luther's writings, to a divinely instituted special ministry.[14] L. Green, for his part, speaks of a development in Luther's position. Luther, early on, was quite similar to other medieval theologians on the matter of ministry, but around 1520/1525 Luther's protest against the clerical priesthood led him to stress a universal priesthood; finally, at the end of his career, he stressed a separate ministry of preaching and administering the sacraments.[15] Robert Fisher responded to Green in a negative way. Fisher interprets the writings of Luther in a way which strongly includes: (a) God's institution of the Church and with this a universal priesthood; (b) God's establishment also of an ordained ministry, which, however, is not separate from the Church.[16]

Manns, for his part, attempts to document the reasons for the unclarity in Luther's writings on official Church ministry. All scholars, Lutheran and Catholic, agree that Luther nowhere presented a systematized and theologically elaborated statement on Church ministry. Manns lists, rather, the varied writings of Luther, in which the theme of ministry is touched on.

> Luther hat seine Auffassung über Amt und Eucharistie . . . nicht in Gestalt einer eigentlichen Lehre entwickelt und vorgetragen, sondern in programmatischen Streitschriften, in pastoralen Ratschlägen, Gutachten und Gelegenheitsschriften, in der Neuordnung und Handhabung der Ordination, sowie in seinen Kommentaren zur Schrift, in seinen Predigten, und immer wieder in seiner Korrespondenz.[17]

On the other hand, Calvin formulated a very systematized theological treatise on Church ministry. This makes the formulation of a Calvinist position somewhat easier than that of a Lutheran position. Clearly, all the problems in the Luther material have not yet been ironed out, but for our present purposes we must realize that even today there are controverted areas of Luther's position on this matter.

One must take into account, then, the fact that Luther's own position on official ministry is, to some degree, unclear. One must also take into account that Lutheran theology on this subject also reflects variant positions. Unlike Calvin and Calvinism, Luther and Lutheranism are not systematically and uniformly clear.

Manns presents us with some important historical details which in serious ways shaped Luther's approach to Church ministry. Very early on in the Reformation period, the Zwinglian influence clashed with Luther's approach, specifically on the issue of "home eucharist" (Hauskommunion). Many of Luther's own followers wanted to celebrate the eucharist at home and in a still setting ("dahaim in ainer stille").[18] Some Lutheran followers at Augsburg were especially desirous of these home eucharists. The eventual development of the *cuius regio, illius religio* principle created a eucharistic need, "eucharistische Notstand," a term which seems first to have been coined by Zwinglian preachers M. Keller, W. Muisculus and B. Wolfart in Augsburg, around 1531.

At the close of 1535, Luther wrote to Wolfgang Brauer, the pastor at Jessen, who had asked about such home eucharists under both species, when the law of the land and the Roman Church forbade communion under both forms.[19] A similar situation, a sort of *casus conscientiae,* was presented to Luther from Freiberg in February 1536.[20] Luther, in his responses, was seriously concerned about the "fanatics," the "Schwarmer," who were connected to Zwingli and Thomas Munzer. Luther was not in favor of these private, home eucharists, just as he had not been in favor of the monastic "Winkelmesse." The Roman practice of private masses was wrong, and so, too, the practice of private masses, simply for the sake of reception of the eucharist under both forms, was wrong. The eucharist was from its Gospel foundation a public affair, not a private devotion: "For Christ instituted this sacrament as a public ministry, so that there might be a memorial of Him in it through teaching and confessing" ("Nam Christus instituit hoc sacramentum in publicum ministerium, ut eius in eo fiat memoria docendo et confitendo").[20] Christ "wanted this sacrament to be a sign of public confession" ("vult hoc sacramentum esse publicae confessionis signum").[21]

Even on the issue of preaching, Luther realized that there was a command of God for parents to instruct their children: "Das aber ein Hausvater die Seinen das Wort Gottes lehret, ist recht und soll so sein; denn Gott hat befohlen, dass wir unser Kinder und Haus sollen lehren und ziehen, und ist das Wort einem gleichen befohlen."[22] There is, Luther writes, a difference between the official ministry (*Amt*) in the Church and that of a parent over the children; these are neither to be merged nor divided ("darum sie nicht zu mengen sind noch zu trennen").[23]

In the second part of his essay, Manns attempts to outline the differences between the position of Luther on Church ministry and that of the Roman Church. He lists four areas:

1. The relationship between official Church ministry on the one hand, and on the other the priesthood of all believers. Manns reaches a conclusion on this matter which closely parallels that of Lindbeck and Reumann, mentioned above, namely, that the official ministry is not identical to the priesthood of all believers, nor does the official ministry derive from the priesthood of all believers. These two aspects

of the Church are indeed connected, but quite distinct as well. In his exegetical writings, especially in his commentaries on Titus and Timothy, Luther clearly states that the word priest is used for all. Luther also maintains that the New Testament in no way allows for a "sacrament of order." This sacramentalizing of Church ministry is, in his view, a creation of the Roman Church. In this respect, one must recall that the sacrament of order reaches its fulfillment, in the theology of Luther's time, in the priesthood, so that one could also speak of a sacrament of priesthood. Generally, Luther speaks of a "ministerium ecclesiasticum," a "Predigersamt," not an ordained or official "priesthood."

2. The second issue which separates Luther's approach from the Roman Catholic approach is, then, the issue of sacramentality. Manns reminds us that the refusal of sacramentality to order was made by Luther on the basis of a particular conception of sacrament and that the sacramentality of order, from the standpoint of the history of doctrine, had raised innumerable questions.[23]

3. The third difference, Manns notes, and this ties in with what was indicated at the very start of this chapter, is the issue of the sacrificial character of the Mass. In this issue, the question of the gratuity of grace over against good works, the full efficacy of the sacrifice of Jesus, as well as justification generally, is raised. In many ways, this is the most important aspect of the division between Lutheran and Roman approaches to ministry, which means that the divisive issue is basically christological and ecclesiological, rather than simply a matter of the sacrament of order itself.

4. Manns brings to his fourth position many other issues, but above all the issue of priests ordaining to priesthood. Since in many areas of the then Lutheran world there were no bishops who would ordain Lutheran candidates, a need developed in the Churches to have adequate provision of official ministry. This, of course, developed into non-episcopal ordinations as a more or less general pattern.[24]

Foundational to an understanding of ministry in this Lutheran context is, however, the preeminence of the Word of God. Specialized ministry in the Church revolves around Word and sacrament. Ministers in the Church are needed for the preaching of the Word and the right administration of the sacraments (baptism and eucharist). Perhaps the profound theological reasons why ministerial office is necessary for Word and sacrament are not totally clear in Luther's own writings and in the Lutheran confessional documents. However, the actuality in the Church of both this ministerial office and its necessary connection with word and sacrament is, for both Luther and the Lutheran documents, not a matter of dispute.

In our present century, far from the heated arguments of this Reformation period, scholars, both Lutheran and Roman Catholic, have reassessed many of the positions which have separated these two Christian communities for so long. In the United States these reassessments have taken the form of a dialogue which has the highest endorsement of the Roman Catholic National Conference of Bishops on the one hand, and of the Lutheran World Ministries, which is the USA National Committee of the Lutheran World Federation of Churches. In the seventh dialogue, or series of conferences, the topic under consideration was justification by faith. The "Common Statement" which the group of theologians finally developed was preceded by a brief but very incisive summation of the history of the question. The authors of this statement write:

> Historical research in recent generations has greatly increased our awareness of the degree to which the debate over justification in the sixteenth century was conditioned by a specifically Western and Augustinian understanding of the context of salvation, which, in reliance on St. Paul, stressed the scriptural theme of *iustitia*, of righteousness. Eastern theologians, on the other hand, generally saw salvation within the framework of a cosmic process in which humanity occupies a place of honor.[25]

The authors then go on to trace this specifically Augustinian approach, with all of its variations, from the fourth century, down to the period of high scholasticism, and finally to the time of the Reformation in the sixteenth century. The issues of grace, merit and predestination are singled out as the centralizing factors [nn. 6–63].[26]

There is no doubt that Augustine's polemic against Pelagius was of serious moment and influence on the way in which the issue of grace and good works was developed, both by Augustine himself and by the Western theologians who followed him. Pelagianism, in the view of the Augustinian critique, undermined the gratuity of God's grace, by Pelagius' allowing for human input into the very initial stages of the salvation process. If men and women take the first steps toward salvation and justification, then grace is no longer grace, i.e., a gift of God, but simply follows on and is even required by this initial step of human endeavor. Grace as gift is supplanted by an earned or merited entity. A good work, which calls for a "reward," is placed before the gift of faith, and it is this inversion which negates all of scripture and the entire work of Jesus. Augustine perceived this most clearly and opposed Pelagius, Coelestius, Pope Zosimus himself, and all others who attempted to agree with this Pelagian defamation of the gospel.

Manichaeism, a later heresy, played its role as well, for in man-ichaeism the human person is irretrievably evil. Justification or sal-vation is simply a facade; it is not a complete transformation of the human person into something pleasing to God, but only a veil, by which God does not have to see the evil in the human heart. In the pelagian framework, the human element is too good; in the mani-chaean framework, the human element is too evil. It is clearly a case of Scylla and Charybdis.

All medieval theologians claimed to be anti-pelagian, but in spite of their claims some were openly accused of pelagian stances and positions. Augustine had stressed the absolute priority of God's ini-tiative and the primacy of his grace, and this was often repeated by medieval theologians; still, in Church practice and spirituality, and even in some medieval theology, the human role in this process was not forgotten and at times quite strongly presented, so that a pelagian framework seemed to reappear. Heiko Obermann, in his volume *The Harvest of Medieval Theology,* which treats of Gabriel Biel and late medieval nominalism, employs pelagianism as one of the major threads which runs through the entire discussion on the medieval and late medieval doctrine of justification.[27]

The common statement on justification, cited above, notes that there were three areas in which these conflicting positions can be found in the medieval theological world:

1. the treatment of grace;
2. the emphasis on merit;
3. the changing attitude toward predestination.

Toward the end of the medieval period, the "emphasis on human freedom was strong especially, though not exclusively, among those influenced by Ockham's nominalism and the via moderna" [10]. In the area of grace, the emphasis was tilted away from uncreated grace (God's own personal presence) to created grace (the transforming effects of God's presence). In some cases this emphasis on created grace verged on pelagianism, and it was this tendency toward a pelagian position which was one of the theological occasions for the Reformation. Again, however, it must be stressed that the Reformation did not occur suddenly; this topic of the relationship between grace and good works had been strongly discussed throughout the medieval period. The Reformation was not a protest against such theological discussions, but rather against the practical application of a good work theory in Church ministry.

The emphasis on merit had taken a major stride in the medieval period, but the indulgence issue only aggravated the situation. Augustine had not "invented" merit by any means, for he had found this theme already in the North African theological tradition, which stemmed from Tertullian and Cyprian. There was also at hand to Augustine a biblical basis for merit in the scriptural passages of reward and punishment. The medieval scholars, for their part, made a distinction between merit *de congruo* and merit *de condigno*. The merit *de congruo* corresponded to the medieval adage: *facienti quod est in se Deus non denegat gratiam* (for to one who does what he or she is able to do, God will not deny grace). Yet, this, too, appeared to lead to a pelagian position: one does something first, and then God will give grace. Or as the authors of the common statement remark: "The precept, 'do what is in one's power' (*facere quod est in se*), according to some historians, contributed to the rampant scrupulosity of the late Middle Ages, and it was viewed by the Reformers as a cause of the 'terrified conscience.' "[12]

The emphasis on predestination also goes back to Augustine, and as scholars point out, his thought on this matter is not clear. There are indications that Augustine at times seemed to inculcate a double predestination: God has predestined some for heaven and has predestined some for hell. Anyone aware of the history of the theology of grace in Roman Catholic theology knows that this has been one of the most divisive questions. Even the struggle between Molina and Bañez and their respective followers, which led to the papal intervention with the well-known congregations called *de Auxiliis,* which began in Rome in 1598, brought no solution to the question of predestination. The very date of these congregations (1598 and following) indicates that the issue of predestination was a disruptive part of the sixteenth century. This bitter and divisive debate on the issue of grace within Roman Catholicism itself was going on at the very same time as some of the sessions of the Council of Trent, since Baius and Jansenius were contemporaries of this council.

The Reformers are not aligned with any single medieval school of thought of this matter, since there was in the late middle ages such a divergence of thought.

> On the depravity of human nature, for example, there are par-
> allels, recognized by Luther himself, between his teachings and
> those of theologians of the Augustinian order such as Giles of
> Rome and Gregory of Rimini. The Reformers' rejection of the
> category of created grace may echo Peter Lombard's identification
> of infused love with the Holy Spirit. In rejecting positions such
> as that of Gabriel Biel, that human beings have a natural capacity
> to merit grace, the Reformers resembled Aquinas and others.
> Their language of imputation, some scholars have argued, has
> similarities to the Scotist notion of acceptation and to the language
> of Bernardine mysticism.[28]

In all of this one must realize that Reformation theology grew out of its medieval rootage, and since that rootage was not totally clear and unencumbered by strange tendencies, with even some of these theological positions bordering on the heretical, one must understand the Reformation doctrine on justification by faith as a continuing struggle to find the correct balance between grace and good works.

By now one can undoubtedly see that Christian ministry can easily become an ally to a pelagian way of thinking: ministers can (a) encourage people to "do what they can" but in a way which means that people should act first and then God will give his grace; and (b) their own ministry itself can be understood as a "good work," which must be done first so that God will give his grace. This latter (b) was perceived as a danger in the way in which the entire sacramental system was, to some extent, being developed. Ministers—priests—had to say the "right words," do the "right actions," and not only after these words and actions, but more importantly, precisely because of these words and actions, God will then give his grace to his Church. The words and actions of the priest are the "good works" which cause

God to give his grace. Indeed, the entire issue between the Roman Catholic theologians, on the one hand, and the Reformation theologians, on the other hand, focused on this particular item: grace and (sacramental) good works. The need of the sacraments, the efficacy of the sacraments, the ritual of the sacraments—all these are brought into question by the Reformers, but the underlying factor remains: grace and good works and the relationship of the two.

The Lutheran position on faith is closely connected with its emphasis on the Word of God. Faith comes through hearing, and we must hear not simply the words of the preacher, nor read the words on a page of the Bible, but we must hear the Word of God beneath the spoken or written words, either of the preacher or of the printed page. God is acting in his revelatory words; this revelation is certainly the Word of God but uttered for our hearing and our perception in the words of men and women. The doctrine on *sola fides* (faith alone) in many ways simply reiterates the items mentioned above under justification: namely, faith alone means God alone, and not a pelagian or semi-pelagian approach to the Christian message. It is not the fact that we do something (make an act of faith) which brings the gift of God's grace; it is, rather, because God has first offered himself to us through the revelation of his own Word in human words that we have this gift of grace. Faith, in this Lutheran view, is our realization and acceptance that all depends completely and absolutely on God: a *fides fiducialis.*

G. Ebeling says that faith in Luther's thought is not some power to do a good work, but it is, rather, a radical, new-becoming (Neuwerden) of the human, a newness, which has within it the death of the old person. Faith is focused on the human person, him or herself; "Das aber kann nicht heissen: eine Änderung in bezug auf das Personsein selbst—das wäre eben nur eine Veränderung bestimmter Eigenschaften und Fähigkeiten—vielmehr eine Änderung der Person selbst."[29] "Faith," he writes further on, "does not, as a power to act, make good works; rather, faith, as a power of good, makes works good."[30]

All of this influences the Lutheran approach to Christian ministry. We might bring this material together as follows:

1. Specialized Christian ministry is a ministry ordained by God; it is not a ministry which originates from the Christian people.

In this, specialized Christian ministry is in complete agreement with the gospels and with a solid doctrine on the priority of grace.

2. This specialized ministry is a ministry of the Word. The Word of God is above all ministry, whether that which comes from baptism or that which comes from holy ordination.

3. Any forms of specialized ministry or any aspects of such specialized ministry which are in opposition to this preeminence of the Word of God are to be rejected.

4. This specialized ministry is only meaningful within the Church; specialized ministry is not above the Church.

5. Only a specialized ministry connected to the Word of God, and consequently a preaching ministry, is in keeping with the gospel. Preaching ministry is the only essential or *de iure divino* specialized ministry in the Church.

6. Included in this specialized ministry is the right administration of the sacraments (baptism and eucharist).

7. Any and all other ministries in the Church are valuable only as they contribute to the ministry of preaching and the right administration of the sacraments.

In the *Confessio Augustana* we read that this ministry is truly *de iure divino:*

To obtain such faith God instituted the office of the ministry, that is, provided the Gospel and the sacraments. Through these, as through means, he gives the Holy Spirit who works faith, when and where he pleases, in those who hear the Gospel. And the Gospel teaches that we have a gracious God, not by our own merits but by the merit of Christ, when we believe this.

Condemned are the Anabaptists and others who teach that the Holy Spirit comes to us through our own preparations, thoughts, and works without the external word of the Gospel.[31]

Along with the constant tradition of the Christian Church, this article of the Augsburg Confession states quite clearly that ministry is from God. We have already seen that this is the first and major characteristic of the ministry of Jesus himself; we have likewise seen that this was the constant teaching of both the early Church and the

Fathers in the high patristic period. It was as well the teaching of all the great medieval theologians. Ministry is not a self-appointment, nor is it an appointment from the community. Ministry comes from God alone. This is the impact of *de iure divino.*

This article of the *Confessio Augustana* states that the basis for saying this is to be found in the Gospel. Scriptures, the very Word of God in most special words of men, remains the foundation of the Christian Church. Gospel ministry is what one must see as *de iure divino.* The condemnation of the Anabaptists, as is evident, focuses on (a) its pelagian approach to the sanctification which comes from the Holy Spirit, and (b) its non-gospel approach, and therefore its privatized approach. There is clearly nothing in this article which of itself would cause problems between Roman Catholics and Lutherans today.

One issue in the summary above, however, needs to be considered in a more thorough way, since it is not self-evident. This is the issue of the essential and almost (in Luther's writings) exclusive connection between the specialized ministry and preaching.

When one looks back, as we have been doing, on the history of ministry, we see that in the early Church teaching and preaching were part of the ministry of the apostles, of the Twelve, of the early ministers with their many names throughout the New Testament. Stephen was one of those, for instance, who was selected to be a "deacon." In selecting these men Peter reportedly says: "It would not be right for us to neglect the word of God so as to give out food; you, brothers, must select from among yourselves seven men of good reputation, filled with the Holy Spirit and with wisdom; we will hand over this duty to them, and continue to devote ourselves to prayer and to the service of the word." Peter insists on this service of the word, which cannot be neglected. Evidently this is a major part of the ministry which he envisioned. On the other hand, the seven were to "give out food," i.e., provide for the needy. It does not seem, however, that providing for food was all that these seven men did, for in the very next section of Acts we find Stephen debating and "always making speeches." Evidently, Stephen engaged in preaching and teaching the Word as well. In other words, in his ministry, too, there was a preaching component.

If one goes through the New Testament writings, one clearly finds that preaching the gospel is very much a part of the Christian ministry.

One also finds, though not as emphasized, the celebration of baptism and eucharist. Word and sacrament, both, not simply one or the other, are involved in the specialized ministry of Christians. This twofold aspect of ministry remains a constant throughout the history of Christian ministry.

In our historical journey we have found some other items of interest which at least might cause one to pause. Luther, of course, did not have access to the historical material which we are privy to today, nor did the Roman theologians of that time. Perhaps our vantage point helps us to modify some of the apodictic statements which were made on both sides at the time of the Reformation. First of all, in the first ordination ritual which we possess, namely, that in Hippolytus' *Apostolic Tradition,* we find that in the ritual for the ordination of the presbyter there is no mention of preaching or teaching, but simply advising the episkopos. If one were to say that the ministry of preaching belongs essentially to the presbyter, one would have to say that these ordinations are quite invalid. But this raises a question for the Lutheran theologians today: on the basis of the silence of this ministry of preaching, are they ready to condemn the ministry which we find in the *Apostolic Tradition* and subsequently in many other rituals of ordination for presbyters in both East and West up to about 500 A.D.? On the other hand if one were to say that the ministry of celebrating the eucharist (i.e., the power to consecrate the bread and wine at the eucharist, which as we saw was the focus of the medieval understanding of Order) belongs essentially to the presbyter, one would also have to conclude that these ordinations of Hippolytus were quite invalid. This latter raises a question for the Roman Catholic theologians. In that ritual of Hippolytus, and in many subsequent ordination rituals for the presbyter, there is mention neither of preaching nor of celebrating the eucharist. It would seem that this aspect of history—involving not simply one document, but a series of documents and indeed an entire theology of the presbyter—cautions us today to modify some of the exclusive statements made during these Reformation times by both sides. If preaching is so essential to the presbyteral ministry, then the ordination to the presbyterate in Hippolytus is essentially inadequate and therefore invalid; if the celebration of the eucharist is so essential to presbyteral ordination, then, once more, the ordination to the presbyterate in Hippolytus is essentially inadequate and therefore invalid.

Another very interesting aspect of this historical data was discussed at the ordination conference at the *Centre de Pastorale Liturgique.* In an informal discussion after Daniélou's address on "The Priestly Ministry in the Greek Fathers," the scholars who attended Daniélou's talk, namely, Liège, Rousseau, Gy, Chavasse, Girault, Lecuyer, Martimort, and Daniélou himself, spoke on an issue, which Liège raised as a first question to Daniélou: "I would like to put a question about the missionary function. . . . You have laid great stress on the 'word' as having a place in the cult, and as being bound up with the rite, but do the Fathers give the word, as such, a place in the ministry of evangelization and place catechesis first in their definition of priesthood?" In their subsequent discussion, these patristic scholars developed this thought, but the consensus was clear that evangelization, i.e., preaching to those outside the Christian community, was hardly ever, if at all, mentioned by the Fathers of the Church. In others words, the ministry of the word, for the Fathers of the Church, was directed to the Christian community. The teaching and preaching was indeed a part of specialized Christian ministry, i.e., of priestly ministry in patristic times, but it was seen as part of the ministry of leadership in the community.

> When the Fathers speak of the ministry of the word, it is essentially the word addressed to the community. But as far as the proclamation of the message to non-Christians is concerned I know of no patristic document which deals with this point.[32]

Liège and Daniélou concluded that the laity apparently were the ones who first brought the message of the gospel to the non-Christian, basically through family and friends. Only when these people were brought to the Church leadership and in some way were enrolled in the catechumenate did the ministers of the Church in a specific, but rather intramural way, begin to teach and preach to them. For John Chrysostom, the minister's basic task was to cooperate with God in his plan to heal the human race. He writes: "[We] are the ministers (*hyperetai*) and fellow-workers (*synergoi*); all we who preside (*prokathezometha*) over others. . . . The aim [of priesthood] is to give wings to the soul, to wean it from the world and to present it to God."[33] In the Eastern Fathers this design of God, *oiknomia,* governs the entirety of theology, including the theology of ministry. For them, it is this special ministry in the oikonomia which is the essential, *de iure,* unalterable character of ministry. In the cosmos, God is at work, and the minister is the co-worker, the *synergos*. Priesthood, Daniélou comments, is essentially defined by its relationship to the history of salvation.

On this salvation history basis, and not exclusively on the basis of "preaching" (the Lutheran approach) or exclusively on the basis of "celebrating eucharist" (the scholastic approach), do the early Fathers build a theology of priestly ministry. As *synergoi* with Jesus, priests continue the very work of the Lord, his work of salvation. But how does the minister do this? What are the functions of this ministry? Without any doubt, the mystery of God's plan is a mystery hidden in God and revealed in Jesus. "The first function, therefore, is to proclaim it lawfully, or, more strictly, the Word of God is at work in the Church, converting, instructing, reproving. Priests [i.e., ministers] are servants of the Word (Acts 6, 2). From this angle the priesthood is essentially apostolic. Its mission is evangelization, the proclamation of the kerygma."[34]

These comments of Daniélou in many ways confirm the Lutheran position that ministry is indeed, and essentially, involved with the preaching of the Word. They critique the Lutheran position, however, by indicating that there is a more profound or, if one could so speak, more essential aspect, namely, cooperating with God in his cosmic plan, revealed in Jesus. In other words, the preaching of the Word of God is itself based on a more profound aspect of special ministry: namely, the very ministry of Jesus.

These comments of Daniélou critique, as well, the medieval position that the priesthood is essentially the power over the eucharist. Prior to either preaching the word or administration of a sacrament, even the most holy of all the sacraments, the eucharist, there is a more profound aspect of priesthood: namely, the very ministry of Jesus.

What is being suggested in the examples above, taken from historical studies, is this: both the Lutheran and Roman Catholic position on the special ministry in the Church, as presented in the sixteenth century, might, if not must, be modified to correspond better with both the New Testament exegesis and the historical tradition in the Christian community. Neither position is wrong, but both positions are too narrowly conceived.

A second issue which needs to be re-considered is the issue of succession: both episcopal succession and papal succession. For Luther ministry was an *ordo* in the Church, as we have seen above. Luther did not see the Church as some sort of amorphous, congregational community with no leadership at all. The historic structures of Church ministry are presupposed in the *Confessio Augustana,* and there is a requisite on the part of the Christian community to obey such leadership and ministry. In the *Tractatus on the Primacy,* Luther assumes that synods and councils constitute legitimate avenues for the Church to exercise its leadership. Lutherans, today, however, are not at one on interpreting these historic structures of Church ministry. Some, and it is a minority, would say that any ministry which does not have episcopal or at least presbyteral succession is thereby defective. In other words, the *de iure divino* character of the ministry is in part dependent on the historic transmission of the office from apostolic origins. This position squares with that of the Orthodox Churches, the Roman Catholic Church and the Anglican Church. On the other hand, the majority opinion of Lutheran scholars today, on the basis of the material in the writings of Luther and the confessional documents, would say that this historical connection is not necessary, i.e., it is not *de iure divino,* and that there might be at times situations when no such historical minister would be available to the community. In these difficult situations the Church should not be deprived of ministration simply because such historically succeeding ministers are unavailable. It is evidently a moot point. Nonetheless, one must note that in the Lutheran writings there is an openness, at least *de facto,* for bishops, as well as presbyters, and deacons. The *Smalkald Articles* are dubious about the value of the papacy, even as a humanly instituted symbol of Christian unity (c. 2, 7–8), but in other writings there is clearly an openness to a papal position, even if only *de facto* (i.e., not *de iure*), provided that the ministry of the papacy is a true ministry of Word and sacrament.[35]

In the late medieval period, indeed just prior to the Reformation, there were instances of the pope allowing a priest to ordain to priesthood. Even the great scholastic theologians, such as Thomas and Bonaventure, note that if the Pope grants such a privilege, it is within his competence. Theologically and practically, then, in the fifteenth and sixteenth centuries, presbyteral, not episcopal, ordination to priesthood (which, it should be remembered, was considered the fullness of the *sacerdotium*) was not unheard of. In the empire at the time of the Reformation, the application of the principle *cuius regio illius religio* often led to the Catholic bishops leaving a region and thereby creating a region which had no episcopal ministry. Presbyteral ministry, accordingly, which included presbyteral ordination to the priesthood, filled this vacuum. In the Scandinavian and Balkan areas this was not the case, and for some places, such as the Finnish Lutheran Church, this has never been the case. Episcopal ministry and episcopal ordination continued for some time, or even down to the present.

In the common statement, developed by the Lutheran-Catholic dialogue on eucharist and ministry, published in 1970, we find the following summary on the issue of ordination, but this statement represents the thinking of theologians in both Churches of the twentieth century, and not that of the theologians in the sixteenth century:

> Entry into the Ministry has been designated by both Catholics and Lutherans as "ordination." This term too has had a variety of meanings. Catholics have seen in ordination a sacramental act, involving a gift of the Holy Spirit, a charism for the service of the Church, and the quality of permanence and unrepeatability. Lutherans, using a different (and more restrictive) definition of sacrament, have generally been reluctant to use "sacrament" with reference to ordination, although the *Apology of the Augsburg Confession* is willing to do so (c. 13, 9–13). Because of post-Reformation polemics, Lutherans became even more reluctant to use the term. The consistent practice, however, shows a conviction concerning the sacramental reality of ordination to the ministry. Lutherans, too, invoke the Holy Spirit for the gifts of the ministry, see ordination as the setting apart for a specific service in the church and for the world, and regard the act as having a once-for-all significance. Thus, there is considerable convergence between the Catholic and the Lutheran understanding of ordination.[36]

This is truly a remarkable summation. As one researches the Reformation period and the subsequent Tridentine deliberations, one would think that there was no possible convergence. The tenor of the theological debate at that period of time was quite apodictic on both sides; the tenor of the dialogues today has become far more irenic, due without doubt to a more critical exegesis of the New Testament and the powerful impact which our knowledge of the history of ministry and ordination has occasioned. Even the issue of "sacrament," which this common statement alludes to as a divisive issue, might find some resolution in the contemporary (therefore not sixteenth century) view that Jesus, in his humanity, is the primordial sacrament, and that the Church is the basic sacrament. Both the Lutheran and Catholic approach to sacrament in the sixteenth century was, as the statement notes, "restrictive." Both groups employed the same definition: a sacred sign, instituted by Christ, to give grace. This definition was never controverted; the controversy was over the extension of this definition. For the Lutherans only baptism and eucharist, given this definition, could be found in the New Testament; for the Catholic, the seven sacraments could be so found, at least in some way or another. No one at that time ever considered the Church as a basic sacrament, much less Jesus as a primordial sacrament. This new sacramental approach has the potential of assisting both communities come to grips with sacramental theology in general, and the theology of the "sacrament" of order in particular.

2. MINISTRY IN JOHN CALVIN'S THEOLOGY

In Book IV of the *The Institutes of the Christian Religion,* John Calvin takes up the theme of Christian ministry.[37] In the format of this volume, Calvin first traces the way in which we come to know God, our creator (Book I); then the way in which God, as our redeemer in Christ, is made known to us (Book II); third, he treats of the way in which we receive the grace of Christ, which constitutes a lengthy treatise on justification itself (Book III); only after all this, and in the last place, does Calvin treat of the external means or aids by which God invites us into the society of Christ and holds us there (Book IV). Among these external means are the visible Church, ministry, sacraments, structures of authority in the Church. One sees in this progression of topics that there is for Calvin both a christological and ecclesiological base to his presentation of the issue of Christian ministry.

The first question about ministry which Calvin raises is this: Why does God need the service of men? Actually, Calvin concludes, God has no such need: "He could indeed do it either by himself without any sort of aid or instrument, or even by the angels; but there are many reasons why he prefers to do it by means of men."[38] From the start, Calvin relativizes ministry; God might have structured his Church in quite a different way, but he has chosen to structure his Church with ministers: "He uses the ministry of men to declare openly his will to us by mouth, as a sort of delegated work, not by transferring to them his right and honor, but only that through their mouths he may do his own work—just as a workman uses a tool to do his work."[39] Calvin, in line with the entire Christian tradition, sees that ministry is essentially from God. Ministers are neither self-appointed nor community-appointed.

Given this free choice of God alone to work in and through his ministers, Calvin then says that "neither the light and heat of the sun, nor food and drink, are so necessary to nourish and sustain the present life as the apostolic and pastoral office is necessary to preserve the church on earth."[40] For Calvin, ministry is not something secondary to the Church, a sort of super-added issue. Ministry—and this means a special ministry, not simply a "priesthood of all believers"—is so much a part of the Church that one cannot think of Church without thinking of a specialized ministry. For Calvin, there was not an original ministry-less Church, which in time developed into a ministry-full Church. The prestige of this ministry in the Church is described by Calvin in highest terms, and he uses the scriptures as his base. God himself has acted in and through human ministers; therefore, we should not "dare despise that ministry or dispense with it as something superfluous."[41]

Calvin takes, as his starting point, the list which one finds in Ephesians 4, 11: "And to some his gift was that they should be apostles; to some, prophets; to some, evangelists; to some pastors and teachers." Of these five, Calvin comments, the first three were for the foundation of the Church or for some special moment in the history of the Church which God alone determines. Only the ministry of pastor and teacher are the "ordinary offices in the church."[42] For Calvin, the apostles were those who preached to the entire world and planted or founded the early Churches; prophets were those who excelled through a special revelation, and not just anyone who might interpret God's will. Evangelists were those Gospel ministers such as Luke, Timothy, Titus, or even the seventy (seventy-two), whom Jesus apointed in a second place after the apostles.[43] Today we might find this exegesis somewhat dated, and in great need of nuancing, but it was representative of Calvin's time, both for those who were in the Reformation group as for those who were in the Roman Catholic group. Apostle, prophet, evangelist were, however, extraordinary ministries, since they did not perdure in any stable way.[44]

This is not true for pastor and teacher. The Church "can never go without" these offices. The pastoral office, for Calvin, has the following charges: the discipline of the community, the administration of the sacraments, warnings, exhortations, scriptural interpretation. The teacher has only the last, so that doctrine might be kept whole and pure among the community of believers.[45] The pastors are compared to the apostles; the teachers are compared to the prophets and evangelists.[46] The pastors have been set over individual Church communities not "to have a sinecure, but by the doctrine of Christ to instruct the people to true godliness, to administer the sacred mysteries and to keep and exercise upright discipline."[47] These pastors are to remain with the individual Christian community or Church over which they are established. Not only a sense of order suggests such a procedure, but it is also, according to Calvin, the ordination of God, since Paul established presbyteroi over individual communities of Christians.[48]

Calvin realizes that in the scriptures the naming of these offices was often not firmly established, and that there is a sort of interchange between episkopos and presbyter as far as a name is concerned.[49] However, he does find that there are two other offices mentioned in Paul which have a permanence about them: government and caring for the poor. He sees the "governors" as a sort of senate, "chosen from among godly, grave and holy men, which had jurisdiction over the correcting of faults." This office was, in his view, necessary "for all ages."[50]

Caring for the poor was entrusted to deacons. These were public figures in the Church who distributed alms; there were also those Christians, such as the widows, who cared for the poor as well, but not in a public nor in an institutional way.[51]

Once more, one might today say that the apostolic Church needs to be interpreted in a somewhat different way than that which Calvin employed, and that many of his statements would need historical qualifications. Still, one finds in this section of Calvin's treatment of ministry many items which belong to the most solid strata of our Christian tradition: that ministry is from God alone; that there has been from the start of the Church a special ministry; that this ministry is meant for the leadership of the community; and that this ministry involves both preaching and sacramental administration.

Calvin then turns to the issue of ordination. If ministry is from God, then there is indeed an inner call, and this is clearly at the center of all true ordinations. Someone is called by God's grace to minister in the Christian Church, and in scripture itself one finds a description of the kind of minister whom God calls. Calvin notes that there are, in many sections of the New Testament, such descriptions. Unfortunately, Calvin does not use Jesus himself as the example, preferring the passages in Titus 1, 7 and 1 Tim 3, 1–7.[52]

If God calls someone, i.e., the inner call, and if the person, in the eyes of the community, measures up to the qualities of a minister enumerated in the scriptural passages, who then chooses and ordains them? The very procedure as a factual item is considered by Calvin as a given: "No sober person will deny that for men to appoint bishops is in every respect consonant with a lawful calling, since there are many Scriptural passages that attest this practice."[53] These scriptural passages are those which speak of the setting apart and laying on of hands. A question arises, however, whether the election should be made by the community at large, or by one's colleagues or by the elders or by a single individual. Arguments for each of these positions had already been formulated at the time of Calvin, and he addresses them carefully. Basing himself not only on passages from Acts, but also on the practice of St. Cyprian, Calvin holds that the consent and approval of the people should be involved, but that other pastors should preside over the election process, so that fickleness, evil intent, disorder do not occur.[54]

This process was simply the "election"; there was also the "ordination." From what we have seen in the medieval Church, the election was indeed one thing, while the ordination was another. In the proprietary Church system, the lord elected the parish presbyter, but the bishop ordained him; in the cathedral system, the canons elected the presbyters, but the bishop ordained. In some cases, it is true, the bishop or the pope had both elected and ordained. The point of this is: there was, at the time of Calvin, a distinction of election and ordination, and Calvin merely discusses the normal procedure for the selection and ordination of ministers for the Church.[55]

The ordination for Calvin is the "laying on of hands." This ritual alone is attested to in the New Testament. Calvin notes that with this ordination or laying on of hands, the person ordained is "no longer a law unto himself, but bound in servitude to God and the church."[56] The ordained person is a public person in the Church and must therefore act as such. In the laying on of hands, the community, Calvin states, was not involved; this was done only by the pastors. Another task of the pastors, or main pastor, then, is the ordination of worthy people to ministry.

Calvin then goes on to consider the early Church, with a brief historical accounting of ministry in the first five centuries.[57] Calvin relies on Jerome to a great extent in his interpretation of ministry in these early centuries. At first, according to Jerome, presbyter and episkopos are the same; then, to assure good governance, one was selected to be in charge, much as the consul was in charge of the senate. Although his oversight of the senate was a position of dignity, the consul was still subject to the assembly of his brethren. In time, we find the names for other ministries: chore-episkopoi, the metropolitans, the archbishops, the patriarchs, etc. Nonetheless, Calvin notes, both bishop and priest preached and administered the sacraments. In all of this, Calvin, in line with the majority of the scholastic theologians, sees that priest and bishop, as far as "orders" are concerned, are equal; the bishop is, however, administratively higher and therefore has a certain honor and dignity.

Just as the bishops, due to pastoral concerns, developed into metropolitans, patriarchs, etc., so, too, the deacons, due to pastoral concerns, developed into various levels: the deacon and the archdeacon. The minor orders that one reads of in history, and which were in practice within the Church at the time of Calvin, were simply preparatory stages for the office of bishop or priest (pastor or teacher). These minor orders were not, in Calvin's view, true ministries in the Church.[58]

One is quite struck at the amount of Church history which Calvin uses in this section on ministry, and even though some of it is outdated or even misleading, the historical thrust is admirable. Once this historical material is laid out, Calvin then claims that the history and even the scriptural base for the election and ordination processes were subverted by the papacy.[59] One is reminded in this section of Calvin's writings of the description of a bishop given by Origen at his time. Calvin's critique of the bishops of his own time parallels that presented by Origen. Lack of learning and lack of solid morality head the list of grievances. The election and ordination of young boys to be bishops is shameless. One of the reasons why the bishops, for many decades, even centuries, prior to Calvin, were unfit for the task was the denial of the community in the election process. He pits Cyprian against Leo I. For Calvin the history of bad episcopal leadership has led to the intervention of the princes at times, which had had both good and bad effects. In all of this, he writes, "ordination is nothing but pure mockery."[60]

Calvin then proceeds to discuss similar difficulties with the election and ordination of priests and deacons. The lack of learning and the lack of moral qualities, of course, head the list, and the ordination of inept and unworthy candidates is a travesty of ministry in the Church and of ordination itself. These abuses in Church ministry, abetted at times by the political powers and above all condoned by the papacy, lead Calvin to say that the form of Church government which "exists today under the papacy" is but a robber's den.[61] Reform was clearly needed, and as we find in a motto that was heard again and again during the Council of Trent, a reform of "head and members." The curia, however, was not overly excited about such reform, and the issue of residency of bishops was stonewalled on many occasions even during the Tridentine council itself.

From chapter VI to chapter XIII, Calvin spends his time on the papacy and all of the problems and evils he sees in the interpretation of papal authority. This present volume, however, is not a book on papal authority, and so any details on this matter need to be passed over here, not because they are insignificant, but because they are not precisely the theme of this volume. However, Calvin believed that the major problem to the issue of true Christian ministry lay with the *way* in which papal authority involved itself in the election process and the ordination process of Church ministers. Men might not be morally sound or well educated, and as such should never be allowed to become bishops, priests or deacons. Nonetheless, it was not the immorality as such or the lack of learning as such, but the involvement of the papacy in permitting and even promoting such people to ordained ministries, which was, in Calvin's view, the root cause for the sorry state of Church ministry both at the time of Calvin himself, as well as in the centuries prior to Calvin's period. We have already noted that the more the papacy took over or the more it intervened in regional and local Churches, the more the collegiality of bishops diminished. What Calvin is saying is that if the popes assume "supreme" power, then they must also give evidence of "supreme" responsibility, i.e., gospel responsibility.

Clearly, Calvin dedicates a lion's share of his treatise to the corruption of the ministry in the Church by the papacy, but this in no way means that he does not revere Church ministry. In fact, the situation is quite the opposite. Because he has such reverence for Church ministry, he is outraged by the decadence of that ministry and above all outraged by the causes which he sees had both brought about and was continuing to bring about these abuses of Christian ministry. He has no *a priori* problem with bishops in the Church, with priests and deacons in the Church, nor with ordination, as long as the ordination was not performed by everyone, but only by legitimate Church officials. All of these ministries he finds warranted by the New Testament itself. It is the practical situation which has, in his words, made a mockery of this ministry, and this overwhelms him with sadness and outrage.

In Chapter 14, Calvin takes up the question of sacraments. After treating sacraments in general, and then baptism and eucharist, Calvin takes up the "other sacraments."[62] In this section, he again returns to the theme of ordination. He begins with the minor orders and their relationship to major orders. Are these but one sacrament or seven (or nine if one follows William of Auvergne)? How can theologians say (he names Peter Lombard and others) that Jesus exercised all the minor and major orders? This is absurd! At the time of Calvin, the minor orders were simply rituals that one went through on the way to priesthood; there was no ministry of any magnitude attached to them.[63]

It is, of course, his discourse on the priesthood, not his discourse on the minor orders, which is central.[64] A theological explanation and understanding of the eucharist is presupposed, since Calvin has previously spent a large amount of his book on the topic of eucharist. The issue of offering a "sacrifice of the mass" is pivotal. To expiate, to offer sacrifice, or whatever term one uses, raises two major issues: namely, the sufficiency of Jesus' own act of expiation on the cross, and the relationship between grace and good works. In other words, a proper understanding of the ministry of priest (as well as that of bishop and deacon) requires a solid christology, particularly as regards the redemptive action of Jesus himself. For Calvin, a theology of priesthood which compromises the sufficiency of Jesus' salvific work is a false theology and one that can only endanger the total Christian teaching. Secondly, if the priest is performing a good work (the mass) in order to merit grace, particularly the grace of forgiveness of sin, then once more the "once and for all" aspect of Jesus' salvific work is placed in jeopardy. The crux of Calvin's criticism of the theology of priestly ministry as presented by the Roman position is most in evidence here. The issue is not priestly ministry per se, but rather the issue of christology (soteriology) and grace.

There is no way to discuss the sacrament of ordination if one does not first clarify its christological and soteriological basis. If the christological foundation is destroyed, as Calvin believes, then ordination cannot be a sacrament. "Surely," he writes, "they are utterly wicked when they dare designate this rite with the title of sacrament. As far as the true office of presbyter is concerned, which is commended by Christ's lips, I willingly accord that place [of sacrament] to it."[65] Or again, Calvin writes: "As I concede that it is a sacrament in true and lawful ordinations, so I deny that it has place in this farce, where they neither obey Christ's command nor consider the end to which the promise should lead us."[66] There is, then, in these passages an openness on Calvin's part to see ordination as a sacrament, although on other occasions, one might add, he does seem to hedge on this matter. What he will not call a sacrament is the ordination ritual and its theology as practiced in the Roman Church of his time, because in it the "once and for all" salvation-work of Christ is denied, and the absolute gratuity of grace is supplanted by good works. Calvin, in this approach, challenges the Roman theologians to show that Christology (soteriology) and the gratuity of grace is completely safeguarded in their approach to ordained ministry.

There is much that is commendable in Calvin's approach to the question of ministry. Since he spends so much time on the historical issues, one might think that the way either to support or to correct Calvin would be to joust with him on the matter of history. Has he read and interpreted the historical data correctly or not? Should one modify the historical data which he presents, and thus modify his conclusions as well? On the other hand, he is a very New Testament-oriented theologian, and so should one not wrestle with him on the basis of the New Testament interpretation? Given today's critical interpretation of the New Testament, would not one have to modify both Calvin's stance and his conclusions? Both approaches seem wise, but I would suggest, even more strongly, that it is the christological issue which must be resolved first. We saw above, when discussing Martin Luther, that his theology of ministry rested on the issue of justification and the issue of grace and good works; so, too, for John Calvin, the issue of justification in Jesus, and thereby the issue of the grace of forgiveness and subsequent good works, must be considered first. A defense of historical data, a defense of New Testament interpretation, even a defense of the papacy is not really getting to the heart of Calvin's understanding of Church ministry. Jesus, and the salvific work of Jesus, is the only adequate place to begin.

Ott, in his brief overview of Calvin's understanding of priesthood and ordination, reaches generally the same conclusions as those presented above. For Ott, Calvin is not opposed to a "sacrament of order," only to the falsification of this important ritual, which had occurred in the Roman Church and which had received, to some degree, theological justification from the time of such theologians as Peter Lombard.[67]

Both Luther and Calvin raise substantive issues vis-à-vis the sacrament of order, as regards both its practice and its theological description. However, it must be recalled again and again in this matter that ministry itself was not a major area of controversy in the Reformation. Far more profound were the christological and ecclesiological issues. Nonetheless, since ministry, and particularly episcopal and presbyteral ministry, structured the Church so essentially and so practically, the views of both Luther and Calvin on priestly ministry were considered a serious threat to the integrity of the Church. The very fabric of the Church was being challenged, not without reason in many areas, but still challenged. Given the momentum of the Reformation program, a momentum toward reform which preceded both Luther and Calvin, and given the monumental task of responding to this cry for reform, even theological reform, a council became inevitable. This council was, of course, the Council of Trent.

9

The Sacrament of Order
and the Council of Trent

In response to the many ideas circulated by Reformation theologians, the Roman Church, after several delays, finally met in a universal council at Trent. It opened on December 13, 1545 and lasted with several stops and starts and with changes of location until 1563. There were three sessions in all; the first at Trent itself, 1545–1547; the second at Bologna, 1551–1552; the third and the last, at Trent again, 1562–1563. It was in the second session that the topic of the sacrament of order was discussed. On November 25, 1551, it was announced that the deliberations on the mass as a sacrifice and on the sacrament of ordination would begin on January 25, 1552.[1]

1. THE PRELIMINARY DRAFT ON THE SACRAMENT OF ORDER

On December 3, 1551, the theologians were given a series of excerpted and abridged statements from the Reformation documents on the questions of the sacrifice of the mass (ten articles) and on the sacrament of ordination (six articles). These were discussed by the theologians from December 7 to December 29, 1551, and the forty theologians all concluded that these articles, as stated, were heretical.[2] On January 20 1552 a draft was submitted to the council, consisting of seven statements on the sacrament of order. These statements were not taken verbatim from the writings of the Reformation theologians; rather, they were based on the Reformers' ideas, but worded in such a way to highlight the problem area.[3] These seven positions are as follows:

1. Order is not a sacrament, but a certain rite for choosing and establishing ministers of word and sacrament.

2. Order is not only not a sacrament, but a human figment, invented by men who were ignorant of ecclesiastical things.

3. Order is not one sacrament; lower or minor orders are not degrees leading to the order of priesthood.

4. There is no ecclesiastical hierarchy, but all Christians in an equal way are priests; however to exercise this priesthood it is necessary to have the consent of the people and the government. Anyone who has been a priest may again become a lay person.

5. In the New Testament there is no visible and external priesthood, nor is there any spiritual power either to consecrate the body and blood of the Lord, or to offer it, or to absolve someone before God from his or her sins. There is only the office and the magisterial task of preaching the gospel, and those who do not preach are not true priests.

6. An anointing is not only not required in the ritual of ordination, but it is pernicious and despicable, as are also all the other ceremonies; nor is the Holy Spirit conferred in the sacrament of order, so that bishops are impertinent when they say: "Receive the Holy Spirit."

7. Bishops are not superior to priests, nor do they have the right to ordain, or if they do have this right, the right is held in common with the priests, and ordinations performed by them without the consent of the people are invalid.

As one can see, these statements are expressed in a very stark way. No reasons for any of these positions were added, so that their presentation might have been better contextualized. On September

18, 1562 the theologians were given these seven articles for discussion, and they were distributed to three groups of these theologians for further study and refinement. Fifteen theologians examined the first three; fifteen theologians were to examine the fourth and fifth; sixteen theologians were to examine the last two. It took many meetings, but on October 3 a commission of eight conciliar members received the results of the theological discussions: this commission consisted of two archbishops, four bishops, and two general superiors of religious orders.[4] One of the issues which provoked a great deal of discussion was the use of the term *de iure divino instituti* for bishops. One notes, right from the start, that the unresolved interrelationship of episcopal power and papal power surfaced and remained a major issue throughout these discussions by the council members at Trent. Finally on October 13, 1562 a new draft was submitted to the council members, sitting in plenary session and in this new draft there was no mention of bishops being established *de iure divino.*[5]

One must realize that the issue of justification had already been formulated (January 13, 1547); the decree on the sacraments in general had been promulgated (March 3, 1547); the decree on the sacrament of the eucharist had been completed (October 11, 1551); the decree on the sacraments of penance and extreme unction had been promulgated (November 25, 1551); the decrees on communion under both species and communion to children, as well as the decree on the mass as a sacrifice, were being discussed at the exact same time as the discussions on the sacrament of ordination (July 16, and September 17, 1562). The bishops were not about to take up material which had already been treated in these other decrees, nor were they in any way open to change what had already been decreed. This means that when one begins to study the sacrament of order in the discussions of Trent, one must never begin simply with the deliberations on order. One must take into account all that had preceded these discussions, particularly in the matter of sacraments and of justification.

Since the bishops had already treated many aspects of sacramental theology, and these were, therefore, not really issues which called for any further discussion, it is interesting to note that between the submission of the draft mentioned above, which took place on October 13, 1562, and the final decree, promulgated on July 15, 1563, one of the main topics, if not the most discussed topic, was that of the relationship of bishop to both priest and pope. We have seen earlier that the scholastic theologians, by and large, had not considered epis-copacy as a part of the sacrament of order. Episcopacy thereby became an office and a dignity. This, of course, was only a theological position; many canonists were not in accord with this separation of episcopacy from priesthood and the sacrament of order. For the scholastic theo-logians, as far as the sacrament of order is concerned, the bishop and the priest (the pope as well) are all equal. Jurisdictionally, the bishop and the pope are higher, but this superiority is only one of jurisdiction. The bishop of Granada, Spain, Pedro Guererro, speaking for the Spanish bishops in particular, took issue with this scholastic way of speaking, since bishops, as Guererro emphasized again and again in his interventions, have been instituted by the Lord himself and are therefore of divine right. This alone makes them quite superior to priests.[6] Discussion ensued on this matter, and historical data was brought to the attention of the conciliar bishops, which in some ways did not always indicate that bishop and priest were distinguished as the superior and the inferior.

The archbishop of Rossano, Giambattista Castagna, who later became Pope Urban VII, defended the opposite position, and became the spokesman for the Italian bishops. In Castagna's view, only the bishop of Rome is instituted *de iure divino* and in a personal way, since he alone, of all the bishops, succeeds not to the apostles generally, but to an individual apostle, namely, Peter. Other bishops can make no such claim to any individual bishop, and therefore, as a group, but only as such, are they the successors of the apostles. In the concrete, individual situation, a bishop is instituted by the pope and receives his authority and jurisdiction through the pope.[7]

J. Laynez, the general of the Jesuits, spoke in a way similar to that of Castagna. Generally, bishops, in the plural, have a jurisdiction directly from God, and in this way they, the bishops, are the successors directly from the apostles. In the case of a single bishop or in the case of a particular issue of jurisdiction, this is not the case. The individual bishops and bishops in an individual jurisdictional situation receive their power directly from the pope. Needless to say, Laynez' ideas were not welcomed unanimously, nor were his positions conclusive. Whether Castagna's, Laynez' and other bishops' ideas on this source of jurisdiction were cogent or not is not the main issue, so it seems. The main issue, the underlying issue, the essential issue, was the col-legiality of the bishops on the one hand and the primacy of the pope, or better the almost mono-primacy of the pope, on the other. We have already seen the seeds of this problem in the instances of the pallium and the instances of jurisdictional interference by Rome in local episcopal matters in the late Frankish Church; we have seen how the separation of episcopacy from the sacrament of order provided a theological base for diminishing the collegiality of the bishops. The more that each individual bishop is tied directly to the pope, the more the collegiality of the bishops is constrained. It was precisely this issue of the collegiality of the bishops and their position in the Church as a collegial body which, though in many ways not stated in these precise terms, became the fundamental issue for discussion in the debate on the sacrament of order at the Council of Trent. The position of the Protestant theologians and above all the reasons for their positions did not receive the same attention as this issue regarding the source of episcopal power and jurisdiction. The Protestant positions were judged heretical, and there was no need to enter into lengthy debates on their positions. Ostensibly, the bishops were discussing the difference between bishop and priest, the meaning of jurisdiction and divine right, the relationship of episcopal jurisdiction and papal jurisdiction, but when one examines the many factors involved, one sees rather clearly that it is the collegiality of the bishops which is at stake and what this collegiality means theologically and practically for the Church.[8]

2. THE DOCTRINAL/PASTORAL STATEMENT ON ORDER

In session twenty-three, July 15, 1563, the bishops at the Council of Trent promulgated the teaching of the Roman Catholic Church on the sacrament of order. The title of the decree indicates the apologetic approach which the conciliar members had taken: *Vera et catholica doctrina de sacramento ordinis ad condemnandos errores nostri temporis* (The true and catholic teaching on the sacrament of order to condemn the errors of our time). In keeping with the procedure already adopted by the council, a doctrinal and pastoral explantory section in four chapters was presented first. This is followed in customary fashion by eight canons, all of which are stated with the usual anathemas.[9] The first part is not simply doctrinal but pastoral. At times, authors forget how pastoral in intent the Council of Trent wanted to be. The bishops clearly wanted to provide the local priests and local bishops with a pastoral guideline for their own preaching and teaching. The bishops had no intention of developing a complete theology of the sacrament of order. This doctrinal/pastoral section is quite different from the one which the bishops had put together on the topic of justification. The justification statement is, in many ways, an attempt at a full-blown summation of the issue. The ordination statement simply highlights certain aspects which, at the time of Trent, were of great concern.

Chapter one of this doctrinal/pastoral section takes up the question of the institution or existence of priesthood in the new law:[10]

> In conformity with God's decree, sacrifice and priesthood are so related that both exist in every law. Therefore, in the New Testament, since the Catholic Church has received the holy and visible sacrifice of the Eucharist according to the institution of the Lord, it is likewise necessary to acknowledge that there is in the Church a new, visible and external priesthood, into which the old priesthood was changed (cf. Heb 7, 12ff). Moreover, Sacred Scripture makes it clear and the tradition of the Catholic Church has always taught that this priesthood was instituted by the same Lord, our Savior, and that the power of consecrating, offering, and administering his body and blood, and likewise the power of remitting and of retaining sins, was given to the apostles and to their successors in the priesthood.

One sees, immediately, that the bishops at Trent have no intention of promulgating anything which one might call "radical." Given the scholastic teaching of that period, the above chapter is quite "traditional." Priesthood is derived from the eucharist; priesthood focuses on the eucharist. This is the way that the New Testament and the tradition is to be interpreted. The scholastic theology of priesthood was essentially a eucharistically oriented theology of priesthood, and this is reiterated by the Council of Trent. No mention of preaching the Word, no mention of leading the community is included. Eucharist is the primary focus and essential power in the Christian priesthood, even though in the final sentence the power to forgive sins, which is secondary according to most of the scholastics, is also enumerated. The standard scholastic approach to the theology of order is repeated by the Council of Trent with no modifications.

In his commentary on this section of the tridentine decree, Michel in the *Dictionnaire de Theologie Catholique,* which is clearly a conservative statement on the matter, notes that the Council of Trent "defines nothing touching upon either the moment or the manner of instituting the priesthood; it is content to recall that the priesthood is above all ordained to sacrifice, a fundamental truth which is manifest in the three laws: the patriarchal law, the mosaic law, and the Christian law, and that the reformers deny this stubbornly."[11]

In the second chapter, the various orders are mentioned:

> The ministry of so sacred a priesthood is a divine arrangement and it is therefore fitting that in the perfectly ordered disposition of the Church there be several different grades of ministers to insure that the ministry be exercised more worthily and with greater reverence (cf. Mt 16, 19; Lk 22, 19; Jn 20, 22). These orders are to assist the priesthood, and they are arranged in such a way that those who are already set apart by the clerical tonsure are to pass through minor to major orders. For Sacred Scripture makes explicit mention not only of priests but of deacons as well (cf. Acts 6, 5; 1 Tim 3, 8ff; Phil 1, 1) and teaches with most solemn words what is to be chiefly attended to when ordaining them. And from the very beginning of the Church names of the following grades and the ministries proper to each one, namely: subdeacon, acolyte, exorcist, lector, and porter, are known to have been in use, although they were not of the same rank. For in the writings of the Fathers and of the sacred councils, in which we very frequently read about the other lower orders, the subdiaconate is regarded as a major order.

This chapter is clearly a defense of the minor/major order system which was in practice at the time of Trent and had been in practice in the Western Church for several hundred years. In the eyes of the bishops at Trent, this system was the tradition. Our knowledge of history today would without any hesitation modify several statements which are expressed here. "From the very beginning of the Church" is, indeed, a sweeping statement which must be qualified immensely. Even though one would write the history of these minor orders in a more careful way today, and even though the major orders would receive a different historical nuancing, the bishops, in their pastoral concern, wanted to revive the status of the minor orders for the Church practice of the sixteenth century. The minor orders, as well as the major orders of subdeacon and deacon, were seen as stages toward the priesthood. They were not ministries of any permanence, but only transitional. In many ways they had become only ceremonial formalities, and Trent wanted to give them a better theological position. The criticisms of the Reformation theologians had also belittled their value, which the bishops at Trent clearly wanted to combat. Therefore, both from within the Catholic structure and from without, there had been a depreciation of the minor orders, the subdiaconate and the diaconate, which the bishops were attempting to counteract. One must realize that in many ways this action of the bishops at Trent did provide, in the decades and centuries which followed, an improved ecclesiastical stance and value both to the minor orders and to the subdiaconate and diaconate as regards Church practice. Only with Vatican II has there been any substantial change to the thrust which Trent gave to these preparatory orders.

There is a deliberate vagueness on the part of the tridentine bishops on the matter of early Church and the minor orders as also on the subdiaconate. The scholastic approach that the minor orders, plus subdiaconate and diaconate, are to be defined in their relationship to the eucharist is sustained, though not defined, and the bishops left open the issue whether each of these orders confers a separate character, or whether they cumulatively imprint only one character, which progressively is enhanced. Even the question of the unity of the sacrament of order is left open: Is order one sacrament or seven? In fact, the council deliberately evades, throughout its sessions, any settlement of intra-scholastic issues. It seems, rather, that Calvin's writings are the focus of this particular chapter, and the council wanted to refute Calvin's position on the lesser orders.[12]

In chapter three, the issue of the sacramentality of order was taken up. The council bishops had already decreed the seven-sacrament position for the Roman Church, and this is simply repeated with focus on the sacrament of order in this particular chapter.

> Since it is very clear from the testimony of Sacred Scripture, from apostolic tradition, and from the unanimous agreement of the Fathers, that grace is conferred through holy ordination, which is effected by words and external signs, no one should doubt that order is truly and properly one of the seven sacraments of holy

Church. For the Apostle says: "I admonish thee to stir up the grace of God which is in thee by the laying on of hands. For God has not given us the spirit of fear, but of power and of love and of prudence" (2 Tim 1, 6; cf. 1 Tim 4, 14).

The council does not attempt to define the sacramentality of orders from a reasoned theological base. The foundation for maintaining that orders is one of the seven sacraments rests on scripture and tradition, particularly the patristic tradition. Grace is conferred through word and sign. Such theologically technical terms as matter and form are avoided. We have seen in the discussion above on John Calvin that here and there, in rather key places in the *Institutes,* he is open to the sacramentality of order, but his argument is that the words which the Roman Church uses direct the ordination in a non-gospel way, namely, that of offering a sacrifice, which Calvin interprets as derogatory to the once-and-for-all sacrifice of Jesus. This chapter in no way enters into a discussion as regards the reasons why Calvin and others refused to call ordination a sacrament. Rather, the bishops, in keeping with a long tradition in the Church, maintain the sacramentality of order and see any denial of it as heretical.

In the deliberations for this particular chapter, some of the bishops and some theologians pressed that the chapter include New Testament indications that Jesus himself had used external signs; e.g., he gave the chalice to the apostles, much in the same way that the bishop gives the chalice to the one to be ordained; or that Jesus blew on the apostles, thereby using an external sign. Because of the tenuousness of such exegesis, the majority of bishops refused to include such material in the final draft.[13]

Both the Catholic and the Protestant theologians in the sixteenth century argued on the basis of an identical definition of sacrament: an external sign, instituted by Jesus, to give grace. This definition was never a controverted issue, and in fact the definition was an essential part of the sacramental theology of both Catholic and Protestant positions. The main argument which the Reformers brought to bear was not on the definition, but on the extent of its application. Nowhere, they said, was there any clear indication in the New Testament that Jesus had instituted such a sacrament. The existence of bishops and priests was taken for granted; that they were so designated by a ritual *which Jesus himself instituted* is not evident. The bishops at Trent did not decide the issue regarding the time that the sacrament of ordination was instituted, and as is clear in the citation in this particular chapter, an ordination by laying on of hands is recalled, but Jesus himself is not mentioned in this reminiscence of the laying on of hands. The citation indicates that it was Paul who had laid hands on Timothy. On the other hand, the bishops and theologians at Trent realized that the scholastic theologians were somewhat divided on the matter as to when Jesus instituted this sacrament, and so they wisely left the question open.

Chapter four is the longest of all the chapters, indicating its significance. It treats of the hierarchical structure of the Church's ministry.

Moreover, in the sacrament of orders, just as in baptism and in confirmation, a character is imprinted which can neither be blotted out nor taken away. Therefore, this holy council rightly condemns the opinion of those who say that the priests of the New Testament have merely temporary power, and that once they have been duly ordained they can become laymen again, if they do not exercise the ministry of the word of God. But if anyone says that all Christians without exception are priests of the New Testament or are endowed with equal spiritual power, it is apparent that he upsets the ecclesiastical hierarchy, which is like an army in battle array (cf. Cant 6, 3), as much as if, contrary to Paul's teaching, all were apostles, all prophets, all evangelists, all pastors and teachers (cf. 1 Cor 12, 29; Eph 4, 11). Therefore, the holy council declares that besides the other ecclesiastical grades, the bishops who have succeeded the apostles belong in a special way to the hierarchical order; and placed (as the Apostle says) by the Holy Spirit to rule the Church of God (cf. Acts 20, 28), they are superior to priests, and can confer the sacrament of confirmation, can ordain ministers for the Church, and they have the power to perform many other functions that those of an inferior grade cannot. Moreover, the holy council declares that in the ordination of bishops, of priests, and of other grades, the consent, call, or authority, neither of the people, nor of any secular power or public authority, is necessary to the extent that without it the ordination is invalid. Rather, it decrees that all those who have been called and appointed merely by the people or by the secular power or ruler, and thus undertake to exercise these ministries, and that all those who arrogate these ministries to themselves on their own authority, are not ministers of the

Church but should be considered as thieves and robbers who
have not entered through the door (cf. Jn 10, 1).

Many items are touched on in this lengthy chapter, and it would
be wise to consider them carefully in an organized form.

1. **The question of sacramental character.** This is a theological
position which had had a long history in the Christian tradition. Very
early on in Church history, the question of re-baptism and re-ordination of those either baptized or ordained in an heretical group became quite vexing. It took centuries to work out the various elements
involved in this complex question. Eventually, the Church decided
not to re-baptize nor to re-ordain. Battles on this matter had been
fought; scars were everywhere; with the theological discussion on sacramental character, a stage was attained when the battles and the
questions and the hesitations seemed to be quite over. If one does not
appreciate this issue of re-ordination, one will never appreciate what
the theology of sacramental character is all about. In the sixteenth
century, to deny the sacramental character of baptism, confirmation,
and order simply reopened these issues all over again. Trent would
not hear of this. By the use of the term sacramental character, the
bishops of Trent stood firmly with the hard-won position that these
sacraments were not to be repeated. There is no description, definition,
discussion on "what" this character might be. Only the fact that these
three sacraments confer a character has been promulgated; the exact
make-up of such a character is an open question.

J. Galot, in his study on sacramental character, *La Nature du
Caractère Sacramentel,* notes that the bishops at Trent were very circumspect on this matter of sacramental character: "Le concile définira
l'existence comme certaine, mais refusera de se prononcer sur la nature
de caractère" (The council defined the existence [of the character] as
certain, but made no pronouncement on the nature of the character).[14]
Again, Galot notes that the council did not want to *define* the sacramental character "as the reason for the non-reiteration of the sacrament."[15] The bishops did not employ the formula: ratione cuius ea
iterari non possunt [in virtue of this [character] they are not repeated].
Rather, after mentioning the character conferred in the three sacraments, they say simply say: unde ea iterari non possunt (Denz. 1610):
"hence, they are not repeated." In this way, Galot indicates, the bishops
at Trent avoided settling the scholastic discussion on the very reason

why the three sacraments are not repeated. The tridentine bishops left the matter open, but they did indicate clearly that the sacramental character is indeed connected to the issue of the reiteration of the sacraments.

2. **The question of priests returning to lay status.** On the basis of this whole re-ordination background, the theology of priesthood which affirms that once a person is ordained there is never any need to re-ordain means that a duly ordained priest (or deacon) always remains a priest, even though he might not exercise his ministry. If one maintains that one might be a priest for a period of time, then return to the lay state, and that if then that person decided to return to active priestly ministry he would need to be re-ordained, then the issue of re-ordination occurs all over again. Trent would have nothing to do with this side of the re-ordination question either.

This was not a new issue in the history of the Church. The Council of Saragosa in 381, the Council of Chalcedon in 451, that of Angers in 453 and that of Tours in 461 had all declared orders to be irrevocable and forbade clerics to return to lay life. Generally, councils do not take up such issues if the contrary practice had not been going on, and their mention in these early documents indicates that such a procedure might have been going on. However, the theology of Augustine on the irrevocableness of order played an important role in providing the substantive basis for this stance. The Council of Trent follows this long-tradition in the Church.

3. **The question of the priesthood of all believers.** The Council of Trent, in this section of chapter four, does not speak about a priesthood of the laity and a priesthood of the ordained. It correctly speaks of a priesthood of all believers. There is an attestation in the New Testament that all Christians are priests; cf. 1 Pet 2, 5; 2, 9; Rev 20, 6. These passages are neither mentioned in the chapter, nor can one find in the chapter any openness to a priesthood of all believers. This negative stance became the normal Catholic stance on this issue. For instance in the 1936 volume of the *Lexikon für Theologie und Kirche,* the article on priest, written by Ludwig Kosters of Sankt Georgen, Frankfurt, has about one sentence on the issue.[16] In the 1963 edition of the same *Lexikon,* there is an entire section devoted specifically to the topic, written by J. Blinzler and by Y. M.-J. Congar.[17] These two entries on the matter in the same *Lexikon,* but at different times, indicate two different stances on the part of Roman theologians to

the issue of a priesthood of all believers: one which reflects the stance of Trent and the other which reflects the stance of contemporary biblical and systematic theologians. It is perhaps, however, more important to realize what the council bishops at Trent did not want to say, namely: the Church originally was a non-hierarchical society. The initial Church structure would then have been "congregational," and only in time did it become "hierarchical." We have seen in the earlier chapters of this volume that such an original "congregational" structure is impossible to verify. That there were ministers from the start is, on the other hand, historically evident. The constant teaching of the early Church was clearly that of a dual-structured Church society, and this from the beginning. One might not be able to use such terms as "cleric" and "lay" in this earliest of Church structures in the sense that we today understand such terms, but one must see that from the beginning there were ministers and there were those to whom they ministered and that ministry in the early Church was connected with community leadership. In this Trent aligns itself with the finest of Christian tradition.

In some ways, the Reformers did not argue so much from the early Church and its initial structures, although at times this was indeed the form of the argument. Rather, they argued at times that if there were, for a variety of reasons, an inability for a Christian community to have such ordained ministry, then the lay persons might celebrate eucharist, etc. The statement of Trent does not refer to this kind of situation; it refers only to the original structure of the Church. To complete the picture, however, it must also be recalled that neither Martin Luther nor John Calvin opposed hierarchical leadership as such; it was the type of leadership which they opposed.

When one compares the statements in Vatican II on the role of the baptized in the Church, which emphasize that simply because of baptism there is a clear basis for the priesthood of all believers, with the lack of any extensive appreciation of this role of the baptized in the statements of Trent, one sees that the appreciation of ministry in Trent clearly needed to be complemented and enriched with a solid doctrine on the priesthood of all believers, which Vatican II has expressed.

4. **The question of the superiority of bishops.** At the Council of Trent it was taken for granted that there was a hierarchy of order and

a hierarchy of jurisdiction. As regards the issue of the episcopacy as a separate but essential stage of the sacrament of order, the Council of Trent did not decide the matter. Bishops were, of course, priests, and therefore in their capacity as priests they were clearly part of the sacrament of order. By becoming bishops, was this only an office or dignity, as the scholastic theologians held, or was it another stage or grade in the sacrament of order, as some of the canonists argued? Trent did not give any definitive statement on the discussion. As late as 1962, for instance, Sola in his section on the sacrament of order for the *Sacrae Theologiae Summa,* published by the Jesuits from the various theological faculties throughout Spain, put forth the thesis: *Episcopatus est verum sacramentum Novae Legis* (Episcopacy is a true sacrament of the new law).[18] "This thesis," he writes, "in so far as it is understood of the episcopacy in differentiation from the presbyterate, is certain and common."[19] Had the Council of Trent defined anything on the matter, Sola would have said that it was *de fide definita,* either *explicite* or *implicite.* Neither is the case; the question remained open, and Sola, availing himself of this open situation, argued, but only in the capacity of a theologian expounding a position not a defined doctrine, that episcopacy should be considered a sacrament and therefore part of holy orders. In the footnote he cites Bellarmine, Soto, Lennerz, and Bozzola in favor of his stance. He notes that Tanquerey goes so far as to call it *de fide.* Gasparri simply says that it must be *firmiter tenenda* (firmly held).[20] Lercher in his manual *Institutiones Theologiae Dogmaticae* notes that the bishops of the Council of Trent "did not wish to define this question."[21] Just as the issue had been debated during the scholastic period, so, too, after the Council of Trent, the issue continued to be debated, with a gathering of force for the inclusion of episcopacy in the sacrament of order. It was not until Vatican II, however, that an official document of the Church presented the episcopacy as included in the sacrament of order, and this was done through the ordinary, not extraordinary magisterium of the Church. In other words, even today, there is no solemn definition of the Church on this matter. It might also be noted that Trent refrained from saying that the bishops are superior to priests *de iure divino* (by divine right), even though this had been a matter of the discussions. The issue was simply passed over in silence. Nor is there any statement whether or not the jurisdiction of the bishop comes directly from God or indirectly through the pope. This, too, was left as an unresolved issue.

Galot, in his volume on the *Theology of the Priesthood,* recounts the debate mentioned above between the Spanish bishops on the one hand and the Italian bishops on the other regarding the *de iure divino* institution of the bishops. He writes:

> In the end, the Council compromised and settled for the formula: "a hierarchy instituted by divine ordinance." This choice of words leaves open the question of whether bishops were instituted by Christ. The phrase "divine ordinance" refers to a will or provision on the part of God but contains no other concrete precisions as to the nature of that ordinance. When interpreting the conciliar text, we must take into account the Council's deliberate intention to refrain from a clear-cut affirmation of a divine institution, or of an institution on the part of Christ directly related to bishops.[22]

What Galot does not refer to in the above summation is that the underlying issue was this: if the bishops are not instituted directly by God or Christ *de iure divino instituti,* then their jurisdiction and power comes indirectly through the pope. If the latter is the case, then episcopacy must be theologically interpreted in a way in which the collegiality of the bishops is at least diminished if not radically altered.

The bishops have the power to confirm, to ordain, and to do "many other functions"; these latter are certain blessings and dedications or consecrations of Church buildings. The practice of the Church at the time of the Council of Trent was clearly this: the ordinary minister of confirmation was the bishop. This was the formulation which the council had already used, allowing, thereby, for extraordinary ministers of confirmation, i.e., certain delegated priests. It is well known, however, that in the fifteenth century there were several cases in which priests (generally abbots) were allowed to ordain, even to ordain to priesthood itself. These ordinations are not even referred to in the tridentine documents, although many of the bishops and theologians at the council might have known of such cases. In the tridentine document, the bishop is simply presented as the ordinary minister of the sacrament of order. In theory, even major scholastic theologians had allowed for "extraordinary ministers" of this sacrament; in practice, it seems, various popes had delegated such power to ordain to simple priests.

On this matter Galot interprets the situation as follows:

> When chapter 4 asserts that the ministers of lower rank have not the power attached to the functions performed by the bishops, it speaks of the empowerment priests receive at ordination. It does not intend to assert that priests may not be empowered by the pope to act as extraordinary ministers of confirmation, or even of ordination, which was the minority's position at the council.[23]

In some ways, Galot over-interprets this fourth chapter. The question really was: Does the empowerment come from ordination to the priesthood itself, or does the empowerment come from a papal fiat? If the first, then priests, in virtue of priestly ordination itself, confirm and even ordain; if the latter, then something has to be superadded to the power of ordination. Trent did not settle this issue, whereas Galot in his comment above seems to assert that Trent disallows the power to confirm and ordain as originating in priestly ordination itself. This latter seems to go beyond the text.

5. **The question of election.** The bishops of the Council of Trent maintained that *the election* to an ordained office did not depend on the call of the people, nor of a political ruler. Secondly, *the appointment* did not depend on either people or ruler. In line with the entire tradition on the matter of Christian ministry, these bishops maintained that the call and the commission is from God. Community appointment has never been a part of solid Christian teaching as regards ministry. In the early Church and in even later periods, the people at times were quite involved, and secular rulers as well were involved, in the selection of popes, bishops and priests. Lay investiture, as the movement in the middle ages was called, had not been, however, uniformly an advantage to the Church, and the tridentine bishops opposed a return to such lay investiture structures. Community elections had also mixed effects, and the council did not want a return to those kinds of elections. However, the underlying motive for denying these past procedures from recurring again was much more the Reformers' doctrine that *unless* the people were involved, or *unless* the secular power was involved, ordinations would be invalid. It was this kind of invalidating connection which was condemned, not simply some sort of participation in the selection process or the appointment process.

Finally, in this issue of election of Christian ministers, self-appointment was roundly condemned as totally against the Christian tradition and the New Testament itself. As we have seen, self-appointment has never been an acceptable position in the Church as regards ministry.

3. THE CANONS

On the basis of this statement of four chapters, the bishops then go on to promulgate eight canons, all of which are so worded that they would incur an anathema if denied by any Catholic. These canons follow directly from the positions expressed in the preceding doctrinal/pastoral statement. In many ways they are repetitious of the material already covered.[24]

> 1. If anyone says that there is not a visible and external priesthood in the New Testament, or that there is no power of consecrating and offering the body and blood of the Lord, and of remitting and of retaining sins, but says that there is only the office and simple ministry of preaching the gospel, or says that those who do not preach are not priests at all, let him be anathema.

One would have to maintain all of the above to be a heretic, formally speaking. In other words, the anathema applies only if someone holds all that precedes it. This is the standard approach in understanding all such anathema-statements. One could focus the issues as follows:

> a. In the New Testament, and therefore in the Christian Church, there is a visible and external priesthood, not simply an internal and spiritual priesthood.
> b. This visible and external priesthood involves the eucharist and the central message of the gospel: forgiveness of sins and life in God.
> c. Priesthood is not simply confined to preaching the gospel, so that priests who do not preach are actually no priests at all.

The basis for this canon is the scholastic definition of priesthood, which essentially focuses on the eucharist. Vatican II, as we shall see, does not say that this approach is wrong, only that it is too narrow. We will consider in a subsequent chapter the position of Vatican II, but for our present concerns one must realize that at Vatican II, the scholastic definition of priesthood (which is the basis for the above tridentine canon) was formally not accepted as the theological understanding of priesthood. Vatican II, therefore, qualifies this first canon of Trent, and does so via the ordinary magisterium of the Church. We, then, today, must acknowledge the good points of the canon (nos. a, b, c above), but likewise acknowledge the limitations of this canon. Unless we do both, we are not in compliance with the magisterium of the Church, which has spoken both at Trent and at Vatican II.

> 2. If anyone denies that in the Catholic Church, besides the priesthood, there are other orders, both major and minor, through which one must pass, as through certain steps, towards the priesthood: let him be anathema.

This canon does not identify the major and minor orders, even though the chapter had done so. At the time of Trent, subdiaconate was considered a major order by the Western Church. Again, documents which have come from the pope after Vatican II require us to qualify this canon in a quite extensive way. In the motu proprio of Paul VI, issued on August 15, 1972, we read: "Consequently, the major order of sub-diaconate no longer exists in the Latin Church" [4]. Again: "What up to now were called minor orders are henceforth called 'ministries' " [2]. Again: "Ministries may be committed to lay Christians; hence they are no longer to be considered as reserved to candidates for the sacrament of orders" [3].[25] Other than the diaconate, no order inferior to that of the order of presbyter remains in the current Church structure. How does one explain this, since Trent places any denial of these minor and major orders under anathema. And yet, one might say that Pope Paul VI officially "denies" them by abrogating them.

In the sixteenth century, the denial of these minor and major orders was more fundamentally a formal denial of Church authority. In other words, it is not the denial of the canon as such which is anathematized as heretical, but rather it is the denial of competent Church authority in these matters which is the heretical aspect. What

H. Jedin has written on the issue of anathema (and he wrote this long before Vatican II and Paul VI) has special significance here:

> It should be observed that at this time [the time of the Council of Trent], the anathema had not yet entirely lost its disciplinary character; it was still a formula of excommunication. For this reason, it was all the more easy to refrain from a nominal condemnation of Protestant authors. The prelates and theologians of the Council, above all Cardinal Cervini, still entertained a somewhat wider conception of faith and heresy than that elaborated by modern theology. Hence, the canons, with their appended anathemas, are not to be regarded without more ado as so many definitions *de fide definita;* what they do is to express the fact that a specific doctrine is in formal opposition to the faith proclaimed by the Church, so that whosoever maintains such a doctrine denies her teaching authority and thereby separates himself from her.[26]

There is much value in Jedin's comments, particularly when one deals with these canons on the sacraments. Historical studies require us to revise some of the tridentine canons in many ways, so that the apodictic or apparently unchangeable nature of their expression is indeed modified. On the issue of these minor orders, the manuals of theology have never formulated any thesis *de fide definita,* even though there is a solemn canon, with anathema attached to it regarding these minor orders. The point that is being made here is this: the mere fact that there is a canon with an anathema attached is not of itself an indication of heresy if the canon is denied. This second canon makes this interpretation quite clear. The Church authority was indeed well within its competence to abrogate the minor orders and the major order of subdiaconate, but this would not have been the case if this second canon had meant that no person, even Church authority, could change the issue of these minor and even major orders.

> 3. If anyone says that orders or holy ordination is not truly and properly a sacrament instituted by Christ our Lord, or that it is a kind of human invention, thought up by men inexperienced in ecclesiastical matters, or that it is only a kind of rite of choosing ministers of the word of God and the sacraments: let him be anathema.

One sees that this canon resembles almost verbatim one of the first statements which were submitted to the council bishops on the matter of the sacrament of order. The council states clearly that ordination is a sacrament of the Christian Church, not some humanly established rite or process of election of ministers. This is a solemn teaching of the Catholic Church, and to deny it would clearly be heresy. One can find many passages in the writings of both Luther and Calvin which would favor the sacramentality of order. In these deliberations on the sacrament of order, Trent did not address itself to the reasons why both Luther and Calvin refused to call ordination in the Roman Church a sacrament. These reasons have already been stated above: namely, that in the Roman Church the ordination to priesthood (and therefore the ordinations to all the other orders, which are essentially focused on the priestly ordination) is defined by its relationship to offering the sacrifice of the mass. How does one describe the relationship between the sacrifice of Jesus, which was once and for all and totally adequate for the expiation of sins, and the sacrifice of the mass, which is also called "expiatory." It is this christological base which must be addressed, so the Reformers argue; otherwise, to admit that ordination is a sacrament, under the terms of eucharistic sacrifice as explained theologically by the Roman Church, is to derogate the sacrifice of Christ. If one does not address this christological issue which divides the Catholic and the Protestant, one will never settle the issue of the sacramentality of ordination.[27]

> 4. If anyone says that by holy ordination the Holy Spirit is not given and thus it is useless for bishops to say, "Receive the Holy Spirit"; or if anyone says that no character is imprinted by ordination; or that he who was once a priest can become a layman again: let him be anathema.

Once more, themes which were enumerated in the first draft appear, indicating that the bishops considered these issues to be of serious moment. Statements by Reformers, denigrating the invocation of the Holy Spirit in the ordination ritual, are clearly in mind. Still, there is no reference as to the reasons why the Reformers might say this. The fundamental reason is, once again, the christological issue. If the ordination ritual, with its injunction to priests to offer sacrifice, is interpreted in a way which diminishes the complete efficacy of the work of Jesus, then an invocation of the Holy Spirit is, indeed, an unworthy prayer. The bishops at Trent had already discussed the matter of the eucharist, but above all they had already discussed the matter of the relationship between the sacrifice of the cross and that of the mass and had worked out a manner of expression which, in their view, seemed adequate to safeguard the full and complete efficacy of the expiatory sacrifice of Jesus. Consequently, when they came to this issue on the sacrament of ordination, they could say without further ado that the invocation of the Holy Spirit is totally legitimate.

The character of ordination and the possibility of someone receiving ordination and then returning to the lay state have been noted in the discussion on the chapter statement itself.

> 5. If anyone says that the sacred anointing which the Church uses at holy ordination not only is not required, but is despicable and harmful, just like the other ceremonies: let him be anathema.

Although this canon is expressed in a clear way, the reasons why many Reformation theologians rejected anointing, as well as other ceremonies, for the ritual of ordination are not mentioned. Calvin in particular took issue with this anointing, using rather blunt language:

> Finally, from whom have they [the Roman bishops] received anointing? They answer that they have received it from the sons of Aaron, from whom also their order took its beginning. They constantly prefer, therefore, to defend themselves by perverse examples, rather than to confess that what they rashly use they have themselves devised.[28]

Calvin goes on to say that oil can be wiped away, with dust and salt, or with soap if needed. "But what has oil to do with the soul?" Moses was commanded to anoint with oil, but he also gives commands about "the coats, the girdles, and the caps," but no one in the Church follows those instructions. Moses commands the slaying and burning of rams, consecrating ear tips and garments with the blood of rams, but none of these are picked up—only that of the anointing. "Obviously, they are attempting something ingenious: to shape one religion out of Christianity and Judaism and paganism by sewing patches together. Their unction therefore stinks because it lacks salt, that is, the word of God."[29]

Anointing is not found in the New Testament, whereas the laying on of hands does appear in the New Testament. As we have seen, in the development of the ordination ritual, many external signs, such as anointing, were added, as also vestings, handing over such instruments as chalice and paten, and other external signs. It is this accumulation of external rites, which are not rooted in the New Testament, that Calvin goes after. There is a *sola scriptura* argument in the approach of Calvin—so much so that details not found in scripture are denigrated.

However, Calvin's argument is deeper than a merely *sola scriptura* approach. In the justification for such things as anointings, the Roman Church, through bishops and through theologians, were basing themselves on Old Testament data: what Aaron did as a priest; what the Levites did; what Moses commanded. However, it is the priesthood of Jesus that is central to the Christian faith, not the Old Testament types. "Therefore," Calvin notes, "while they long to emulate the Levites, they become apostates from Christ, and abdicate the office of pastor."[30] The bishops at Trent, however, did not invent this ritual of anointing in connection with ordination; this anointing ritual goes back to the patristic period, and it had become traditional in the Church. The bishops perceived that an attack on such a tradition of long standing was an attack on the authority of the Church itself. The bishops did not enter into the question of the origin of this rite of anointing and the way in which anointing relates to the priesthood of Jesus. They simply accepted them, and felt that a denial of them would include a denial of the authority of the magisterium of the Church.

A third item which Calvin finds fault with in such anointings is this: the Roman theologians see such actions as "conferring grace," "imparting the Holy Spirit."[31] What is at stake here is the causality of the sacraments: what does the priest or bishop actually do? what do the actions accomplish? what causality is to be found in material things such as oil, bread, wine, water, etc.? what efficacy do the words of the priest or bishop have? This sacramental causality was in profound ways challenged by the Reformation theologians: the basis of their challenge is the relationship between grace and good works. By the time the tridentine bishops arrived at the discussion on ordination, they had already treated the sacraments in a general way, and this general treatment had included a very modest and, as far as the inter-scholastic debate on the matter was concerned, quite non-committal discussion of sacramental causality. There were various theories on sacramental causality at the time of the Council of Trent, particularly theories which divided the Dominicans and the Franciscans. The council bishops refused to settle this inter-scholastic debate and left all positions open for further discussion. Nonetheless, in each of these scholastic positions the fundamental issue of grace and good work was evident.

This rather simple, straightforward canon five, as we can see, has a host of ramifications, none of which are addressed directly at this juncture of the council deliberations. However, not to see these implications, would be a total misinterpretation of the canon.

6. If anyone says that in the Catholic Church there is no divinely instituted hierarchy consisting of bishops, priests, and ministers: let him be anathema.

It has been one of the major issues of this present volume to indicate that from the very beginning there was in the Church those who were the ministers. This, indeed, means a division between those who are the ministers and those for whom and with whom this ministry occurs. In the course of Church history, this division was named hierarchy, and the hierarchical structure was legitimated by many theological bases. A late such theologizing is that of Dionysius the Areopagite, although Ignatius of Antioch clearly presents us with an early hierarchical theology. The bishops of Trent remain solid in this tradition that from the first there were ministers, here called hierarchy, in the Church. Since the Church is divinely instituted, one can say that ministry in the Church is divinely instituted. Therefore, this division is not a human structure imposed on the Church. To deny this ministerial division, commonly called hierarchy, would be a denial of the Church itself, and therefore heretical.

When one comes to the issue of the three grades: bishop, priest and ministers, some modification of the canon is required. It is by no means historically evident that from the very beginning of the Church we have these three grades. Indeed, the naming of ministry was by no means uniform in the apostolic Church, and the eventual standardizing of ministerial names did not come until the end of the second century. The bishops at Trent, as well as the theologians, did not have the clarity of this historical background on ministry which we have today, and although they realized that the episkopos/presbyter issue was somewhat cloudy in the New Testament, they also realized that the gradation of bishop, priest, other ministers, had a lengthy tradition in the Christian Church. Here, I think, Jedin's comments help, since there is an excommunication-factor in the anathema, and not simply a heresy-factor. In the sixteenth century, the bishops seem to be saying, the Church is made up of this gradation: bishop, priest and other ministers. If one does not wish to accept this kind of structure, then that person should be considered excommunicated. The excommunication is not made on the basis of heresy, but on contempt for current Church structures. If some modification or interpretation along these lines is not made, then one is quite constrained to explain the solemn statement at Trent on bishop, priest and other ministers, on the one hand, and the lack of historical evidence for such a gradation, on the other hand, or, even more to the point, the historical evidence that contradicts a gradation of episkopos/presbyter in the apostolic Church.

Galot presents a similarly qualified judgment on the tridentine position:

> The Tridentine declaration is somewhat obscure also with respect to ranks in the hierarchy. It does not say that the three ranks listed in canon 6 were instituted by divine ordinance. It says this only of the hierarchy itself. The word "minister" too raises a question. Does it refer to deacons only, or to all the orders below priesthood? Since the phrase "and other ministers" was explicitly amended to read "and ministers", it is more likely that only deacons were meant. Yet the fact remains that deacons were not explicitly named.[32]

Today, with the ecumenical thrust to Christian deliberations, might one see in this "obscurity," these raised questions, the possibility of a non-episcopal hierarchy? Note well that hierarchy alone is the thrust of the canon, not the episcopalness of the hierarchy. Such considerations need to be explored along ecumenical lines.

7. If anyone says that bishops are not superior to priests, or that they do not have the power to confirm and ordain, or says that the power they have is common both to them and to

priests; or says that the orders conferred by them are void
without the consent and call of the people or of the secular
power; or says that those who have not been rightly ordained
by ecclesiastical and canonical power and have not been sent,
but come from some other source, are lawful ministers of the
word and of the sacraments: let him be anathema.

This is the longest of all the canons in this section, and there are
many inter-connected items expressed in it. Following on canon six,
the council states that bishops are superior to priests. The basis for
this superiority is expressed in their "power to confirm and ordain."
As ministers of confirmation, they were already called the "ordinary
ministers." This distinction is not applied to the power to ordain; in
fact, nothing is said to indicate whether priests might also be "extraordinary ministers" of ordination, a position found in the works
of Thomas, Bonaventure, etc., and a position which was mentioned
at the Council of Trent by several theologians and bishops. Since the
issue of the superiority of the bishop over the priest had consumed
much of the time for discussion prior to this final decree, the brevity
of the statement is in itself noteworthy. The reasons for such superiority
of bishop over priest are left as open questions; the fact of the superiority is not.

In this canon, moreover, once more the question of the role of
the lay people in the selection of those to be ordained is brought up,
whether this be the people generally or secular political figures more
specifically. Such voices, the council states, are not needed as far as
the validity of order is concerned. The bishops reject any theology of
ordination which is based on ordination by the community, and they
do this in keeping with the best of the Christian tradition. That the
people might play some role is not the issue; the issue is whether
community appointment alone determines the validity. Community
appointment, however, has never been an acceptable position in the
Christian Church as far as the validity of Christian ministry is concerned.

The final section of the canon deals with self-appointment, i.e.,
an appointment to ministry which is not made in any way by the
Church. Ministry can only be seen within a solid ecclesiology. Any
exclusion of Church in the matter of ministry vitiates the ministry.
The bishops maintain this connection of ecclesiology and ministry,
and they do this on the most solid of theological foundations.

8. If anyone says that bishops chosen by the authority of the Roman Pontiff are not legitimate and true bishops, but a human invention: let him be anathema.

It is interesting to note that this is the only place in the entire decree on the sacrament of ordination that mention is made of the Roman pontiff. It was added as a separate canon because of the lengthy discussions on the issue of the relationship of bishop to pope. At the time of Trent, the popes had instructed the papal legates to make sure that the prestige of the papacy was not diminished in any way, even the slightest. Many bishops, in their interventions defending the papal conferral of episcopal jurisdiction, reminded their fellow bishops that the opposite view, the *de jure divino* view, might easily be read as a dimunition of the papacy.[33] The decree, both in its doctrinal/pastoral section, and in its canons, is, as a point of fact, not dominated by a theology of papacy. Historical data, known to the bishops at the Council of Trent, and known to both Catholic and Protestant theologians at the time of Trent, indicated that bishops had, in the past, not been appointed by the Roman pontiff, but had been appointed more locally and through a variety of ways. Appointment of bishops by the Roman pontiff and confirmation of bishops by the Roman pontiff were historically a late medieval practice in the Church. One can see that the complaint of "human invention" might easily be made, since the apostolic Church, the early Church, the patristic Church, and the early medieval Church did not know of this practice. On the basis of this rather late institution in the Church, the question of its validity clearly arose. The canon defends the practice of the Roman Church. To absolutize this canon into a divine right of the pope, as if only through papal election can bishops be legitimate, goes far beyond the intentions of the Council of Trent.

However, there is more to this canon than simply a late historical development. Calvin, in book IV of the *Institutes of the Christian Religion,* discusses the ministry in the early Church, but then from chapter five through chapter thirteen takes up the issue of the papacy. He shows his hand, as it were, in the very title of chapter five: *The Ancient Form of Government Was Completely Overthrown by the Tyranny of the Papacy.* Calvin believes that the intervention of the papacy into the government of the Church produced the major problems in the Church.[34] The same could be said of Martin Luther and his book on *The Babylonian Captivity of the Church.* Whatever the pope touched, they seemed to imply, invalidated the gospel message, not simply because of the popes themselves, but because of the basic issues of (1) justification and (2) grace and good works, which the popes were, in the minds of Luther and Calvin, perpetuating. These two issues undergird all the objections which the Protestants brought against the Roman Church. Since the two themes had been discussed in previous sessions, the bishops at Trent did not raise the matter anew here. They simply upheld the Roman Pontiff's authority as it was actually practiced at that time to appoint bishops. However, if one misses the Reformers' objections to papal power, which rest on the doctrines of justification and of grace and good works, one will miss the fundamental elements behind this canon.

4. AN OVERVIEW OF THE TRIDENTINE TEACHING ON THE SACRAMENT OF ORDER

We have considered above the initial draft, the doctrinal/pastoral statement, and the canons of the tridentine discussion on the sacrament of order. What can one say in general about this material. Ott summarizes his discussion on Trent and ordination by simply enumerating the eight main issues found in the eight canons: "Zusammenfassend sei gesagt, dass durch das Konzil von Trient folgende Lehrpunkte als amtliche Lehre der Kirche festgestellt wurden. . . . " (In conclusion, it can be said that in the Council of Trent the following doctrines were established as official teaching of the Church.)[35] One might ask if this is adequate.

A. Duval, in his analysis of the Council of Trent and the sacrament of order, speaks of the decree which we have just considered, but also notes that side by side with this decree, one must consider as well the *Decreta super reformatione,* consisting of eighteen canons, which are disciplinary in nature. This second group of texts

> is not merely the practical application, the pastoral corollary, as it were, of the doctrine expounded in the first. For these texts imply a theology which is not strictly that expressed in the dogmatic decree. It is clearly not opposed to it, indeed it assumes it, but it incorporates more or less coherently other elements as well. It is a theology which is trying to get its bearings, which is in the process of being worked out, inspired by those pastoral efforts which were going on at the time, of which the council

itself was to a certain extent a result. In fact, on the practical level, particularly as far as the administration of the sacrament of Orders and its exercise were concerned, the Council of Trent is as much a point of culmination as of departure.[36]

Duval helps us immensely here. (a) he says that there is more to the theology of ordination or priesthood than one might find only in the dogmatic decree; one finds other elements in these disciplinary decrees. (b) Duval notes, too, that a theology of priesthood was in the process of being worked out, and so we do not have a final word or completed theology in the tridentine material. (c) Third, he notes that Trent needs to be seen not simply as a culmination, but as a beginning. These three points which Duval makes help us move in Roman Catholic theology from Trent to Vatican II, i.e., from a theology of priesthood presented at Trent, but not in a completed or finalized way, to a theology of priesthood presented at Vatican II, although again not in a completed or finalized way. Unless one appreciates this openness to development from the tridentine material, the teaching on priesthood in the documents of Vatican II might be seen as disruptive and not as constructive.

What were these disciplinary issues? The decree is quite lengthy, but we can summarize the eighteen points topically as follows:

1. The residency prescription of bishops.
2. The allowed interval to accept consecration as bishop and the place of this consecration.
3. The obligation of bishops to ordain.
4. The conditions required for first tonsure.
5. The conditions for the conferral of minor orders.
6. The age of a candidate for tonsure and minor orders and his living circumstances; the conditions for married minor clerics.
7. Prior to every ordination, there is to be an examination of the candidate's intellectual ability and an investigation of his moral character.
8. The place of ordination and the proper bishop for such ordinations.
9. The ordination of candidates not under the jurisdiction of a local bishop.
10. Restrictions on abbots and others who had previously had the right to confer tonsure and minor orders.

11. The intervals between the various orders.
12. Subdiaconate is to be conferred on candidates who have reached the age of twenty-two; diaconate at the minimum age of twenty-three; priesthood at twenty-five.
13. The instruction on celibacy for candidates to the subdiaconate and diaconate; the interval between the conferral of major orders.
14. The conditions for promoting a deacon to priesthood.
15. The faculties to absolve are to be given to priests only after suitable examinations and the permission of the bishop to do so has been obtained.
16. Ordination of any candidate must be justified by the pastoral needs of the Church.
17. Bishops are to see that minor orders and subdiaconate and diaconate are exercised by those so ordained.
18. Seminaries are to be established. This is the longest of the disciplinary decrees.

These decrees are helpful for us today to obtain some idea of the actual situation in the Roman Catholic hierarchy at the time of the Council of Trent. Not only in these decrees but elsewhere, the residency of the bishops was enjoined. Bishops were notorious at this period for not staying home. This resulted, clearly, in poor, often scandalous, leadership throughout a diocese. Secondly, there were at the time of Trent and the period prior to Trent (therefore all during the Reformation period) too many priests and clerics.[37] This overgrowth of priests had been mentioned at the Council of Sens in 1528, and at the Council of Trent in 1547 and again in 1562. Not only were there too many priests, but it seems that a large group of them were morally deficient, intellectually unqualified and professionally incompetent. Men became priests simply for economic reasons, poorer people in order to have a modicum of economic security, those better off in order to have an affluent life. The cause for this seems from all the data of history to lie with the benefice system.

There is no doubt that the theology of ordination espoused by the Council of Trent and the disciplinary action which Trent backed helped in the decades and centuries which followed to revitalize the moral and spiritual dimension of priesthood in the Roman Church. For approximately four hundred years the theological synthesis on priesthood espoused by the Council of Trent influenced the entire teaching on priesthood in the Roman Church. All the manuals of theology used in the seminaries were strongly dependent on the tridentine material. There was and is a certain unity to the view on priesthood and ministry which Trent presents. This internal coherence to the material offered a solidity to the understanding of bishop, priest, deacon, and other ministers. Trent, of course, did not originate this coherence, since it was in the *summas* and commentaries on the sentences which the scholastic theologians of the twelfth to the fifteenth centuries had put together.

A second factor that contributed in no small measure to the long-lasting influence of Trent on priestly theology and priestly practice in the Roman Church was the strong opposition to Protestantism which became entrenched from the seventeenth to the twentieth centuries. Naturally, this entrenchment worked both ways. Protestant theology and practice of ministry solidified because of their opposition to the Catholic positions. Whenever there is an enemy to fight, the home positions are not challenged and become hardened.

Other factors might also be invoked, but one can only marvel at the long-standing influence which the tridentine material had on the issue of the sacrament of order, theoretically and practically, in the Roman Catholic Church. As the decades and centuries went on, a certain stagnation began to take place. Catholics began to absolutize more and more the tridentine material. It was seen as a culmination, not in any way as a beginning of a theology of ministry and ordination. Vatican II and the theological and historical studies that led up to Vatican II have altered this situation, as we shall see in a later chapter.

A major limitation to the approach which Trent took on the matter of the sacrament of order is the almost total silence on Jesus' own priestly ministry. The eucharist, of course, is mentioned as the essential focus of the priesthood, and the eucharist is indeed the real presence, sacramentally, of the Lord. Jesus is mentioned briefly when the priesthood is mentioned as being instituted by the Lord (chap. 1 and can. 3). Jesus' own ministry as the source of all Christian ministry is never alluded to. The characteristics of that ministry of Jesus, as portrayed in the gospel, are not used as the criterion for Christian ministry. The Church, on the other hand, is defended; the hierarchy and its position is defended; power and jurisdiction are defended— no doubt because they were precisely the areas that the Protestants were challenging. Nonetheless, no adequate theology of priesthood can be developed without a thorough christological base.

A second limitation to the tridentine approach is its exclusive focus on the eucharist as the center of a theology of priesthood. This limitation, of course, applies to the standard scholastic approach to priesthood as well. The preaching of the Word is only mentioned in a secondary or even tangential way. Again, the Reformers' position that preaching the Word was the essential element of Christian priesthood accounts for the tridentine over-emphasis on eucharist and under-emphasis on preaching. Moreover, leadership of the Christian community is not given any major place in the tridentine discussion of priesthood, whereas it is more clearly evident in the tridentine discussion of bishop.

These indications of limitation to the tridentine approach on the sacrament of order are not meant in any way to belittle the Council of Trent, but unless one appreciates not only the value of Trent but also its limitations, the theology of priesthood which one finds in Vatican II will not make sense. Vatican II does not say that Trent was wrong; it does, however, find the tridentine approach to be too limited, too narrow. Pinpointing these limitations helps one see the areas in which Vatican II complements and enhances the Roman Catholic understanding of ordained ministry.

It is difficult to summarize the main points which the Council of Trent has established. Ott, as noted above, simply expresses in summary form each of the canons. Galot expresses it this way:

From the declaration of Trent, we must retain the following assertions:

1. In the power of order there is a hierarchy which comprises several ranks but without detriment to the unity of the sacrament. Since there are only seven sacraments, the sacrament of order must count as one.
2. The hierarchy has been instituted by virtue of a "divine ordinance" or provision.
3. It is defined that, in this hierarchy, bishops rank above priests. They have powers of their own, especially the power to confirm and ordain, yet the possibility of priests being empowered by the pope to function as extraordinary ministers is not excluded.
4. In addition to bishops and priests, the hierarchy includes ministers, but the import of this term is not determined with pre-

cision. The Council focused attention on the power of bishops. It did not delay over lower ranks.[38]

Other theologians might word the summation of Trent differently, emphasizing here and there other items than those which Galot emphasizes. This does not mean that there will be radically different views by a variety of Catholic authors, but there will not be total agreement either, since Trent left so many issues fairly open and since many of the expressions used by the bishops in the document are imprecise to some degree.

The spiritual concern for the quality of priest, deacon and other ministers is certainly evident in the *Decreta de reformatione,* although even in this document the role of Jesus as priest is at best tangential. Minor orders are given greater respectability, but all the minor orders and the two major orders, subdeacon and deacon, are seen only as transitional stages toward priestly ordination. In this respect, a theology of deacon is not enhanced in any profound way by Trent.

The relationship between bishop and priest, on the one hand, remained an open question, and continued to be discussed in the centuries following Trent. By the time of Vatican II, some major steps had been made in this matter, so that the relationship, theologically, came to be seen with more clarity and profundity.

The relationship between bishop and pope, on the other hand, has remained not simply an open question, but one that is quite vexing. Even Vatican II, with all its insights, did not resolve the issue, and the many struggles, even one might say confrontations, between the pope and the bishops in the aftermath of Vatican II indicate that not all is resolved. However, let us continue our historical overview as we turn to counter-Reformation theology on the ministry in the Roman Catholic Church.

10

The Sacrament of Order in Counter-Reformation Theology

This chapter is concerned with the Roman Catholic approach to the sacrament of order from 1600 to 1950. Although this is a lengthy period of time, the basic theological structure regarding this sacrament remained fairly unchanged in Catholic theology throughout this period. This lengthy and consistent approach to holy order was due to several circumstances:

1. Counter-Reformation Catholic theology tended to be defensive or apologetic. The positions maintained by the Council of Trent were repeated over and over, against the Protestant positions.
2. In Lutheran theology a period of "orthodoxy" set in, shortly after Luther, and this Lutheran orthodoxy was for the most part quite rigid and apologetic as well. Pietism in Lutheran circles developed in the latter part of the seventeenth century and into the middle of the eighteenth century as a reaction to the formalism of such orthodoxy. When Reimarus, Schleiermacher, Bauer, and others began to restructure Protestant thought, at the end of the eighteenth and throughout the nineteenth century, the official Roman Catholic approach was negative to these new approaches. Catholics who seemed to side with this new Protestant approach were suspect of modernism. The antimodernist stance of the official Church

was stringent, with the result that a conservative approach to theology continued to dominate.

3. A few, but very ineffective, measures toward ecumenical dialogue did take place during this period of time, but such occasions had no lasting effect. Rather, a non-ecumenical, even antagonistic attitude prevailed in Roman Catholic theology vis-à-vis Protestant theology.

Catholic authors who trace the history of the sacrament of order, such as Michel[1] and Ott,[2] agree that this lengthy period was, theologically speaking, quite uniform. It is not, then, inappropriate to consider Roman Catholic theology on priesthood as a fairly single entity from the end of the Reformation down to the middle of the twentieth century. Our chapter, then, will begin with Robert Bellarmine, who, more than any other Catholic scholar, immediately after the Council of Trent established the patterns for discussing this sacrament. Second, we will consider the influence of the *Traité des Saints Ordres,* ascribed until recently to the Sulpician Jean-Jacques Olier, which contains a program on priesthood that dominated the seminarians' spirituality in the Western Catholic Church from post-tridentine times down to the present century. Third, we will consider, but in a brief fashion, some of the more significant efforts made by Catholic scholars in the eighteenth and nineteenth centuries on the issue of the history of this sacrament. Fourth, we will consider some of the major official statements of the Church hierarchy on the priesthood which were issued during this period. Lastly, we will indicate the major contributions to the theology of the sacrament of order which the Catholic Church made during this rather lengthy period.

1. ST. ROBERT BELLARMINE AND HIS PRESENTATION OF THE SACRAMENT OF HOLY ORDER

Robert Bellarmine (1542–1621), a Jesuit scholar of keen intelligence, taught at Rome from 1576 to 1588, and it was during this time that he composed his *Disputationes de controversiis christianae fidei adversus huius temporis haereticos.*[3] In this work he devoted a small section on the sacrament of holy order. In many ways, this *Liber Unicus de Sacramento Ordinis*[4] became the model for presenting the

Catholic view on priesthood for the next three hundred years. Bellarmine approaches the topic from an orderly and scholastic standpoint; he asks a series of questions and his replies present the major theological material on the particular subject. His questions are as follows:[5]

1. Is the ordination of ministers truly and properly called a sacrament?
2. Is the ordination of all or of only some of these ministers a sacrament?
3. What is the matter and form of this sacrament?
4. What is the effect [of this sacrament]?
5. Who is the minister [of this sacrament]?
6. By which ceremonies is this [sacrament] conferred?

Bellarmine's method in treating each of these questions is quite noteworthy. First of all, he has read the writings of Luther, Calvin, Melancthon, Chemnitz and other Reformation writers. He cites them in each of the questions, indicating specific writings and specific passages. In many ways, Bellarmine is indebted to these Reformation theologians for the very way in which he presents his response to them. First of all, since the Reformation theologians themselves had based their arguments strongly on scripture, Bellarmine spends a great deal of time on the New Testament foundation for the Roman Church's position, even utilizing the Greek text. Secondly, Bellarmine responds to the Reformation positions by citing tradition, particularly, the tradition of the early Church. The New Testament, in Bellarmine's pedagogical approach, remains, of course, the basis for his argument. This New Testament basis is the Word of God in Christ, and today we might consider this aspect of Bellarmine's thought to be the christological base. However, for Bellarmine there is more than just scripture; there is also the ecclesial aspect. The theological understanding of the sacrament of order formulated by the Roman Catholic Church in Bellarmine's time is presented as the true interpretation of the New Testament data, precisely because it corresponds to the interpretation of that same data by the ancient Church. If the theological approach to the sacrament of order in the Roman Catholic Church of the sixteenth and seventeenth centuries agrees with the approach of the ancient Church, then, in Bellarmine's argument, this approach must be superior to that of the Reformers, who have no such early Church basis.

It is remarkable that Bellarmine, who had been the first Jesuit professor to teach publicly, with the permission of the University of Louvain, a course on the *Summa* of St. Thomas, refers to Thomas Aquinas most often only obliquely: "ab antiquis nonullis Scholasticis,"[6] "ex communi sententia Theologorum" [with only Durandus and Cajetan disagreeing],[7] "omnes veteres Scholastici, Durando excepto,"[8] In discussing the imposition of hands as an essential part of the sacrament, Bellarmine cites St. Thomas directly.[9] On the other hand, Bellarmine cites the Magister [Peter Lombard] on several occasions, and other theologians, such as Scotus, Bonaventure, Paludanus, Francisco Vittoria, Pedro de Soto, Martin Ledesma, and a few others. All of these, including St. Thomas, are mentioned merely as indicative of Roman Catholic theological thought. There is no argument in Bellarmine "from St. Thomas." Moreover, he cites the Council of Trent on only three occasions,[10] while other councils, particularly those held in the early Church, are cited more frequently. Bellarmine, in other words, does not counter the Reformers' positions by recourse to the Council of Trent; rather, his methodology is based on the New Testament and on the early Church.

Bellarmine's initial question on the sacramentality of order is handled, both in its New Testament presentation and in that of the early Church, in its ritualistic form. Great concern is shown for those passages in the New Testament which deal with the imposition of hands, and the promise of the Holy Spirit. Bellarmine cites the Fathers of the Church, particularly using those quotations which indicate that ordination is a holy ritual in the Church. Nowhere does Bellarmine treat of the ministry of Jesus himself. This ministry is not seen as the very center or heart of the sacramentality of ordination. Nor does Bellarmine, in this treatise, allude to the underlying reasons for the Reformers' positions. For instance, Bellarmine in dealing with Calvin's stance on the sacramentality of Order, notes that Calvin appears to be somewhat open to its sacramentality. However, Bellarmine does not indicate the foundational reasons why Calvin denigrates the Roman position on the sacramentality of order, namely, as we saw above, the christological issue on the full efficacy of the sacrifice of Jesus.[11]

In a lengthy chapter, chapter five, Bellarmine takes up the issue of the sacramentality of the episcopacy. He gently mentions that some of the older scholastic theologians had denied episcopal sacramentality, but he makes no further comments on their opinion. Rather, he goes to the early Church and to the canonists. That episcopacy is part of the sacrament of order is called *certissima*. It is not, as Bellarmine well understood, a defined position of the Roman Church, since Trent had left the question open. Bellarmine rests his case on the evidence of the New Testament, even mentioning that in Acts 13 Paul and Barnabas are ordained to the episcopacy (!).[12] More importantly, however, he bases his argument on the data from the early Church. As we saw above, the patristic Church saw in the episcopos the apex of priesthood. Bellarmine makes his own the position of Hugh of St. Victor, namely, that priesthood has two grades: that of the presbyter and that of the bishop. The bishop is called the *summus sacerdos,* the *primus sacerdos,*[13] or bishops are called the *maiores sacerdotes.*[14] "We compare bishops with presbyters, when we say that some are superior, others inferior; nonetheless, if one compares the character which a bishop has from his second consecration with the character which one has from presbyteral ordination, then the latter is greater intensively, for it entails the highest power: one is able to consecrate the eucharist; the former is greater extensively, since it extends to a plurality of powers."[15]

However one might evaluate Bellarmine's arguments for the sacramentality of the episcopacy, it remains clear that he has done a great service to Catholic theology by insisting that episcopacy is *certissime* a sacrament. Bellarmine's stance will influence many Catholic theologians in the centuries that follow, and the re-introduction of the episcopacy into the sacrament of order was a needed step for a solid theology of order.

For Bellarmine, diaconate, *valde probabile,* was a sacrament.[16] He evaluates the sub-diaconate in the same way. Along with Peter Lombard, Bellarmine bases his position on the eucharist and the ways in which these two ministries relate to the eucharist. Indeed, throughout this treatise, it is clear that the center of the sacrament of order, for Bellarmine as for scholastic theology generally, is the eucharist.

An issue which will dominate the discussion on the sacrament of order in the Roman Catholic Church from counter-Reformation times onward is that which concerns the laying on of hands and/or the presentation of the sacred vessels. This chapter, chapter eight, is the lengthiest chapter in the entire treatise. One of the reasons for this length is its importance to the efforts for reunion of Eastern and Western Churches. Following Scotus, Bellarmine emphasizes the two powers given in the sacrament of ordination: the power to celebrate the eucharist and the power to forgive sins, and therefore, Bellarmine concludes, both ceremonies are essential: the presentation of the sacred vessels for the conferral of the power to consecrate the eucharist and the imposition of hands for conferral of the power to forgive sins.

Bellarmine provided the Roman Catholic scholar with a basic outline for a presentation of the sacrament of order. Later Catholic authors will base their arguments more on the writings of St. Thomas and the statements of the Council of Trent, but the fundamental format will remain quite constant. The questions Bellarmine proposed will become the standard questions for almost all treatises on this sacrament. Bellarmine's awareness of the Reformers' writings will, however, not be as deeply repeated by subsequent theologians, so that their writings will become much more intramural. But in general, both the strengths and the weaknesses of Bellarmine's approach will, however, remain the strengths and weaknesses of future Catholic writers. Among these weaknesses is the lack of any strong connection of a study on the theology of the sacrament of order with the very ministry of Jesus himself.

2. JEAN-JACQUES OLIER AND HIS THEOLOGY OF THE SACRAMENT OF ORDER

Jean-Jacques Olier (1608–1657) was the founder of the society of priests of St. Sulpice. Although his early life was not focused toward a religious bent, Olier, in his twenties, decided to become a priest and was ordained in 1633 and began to work in parish missionary work with St. Vincent de Paul. In 1641 he laid the foundations of a seminary for future priests in Vaugirard near Paris, but in 1642 he became the pastor of the parish church of St. Sulpice in Paris. He then transferred the fledgling seminary he had established to the St. Sulpice area, and the group of priests he gathered about him for this work took on the name of the parish, St. Sulpice, and the Sulpician movement spread effectively throughout the Roman Catholic world. Olier and the Sulpicians had an enormous influence on the training of priests in the Roman Catholic Church throughout the period we are presently considering.

Until recently, a volume, *Traité des Saints Ordres,* had been attributed to Olier. This work first appeared in 1676, eighteen years after the death of Olier. It was re-edited twice at the end of the seventeenth century, and again at the beginning of the nineteenth century, precisely at the time when Catholic seminaries were being re-established throughout France in the wake of the French Revolution. This work became a classic for the spirituality of diocesan priests throughout all this time.

Gilles Chaillot, Paul Cochois and Irenee Noye, all three Sulpician priests, have studied this work in a most thorough way and presented their findings in a critical edition: *Traité des Saints Ordres (1676) compare aux Ecrits Authentiques de Jean-Jacques Olier (d. 1657).*[17] It seems that Olier himself did not write the volume; rather, the third superior general of the company of St. Sulpice, Louis Tronson, drew up the volume, but using writings from Olier. In the preface to the critical edition of this work, C. Bouchard notes that Olier's approach was essentially paschal, baptismal and mystical, while that of Tronson was more clerical and more ascetic.[18]

Tronson published this *Traite* under the authorship of Olier to preserve the movement of the Sulpician founder and to provide a sort of manual for those to be ordained: a spiritual directory for seminarians. And yet it seems that the priestly spirituality which Olier himself had inculcated was in no small degree modified by Tronson. More specifically, the three authors mentioned above call attention to these elements:

1. The relationship between the apostolic dimension of the priest and the religious dimension;
2. The relationship between the mystical dimension of grace and ascetical practices;
3. The organic relationship between priest and bishop;
4. The relationship between priest and the baptized.

As regards the first, Olier understood, at least from 1642 on, that "the entire missionary life of the Church was a true and living sacrament of the universal salvation in Jesus Christ." Tronson, however, limits this vision of sacramentality to priests alone and makes of it a sort of "religious state." Priests, according to the primitive order of the hierarchy of the Church, are by their state above all other religious (i.e., those who take vows). This "religion" is centered by Tronson on cultic functions; Olier, for his part, was far more apostolic. Nonetheless, it is the text of Tronson, not the ideas of Olier himself, which has been influential in forming a strongly clerical and cultic understanding of the priest throughout the counter-Reformation period.[19]

As regards the second issue, Olier's own writings see the mystical life flowing from the baptismal waters, and this for all Christians. It is this gift of the Spirit which allows each and every Christian to turn more and more from earthly things and live in the Spirit. Tronson, however, stressed the denial aspect in spirituality as the means to enjoy heavenly gifts. This present earth is evaluated negatively; only the heavenly life is worth our efforts. Ascetical efforts, therefore, are needed to curtail the desires of the flesh. The *Traité*, with the emphases given to it by Tronson, developed in the counter-Reformation clergy of the Catholic Church a spirituality which in many ways rejects the world and sees the only worthy life in the after-world. Priestly spirituality is presented as an other-worldly spirituality. When Jansenism began to influence this type of spirituality, a profoundly negative spirituality established the spiritual ideals of the priest.[20]

Third, Olier understood the bishop as the fullness of the priesthood, but he explained this in a very mystical way. A true bishop should be filled with the Spirit, for his rank as the highest priest means that he should be a holy person in an eminent way. Because the bishop should primarily be a man of the Spirit, it follows that wherever he goes he is to bring holiness and grace. For Olier a theology of bishop is essentially connected to a theology of grace, not of office or of jurisdiction. A spiritual bishop will ask himself not about fulfillment of duties, but about the sharing of grace, since it is precisely grace itself which makes the bishop the fullness of the priesthood. In the bishop the priest ought to be able to see the fullness of his spirituality. It is this spiritual dimension of the episcopacy which Tronson omits to a great degree. The editors of the critical edition write:

> L'episcopat est ainsi le dépositaire de 'la plénitude de l'Esprit" sacerdotal et apostolique du Christ pour l'illumination du monde entier: on ne saurait mieux exprimer la théologie olerienne du sacrement de l'Ordre. Il est d'autant plus regrettable que cette inspiration théologique dionysienne ne soit pas davantage explicitée dans le *Traité*, avec les consequences spirituelles, pourtant

si importantes, qu'elle impliquait pour le fondateur de Saint-Sulpice.[21]

Finally, Olier stresses the call to holiness of all the baptized, and sees the priestly holiness within this baptismal call. Tronson, for his part, makes the holiness of the priest something singularly special and highly cultic. There is a clerical holiness, quite apart from the baptismal holiness of the ordinary Christian. It is this latter which influenced the priestly world in the counter-Reformation Church.[22]

It is remarkable, the three authors note, how close Olier is to the priestly theology presented in the documents of Vatican II, but it was, unfortunately, not the thought of Olier which dominated priestly spirituality during the counter-Reformation period, but rather that of Tronson, who had reworked the *Traité*. In spite of these changes in emphasis, the *Traité*, through its wide influence, did help to center in many ways the theology of priest on Jesus Christ himself. The sacrament of order was, to some degree at least, seen as the very sacrament of the ministry of Jesus. This was a healthy counterbalance to the scholastic approach to ordination. This does not in any way, however, minimize the negative qualities which Tronson emphasized, thereby suppressing the actual intent of Olier. Still, it can be said rather honestly that the theological writings on the sacrament of order by Robert Bellarmine and the spiritual approach of the *Traité des Saints Ordres* were the two most influential set of documents on priestly ordination which were developed during this entire period.

3. OTHER SIGNIFICANT CATHOLIC SCHOLARSHIP ON THE SACRAMENT OF ORDER IN THE COUNTER-REFORMATION PERIOD

Michel, in his lengthy treatise on holy order, adds some significant data to this post-tridentine period of Roman Catholic theology.[23] In the early part of the seventeenth century, Denis Petau (d. 1652), a Jesuit, wrote an apologetic book, *De ecclesiastica hierarchia,* which attempts to answer Luther and other Protestants from an historical base. Jean Morin (d. 1659), an Oratorian, in his volume, *Commentarius de sacris Ecclesiae ordinationibus,* addresses the issue of plurality in the ordination rituals in history. For a scholar interested in this field of the history of the sacraments, and particularly the history of the sacrament of order, it is important to mention Jean Mabillon (d. 1707), a Benedictine, who, together with his confreres of the Abbey of St. Maur, published during this period the *Ordines romani* together with a commentary. Edmond Martene, following in Mabillon's steps, published *De antiquis Ecclesiae ritibus* in four volumes (1700) as also *De antiquis monachorum ritibus* (1690). Abbot Chardon and P. Merlin wrote treatises on the history of the sacraments, order included, during this early period. Eusebe Renaudot, an orientalist and a member of the French Academy as well as of the Accademia de la Crusca, published, in 1715, the *Collectio liturgiarum orientalium*. All of this historical research was indeed massive and of lasting significance; it gave impetus to establish solid and critical texts of early Church history, both East and West, but unfortunately it did not have the same widespread influence which a similar impetus to history has had in our own century. The pressing need for an apologetic approach, rather than a more open historical approach, tended to dominate the theological scene in Catholic thought. Michel even entitles one of his sections which deals with Peteau and others: "La théologie positive au service de l'apologie catholique."[24] Although apologetics clearly dominated the field during these many centuries, there were, from time to time, some highly significant attempts to move beyond the polemics. One can rightfully say that this early work of solid historical research on sacramental and liturgical theology helped pave the way to the more intense studies in these areas in the twentieth century by both Catholic and Protestant scholar alike.

The eighteenth century saw a number of books on the sacrament of order. The bishop of Cavaillon, Francois Hallier, in the middle of the seventeenth century, had published his *De sacris electionibus et ordinationibus, ex antiquo et novo Ecclesiae usu*. This volume was very much in demand and influenced in some ways the writings of the eighteenth century. Noel Alexandre, in 1703, published *Theologia dogmatica et moralis secundum ordinem concilii Tridentini*, which was based on a different approach from that of Robert Bellarmine. Boucat in 1739 published his *Theologia patrum scholastico-dogmatica, sed maxima positiva*. This author tried to bring together all the dogmatic, pastoral, moral and canonical questions on the sacrament of order, a truly comprehensive undertaking, but indicative of the multidimensional aspect of the theme. Other authors, such as Tournely, Gonet, Frassen, etc., could also be mentioned. These treatises, heavily dogmatic in emphasis, prepared the way for the manuals of the next two centuries.

Of greater influence were the many treatises on the formation of the clerical student, which began to appear after Trent with the establishment of the seminary system. We have already considered Olier and Tronson, but Lantages might also be mentioned. St. Alphonsus Ligouri (1696–1787) published many small volumes on this matter, and his guidelines for confessors were often a practical picture of the good priest. In the nineteenth century Lacordaire and d'Hulst wrote on the priesthood and even today their works are still cited. Cardinal Manning in England, in 1884, wrote *The Eternal Priest,* and Cardinal Gibbons of Baltimore wrote, in 1896, *The Ambassador of Christ.* Cardinal Mercier (1851–1926) published his book *La vie interieure, appel aux ames sacerdotales.* All of these volumes encouraged a deep spirituality for the Catholic priest as well as for the seminarian looking forward to ordination to the priesthood.

The nineteenth and twentieth centuries were the centuries of the theological manuals: Perrone, Hurter, De Augustinis, Billot, and eventually, Tanquerey, Lercher, Van Noort, Herve, etc. These manuals tended to be heavily repetitious. Even Michel notes: "Rien ne serait fastidieux comme de parcourir tous les traités du sacrement de l'ordre. Dans nos manuels, on le retrouve partout a peu près le même, avec les mêmes formules, les mêmes arguments, souvent propose dans le même cadre." ("Nothing would be more irksome than to run through the treatises on the sacrament of order. In the manuals, one finds almost always the same things, with the same formulas, the same arguments, frequently proposed in the same schematic way.")[25]

Catholic moral theology, during this entire counter-Reformation period, tended to distance itself from dogmatic theology, with the result, in the case of the sacrament of order, that order in moral theology stressed the issues of canonical impediments to ordination, and the moral obligations of those who ordain and those who are being ordained. These books stressed the laws of the Church connected with the sacrament of order, and the dogmatic aspects of these volumes tended to cite verbatim passages from the Council of Trent.

All of these many publications, dogmatic, historical, moral and ascetic, together with the seminary system, produced numerous educated and holy men in the priesthood. When one looks at the condition of the priesthood at the time of the Council of Trent, and compares that condition with the condition of the priesthood in the Catholic Church at the end of the nineteenth and beginning of the twentieth century, one can only be amazed at the enormous difference and quality of priest. Nonetheless, the training of the priests during this entire period, with the exception of the efforts of Lammenais, reflected the mainstream of Catholic thought: fairly traditional, scholastic, apprehensive of current movements in the wider world. Modernism and the severe reaction of Rome to it did not create a seminary system that was open to creativity. This does not mean that there were no fresh theological ventures in the Roman Catholic Church during the nineteenth century. The main scholars of the Catholic Tübingen School, as also Georg Hermes, Anton Gunther, Ignaz von Dollinger, A. Rosmini, M. J. Scheeben, John Cardinal Newman, Maurice Blondel, Alfred Loisy, Baron von Hugel, George Tyrell—these are but a few names which immediately come to one's mind. Still, almost each of these engendered some sort of resistance. They were not the traditional, the scholastic, the approved scholars, and as a result their ideas do not represent the general attitude of the Roman Catholic Church on the sacrament of order during this period of time.[26]

Roger Aubert, who has perhaps researched nineteenth century Catholicism more than any other scholar of our age, portrays a picture of the Catholic clergy in his essay, "Light and Shadows of Catholic Vitality."[27] Prior to 1850, Aubert notes, one might have seen a rather worldly priest taking on the role of an intellectual in the salons of Paris. Or one might have found a priest with rather wealthy benefices who had the leisure time to devote his hours to study. Another priest, living in a rural and isolated village, might have differed from the townspeople only by his liturgical garb, but surely not by his moral behavior.[28] In this same century, there was always a need for village or rural priests, but increasingly there came a demand for priests in industrialized areas and large urban, but poor, populations. In Spain there were priestly deans in the university system; in the United States and Canada there were priests needed for large-scale immigrant populations.[29] Remarkably, Aubert notes, after 1850 exceptional cases begin to disappear, and the "distinct rise in the spiritual standards of the clergy was one of the most characteristic aspects of Church history in the course of the pontificate of Pius IX."[30] This spiritual development was due to the education which priests received, an education which often started in childhood and lasted for many years. From 1850 onward, only a small part of the German and Austrian clergy were still trained at universities. Such a seminary training was, in many respects, a "hothouse" approach to education. The ideal had been formed by St. Sulpice, which "directly or indirectly served as model for all of Europe and America."[31] Many bishops inculcated the ideals and value of this model for their seminaries. The wearing of the soutane became mandatory, particularly in the Latin countries. A more profound spirituality, a more solid education, and a clearer self-image of priest were positive signs of this seminary system. Some negatives have also been expressed: G. Martina has asked whether the emphasis on clericalism in this system is not actually one of the very causes of anti-clericalism and the secularization of everyday life;[32] Daniel-Rops asks: "Did the reaction to the excessive freedom of the period of crisis and the concern with discipline encourage the priests to live in a compartmentalized world, a world without windows on the real life of the people?"[33]

The priest in the nineteenth century became a "man apart." However, this cannot be generalized, since we find in this period of the nineteenth century efforts by priests to focus on specific apostolates: the youth, the workers, child education, etc. These early efforts toward apostolic specialization were far more cultivated in the twentieth century than in the nineteenth, but it did demand that such priests enter more closely into the lives of the people they served. Don Bosco and d'Alzon started communities, in which priests were involved, along these lines. Dupanloup encouraged, in his rural areas, priestly visitation of homes. Many parish priests, urged both by Rome and by their local ordinary, pushed for parochial schools. Associations of workers and young people, with priests involved, a school system which was independent of the public school programs, Catholic magazines and papers, and in some areas Catholic political parties—all of these tended to disassociate both the priest and the Catholic people from the surrounding world. The very involvement in these movements was one characterized by defense, i.e., against those who were without true faith. These observations indicate that there were both positive and negative aspects both to the seminary system and to the kind of priest which this system produced.

4. ROMAN STATEMENTS ON THE PRIESTHOOD IN THE COUNTER-REFORMATION PERIOD

Officially, the popes and the Roman curia did not speak out in any great detail on the matter of the sacrament of order during this period: 1600 to 1950. However, five occasions of papal pronouncements do merit mention.

A. PIUS VI, "AUCTOREM FIDEI"

The synod held at Pistoia in Tuscany was a local synod called by Archduke Leopold II. The synod was concerned with many issues connected with the Jansenist debates, and only in a most tangential way discussed an issue connected with holy order. In 1794 Pius VI promulgated his apostolic constitution, *Auctorem fidei,* in which many positions taken by the Synod of Pistoia were condemned. As regards the ordained ministry, those who had gathered at Pistoia wanted to return to a pattern of ministry, which they considered more in keeping with ancient times. This pattern had to do with the promotion to higher orders and the incumbency of the minor orders. The bishops at Pistoia argued on the basis of history. Pius VI, however, did not base his response on the issue of history; rather, what the bishops at Pistoia desired was seen as "a false teaching in each of its parts, rash, disruptive of the orders which had been established for the necessity and benefit of the churches, and injurious to the discipline which had been approved by canons and especially by the decrees of Trent."[34] The Synod of Pistoia and the responses both of Pius VI and of others did not alter the general understanding of the sacrament of order in any substantial way. It does indicate, however, that even at the end of the eighteenth century, historical questions were beginning to surface, questions which had to do with the history of priesthood and order in the Church. For the bishops gathered at Pistoia, the "ancient tradition" was considered quite normative. Additions and changes had taken place because of abuses. Scipio dei Ricci, in defense of Pistoia, wrote: "To admire the ancient discipline and to regret the advent of a new order is not to attack the latter but rather the circumstances that brought it into being."[35] The official Church, however, considered the issues relating to the sacrament of order which the synod of Pistoia promulgated as derogatory of Church authority, rather than historical issues which had in their time required a remedy. The proposals of Pistoia regarding the sacrament of order were, indeed, condemned by the pope, but the questions which originated in Church history have remained with us down to the present century.

B. LEO XIII AND THE QUESTION OF ANGLICAN ORDERS

At the time of the Reformation, the English Church did not, at first, break away from Rome on doctrinal issues, but rather on the issue of papal power. Only from 1537 onward does one find some heretical inroads, which even Henry VIII fought against. It was under Edward VI (1547–1553) that a thoroughgoing revision of the *Order of Communion* (1548) and the *Prayer Book* (1549) took place. These were met with strong opposition particularly in the western and northern part of the kingdom. In 1550 a new ritual of ordination, developed by Cramner above all but by others as well, was published. The fundamental reasons for changes in this ordination ritual were quite similar to those which we have seen above in our discussion of both Luther's and Calvin's opposition to the theology of holy order presented by the Roman Church, namely, the sacrificial character of the mass and the scholastic theory of transubstantiation. When Mary became queen of England and restored Roman Catholic faith (1553–1558), this ordination ritual was declared by the queen to be invalid. However, her successor, Elizabeth I, (1558–1603), restored the Edwardian ritual, and it was used in 1559 for the consecration of the new archbishop of Canterbury, Matthew Parker.

The Roman Church reviewed this ritual in 1675, 1704 and 1875, and on each occasion reached the conclusion that the ordination ritual was invalid. At the end of the nineteenth century Lord Halifax and Abbé Portal raised the issue of the validity of Anglican orders anew. Some Catholic scholars, such as Louis Duschesne (1843–1922), a renowned Church historian, and Pietro Gasparri (1852–1934), a canonist, leaned to the view that Anglican ordinations were valid.[36] Pope Leo XIII established a papal commission to consider the issue once more. Cardinal Rampolla advised that there be a balanced group of men to discuss the issue, and so there were on the commission four who were against the validity of Anglican orders, and a balancing four of men who either favored the validity of the orders or considered them to be doubtfully valid. Cardinal Vaughan insisted that all eight be Catholic. Gasparri, however, was allowed to bypass the secrecy imposed on the membership of this commission and to discuss the issues with two Anglican experts who had come to Rome with official approval of their Anglican superiors but who themselves had no mandate from the Church of England. Twelve sessions were held during the period of March 24 and May 7, 1886. A document, which had been prepared by the members who had been delegated to the commission by Vaughan, proved to be one of the central documents which the commission considered. Recently, J. J. Hughes in his volume *Absolutely Null and Utterly Void* has indicated the errors and omissions of this document.[37] The final votation of the commission was four for nullity and four for validity or at least doubtful validity. It does not seem, however, that this commission was actually a commission of experts: "in fact [it] contained no real experts."[38] Since the commission was only consultive, the final decision rested with the Holy Office. Moreover, R. Merry del Val had become the pope's advisor on English issues rather than Rampolla. In July 1886 the cardinals of the Holy Office came down on the side of invalidity and the pope sided with the Holy Office. The cardinals of the Holy Office deliberated for two hours, with Leo XIII present for these deliberations, but Rampolla was not present. The decision of the cardinals of the Holy Office was unanimous. On September 13, 1896, Leo XIII promulgated *Apostolicae curae et caritatis,* in which he declared that "ordinations performed in the Anglican ritual were totally null and utterly void."[39] The text had been drafted by Merry del Val with the help of Dom Gasquet, an English Benedictine and a friend of Cardinal Vaughan. In this document, Leo presents the case using basic, scholastic categories, such as matter and form. The form used in a sacrament indicates the significance of the matter and the perceptible ritual generally. For the sacrament of order, then, the visible sign is the imposition of hands (the matter), which of itself does not signify anything special. The words, therefore, i.e., the form, give the special signification to this laying on of hands. In the ordinal of Edward VI the formula did not indicate that the one to be ordained was going to receive the "power of consecrating and offering the true body and blood of the Lord, through that sacrifice, which is not a mere commemoration of the sacrifice of the cross."[40] Rather, the Edwardian ritual merely states that the one is to be ordained for the office and work of a presbyter.

In dealing with the episcopacy, Leo XIII openly states that episcopacy "ad sacramentum ordinis verissime pertinet atque est praecellenti gradu sacerdotium" ("most truly belongs to the sacrament of order and is a priesthod of excelling dignity").[41] Leo refers to the Fathers of the Church and to the Roman Ritual itself, both of which call the episcopacy *summum sacerdotium, sacri ministerii summa.*

> Since the sacrament of order and the true priesthood of Christ is totally excluded from the anglican ritual, and therefore in the episcopal consecration of this same rite a priesthood is in no way conferred, and even further since among the first tasks of the episcopacy is that, namely, of ordaining ministers for the holy eucharist and the sacrifice . . .

the Anglican episcopacy is itself null and void.[42] As one can see, whether the issue is the ordination to priesthood or ordination to episcopacy, the argument which Leo brings centers around:

a. **The form**: Priesthood is the conferral of the power to celebrate the eucharist, which is understood as a sacrifice.

b. **The intention**: Episcopacy is itself part of the sacrament of order and is therefore the conferral of the highest power of this order, which includes the power to ordain men to celebrate the eucharist.

Leo XIII took into account the countering view that many of the accompanying prayers and ceremonies gave evidence that a priesthood was intended, according to the mind of Christ. However, in the view of Leo, the Edwardian ordination ceremony itself rejected a consecrating and sacrificing priesthood, and for this larger reason as well as that based only on the form and the intention, Leo drew his negative conclusion.[43]

Recently, J. Hughes has reviewed all the material on this matter as well and published his findings.[44] The first two investigations ended in negative judgments; Hughes' views are much more positive. It seems that even in spite of *Apostolicae curae,* a scholarly interest in the subject, on the part of Roman Catholics, has continued. In some ways, then, it does not appear as if the case is completely closed. The following two points, based on the material gathered in this present volume, raise some issues which likewise need to be taken into account as far as an evaluation of Anglican orders by Roman Catholic theologians is concerned.

First of all, at the time of Leo XIII the *Traditio Apostolica* of Hippolytus had not yet been discovered nor analyzed, and even in the early years of the twentieth century, this document had not yet attained its prominence. Still, the ordination passages in this compilation by Hippolytus must be considered in any discussion of Anglican orders, since there are some similarities between the ordination ritual of Hippolytus and that of Edward VI. As we have seen above, in this first ordination ritual extant to the Church historian, the ordination rite for priesthood did not mention any ordination to celebrate the eucharist, i.e., "a consecrating and sacrificing priesthood." Actually, the ritual of Hippolytus envisioned the presbyter as an advisor of the episkopos, and it was to this ministry of consultation that a man was ordained a presbyter. Moreover, if one considers the other prayers or ceremonies in the Hippolytan ritual, there is still no evidence of a eucharistic priesthood, in the sense of that envisioned by the scholastics and subsequently by the Council of Trent, and that envisioned by *Apostolicae curae.* If this lack, either in intention or in form, is the very reason, according to the Leonine document, which nullifies the Anglican orders, then it must be likewise stated that the presbyteral orders conferred through the ritual of Hippolytus—and, it ought to be remembered, this ritual was the basis for many similar rituals, East and West, in the Patristic Church—should be considered nullified as well. It would seem, however, that no scholar, Roman Catholic or otherwise, would want to do this. Moreover, in the ritual of Hippolytus, the ordaining episkopos does not have the intention to ordain "a consecrating and sacrificing priest." If this intention according to the Leonine document was lacking in the Edwardian ordinal, then the lack of such an episcopal intention would, seemingly, nullify the ordinations which were celebrated according to the Hippolytan ritual. Some consistency in the way in which Hippolytus is treated and the Anglican ritual is treated, so it seems, needs to be better established.

A second observation is also in order. Since the intention both of the ritual itself and of the ordaining minister is essential to the Roman Catholic approach to sacramental theology, and rightfully so, it should also be kept in mind that the major scholastics, St. Thomas and St. Bonaventure among them, did not see the episcopacy as part of the sacrament of holy order. This view, which excluded episcopacy from the sacrament of order, was the common view of theologians throughout high scholasticism and was defended by bishops and theologians at the Council of Trent. This raises a very difficult set of questions. At the ordination of a bishop, during those high middle ages, there most certainly could have been, and rather often at that, consecrating bishops who themselves did not think they were consecrating a priest to be bishop in the sense of a sacerdos-bishop, nor would they have thought that they were conferring a sacrament, i.e., an ordination of the *summus sacerdos.* Rather, in keeping with the best of theology of that period, those bishops would have thought and therefore intended to consecrate the priest merely to an office and a dignity in the Church. If one were to apply the same criteria for episcopal consecrations in the Edwardian period, i.e., those used to evaluate the consecration of Parker, it would seem that medieval consecrations of bishops would likewise have to be considered null and void, which would mean, as in the case of Parker, that any subsequent ordination by those medieval bishops so consecrated would likewise be null and void. The consequences of this line of thought are quite dire. History, at times, has the benefit of substantiating positions; at other times, however, history can challenge positions. The comparison of the issue of Anglican orders with the orders in Hippolytus and the orders in medieval bishops who would have held that episcopacy is not a sacrament requires the application of similar criteria.

C. PIUS X AND THE DECREE "LAMENTABILI"

On July 3, 1907, the Holy Office promulgated the decree *Lamentabili* in which the errors of modernism were rejected. Only one statement in this decree touched on the sacrament of order:

> Mature people, who exercised vigilance in the gatherings of Christians, were appointed by the apostles as presbyters or episkopoi to provide for the necessary surveillance of the growing communities, but not properly to perpetuate the mission and power of the apostles.[45]

Lamentabili was much more concerned about ecclesiology than about the particular sacraments, so that this mention of the sacrament of order must be seen against the larger picture of the Church structure itself. The ecclesiology of some of these modernists was in direct opposition to the ecclesiology, taught by the Roman Catholic Church. When one studies this modernist approach to ecclesiology, even with its excesses, one sees that the question of history involved the history of the naming and function of the early ministers, the presbyteroi and episkopoi. From Pistoia to *Lamentabili* to the present day, the answers might be different, but the historical questions remain quite current. All the issues of the early Church and its ministry, particularly that of episkopos and presbyter, are certainly not yet resolved, and once again history is seen as challenging to some degree, and not as substantiating held positions.

On August 4, 1908 Pius X issued an apostolic exhortation, *Haerent Animo,* on priestly holiness and ministry.[46] In this exhortation the pope first described the holiness or personal spirituality of the priest, and only in the second part does he discuss the apostolate of the priest. In other words, the standard (by then) approach was followed: personal piety first, apostolic work second. In his understanding of priesthood, Pius X adhered to the basic scholastic approach, focusing priestly spirituality and ministry in the eucharist.

D. PIUS XI AND THE ENCYCLICAL LETTER "AD CATHOLICI SACERDOTII"

On Christmas Day, 1935, Pius XI issued his encyclical letter on the priesthood, *Ad catholici sacerdotii.*[47] He wrote this on the occasion of the anniversary of his own priestly ordination, and prior to 1935 he had been very active in promoting seminary education. This was a letter to help all the faithful appreciate the priesthood better, to help non-Catholics understand the priesthood, and to encourage those who were called to the priesthood. The theology is dependent on Trent, but in the encyclical Pius XI widens the understanding of priesthood from that of merely power over the eucharist to that of power over the mystical body of Christ as well. This is clearly not a new idea, since it was emphasized by a few scholars in the middle ages, particularly Scotus, but the major thrust of Roman Catholic theology had been, even at the Council of Trent, to focus almost exclusively on the eucharistic power.

In the letter, the holiness and the education of the priest is treated at great length, with a lion's share being devoted to holiness. In part three, the pope takes up the question of priestly training, and sees that this is certainly a task for seminaries, but also for Catholic parents, who should encourage their sons to consider this vocation. All in all, the encyclical was a letter basically of encouragement and concern for solid spiritual and intellectual training of priests. In the Catholic world of that time, it did stir up a renewed interest in the theology and practice of priestly life. In some ways, also, it moved the theology of the priesthood from an exclusive centering on the eucharist, and thus the letter to some degree prepared the way for the more apostolic view of the priest which Vatican II expressed in its documents.

E. PIUS XII AND THE ENCYCLICAL "MEDIATOR DEI"

Pius XII's encyclical *Mediator Dei*, issued on November 20, 1947, was primarily a treatise on liturgy.[48] However, in the course of the pope's discussion on liturgy he mentions in a special way the priesthood of all believers (*sacerdotium fidelium*). After enumerating some false concepts regarding this term, Pius XII goes on to provide guidelines for a genuine understanding of the term. At issue was the position, raised by some historians, that at the very origin of the Church all the faithful were "priests," since it is only they who are called priests in the New Testament beyond Jesus himself and the Jewish priests. Therefore, some of these writers concluded, any baptized Christian could celebrate the eucharist. Pius XII maintained that there was from the beginning of the Church onward a special ministry. He cites Innocent III and Robert Bellarmine in particular, but his argument is derived primarily from the sacrificial nature of the eucharist, which therefore requires a special priesthood. This, of course, was the common teaching of Roman Catholic theologians. Still, it must be noted that in this official document of the Roman Church room was truly given to a "priesthood of all believers." Since this had been one of the major issues at the time of the Reformation, the Catholic stance had most often been quite negative to such a priesthood. This official mention of the priesthood of all believers can, therefore, be seen as a major ecumenical breakthrough.

F. PIUS XII AND THE APOSTOLIC CONSTITUTION "SACRAMENTUM ORDINIS"

On November 30, 1947, just ten days after the encyclical *Mediator Dei*, Pius XII issued the apostolic constitution *Sacramentum Ordinis*.[49] This document caused a great stir among the Roman Catholic theologians, since it apparently brought to an end one of the major controversial topics on order with which the counter-Reformation theologians had dealt.

> By virtue of Our supreme Apostolic Authority We declare with certain knowledge, and, as far as it may be necessary, we determine and ordain: the matter of the holy orders of diaconate, priesthood, and episcopate is the laying-on of hands alone; and the sole form are the words determining the application of the matter, whereby the effects of the sacrament are unequivocally signified—that is, the power of order and the grace of the Holy Spirit—and which are accepted and used as such by the Church. This leads Us to declare . . . and ordain that . . . if it has ever been lawfully laid down otherwise . . . at least in the future the handing over of the instruments is not necessary for the validity of the holy orders of diaconate, priesthood and episcopate.[50]

Whether the ritual of ordination was simply the laying on of hands, or simply the presentation of the sacred vessels, or both, had been disputed for centuries. Pius XII makes no judgment on the past; for the future, and only for the future, the presentation of the sacred vessels, which had been part of the ordination ceremony in the West since the early middle ages was now no longer an essential part of the ordination ceremony. However, since many qualified theologians had considered this presentation to be "ad validitatem" for the sacrament of order, a question was immediately raised: whether or not the pope had changed the very matter and therefore to some degree the essence of this sacrament. By and large, however, the Roman Catholic theologians found Pius XII's decision a helpful step, and especially in the Roman Catholic relationship with the Eastern Churches this step was very welcome, since in the East, from earliest time onward, only the imposition of hands had been required.

In 1950, Pius XII issued an apostolic exhortation, *Menti nostrae,* in which the standard format, (a) priestly holiness first and then only (b) priestly ministry, is followed.[51] In the final section of the document, Pius XII stressed the need for priestly vocations, the nurturing of these vocations in the home, and the demand for academic excellence in seminary training. He raised again the dangers of contemporary philosophies and pointed out the economic stress which afflicted many priests. In this exhortation there is nothing new theologically regarding the priesthood.

In 1959, John XXIII wrote an encyclical on the priesthood, *Sacerdotii nostri primordia.*[52] It is an exhortation for priestly spirituality with continual references to St. John Vianney. John XXIII begins with the sanctity of life of the priest and only then does he discuss the ministry of the priest. He stresses prayer, poverty, penance, and service to the people especially in priestly dedication to the sacraments of eucharist and reconciliation.

Such were the main papal or Vatican statements on the sacrament of order during this period. One additional issue might be mentioned, even though it does not deal with the papal writings of the counter-Reformation. Nonetheless, it was precisely during this period that these former papal writings were discovered in the Vatican library. The discovery and publication of these papal writings caused no little stir among Roman Catholic historians, theologians, and canonists.

It was the unanimous view of the post-tridentine theologians that only a bishop could ordain. Even an heretical or schismatic, an excommunicated or suspended, even an uncanonically established bishop could ordain validly. Negative as this might sound, the theological principle underlying this belief is extremely positive and unquestionably important: namely, the power of a bishop comes to him directly from the Lord, not in a delegated way through the pope. If the power to ordain had to be delegated to a bishop through the pope, then the power to ordain of the excommunicated, suspended, heretical, etc. bishop could be removed by means of a removal of delegation. If, however, ministerial power is not a matter of delegation but one which belongs intrinsically to ordination itself, then this power is bestowed immediately on the individual by the Lord, not in any delegated way, e.g., through the pope. The power of the deacon is not a delegated power from the bishop; the power of the priest is not a delegated power from the bishop; the power of the bishop is not a delegated power from the pope.

It may be recalled, however, that Thomas, Bonaventure, Scotus, and others had claimed that the pope could, through special delegation, empower a priest to ordain. The possibility of such delegation was a disputed topic in the post-tridentine period. Hadrian VI (1522–1533) claimed that it was impossible, since only the bishops had been granted such power, and no pope could change this divine institution. For the minor orders and even the subdiaconate, however, there were many documents in Church history which seemed to allow the simple priest to ordain to these orders. During this post-tridentine period, the chore-episkopos was considered by many to have been simply a priest not a bishop, and these chore-episkopoi had ordained men to minor orders and to the subdiaconate. Priestly power to ordain at least to those orders did not seem to be theologically impossible.

Ordination to the diaconate or to the priesthood itself by a priest (usually an abbot) was quite a different matter. For those scholars who thought that the chore-episkopos, or at least some of them, were bishops, there was the documentation of these chore-episcopal ordinations to diaconate and to priesthood. It was, however, a papal bull of Innocent VIII, allowing certain Cistercian abbots to ordain up to and including the diaconate, which created a major problem. This was a privilege given on April 9, 1489. According to some theologians and canonists, the Council of Trent had revoked it, at least indirectly; according to other scholars, its very authenticity was challenged. Giovanni Mercati (1866–1957), a very learned scholar who later in his life became a cardinal, found a copy of this bull in the Vatican archives, which made its authenticity indubitable.

Other such bulls were also found: one by Boniface IX, from 1400, granting to the abbot of the monstery of St. Ossyth, in the diocese of London, delegation to ordain even to priesthood. This bull, however, was interpreted by many as only granting the abbot the privilege to provide dimissorial letters, not to ordain. A similar bull, dated November 16, 1427, written by Martin V, was sent to the Cistercian abbot in the monastery of Cella S. Mariae. All of these documents produced a host of speculation and discussion. From the time of the Council of Trent down to the discovery of these documents in the early twentieth century, Catholic theologians had for the most part denied the possibility of a priest ordaining to priesthood. Such papal delegations have raised innumerable questions, particularly those which deal with the relationship of bishop and priest. For our own day and age, presbyteral ordination to the priesthood has far-reaching ecumenical implications. We will return to the ecumenical issue in a later chapter.

5. SOME GENERAL OBSERVATIONS ON THE COUNTER-REFORMATION PERIOD AND ITS THEOLOGICAL PRESENTATION OF THE SACRAMENT OF ORDER

Let us consider some of the issues on the sacrament of order which theologians in this period of Catholic thought discussed and developed. Through this theologizing, the counter-Reformation period in many instances prepared the way for the theological positions of Vatican II on the ordained ministry.

a. As the decades and centuries moved on after the Council of Trent, more and more theologians came to see that episcopacy clearly had to belong to the sacrament of order and not simply be an office and dignity in the Church. In what way this episcopal relationship to the sacrament of order might be best understood was disputed; but the insight that episcopacy cannot be simply an honor and a function gradually became more and more clear. This appreciation of a priestly episcopacy constituted a definite enrichment to the theology of order.

b. The obverse side of this same issue, of course, did cause some theological and even practical difficulties. If episcopacy is only an office and a dignity, then the one who conferred such an office and a dignity might both delegate such privileges and likewise restrain such privileges. This issue of a bishop as delegate of the pope became quite controverted during the entire discussion of papal infallibility at Vatican I.

c. The issue of papal infallibility, which alone was promulgated by Vatican I, due to the early closing of the council, left many issues dealing with a theology of episcopacy unanswered. Indeed, the atmosphere in the Vatican, which seemed to resent any questioning of papal infallibility by either an episcopal infallibility or an ecclesial infallibility, prevented a full discussion on episcopal authority and therefore on the priestly authority of the bishop.

d. The entire discussion on matter and form of the sacrament of order, so foreign to the Greek and Eastern approach to Christian theology, and so foreign to contemporary Protestant theology, caused the Roman Catholic scholars to delve into the historical material available to them. The history of the imposition of hands for ordination, the history of the consecratory form of ordination and its mention of eucharistic power, the history of presbyter and episkopos—all these raised questions as regards the Catholic position on the matter and form of this sacrament. The array of opinions presented by Catholic theologians during this counter-Reformation period which attempted to mesh historical data on the one hand, and the theological positions of scholastic thought on the other, is remarkable. Some of the historical data, which they used, has proved to be incorrect, but still the confrontation with historical data has been enormously helpful in sifting out the multiple factors involved. All of their endeavors paved the way for the enormous historical research on sacramental history which took place in the twentieth century.

e. The collegiality of the bishops remained a major issue. Direct papal involvement in the local diocese and, at times, regions had as its side-effect the lessening of the collegial influence of the bishops. Still, theologically, collegiality was seen throughout this period as an essential part of the full meaning of episcopacy.

f. The lengthy debates on the diaconate, which had in many ways become a mere stepping stone to the priesthood, helped to place the theology of the deacon in a much more profound and reverenced place. The opposite side of this coin, however, was the gradual demotion of the subdiaconate from a theologically considered (not defined) major order to a simple minor order. Likewise, the more that the diaconate alone was stressed as one of the major orders, the more the lower orders were disengaged from the understanding of the sacrament of order itself. This entire study, of course, prepared the way for the radical step of eliminating all minor orders, including subdiaconate, in the renewal of Vatican II.

g. A major enrichment of the priesthood during this lengthy period was the solid development of an educated and a spiritual clergy. We have seen above that from 1850 onward a rather unified priestly group in the Roman Church was observable. A common education in the seminary system and a common spirituality of priesthood clearly produced a clergy which was respected by the Roman Church at large and by many outside the Roman Church as well. This common educational and spiritual development of the priest had, of course, its shadow side, as we saw above.

Other factors in the nineteenth and early twentieth centuries affected all of sacramental theology. Although these factors played a role in the theology of the sacrament of order, they are much too general and comprehensive for discussion in this volume. These factors were: (1) the rise of historical consciousness; (2) the philosophical movement of existentialism and phenomenology; (3) the development of the ecumenical movement; (4) the rise of social consciousness, leading directly to liberation theology. All of these affected Catholic sacramental theology in one way or another, and all of these factors, plus the efforts made during the counter-Reformation period, set the stage for the theology of Vatican II.

11

Ministry in the
Documents of Vatican II

In Roman Catholic theology of the twentieth century, as far as ministry is concerned, the Second Vatican Council holds a commanding place. The Second Vatican Council presented the Roman Catholic Church with a theological understanding of ministry which will continue to exert an influence for decades, perhaps even centuries to come. This theological understanding of ministry is found not only in the documents of Vatican II themselves, but also in the renewed rituals both for ordination and for the conferment of ministries which the Second Vatican Council engendered.

In the wake of this council, a phrase began to appear in theological writings: namely, "Vatican II theology." It would, however, be incorrect to assume that this "Vatican II theology" refers only to the theological positions found in the documents of the council. Rather, it refers to the entire spectrum of theological work which (a) preceded the council, (b) received confirmation in the council itself, and (c) spawned a number of renewal activities within the Church after the council. It is well known, too, that the Second Vatican Council did not produce documents which were meant to be comprehensive theological treatises, covering all aspects of a given topic. The documents are, rather, statements of the episcopal hierarchy which are addressed to Catholics throughout the world (in some cases to all people of good will), and which treat a number of serious issues affecting the Church in the late twentieth century. These documents represent, in general, what is called in theology proper the ordinary magisterium of the Church.

In these documents nothing has been defined in any solemn way. Because there was no solemn definition on any issue, one sees that there is a major difference between the conciliar documents of Nicaea, Ephesus, Chalcedon, Trent—all of which include solemn, defined statements, or what is called in theology proper the extraordinary magisterium of the Church—and the conciliar documents of Vatican II. As the ordinary magisterium of the Church, however, these Vatican II documents offer us more than a mere guideline for teaching and Church practice; they offer an official program or schema on both specific topics of theology and on Church pastoral practice which the Church leadership wants followed at this time. Some future council might indeed make modifications in any and all of these documents, but for the Roman Church of this age these documents provide Catholics with a framework, both for theological work and for Church practice. One should also realize that the official book of rites, which the various commissions appointed after Vatican II produced, and which were promulgated by highest Church authority, is still another expression of the ordinary magisterium of the Church, and these rituals clearly affect the understanding of the sacraments generally, and, for our present concern, the sacrament of order on the one hand, and the ecclesial ministries on the other.

In this chapter we will consider first the history of the document on priestly and episcopal ministry, since these are two ministerial issues which the council focused on in an extensive way. Second, we will consider the major structures of ordained and to some degree non-ordained ministry which Vatican II presents to us as Church teaching. Third, we will single out those major issues concerning the sacrament of order which, in substantive ways, modify the traditional understanding of ordained ministry. Lastly, we will consider some of the unfinished agenda which theology in a post-Vatican II age should consider and develop.

1. HISTORY OF THE DOCUMENT ON EPISCOPAL AND PRIESTLY MINISTRY

The history of these conciliar documents has been traced in detail in several works, and it is not our purpose here to reproduce that material.[1] Rather, let us consider those major elements in this historical approach to the documents of Vatican II in which the council modified to some degree the prevailing approach to the sacrament of order. In this way, as we shall see, we will be building on the material that has been developed in the historical overview in this present volume.

It is well known that in the earliest agenda for the council there was scant mention of any scheduled, special discussion on the priesthood. The mystery of the Church itself was certainly the major theme of the proposed council agenda, and this theme remained central throughout the council's proceedings. Indeed, Vatican II can be called a "Church council," in the sense that its one, single, integrating subject was the Church in our times. Quite naturally, then, bishops and their role in the Church were part of the original agenda. A lengthy discussion on priests, deacons, subdeacons and the other minor orders was not envisioned. Nonetheless, it became apparent from the answers to the initial questionnaire sent out to the bishops of the world by John XXIII, shortly after his announcement of the council (January 25, 1959), that the life of the clergy was too important a topic to treat only in a passing way.[2] The responses on this issue of clergy were compiled by a special commission in book form, the very size of which indicated the worldwide concern for clerical life, particularly priestly life, but the approach of these responses was largely juridical in nature. Such issues as the duties of the priest, his obligations to engage in spiritual exercises, his promises of celibacy and of obedience tended to dominate the concerns which the bishops who answered the questionnaire voiced.[3]

A preparatory committee was then established: *Commissio de Disciplina Cleri et Populi Christiani* (June 5, 1960), which, after many lengthy sessions, prepared a number of "schemata" or drafts which were to serve the council members themselves in their discussions on this matter of the clergy. At this stage, the term "clergy" was the preferred term, even though the major focus was on the priest alone. Three of these schemata played a prominent role:

a. On the holiness of clerical life;
b. On the distribution of the clergy;
c. On the offices and benefices of the clergy.

However, it was not until November 1963 that the council members, i.e., the bishops and some major religious superiors, met in plenary sessions, discussing the work of this commission. The bishops asked that the name of the text be changed to *De Sacerdotibus,* since the focus of the text was basically on priests, not on clergy generally. We will see, however, that even this name, *De Sacerdotibus,* did not perdure. A second issue, which the commission was requested to change, was the introductory section. The bishops clearly desired that at the very beginning of the document the threefold ministry of Jesus, i.e., teacher, priest and pastor, be mentioned, and in this threefold designation of ministries the first to be named was that of teacher, i.e., the ministry of preaching the Word. This use of the threefold ministry marks a definite change of emphasis as regards the sacrament of order, at least as far as official teaching of the Church was concerned, and because of this important change of emphasis let us consider some of the background on this threefold ministry.

There has been a long history on this threefold ministry of Jesus.[4] The New Testament nowhere puts them all together in this triadic way, but various sections of the New Testament do mention that Jesus was a teacher, even a prophet. Other sections highlight his leadership and pastoral care. The letter to the Hebrews is the only document which explicitly calls Jesus a priest, although other New Testament passages, particularly those that relate to his arrest and death, have been interpreted as "priestly." Nonetheless, the New Testament no-where explicitly states that Jesus was prophet, priest and king, in this threefold form of expression, nor does it explicitly state that these three tasks sum up the mission and ministry of Jesus. The formulation of a threefold ministry of Jesus, therefore, is a theological construct, not a matter of divine revelation.

A few of the early Fathers of the Church had used these three titles of Jesus, namely, priest, king and prophet, but most often singly. Seldom does one find a threefold enumeration in the writings of the Fathers of the Church. More often, one finds only two titles mentioned together: namely, those of priest and king. Didymus the Blind, in his *Commentary on 1 Peter,*[5] and Augustine in both his *City of God*[6] and his *Sermon on Psalm 26,*[7] use these two titles together, but do not add the third. When the Fathers of the Church spoke of Jesus as the Christ or "anointed one," they often would mention that in the Old Testament priests were anointed, or that kings were anointed, or that prophets were anointed. They also spoke of the baptized sharing in this threefold anointing of Jesus. There is, then, some patristic basis for this threefold approach to the mission and ministry of Jesus himself.

When, however, the Fathers of the Church spoke about episkopoi (bishops) or presbyteroi (priests), they did not use this threefold ministry as a basis for their teaching on ordained ministry. In other words, the explicit connection between the ordained minister of the Church and this threefold structure of the ministry of Jesus was not part of the patristic tradition.

In the middle ages, during the scholastic period of theology, it was primarily Bonaventure who utilized this theme of the threefold anointing. Bonaventure's *Lignum Vitae* returns to this threefold structure quite often (39, 40, 42, 45).[8] Still, in his *Commentary on the Sentences* of Peter Lombard, a professedly theological work, Bonaventure, like every other major scholastic theologian of that time, does not utilize the threefold format to elucidate the meaning of the sacrament of order. Thomas Aquinas nowhere utilizes this threefold structure. Because of this non-usage of the threefold structure for ordained ministry in scholastic theology, we can say that this threefold description of ministry in relation to ordination and the sacrament of order did not become a part of the theological tradition on priesthood. The sacrament of order was, as we saw previously, focused on one area only: namely, the eucharist.

It was actually John Calvin who systematized this threefold office of Jesus and thereby brought it into the mainstream of theological thought. In his *Institutes of the Christian Religion,* Calvin outlines first the prophetic office of Jesus, which is Jesus' teaching office. Jesus has brought a perfect doctrine, Calvin reminds us, and in this sense he has "made an end to all prophecies."[9] For Calvin, Jesus is not only a prophet, but the greatest of all prophets, who renders further prophecy useless. Calvin then considers the kingly office of Jesus, in which he speaks of the complete dominion of Jesus over everything, including death and Satan. Jesus continues to rule in his Church, and "no matter how many strong enemies plot to overthrow the church, they do not have sufficient strength to prevail over God's immutable decree by which he appointed his Son eternal King."[10] In this section Calvin lays great stress on the spiritual, not the temporal and political nature of Jesus' kingly office. Lastly, Calvin treats of Jesus' priestly office, which is one of reconciliation and intercession. It is here that Calvin uses such theological terms as expiation and sacrifice. He writes: "Thus we see that we must begin from the death of Christ in order that the efficacy and benefit of his priesthood may reach us."[11] Jesus' sacrifice,

Calvin reminds us, can never be repeated, and such Roman phrases as "sacrificing anew" or "the Mass as the sacrificing of Christ" were anathema to Calvin.[12] This connection of the threefold office expressed in a theologically systematized way with the major issue of the Reformation, grace and good works, probably accounts for the Roman Catholic disregard of such usage.

Moreover, Lutheran theologians, but neither Martin Luther himself nor Melancthon, began to utilize this threefold office of Jesus, so that by 1650 or thereabouts, the theme had become quite common in theological treatises by Lutheran scholars.[13] Given this Protestant approach to the threefold office of Jesus, Catholic scholars almost unanimously tended to avoid using it. There were some exceptions, but very few. Peteau early on referred to it in his *De Incarnatione*,[14] but in this he had few Roman Catholic followers. Only at the end of the eighteenth century and the beginning of the nineteenth century do Catholic scholars begin to treat of this threefold office of Jesus (not ministry), with the result that gradually Catholic theologians more and more began to deal with this topic. Subsequently, Catholic authors dealing with the spirituality of the priesthood found this threefold office of Jesus of special value for their treatment of ordained ministry. Catholic canon lawyers also found this threefold description helpful.[15] By the twentieth century this theme, which had been considered by Catholics as rather "Protestant," had become part of the normal way of speaking, both as regards Jesus' ministry, and as regards priestly ministry. Jesus was priest, prophet and king; the ordained priest was also priest, prophet and king. It might be noted that Catholics generally preferred to follow the order: priest first, then prophet and finally king, rather than begin with the office of teaching (prophet). Although this threefold way of speaking about priestly ministry was common in spiritual and theological literature, no formal Church document used it. Pius XI, in his encyclical on the priesthood, preferred to use the scholastic approach of the twofold power: namely, the power over the eucharistic body of Jesus and the power over the mystical body of Jesus.

Vatican II, however, not only mentioned this threefold office of Jesus and a corresponding threefold office of Church ministry, but the council has made it the very structure for its theology of ministry. The vicissitudes of its history, related above, are important, for in the very use of this threefold schema as part of the ordinary magisterium,

Vatican II departs from the traditional understanding of priesthood, namely, a theology of priesthood defined or centralized by the eucharist. Moreover, in adopting a structure which traditionally had been more at home in Protestant theology than in Catholic theology, another ecumenical opening was formed which will greatly help in post-Vatican II discussions with Anglicans and Protestants on the issue of Church ministry. In the next section of this chapter we will analyze Vatican II's approach to the priesthood from this format of a threefold mission and ministry, but this brief digression on the threefold structure seemed necessary, since without some understanding of its foundational status to the documents of Vatican II on ordained ministry the very history of the documentation would be unintelligible.

Let us return now to the history of the documents on priesthood. After the commission had gone over these changes and other numerous suggestions of the bishops on almost every point of the various schemata, and had presented a revised draft of *De Sacerdotibus* to the council members, the bishops in their discussions of December 28, 1963 and January 15, 1964 decided that the decree should be pared down and reformulated into a small number of guiding principles. The commission was requested to do this, and it reduced the document to ten guiding principles, which in April 1964, together with a *relatio* describing the history of the document and the rationale of its structure, written by Archbishop Marty, were sent to the council members for their further consideration. On September 14, 1964 the council officially took up this draft and once again made substantial changes in it. No longer was it called *De Sacerdotibus,* but rather *De Vita et Ministerio Sacerdotali.* But it was precisely this reduction of the discussion on priests to a small number of guidelines (eventually enlarged to twelve), good as these were, which a number of bishops felt inappropriate. In many ways, the discussion on this issue of reducing the material to simply a few guidelines was a major turning point on the topic of the theology of priesthood. Priests throughout the world, several bishops argued, would feel neglected and to a degree overlooked if only a few guidelines were established by this major council. A better conciliar message, they argued, had to be framed.[16] From October 13 to November 15, forty-one council members spoke on this subject of the priestly document. The dissatisfaction of the bishops was clearly and strongly stated and reiterated time and again. Even while the bishops were speaking on this matter, approval to formulate a new draft had been made and the commission worked under pressure to present as quickly as possible this better message of the council on the subject of the priesthood. A first drafting of this new message was given to the council on October 29, 1964. It was mandated that suggested changes were to be sent in to the commission by the end of January 1965. A major leader in this reworking of the document was Francois Marty, then the archbishop of Riems, who had actually been working with the commission almost from the beginning. Marty's leadership cannot be underemphasized.

From February through May 1965, the suggestions (*modi*) of the bishops were discussed by the commission and, if accepted, worked into the document. It was at this time that the linkage between priest and bishop was substantially strengthened in the document's wording. This linkage had already been done in other documents, but it was now clearly imbedded in this statement on the priesthood. We will see later how theologically important this was for an understanding of priestly ministry.

On October 14, 1965 the revised statement became the topic for plenary discussion, but only three days prior to this, on October 11, Tisserant had read a letter to the general assembly from Paul VI in which the pope said the topic of priestly celibacy was inopportune. Many bishops had wanted an open discussion on this issue, but the intervention of the pope disallowed it.[17] On October 16, the draft on the ministry and life of priests was overwhelmingly approved (only twelve negative votes) by the council members. Minor revisions were, of course, still allowed, and the commission worked with these new suggestions to prepare the final text. On December 2, 1965 the council approved the final text and the pope promulgated it on December 7, 1965.

This document had been given several titles during its historical development:

1. *De Clericis*
2. *De Sacerdotibus*
3. *De Vita et Ministerio sacerdotali*
4. *De Presbyterorum Ministerio et Vita*

Cleric is a term that encompassed everyone from first tonsure to bishop and pope. This was changed to *sacerdos,* but in Christian tradition, particularly patristic tradition, *sacerdos* referred to both bishop and presbyter. Since presbyter goes back to New Testament times, and since the stabilization of the names of Church hierarchy had eventually placed presbyter in a subordinate role to episkopos, it was selected over *sacerdos*. In the third title listed above, we see that the initial focus is on the life of the priest and secondly on the ministry. The final title reverses the order: the initial focus is on the mission and ministry; only then does the document take up presbyteral life. As F. Wulf notes: "With each change in title there resulted a concomitant change in the content of the decree." As regards the issue of reversing "life and ministry" to "ministry and life," he adds: "The office of the priest is to be viewed first and foremost in terms of its function and not of its status."[18]

Such, in broad outline, is the history of the text. What one finds in the 1965 text is clearly different in tone and in emphasis from the early statements of 1959/1960. Let us now analyze in more detail the major areas of difference between the traditional or scholastic interpretation of the sacrament of order and the teaching on order in these conciliar documents, since it is precisely these different emphases on priesthood which have now become part of the ordinary magisterium of the Church for our time.

2. MAJOR STRUCTURES OF ORDAINED AND NON-ORDAINED MINISTRY

A. THE VERY DEFINITION OF PRIESTHOOD

As we have seen previously, the manual theology of the nineteenth and twentieth centuries reinforced, almost unanimously, the scholastic approach to priesthood which defined the priest in terms of his relationship to the eucharist. This was the "traditional" doctrine, or scholastic doctrine, which was standard in the Catholic Church at the onset of the council. This eucharistic approach was not only the basis for a *theology* of the priesthood, but it was also the basis for the *spirituality* of priesthood and for the ordination ritual. It was precisely this definition which was set aside, changed, or modified by Vatican II. This does not mean that the scholastic understanding of priesthood was rejected as wrong; rather, it was deemed too narrow and needed to be enriched and enlarged. Marty, in a plenary session, spoke quite clearly on this matter:

The commission cannot agree with those Fathers who think the position paper should have followed the scholastic definition of priesthood, which is based on the power to consecrate the eucharist. According to the prevailing mind of this Council and the petition of many Fathers, the priesthood of presbyters must rather be connected with the priesthood of bishops, the latter being regarded as the high point and fullness of priesthood. The priesthood of presbyters must therefore be looked at, in this draft, as embracing not one function, but three, and must be linked with the Apostles and their mission.[19]

These are forthright words, indeed. Three issues are of paramount importance: (1) episcopacy is not simply an office or dignity beyond the priesthood, but the fullness of the priesthood itself. Moreover, (2) priests can only be understood in and through their relationship to episcopal ministry, but this likewise means that bishops can only be understood in their relationship to priestly ministry. Such a relational approach to both bishop and priest is, of course, found from the New Testament times down to the scholastic era. When episcopacy was severed, theologically, from the sacrament of order, its description and definition tended to lose and, at times in theological works, actually did lose its relational identity to the presbyters. One also sees in Marty's statement that (3) both episcopal and presbyteral ministry can only be understood in its apostolic relationship or dimension, which means its christological relationship or dimension. This christological dimension, however, is threefold: teaching, sanctifying, leading, and therefore all ministries based on Jesus will also have a threefold characteristic.

The interrelating of these three issues form the very definition of priesthood as expressed in Vatican II. In this sense, then, Vatican II presents to the Catholic world, on the basis of the ordinary magisterium of the Church, a definition of priesthood which is clearly not as narrow as that of scholastic theology. It is this "new definition" of priesthood which Catholic theologians and spiritual writers today must incorporate into their teaching and writing. We will specify the elements of this "new definition" in the sections which follow; of importance at this stage of the presentation of the material from Vatican II is the realization that the very understanding of ministry, particularly ordained ministry, has been reformulated by this solemn synod of bishops. This reformulation by Vatican II bases itself in the very mission and ministry of Jesus.

B. THE CHRISTOLOGICAL BASE OF CHRISTIAN MINISTRY

The christological foundation for ministry is one of the most important aspects of Vatican II theology on ministry. Jesus himself is the basis of ministry, and one must begin with the very ministry of Jesus to comprehend the meaning of all Church ministry. In the preceding chapter on the scholastic theology of priesthood, it was mentioned that in the great scholastic writers, Thomas, Bonaventure, Albert, Scotus, the actual ministry of Jesus played no role at all in their theologizing on priesthood. Vatican II, however, instructs us to see in the very mission and ministry of Jesus the foundation for any and all definitions, descriptions, spiritualities of each and every Church ministry.

This ministry of Jesus, which we find delineated in the gospels in a most special way, but mentioned as well in other New Testament writings, is threefold.

a. Jesus the teacher   By his words and by his life itself, Jesus proclaimed the good news. The name teacher, of course, corresponds generally to the more traditional term in theology: prophet.

b. Jesus the priest   We have seen that only Hebrews calls Jesus "priest." Still, Jesus is portrayed in the gospels as one who brings holiness to people. Jesus is a sanctifier.

c. Jesus the pastor   Jesus is the good shepherd, the leader, the pastor. In traditional theological terms he has the title: king.

M. Schmaus, in speaking of this threefold office of Jesus, summarizes these offices as follows: "One understands in this phrase [the three offices] the full empowerment of Christ for those offices, which Jesus had to fulfill, in virtue of his sending by the heavenly Father: as teacher (prophet), priest and king (shepherd), and accordingly one speaks of his office as teacher (office as prophet), his office as priest, and his office as king (office as shepherd)."[20] Schmaus, in this description, notes that the mission and ministry of Jesus is from the Father, a major theme of Christian ministry, as we have noted again and again. Schmaus calls this a "full empowerment," i.e., in these three offices of Jesus we will find the power of the gospel, i.e., the entire divine intent of the incarnation. In many ways, this threefold structure is almost a summation of christology, and so Vatican II is not basing Church ministry on some tangential aspect of the mystery of Jesus, but on the very core of the mystery of Jesus. In *Lumen Gentium* we read: "It was for this purpose that God sent his Son, whom he appointed heir of all things (cf. Heb 1, 2), that he might be teacher, king and priest of all, the head of the new and universal people of God's sons" (n. 13).

C. THE ECCLESIOLOGICAL BASIS OF ALL CHURCH MINISTRY

It is this threefold mission and ministry of Jesus which lies at the base of the council's approach to Church ministry in all its forms: episcopal, presbyteral, diaconal, and lay. Indeed, the mission and ministry of the Church itself is a reflection of Jesus' own ministry. The very title of the most solemn of all the council's documents, the dogmatic constitution on the Church, *Lumen Gentium,* emphasizes this. The "light of the world" is not the Church, but Jesus; the Church is the reflection of that light. In other words, the Church in its totality reflects the very mission and ministry of Jesus, and if the mission and ministry of Jesus is to be described in a threefold manner, then the mission and ministry of the Church is to be described in a similar way. All baptized share in the "priestly, prophetic and kingly office of Christ," as *Lumen Gentium* states (n. 31).

Kloppenburg has written rather eloquently on this matter:

> The Council begins its Dogmatic Constitution of the Church with the word *Lumen Gentium.* But this "light of the nations" is not the Church: "Christ is the light of all nations" [LG 1, 14]. From its very opening words, therefore, Vatican II seeks to give a completely Christocentric and thus relativized idea of the Church. We can understand the Church only if we relate it to Christ, the glorified Christ. The Church lives by Christ.[21]

Kloppenburg then goes on to consider Jesus as this light of the world. Jesus is like the sun, the sole source of light. The Church, then, is like the moon, which has no light of its own, and receives its only light from Jesus. Just as the moon reflects the sun, so, too, must the Church reflect the spiritual sun, Jesus. Indeed, only when the Church reflects Jesus is it really the Church.[22] Since Jesus is teacher, sanctifier and leader, the Church must reflect these teaching, sanctifying and leading aspects of Jesus. Schematically, we might indicate this as follows:

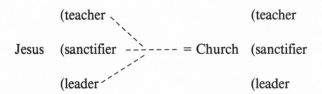

(teacher   (teacher

Jesus (sanctifier --------- = Church (sanctifier

(leader   (leader

In this approach we have the primordial christological base of the Church itself as ministerial (the theology of the Church), and the main ecclesiological base for specialized Church ministry (the theology of ministry). Only against the background of Jesus as teacher-sanctifier-leader can the Church be understood as teacher-sanctifier-leader. This accords well with the contemporary approach to sacraments which presents Jesus himself in his human nature as the primordial sacrament and the Church as the basic sacrament. And only against the background both of Jesus as teacher-sanctifier-leader and of the Church as sanctifier-teacher-leader can there be any theology of specialized ministry.

Wulf notes, however, that the document on the priesthood of Vatican II remains somewhat tentative on this matter.

> Unfortunately, the spiritual, theological unity between the official priesthood and the priesthood of the Church is not made sufficiently clear. It is not stated that the fundamental priesthood in the Church is that of the Church, the whole People of God, and that hence the official priesthood, in spite of its institution by Christ—not the Church—finds its immediate theological setting within the priesthood of the Church.[23]

Even though the documents of Vatican II do not develop in any overwhelming way the priestly role of the Church itself, the prophetic role of the Church itself and the shepherding role of the Church itself, the ground is surely prepared, and even more than just prepared, for this development. This ecclesiological dimension of ministry has been given a solid endorsement by the Council, so that theologians should feel strongly encouraged to pursue this line of thought. Indeed, all that such theologians as K. Rahner and Schillebeeckx have written on the Church as basic sacrament dovetails well with this conciliar approach to Church ministry.

The council, however, having established this christological and ecclesiological fundamental approach to all Christian ministry, then goes on to present the specialized Church ministries. First, let us consider the ministry of bishop. The bishop is seen by the council as teacher, sanctifier, leader. In a key passage from *Lumen Gentium* we read: "Now, episcopal consecration confers, together with the office of sanctifying, the duty also of teaching and ruling, which of their very nature can be exercised only in hierarchical communion with the head and members of the college" (n. 21). This approach to episcopal ministry is consistent throughout the documentation of Vatican II. "Bishops, in a resplendent and visible manner, take the place of Christ himself, teacher, shepherd, and priest, and act as his representatives (*LG* n. 21; cf. also *PO* 12; *LG* 6).

It is evident that the bishops are envisioned in a collegial way, and not in an individualistic way. On the other hand, individually they are bishops. Not all the tensions, perhaps, are worked out, but Vatican II in a most definite way re-emphasized the collegial nature of the episcopacy.

When the council considered the ministry of the priests, the same threefold mission and ministry was expressed. "Priests represent Christ and are the collaborators of the order of bishops in that threefold sacred duty which, of its nature, pertains to the mission of the Church" (*AG* n. 39; cf. *PO* 1; *LG* 28) Just as the bishops participate in the threefold mission and ministry of Jesus, so, too, do the priests participate in the threefold mission and ministry of Jesus. In what way bishop and priest differ in this participation might not be totally clear; but the identifying of priest to this threefold mission and ministry is quite clear. There is a conciliar consistency to this approach to the mission and ministry of priests.

When one considers the diaconate, there is unfortunately a lack of extended material. The documents of Vatican II mention the diaconate in only the briefest way, but mention is made of this threefold ministry: "In the lower grade of the hierarchy are deacons, on whom hands are laid 'not for the priesthood, but for the ministry.' Strengthened by sacramental grace, they serve the people of God in the *diakonia* of liturgy, word and charity, in communion with the bishop and his presbyterium" (*LG* n. 29). This passage is cited by Paul VI in his apostolic constitution *Pontificalis Romani Recognito* of June 18, 1968 introducing the new ritual for the ordination of a deacon, and by his apostolic letter *Ad Pascendam* of August 15, 1972 containing norms for the order of diaconate. Liturgy is the sanctifying ministry; word, the teaching or preaching ministry; charity, the leading or pastoral ministry.

When one studies the issue of lay ministry in the Church which the documents of Vatican II described, the same pattern of the three-fold mission and ministry of Jesus is maintained. In fact, the Vatican II doctrine on the nature of the laity is, in Kloppenberg's phrase, "generous indeed."

> From Vatican II's abundant instruction on the laity, we learn that all the baptized "share a true equality with regard to the dignity and to the activity common to all the faithful for the building up of the body of Christ" (*LG* 32); that all share "in the mission of the whole Christian people with respect to the Church and to the world" (*LG* 31); that all "have an active part to play in the life and activity of the Church (*AA* 10).[24]

He goes on to cite and comment on passages from *Lumen Gentium:* paragraph 34, which deals with the lay person's sharing in the priestly function of Jesus; paragraph 35, which deals with the layperson's sharing in the prophetic office of Jesus; and paragraph 36 which deals with the layperson's sharing in the kingly or pastoral office of Jesus.[25] Klostermann, in his commentary on this section of *Lumen Gentium,* echoes the interpretation of Kloppenburg.

> As the following three articles [34,35,36] show, the Council is aware that baptism and confirmation do not merely confer a share in Christ's priesthood but also a share in Christ's office as prophet and king. . . . Baptism and confirmation each provide the foundation for a general Christian apostolate, an apostolate of all Christians.[26]

The source of this ministry is not a delegation by a pastor, a bishop, a pope, but arises from the sacrament of initiation itself (baptism-confirmation-eucharist). By stressing the sacramental, not jurisdictional foundation of the ministry of all Christians, the emphasis is on God/Jesus as the source of all ministry. Moreover, the document is not simply concerned with an internal and spiritual growth of a Christian, but with an external and active part in the very mission and ministry of Jesus. "The lay apostolate is correctly defined as 'a share in the very sanctifying mission of the Church'; it is nothing less than that."[27] Any other interpretation, Klostermann adds, "would be inconsistent with the whole idea of the Church which is set forth in the Constitution *De Ecclesia.*"[28]

The entire emphasis on the threefold ministry of Jesus and thus on the threefold ministry of the Church and therefore of the ordained priest seems to be contradicted by *Presbyterorum Ordines,* n. 2, in which one reads: "These men [ordained priests] were to hold in the community of the faithful the sacred power of Order, that of offering sacrifice and forgiving sins, and were to exercise the priestly office publicly on behalf of men in the name of Christ." Explicit reference for this statement is made to the Council of Trent. This description of the ordained ministry is surely not the understanding of priest, based on the threefold mission and ministry of Jesus, but rather on the understanding of priest as a man of the eucharist. Without any doubt at all, this section of the document reiterates the traditional scholastic understanding of priesthood, but as Wulf notes in his commentary, the total document clearly indicates a wider understanding of priestly ministry. A single text alone cannot blunt the overwhelming portrait of priestly ministry found in the documents of Vatican II as described above.[29] Wulf concludes his remarks on the section [2] with the questions: "What are the chief marks of the theological image of the priest as sketched by Article 2 of the decree, and how does this image differ from that of Catholic tradition—at least of the Middle Ages?"[30] Note well that there is a difference between the traditional, scholastic approach to priesthood and the approach of Vatican II. Wulf's questions substantiate what Marty said quite officially at the council itself, namely, that the majority of the bishops did not follow the scholastic definition of priesthood, which is based on the power to consecrate the eucharist. Unless one appreciates the "new" or more comprehensive understanding of priestly ministry, stated by Vatican II, and therefore the non-alignment with the scholastic view of priesthood, one will not fully understand this teaching on priesthood by the ordinary magisterium of the Church.

Wulf lists the following differences:

1. The uniqueness of Christ's priesthood is taken seriously. Christ alone is the priest, and his priesthood is an eschatological one. The primary purpose of the priesthood in the Church is to

preach the salvation accomplished once and for all by Christ. This announcing of Christ's redemptive act is also made known by sacrament and by leadership.

2. The scholastic approach saw the presbyter as the fullness of ordained priesthood; Vatican II sees the episkopos as the fullness of the priesthood.

3. The one-sided cultic character of the Catholic priesthood has been absorbed into the wider apostolic ministry, which has found expression above all in the three offices of Christ. The scholastic view was one-sided, static, personal; the view of Vatican II is multiple, dynamic and ecclesiological.

4. The connection between the universal priesthood and the ordained priesthood has not been totally successful in the documents of Vatican II, but the orientation presented by the conciliar documents helps one understand both the basic priesthood of all believers (the ecclesiological element) and the ordained priesthood.[31]

One other item on this matter, however, is important to note. In all of these various sharings in the threefold ministry of Jesus, Vatican II states that it is Jesus who calls to such ministry and it is Jesus who commissions such ministry. This is in keeping with the best of Christian tradition, in which ministry is never self-appointment, nor community-appointment. Using our framework or diagram started above, we can now complete the structural picture of Vatican II's understanding of ministry:

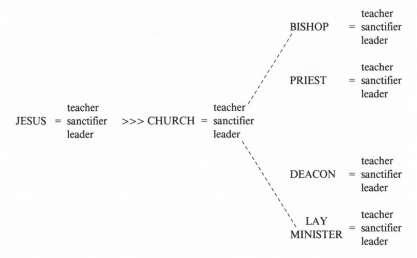

```
                                                                  teacher
                                              BISHOP    =  sanctifier
                                            /                     leader

                                          /                       teacher
                                        /     PRIEST    =  sanctifier
                                      /                           leader
                                    /
          teacher                 teacher /
JESUS = sanctifier  >>> CHURCH = sanctifier
          leader                  leader \
                                          \                       teacher
                                           \  DEACON   =  sanctifier
                                            \                     leader

                                             \  LAY        teacher
                                              \ MINISTER = sanctifier
                                                                  leader
```

Add to this schematic diagram the indication that it is Jesus himself who calls to these ministries and commissions them, and one has a framework or basic image of the teaching of Vatican II on the issue of Church ministry. One sees in this diagram: the christological foundation to all Christian mission and ministry; the ecclesiological basis for all specialized ministry; and precisely that area in which the ministries of bishop, priest, deacon and lay minister fit. Moreover, one sees that the fullness of the ordained priesthood is in the episcopacy; beneath this is the presbyter and only then the deacon. Although not ordained, the lay-ministry is also essentially connected to each and every aspect of Church ministry. In the actual Vatican II documentation the term "ministry" was reserved for the three offices of the ordained ministry. In the case of the lay minister, the documents of Vatican II consistently employ the term "apostolate." This distinction of terms—"ministry" = ordained; "apostolate" = unordained—was deliberately done to indicate the "essential difference" between the ordained and unordained ministries in the Church. However, after the council closed, this distinction in naming has not been followed, even by documents which have come from the Roman curia itself. Today official Church statements, liturgical rituals, theological discussions, religious education at all levels, and pastoral directives speak of ministry for both the ordained and the non-ordained. The term apostolate for lay ministry has not been carried through. The documents of Vatican II, however, teach that there is an essential difference between the ordained minister and the unordained minister; cf. LG 10. Nowhere do the documents attempt to give a theological description or definition of this essential difference; such a description or definition is left to the theologians to elaborate in accord with Christian tradition.

We will return to this understanding of priestly ministry and ministry in the Church generally which Vatican II has presented, but let us consider another major aspect of ministry which Vatican II teaches.

3. MAJOR ISSUES WHICH MODIFY THE THEOLOGY OF PRIESTHOOD IN A SUBSTANTIVE WAY

A. THE BISHOP AS THE FULLNESS OF THE PRIESTHOOD

In 1962, at the very beginning of the council, F. Sola published his treatise on the sacrament of order in the theological manual *Sacrae*

Theologiae Summa. In many ways, this theological manual, written by the Jesuits from the various theological faculties in Spain, is one of the best which was written. The material not only in the section on the sacraments by Sola, but in the other sections of dogmatic theology as well, is very current and well researched, intensively and extensively. At this late date, 1962, Sola, in speaking of the episcopacy as a sacrament, will only indicate that the opinion is "certain and common."[32] Wulf writes:

> Whereas from the Middle Ages until Vatican II the presbyterate was seen as the fundamental priestly order, to which something extra was added by jurisdiction in order to produce the episcopate, now it is the episcopate that is seen as basic, the presbyterate being a participation in the episcopate as the plenitude of official ministry.[33]

We have seen that long before Vatican II most Catholic theologians leaned in the direction of episcopacy, in some way or another, as part of the sacrament of order, but they could not substantiate this theological opinion with any official, solemn Church statement. Trent had not settled the issue, and from Trent to Vatican II there was no official, mandatory Church statement to draw on. This situation, as is evident, is clearly changed by Vatican II, so that it is now the teaching of the ordinary magisterium that episcopacy is the fullness of the priesthood, which is to be understood no longer simply in terms of eucharist, but rather in terms of Christ's own mission and ministry as teacher, sanctifier and leader.

G. Philips notes that the term the council chose was "fullness of the priesthood," and not "the highest degree" of the priesthood. "This does more justice to the structure of supernatural realities which descend from above: the participation in the sacrament which Christ bestows on priests is granted in full to the bishop."[34]

Episcopacy as the fullness of the sacrament of order has a dual implication: one inward to the Roman Catholic community itself, and one outward to the Christian community generally. Inwardly, the Roman Catholic Church distances itself from any position in which the bishop is seen merely as a delegate of the pope. By ordination, not by delegation, are men made a part of the episcopal college. Moreover, throughout the documents episcopacy is defined or described in its priestly-prophetic-pastoral aspects: "Now, episcopal consecration confers, together with the office of sanctification, the duty also of teaching and ruling" (*LG* 21). The Dogmatic Constitution on the Church goes on to say: "Among the more important duties of bishops that of preaching the Gospel has pride of place" (24). In these and many other documentary remarks on bishops we see that: (a) the bishops receive both their call and their basic commission from Christ himself through ordination, not through papal delegation; (b) the bishops, *qua* bishops, are related to one another in a form of "college"; (c) this collegiality is also part of the call and commission which comes through ordination, not through any delegation; (d) the local bishop forms, as well, a collegial structure with the priests of his own diocese, and this collegial structure of a local bishop and his priests constitute a "presbyterium"; (e) the local bishop individually has an intrinsic relationship to the lay ministers of the diocese; (f) the bishops, regionally and universally, have an intrinsic relationship to the total Church, i.e., all the baptized; (g) each bishop individually and the bishops collegially have a relationship to the pope, but not in the sense that either individually or collegially they are *qua* bishops delegates of the pope. This ministerial networking (a to g above) prevents an isolated understanding not only of bishop, but also of all the ministries mentioned above. The very term "fullness" connotes a participatory situation, an interrelational dynamic. A bishop is, consequently, not the fullness of priesthood all by himself, but only insofar as the bishop is fully related to all these other various Christian ministries. The very definition of bishop, then, is not individual but collegial, and this essentially.

Outwardly considered (i.e., in respect to non-Roman Christian communities), this essential connection of episcopacy to the sacrament of order helps smooth out the ecumenical discussions on episcopal ministry, above all with the Eastern Churches, but also with the Anglican Church and several Protestant Churches as well. On the one hand, the full inclusion of episcopacy into the sacrament of order by these conciliar documents helped assuage the Eastern Churches' view that the Latin Church had, over the centuries, downplayed the episcopal dignity. On the other hand, the full inclusion of episcopacy into the sacrament of order helped convince the Anglicans that their own episcopal structure would be taken seriously. We will return to these ecumenical issues in the final chapter.

B. THE COLLEGIALITY OF THE BISHOPS AND PRIESTS

Even though we have already mentioned episcopal collegiality in the section above, let us turn our attention to the matter in a more detailed way. Collegiality, however, was one of those issues at Vatican II which caused strong polarization. Collegiality appeared "suspect" in the eyes of many bishops. The weightiest argument against it was this: the collegiality of the bishops might endanger the primacy of the pope. Naturally, none of the bishops intended this, but it seemed that if one were to emphasize the collegiality of the bishops, the role of the pope would be diminished. On the other hand, if the role of the pope is emphasized, the collegiality of the bishops seems to be diminished. How could the council walk a more centrist path?

The theme of collegiality was not new. Already in the First Vatican Council, the bishops treated the topic. J. P. Torrell in *La Théologie de l'Épiscopat au premier concile du Vatican* indicates that the bishops of that First Vatican Council discussed at least part of the issue as they considered this theme: the primacy of jurisdiction of the pope does not harm the power of the bishop in his diocese. Since no episcopal power suffers any loss by this supreme papal jurisdiction, then there must be a participation by the bishops in the supreme power of the Church. Cardinal Schwartzenberg was the first to bring the matter to the plenary session, indicating the collegial nature of episcopacy. Other bishops followed his approach, while still others spoke of a monarchical Church structure (the pope), but one which was tempered by an aristocracy (the bishops). Still others attempted to elucidate the relationship via a Petrine-apostolic Church structure. Indeed, the entire discussion of the collegial nature of the bishops at Vatican I focused almost exclusively on the relationship of episcopal power and papal power.[35]

Collegiality, however, without further qualification is not something which either exists or does not exist in an unchanging, always identifiable way. Its exercise can be more fully realized at times and less fully realized at other times. A major council such as Vatican II presents a clear example of episcopal collegiality, which one does not find in actuality during a non-conciliar time. In recent times, moreover, the pope has polled the bishops on serious matters through letter (e.g., the question of the assumption of Mary), and this has a clear collegial dimension about it. It was suggested at the Vatican II that an episcopal council or senate might, from time to time, consult with the pope. Since the council, there have been a number of such "synods" of bishops, meeting at Rome in consultation with the pope. This suggestion of a synod was proposed at Vatican II somewhat hesitantly, since the Eastern Churches have a form of episcopacy which includes a patriarch, with strong regional collegiality and therefore regional synods. More in keeping with that Eastern approach are, since Vatican II, the national conferences of bishops, which have received renewed importance in the life of the Church, without, however, any form of a patriarch. Even in the votation for the final text of *Lumen Gentium*, the issue of collegiality met with more resistance than any other single issue, but not enough to sway the total votation. However, this opposition to collegiality did make it necessary to add many caveats throughout the document on the primacy of the pope. Philips notes as regards these additions:

> A perusal of the text shows that it is full of additions designed to block at the very start every attack on the primacy of the Pope. The overloading of the text with all these soothing precautions makes it somewhat prolix and hinders the flow of the style—as can easily be seen if one puts the reassuring clauses in brackets. These redactional touches succeeded in lessening the misgivings of many Western bishops, but weakened the text in the eyes of the Eastern Churches, who needed to be convinced that the Catholic Church really accepted and revered the divine institution of the episcopacy.[36]

In *Lumen Gentium*, n. 21, we read, as cited above: "Episcopal consecration confers, together with the office of sanctifying, the duty also of teaching and ruling." Scholars have attempted in various ways to understand this notion of consecration and the theological distinction between *potestas ordinis* and the *potestas jurisdictionis.* The first power comes through the sacrament of order, so it is taught; the second, through a *missio canonica* of the pope or some other qualified Church official.[37] However, in the above citation of Vatican II we see that at ordination itself a bishop receives the power to teach and rule, and this not through any *missio canonica,* but directly from the Lord. To date, totally satisfactory answers have not been developed, and authors continue to wrestle with the interconnection of these many ideas.

Kloppenburg expresses his interpretation as follows:

> We must stress the deeper meaning of this important conciliar doctrine. It frees us once and for all from a predominantly juridical conception of the bishop. According to this conception, the bishop was a priest who had received a special jurisdiction from the pope, a head of a diocese, a kind of governor and admin-

istrator who, in the measure that he had received jurisdiction, could more or less exercise an immediate and ordinary pastoral function. All the power he had, he had by favor of the Holy See, which could also restrict or entirely remove the jurisdiction that had been freely given. In other words, this kind of bishop was not a vicar of Christ, but a vicar of the pope.[38]

Kloppenburg goes on to say that the new conception of bishop which comes from Vatican II is predominantly sacramental.

> The bishop is the recipient of a charism, a power received directly from God; the power must, of course, be exercised within the bonds of hierarchic communion (and therefore is subject to juridical regulation), but it binds him directly to Christ and, as part of the college, to the apostles, making him a vicar of Christ and a member of that college.[39]

K. Rahner differentiates between *munus* and *potestas,* but notes that the constitution *Lumen Gentium,* "using the pattern of the three offices, affirms that all three (the power to sanctify, teach and govern) are conferred by consecration [to episcopacy] itself, which means by the simple fact of ordination."[40] For this reason, not only diocesan bishops, i.e., ordinaries, but also titular bishops and auxiliary bishops have the right to attend a council. Rahner notes that the constitution *Lumen Gentium* ignores any distinction between diocesan and other bishops throughout its discussion, indicating that the council members were simply talking about bishops, and that all belonged to the college of bishops, because of their ordination, not due to their appointment to some jurisdictional entity.

The addition of the phrase "of their very nature" to *Lumen Gentium* (21) because of the pope's wish, i.e., "of their very nature can be exercised only in hierarchical communion with the head and members of the college," is more a condition than a source. It seems that the consistent and overwhelming view of the Vatican II documents is that the bishops receive their power and office from the Lord himself, not via delegation.[41]

Nonetheless, the emphasis on the collegiality of the bishops has given greater significance to episcopal leadership in the Church, particularly at the regional level. The topic of collegiality has opened the doors for much more theological study of the very meaning of episcopacy, particularly the interrelationship of bishop to bishop. Collegiality has stimulated the interrelational study and practice of bishop to presbyterium. It has opened the door to better relationships with the Eastern Churches. It has asked the non-Catholic Churches of the West to rethink, with the Catholic Church, the role of bishop in the totality of Christian ministry. All in all, it has had by far a most enriching effect on the theology of the sacrament of order, an effect which continues to have increasing value as more and more studies and reflections on the subject appear.

Cardinal Dearden in his address to the United States bishops at their assembly for prayer and reflection, held in 1982 at St. John's University, Collegeville, spoke at length of collegiality. He cited John Paul II's encyclical *Redemptor Hominis,* in which the pope spoke of the new life that has come from this emphasis on collegiality of bishops. John Paul singles out the various synods which helped considerably to renew the Church after Vatican II. Dearden notes that "ordination to the episcopacy entails sacramental insertion into the college of bishops. There is a link between sacramentality and collegiality."[42]

If there is a collegiality of bishops, and one that involves the pope as the leader of this college, then one must say that bishops, theologically, can only be understood in their relationship to one another and in their relationship to the pope. The documents of Vatican II stress this again and again. But the opposite is also true. The pope can only be understood, theologically, in and through his relationship to the bishops. The bishops, without the pope, are not really a college, but the pope without the bishops is not really a pope. Papacy implies episcopacy, just as episcopacy implies papacy. This reciprocity simply stresses the importance of the doctrine of collegiality. Vatican I defined, for instance, the infallibility of the pope, it is true, but this infallibility cannot really be understood apart from the infallibility of the college of bishops on the one hand or apart from the infallibility of the Church itself, on the other hand. Vatican II has in many ways helped to complete the unfinished agenda of Vatican I.

There is, however, equally a collegiality of priests which Vatican II called the *presbyterium.* In the documents of the council, the stress on this priestly collegiality is eminently clear. First of all, Vatican II states, the priests are empowered by the Lord himself. Priests:

are "living instruments of Christ, the eternal priest" (*PO* 12);
"ministers of Jesus Christ among the nations" (*PO* 2):

"represent Christ" (*AG* 39);
"ministers of the Head" (*PO* 12);
"assumes the person of Christ Himself" (*PO* 12);
"act in the person of Christ the head" (*PO* 2);
"act as Christ's ministers" (*PO* 5).

The pattern for the presbyters corresponds to that mentioned for the bishops. The call and the commission is from the Lord himself; it is not delegated to a priest through the bishop. Some bishops wanted it stated that the powers which the priests received in ordination originated solely in the ordaining bishop. This was urged to avoid any "apostolic succession" of the priests. The bishops have the "full power" of the priesthood, and they, through ordination, confer some of that power to the priests.[43] This view was rejected by the council. The threefold ministry of Jesus is conferred on the priests in ordination, and they receive this mission and ministry from the Lord himself. Theologically speaking, then, it is not in accord with the teaching of Vatican II to say that priests are ministers of the Church. Rather, they act in the name of the Church, but they are really ministers of Christ himself.[44] Moreover, theologically one must be careful with such phrases as "priests act in the name of the bishop," as though they were mere delegates of the bishop. Strictly speaking, priests do not act in the name of the bishop, but in the person of Jesus.[45] Priests are ministers or priests of Christ, serving in the diocese of . . . serving with Bishop. . . .

Priests are indeed coworkers of the bishop, and this is stressed again and again throughout the documents of Vatican II. This is clearly what is meant by the presbyterium: a college of priests led by their local bishop. The priests alone as a group do not make up the presbyterium; the bishop alone is not the presbyterium. Priests and bishop together make up the presbyterium. One should also note that a single priest is not a presbyterium either. Ordination affects the individual, it is true, but he is brought into an ordo of priests. To some degree Vatican II theology sees the presbyteral college in a local and regional way, i.e., the diocesan meetings of the priests, and the regional meetings of bishops and priests. The episcopal college, however, is seen in a worldwide way, but also in a regional way.

Several items are important to notice here. First of all, when the main local Church minister was acknowledged rather universally as "episkopos" in the early Church, the second rank of ministers was called presbyters. Generally, the name was in the plural, indicating a sort of "college." These presbyters acted as a council to the episkopos. In other words, when Church leadership reached a sort of normative stage, the local episkopos and the presbyters formed a college. This is re-emphasized by Vatican II in a strong way.

Second, the presbyters at that early stage were counselors of the episkopos. Since Vatican II, every diocese is mandated by canon law to have a presbyteral council. There is, then, something in the very understanding of presbyter which includes this dimension of counselor. It would, of course, be worthless to have a presbyteral council in a diocese if the bishop did not have to listen to his presbyters and even at times abide by its decisions. The new code of canon law tentatively spells out these relationships, but more basic than the areas of con-sultive action is the very basis of such consultive action: the essential, relational understanding of both priest and bishop. Both must be teacher-priest-leader with the other. More profoundly stated, a bishop can only be understood theologically in and through his relationships to a presbyter, and vice versa only in and through a priest's relationship to a bishop can he, too, be theologically understood.

Third, episkopoi/bishops have been theologically associated with a local area. Some of the Fathers of the Church even spoke of the episkopos being wedded to his diocese. Even titular bishops need a titular area. In the middle ages and at the Council of Trent, the issue of episcopal residency was seen as a major issue of reform. Likewise, presbyters were, by ordination, linked to a specific area. "Absolute" ordinations, as they are called, did occur from time to time. Crouzel notes that these "absolute" ordinations existed prior to the Council of Chalcedon, at which canon 6 required a presbyter to be ordained for a community. The fact that such absolute ordinations took place is beyond historical doubt, and "in many cases it is impossible to say whether they aroused any kind of disapproval."[46] Origen, Jerome and Paulinus of Nola in the early Church are striking examples of these absolute ordinations. Nonetheless, the overwhelming tradition is for priests to be ordained for a diocese or for some localized area (as in the case of religious order priests). This very regionality helps one to understand collegiality. Bishops do not belong only to some undif-ferentiated worldwide "college." Bishops are collegial in a territorial way, even a regional way. This is historically quite clear from the second century onward. Priests, too, do not belong to some spiritual, a-temporal or a-spatial "presbyterium." They belong to a regional presbyterium, under the leadership of a very definite, regional bishop.

Even religious order priests must be seen in this way. If these latter are working in a diocese, they are, of course, an integral part of that particular presbyterium. If they have no *cura animarum* in a diocese, but are more monastic in life structure, then their presbyterium, within the religious order, needs to be clarified. Perhaps this Vatican II emphasis on presbyteral collegiality raises the question anew as regards the clericalization of many religious communities of men, so that the clerical predominance in a given religious community or the total clericalness of a given religious community must be re-addressed along the lines of this conciliar theology of priesthood.

It can be said in all honesty that Vatican II, more than any other Church council, took into account the many issues of Church history. The documents of Vatican II do not, of course, enter into an historical background of the material they treat, but the bishops at the council were significantly aware of the historical nuancing. This is eminently true in the issue of episcopacy and presbyterate. The statements about the apostles and the succession to the apostles is handled rather cautiously. Even the words, "Do this in remembrance of me," which Trent indicated was the institution of the priesthood, has been modified by Vatican II, precisely because of New Testament and historical studies on this matter.

C. PRIESTLY SPIRITUALITY

It would be totally misleading if one stopped with the doctrinal issues on priesthood as far as Vatican II was concerned. The bishops were clearly concerned about the spiritual life of priests. Although the spiritual life of the priests constituted the initial chapters of the document in earlier drafts, the change to the pastoral ministry of priestly life first (chapters one and two) and only then to the spiritual life of the priest (chapter three) is itself significant. In the final decree the pastoral ministry of priestly life is placed first since it is the key to an understanding of priestly holiness.

> In discussing the title of the decree [Presbyterorum Ordines] it has already been stressed that in forming a notion of the office of the priest it is important first to think of his ministry and only

then of his life. It was affirmed that the office of the priesthood would be viewed primarily in terms of its function and not of its status. A consequence of this is that the priest's whole life—his spiritual life, his spirituality, his relationship to the world, to things and to men—must be decisively defined and stamped by his ministry, his function, his mandate and mission. The purpose of chapter 3 of the decree is to demonstrate precisely these things.[47]

The spirituality of the priest, in this decree, is focused directly on Jesus: priests are configured to Christ the priest (n. 12). This is fully in keeping with the conciliar presentation that all are called to holiness, i.e., the holiness which Christ both is and shares. In this sense, there is no distinct holiness for the ordained minister which the unordained does not share in. However, as a public person in the Church, the ordained minister has committed himself to be a public holy person in the holy Church. This means a configuration with Christ in his very mission and ministry, which includes the preaching, sanctifying and teaching mission and ministry. We see immediately that the threefold structure not only shapes the doctrinal part of the decree's discussion on the priest, but also the spiritual part of priestly existence.

First of all the priest is like Jesus a teacher. The Word of God lies at the heart of priestly spirituality, and therefore the priest must read and re-read the holy scriptures. This familiarity with the Word of God will, as a result, flow over into his teaching. Priestly ministry is, thus, not separated from priestly spirituality.

By keeping in mind that it is the Lord who opens hearts and that the excellence comes not from themselves but from the power of God, they will be more intimately united with Christ the Teacher and will be guided by his Spirit in the very act of teaching the Word (n. 13).

Vatican II does not elaborate on the priest's role in the magisterium of the Church, but since the priest, through ordination, shares in the teaching mission of the Lord, and through his meditation on the Word of God, as the document mentions, unites him with Christ the Teacher, so that his own teaching will be more fully guided by the Holy Spirit, then it is evident that the priest does indeed share in some way in the magisterium of the Church. Vatican II, however, did not address this issue nor indicate in what ways the theology of ecclesial magisterium might be altered by this stress on the teaching mission and ministry of the presbyter.

The relationship of the priest to Christ the priest and its connection to spirituality is addressed in second place. Emphasis in this section is on the eucharist and the other sacraments. The holiness of these sacraments requires that the ministers themselves be holy. Sacraments, however, are not personal actions, but ecclesial actions or public actions, and thus again the connection between priestly spirituality and priestly ministry is underscored. In this section, however, it is mentioned that the eucharist is the *munus praecipuum,* the principal function, of the priest. In the Constitution on the Church, n. 28, it says even more explicitly that the priests "exercise this sacred function of Christ (*munus sacrum*) most of all (*maxime*) in the eucharistic liturgy." In the same dogmatic constitution, we read that the bishops, who have the fullness of priesthood, are eminent teachers or preachers: "Among the principal duties of bishops, the preaching of the gospel occupies an eminent place" (n. 25). Moreover, in *Presbyterorum ordinis* the first place in the threefold structure is generally given to that of teacher (prophet). The priest-aspect is listed second. At the council there was indeed a small group of bishops who wanted to retain the scholastic theology of priesthood, with its centralizing focus on the eucharist. They did not carry the council. Still, here and there in the documents there are indications of this scholastic approach to priesthood, and we may have one of these indications in the citation above. Wulf, in order to explain such terms as *munus praecipuum* and *maxime,* argues that in the threefold structure, first place is given to preaching the Word, and in the second place there is the priestly or sanctifying function. In this second office of the threefold structure the eucharist is pre-eminent. In other words, only when the office of sanctifier (priest) is considered, can we say that the eucharist is the *munus praecipuum*.[48] When we consider the total of threefold ministry of episkopos/priest, the *munus praecipuum* is teaching-preaching.

The office of leader (king) is then discussed. This priestly role is joined to the very love of Jesus, a love which led to the laying down of his own life. Moreover, priests will renounce their own conveniences and be of service to the Christians of their community, modeling their lives after Jesus, again, who washed the feet of his disciples. One sees here, once more, that the spiritual dimension is intimately connected with the pastoral ministry. Priestly spirituality is not an individualistic matter. The priest in all that he is and does is missionary (n. 14).

Articles 15, 16 and 17 deal with the evangelical counsels: obedience, celibacy, and poverty. In developing this section of the document, many bishops wanted a lengthy treatment of celibacy. Indeed, in an early draft, the section was entitled: "Perfect chastity and the other evangelical counsels." The majority of bishops, however, felt that this gave too much attention to celibacy over other important elements of priestly spirituality. The final structure represents, then, a formulation with which almost all of the bishops concurred. One cannot read into the text, therefore, any programmatic significance to the positioning of obedience first. Priestly existence can only be understood, theologically and spiritually, as Church existence. The obedience promised to the bishop at ordination is a public declaration of obedience to the Church itself, or more carefully stated an obedience to Jesus himself. In this section only the obedience of the priest himself is treated; there is no corresponding discussion on the obligations of those in authority over the priest. Since it is only in the correlation of obedience on the one hand and the rightful use of authority on the other that a full understanding of obedience is possible, there is clearly additional development needed on this topic.

A similar hesitation arises with the discussion on celibacy (n. 16). Paul VI had intervened, as mentioned previously, disallowing a conciliar treatment of priestly celibacy. As a result, there is nothing new in this article. The document states that there is no intent to change the existing practice. It briefly mentions and in a benevolent way the opposite practice, namely a married clergy, among the Eastern Churches. The document rightly says that celibacy for the clergy was, in the early Church, quite optional. Afterward, in the Latin Church, it was imposed by law. "This sacred Council approves and confirms this legislation as far as it concerns those destined for the priesthood." The document clearly sees priestly celibacy as a law of the Church. Celibacy is not seen in any way as an essential element of priestly life. This same approach is taken by Paul VI in his encyclical *Sacerdotalis Caelibatus,* issued June 24, 1967: "Hence we consider that the present law of celibacy should today continue to be firmly linked to the ecclesiastical ministry" (n. 14). Earlier on, Paul VI notes that the New Testament and therefore Jesus did not indeed make celibacy a prerequisite for ministry, and this is surely true (n. 5). Moreover, he writes: "The gift of the priestly vocation dedicated to the divine worship and to the religious and pastoral service of the people of God is undoubtedly distinct from that which leads a person to choose celibacy as a state of consecrated life" (n. 15). In all of this, one sees that there is no essential connection between priesthood on the one hand and celibacy on the other. Attempts to create an essential connection between these two gifts of God distort the theology of each. Accordingly, both the document of Vatican II and the encyclical of Paul VI concern themselves with the "fittingness" of priestly celibacy. In other words, the theology of priesthood, and the spirituality based on that theology, have no essential connections to celibacy. It was, unfortunately, not permitted to the bishops at Vatican II to pursue this fundamental line of thought, with the result that this section on the priestly celibacy remains unfinished.[49]

In the discussion on priestly poverty (n. 17) the example of Jesus is central. As public persons in the Church, the bishop and priest are to give evidence of the simple life of the Lord himself. Whatever they obtain that is not needed for their own livelihood should be spent on others. The focus in this article, however, is not simply on poverty for poverty's sake, but rather the centrality of Jesus and the gospel values are primary.

The concluding sections on the spirituality of the priesthood treat of various helps which the individual priests can and should use to grow in holiness. However, the threefold structure of priestly spirituality is the essence of this entire chapter. The discussion on the three evangelical counsels is secondary, and, as noted, still unfinished in many ways. What appears in the documents of Vatican II as a definite modification is the pastoral or missionary aspect of priestly spirituality. Tronson's *Traité des Saint Ordres* which had dominated priestly spirituality for so long in the Roman Church has been modified considerably by this brief section of *Presbyterorum ordinis* on priestly spirituality.

4. UNFINISHED AGENDA FROM VATICAN II

When one considers the total picture of priestly ministry developed by Vatican II, one is clearly struck by the substantial issues which the bishops considered and the way in which they related a theology of priesthood to the total ministry of Jesus. It can be said that the theology of ministry which Vatican II formulated is a Christ-centered theology. For this reason, alone, the council has succeeded well in its efforts.

If we compare the documents on priesthood with the themes on Jesus' own ministry described in the opening chapter of this volume, we see that Vatican II teaches:

1. That just as Jesus' own call was from the Father, so, too, the call of the ordained minister is from the Lord. The emphasis that both for bishop and priest the threefold office is conferred by ordination itself, and not by a delegation or *missio canonica,* makes this clear.

2. That just as Jesus' own mission and ministry was one of love, so, too, it is love of God and of others which is basic to the very theology and spirituality of both bishop and priest. This spirituality is pastoral and ministerial in nature, not privatized or individualistic.

3. That just as Jesus' own mission and ministry was one of service, so, too, it is service which Vatican II uses to describe priestly work. The Council of Trent had focused more on power, i.e., the power to consecrate the eucharist, the power to forgive sins, the power to ordain, etc.; the Second Vatican Council focused on service as the operative factor in priestly ministry. It did this by the constant referral to the threefold ministry of Jesus as the very foundation of ordained ministry.

4. That just as Jesus' ministry was to some degree political, so, too, the ministry of *every* baptized Christian is political, because this mission and ministry is not only inwardly directed (to the Church community) but also outwardly directed (to the world at large). Since this baptismal mission and ministry, i.e., the priesthood of all believers (lay and cleric), is foundational for a theology of the ordained minister, there is some political aspect to ordained ministry as well.

5. That just as Jesus' own ministry was a ministry of preaching, so, too, the ordained ministry is pre-eminently characterized

by the office of preaching, although not in an exclusive way, since there are also the offices of sanctifying and of leading. Preaching the Word, however, is often mentioned in first place.

In all of these items, the priestly theology of Vatican II corresponds well with the New Testament teaching on the very ministry of Jesus himself, the source of all ministry in the Church. However, there remain items which need further theological development, although the basic orientation has been provided by the council itself. Let us consider some of the major issues which remain unfinished and need the theological acumen of post-Vatican II scholarship.

1. The structuring of priestly ministry around the threefold mission and ministry of Jesus is indeed a helpful step, since it makes the theology of the priest far more comprehensive than a theology focused exclusively on the eucharist. This structuring is christological, and that is its value. However, since neither scripture nor the early Church nor even the scholastics used this threefold structuring, the format itself can only be seen as a theological aid, not a part of revelation itself. Indeed, there are some questions as to the terminology used in this threefold structure. For instance, to say that Jesus should be called a prophet has been questioned by some biblical scholars, since Jesus does not fulfill all the characteristics of the Old Testament prophets; nor can Jesus be called a rabbi, an official Jewish teacher of that era. Still, Jesus was, indeed, a teacher, although certainly not a rabbi and possibly not a prophet. Christian ministers must certainly reflect Jesus, the teacher, but this reflection includes more than simply the fact that the ministers are teachers. What they teach, i.e., the content, is even more fundamental. This content of teaching takes us back to the first chapter of this present volume, in which we discussed the content of the message of Jesus, utilizing the theological schematic of Jeremias. The teaching office of the Church and of the ordained ministry not only involves a fact of teaching, but it involves as well the content of that teaching, which must reflect the very message of Jesus. That there is a magisterium in the Christian Church is important, but what that magisterium teaches is even more important. In this sense, one can say that the Word of God is above the magisterium.

2. A second issue which flows from the teaching office of Jesus and the Church is the role of the presbyter, as well as deacon and lay minister, in the magisterium of the Church, since each of these min-

istries shares in the teaching office of Jesus himself. If the threefold structure of ministry, as developed by Vatican II, is pursued in a consistent way, then it is clear that the magisterium of the Christian Church cannot be confined to the hierarchy of pope and bishops. To define the presbyter (and the deacon and the lay minister) as teacher implies magisterium.

3. The second function of the threefold structure to ministry is that of "hiereus," but in the New Testament only the letter to the Hebrews calls Jesus "hiereus," or "priest." Moreover, in this letter, the priesthood of Jesus is eschatological, i.e., a heavenly priesthood, not one of this earth. In the letter to the Hebrews it is not so much Jesus' dying on the cross that is priestly, as it is his sitting at the right hand of the Father, making intercession for us. In the course of Christian theologizing on the redemption of the Lord, various views have been formulated: Christ as Victor, Christ as Victim, and Christ as Illuminator. Perhaps in certain schools of Christian theology too much emphasis has been placed on the death of Jesus as the priestly sacrificial act (Christ the Victim theory), whereas it is his entire life, death and resurrection which has brought to every man and woman the grace of salvation and sanctification. The connection of the priestliness of Jesus with his death on the cross might be far too narrow. Even a "heavenly priesthood" might be too one-sided. Rather, the content of Jesus' priestly life, priestly death and priestly resurrection needs to be more profoundly studied, and only then will this office of priest (sanctifier) be clarified. Simply to assert that the ordained minister shares in the "priestly office of Jesus" is not enough. What remains unfinished, in both Catholic and Protestant thought, is a clarification of this priestly ministry of Jesus himself.

4. Collegiality remains quite unfinished. There are too many unanswered questions regarding collegiality. For example, in what way do the Eastern bishops share in the collegiality of the episcopacy? If collegiality is essential to the very sacrament of episcopacy, then in some way do not all the Eastern bishops share with the Western bishops in the collegial episcopacy? According to the documents of Vatican II, one is not first a bishop, and then eligible to be accepted into the college of bishops, but only on the condition that one accepts the papal primacy. In the documentation studied above, we saw that the very being a bishop means being a part of the college of bishops. Unfinished work remains on this important matter.

5. The relationship of the pope to the college of bishops has not been satisfactorily worked out. The entire discussion on *munus et potestas,* referred to earlier, indicates that there remains a great deal of unclarity. Can a bishop at one and the same time remain the ordinary of a diocese and yet be deprived by the papacy of some episcopal powers? In what way is the bishop dependent on the pope, and correlatively what are the limits of papal authority vis-à-vis the sacramental nature of episcopacy? Again, these are unfinished items, but serious ones which need clarification.

6. The celibacy of the ordained minister remains an unfinished question. Although the pope curtailed the discussion by calling it untimely, the issue has not gone away, and further clarification is clearly needed on this matter, a clarification which does more than merely mention in a kindly way the entire tradition of the Eastern Churches. If celibacy for the ordained minister is merely a law, then to what extent is breaking the law immoral? An emphasis on the legal connection of celibacy to the ordained ministry has very serious ethical implications, implications which revolve around the distinction of what is merely illegal and what is both illegal and immoral.

7. The relationship between ordained and unordained ministry needs to be further developed. *Lumen Gentium* 10 states that there is an essential difference, and this is mentioned on other occasions in the Vatican documents, but the documents nowhere define what this essential difference might be. Indeed, during the debates, a number of suggestions as regards terminology were made by the bishops to bring out this distinction, but the issue was not completely developed in the final documentation.

8. A further need for development centers on the relationship between the mission and ministry which comes from baptism (the priesthood of all believers) and the specialized ecclesial ministry. The council clearly opened the discussion and certainly provided a major impetus to a deeper appreciation of the sacrament of baptism. Nonetheless, not all the details have as yet been satisfactorily settled, so that one can see clearly both the relationship and the distinction between baptism on the one hand and holy order on the other.

9. In much of the documentation both the call and the commission to ministry, at all levels, is described as the work of the Lord. If this direct calling and commissioning by Jesus is a major part of the theology of ministry, the question arises as regards the significance

of ordination. The council did not address the ordination issue, but it would seem that the theology of ordained minister formulated and promulgated by Vatican II would necessarily require at least a review of the theology of ordination, so that the interrelationship of these two factors might be more clearly seen.

10. The political position of both bishop and priest must be further addressed. In recent times, Pope John Paul II has spoken out against the involvement of priests in political matters. However, it seems that the very ministry of Jesus did have political overtones which themselves need to be clarified. Moreover, the office of teaching will often make an ordained person more of a public figure than perhaps desired, and some involvement in the political structures can almost be mandated if the gospel teaching is to be preserved. The painful experience of Germany under the Third Reich has made this keenly evident. Furthermore, the office of leadership in the Church, which is part of the priestly mission and ministry, can often lead to a more public situation than desired, even confrontational with ongoing political forces. Serious questions are involved in this issue and clearly require further study.

There were some additional and serious issues on ordained ministry which the council itself did not directly address: namely, the ecumenical questions on ministry and the issue of the ordination of women. Since these were not part of Vatican II, at least in any focused way, let us turn to these two major issues in the concluding chapter.

12

Christian Ministry in
an Ecumenical Perspective

In the period after Vatican II, the Roman Catholic Church has entered into serious dialogues with the total Christian world. Since this present volume deals with the history of ordained ministry in the Roman Catholic Church, a full-scale investigation of the diverse issues on the theme of Christian ministry from an ecumenical aspect far exceeds the ambit of this book. Nonetheless, Roman Catholic theology of ministry, in this post-Vatican II era, cannot be pursued without taking into consideration the theologies of ministry which other Christian ecclesial communities have developed.

In this chapter, then, we will consider only some of the major issues, and these only in outline. First of all, this chapter will consider the major issues on ministry which separate the Eastern Churches from the Roman Church. Second, we will consider the issues on ministry which divide the Anglican Church from the Roman Church. Third, we will consider those aspects of Church ministry which separate the mainline Protestant Churches from the Roman Church. Last, we will consider another important issue which clearly has ecumenical implications, namely, the ordination of women. Each of these topics will be treated only from the standpoint of the Roman Church, i.e., from the standpoint of those matters which the Roman Church needs to consider in more theological depth.

1. CHRISTIAN MINISTRY AND THE ISSUES WHICH DIVIDE THE EASTERN CHURCHES FROM THE ROMAN CHURCH

Basically, the main issue which must be addressed on this East/West ecumenical dialogue is ecclesiology, not the question of ministry per se. The question of the primacy of the pope is simply part of this ecclesiological difference, so that to begin with the papacy is to begin in the middle of things. Central to this ecclesiology, however, is the episcopacy. Vatican II, as we have seen, stressed the threefold structure of ministry, which is conferred by the sacrament of order, not by delegation. In theory, this is indeed a major step toward a better unity with the Eastern Churches, since the sacramentality of the episcopacy is a cornerstone of Eastern ecclesiology. Nonetheless, it was pointed out that the question of episcopal powers has not been fully clarified in the Roman Church. The Council of Trent, in its time, wrestled with the issue of episcopacy; the First Vatican Council took up the topic again; Vatican II addressed the issue in a forthright way. The perdurance of the theme indicates the seriousness and complexity of the issue. The statements of Vatican II, by themselves, cannot possibly remove all these complex and serious factors, but they do move the Roman Church into an ecumenically clearer ecclesiological framework. The teaching of Vatican II that episcopacy is not only part of the sacrament of holy order but also the highest expression of this order is now part of the ordinary magisterium of the Roman Church. By ordination, then, every bishop shares in the threefold ministry and mission of Jesus himself: every bishop is a teacher, a sanctifier and a leader. These offices come to a bishop through the ordination itself. Moreover, to be a bishop is to be part of the college of bishops. Collegiality is not a "second step," conferred only after episcopal ordination on those who accept the papacy. Collegiality is also connected to sacramentality, i.e., to ordination. All of these Vatican II approaches can only be seen as helpful stages toward a fuller unity with the Eastern Churches.

However, the relationship of these episcopal, sacramental ideas with papal jurisdiction has not been satisfactorily elaborated. This was evident even during the council and has not been clarified totally after the council. There remains as yet an unresolved tension between these two poles: collegial episcopacy and papal primacy. The resolution will surely not be reached by a concentrated study on the papacy alone. Only if both poles of the tension are honestly considered can a resolution be established. This means, of course, that a discussion on episcopacy, even with some possible criticism of some past papal practices, might be necessary.

In the course of this volume, we have seen that the key to a theology of ordained ministry does not lie primarily with the presbyter, but rather with the episkopos. This was true in the study of the subapostolic Church. This was clearly the situation in the study on the patristic Church, in which the episkopos was indeed the *summus sacerdos*. We saw that the West began to lose a sense of collegial episcopacy in the early medieval period, with the involvement of the papacy into the diocesan and regional levels. The scholastic period theologically removed episcopacy from the sacrament of order, and this had drastic consequences both for Church theology and for Church practice. In the post-Reformation Catholic theology, the effort to restore the episcopacy to the sacrament of order proved to be an upward struggle, although at the very same time the spirituality of priesthood, which was being taught, was still centered on the scholastic notion of the priest as eucharistic minister, and therefore focused not around the episkopos as the fullness of the priesthood, but around the presbyter. Only with Vatican II has episcopacy been restored officially to the sacrament of order. This Western and Roman fluctuation on the role of the bishop in the sacrament of order has in many ways affected the ecclesiology in Roman Catholic theology. From Trent through Vatican I to the eve of Vatican II, an ecclesiology prevailed which overly focused on the papacy. During and after Vatican II, it would seem, an ecclesiology which truly takes into consideration the sacrament of the episcopal order not only is bringing a balance to Roman Catholic ecclesiology, but is also providing a major step toward a richer and more profound unity with the Eastern Churches.

A study of the episcopacy/papacy issue in the West deserves a similar consideration of the episcopacy/patriarch of the East. W. de Vries commented on this latter situation about the year 1000 A.D. as follows:

[The primacy of the patriarchs] is conceived as a participation in the supreme power of the pope and is consequently bestowed by the pope upon the occupants of the patriarchal sees as a privilege. Thus the confirmation of the patriarchs becomes logically a bestowal of office. The primacy of the patriarchs consists no longer in the ordinary right of autonomous jurisdiction in matters of the liturgy, canon law, and discipline, but in the sum total of a number of strictly circumscribed and limited privileges freely granted by Rome, all of which taken together mean much less than the old autonomy of the first ten centuries.[1]

When we compare this approach to patriarchal episcopacy with the general approach of Rome to Western episcopacy at the same time, as we noted above, there is a clear similarity. The pope "delegates" the privilege of being a bishop to the local incumbent. As we pointed out, this papal procedure contributed directly to the scholastic understanding of the bishop as merely an office and a dignity, not a part of the sacrament of holy order. The development in the West of large sees, in which several bishops resided, but only one with the title of archbishop, raises new questions regarding collegiality today, with the teaching of Vatican II on the threefold office of every bishop. How can there be several bishops in the same see, each with the office of teaching, sanctifying and leading? In what ways is the teaching, sanctifying and leading of the archbishop related to the teaching, sanctifying and leading of the suffragan bishops? If the threefold office comes through ordination and not through delegation, then in what way is one of these bishops "superior" to the others? Undoubtedly, the answer to these questions, based on the magisterial teaching of Vatican II regarding episcopacy, will aid greatly in evaluating the episkopos/patriarch relationship of the Eastern Churches.

It would be simplistic to say that only this issue divides East and West, but it is not simplistic to say that the basic issue which divides these two sectors of the Christian world is clearly ecclesiology and that in the theology of the Church the theology of the episkopos plays a central role. With a better understanding of the history of ordained ministry in the West, the dialogue between East and West can only be enriched and even to some degree lead to a deeper unity of these two spiritual dimensions of Christ's own ministry.

2. CHRISTIAN MINISTRY AND THE DIALOGUE BETWEEN THE ROMAN CHURCH AND THE ANGLICAN CHURCH

We have already alluded to the Anglican Church and the question of Anglican orders. Two areas on the theology of ministry seem to be fundamental in this Anglican/Roman Catholic dialogue: (1) the continued discussion on the matter of Anglican orders; (2) the theology of episcopacy. It should be remembered that in the West, as far as the Roman Catholic Church is concerned, the dialogues with the Anglican Church have been pursued at the highest level of Church involvement. These dialogues have often been conducted under the auspices of the Secretariat for the Promotion of Christian Unity at the Vatican, on the one side, and the Lambeth Conference on the other. There have as well been common statements issued by both the archbishop of Canterbury and by the pope. Besides these discussions and statements, there have also been national discussions, enjoined by the national council of bishops. *Called to Full Unity* is a volume recently published which gathers together these significant agreements and statements, dating from 1966 to 1983.[2]

In 1979 a common statement was issued by the joint study group of the Roman Catholic Church in Scotland and the Scottish Episcopal Church on the topic of *Priesthood and the Eucharist.*[3] The Anglican-Roman Catholic International Commission, meeting at Canterbury in 1973, developed a statement on *Ministry and Ordination.*[4] This was followed by an *Elucidation* from the same commission, issued in 1979, on the topic of ministry and ordination, gathering together some of the significant responses to the original document of 1973. Moreover, the issue of priestly ministry was discussed in the various dialogues concerning the eucharist.

In the 1973 document and the *Elucidation of 1979,* a re-examination of *Apostolicae Curae* was called for. "We are fully aware of the issues raised by the judgment of the Roman Catholic Church on Anglican Orders. The development of the thinking in our two communions regarding the nature of the Church and of the ordained ministry, as represented in our Statement, has, we consider, put these issues in a new context."[5] "This calls for a reappraisal of the verdict on Anglican Orders in *Apostolicae Curae* (1896)."[6] In the discussion on this matter above, it was pointed out that two factors, among others, need to be involved in this reappraisal:

1. The judgment on Anglican orders must be judged by the same criteria with which one judges the ordinations conferred by the ordinal of Hippolytus.
2. Episcopal consecrations in the scholastic period, in which the bishop did not consider himself, *qua* bishop, as ordained, and did not intend to confer a sacrament in episcopal consecrations, should be judged by the same criteria as those which *Apostolicae Curae* used for the consecration of Bishop Parker.

Historical research into the Leonine commission on Anglican orders has raised serious questions on the issue of its credibility, and these factors must also be honestly taken into account. Moreover, the reaction of Anglican scholars to the position taken by *Apostolicae Curae* must also be seriously considered, since in many of these reactions, made by qualified Anglican scholars, the import of the Leonine statement that the Anglican Church did not intend to act in the name of the Church was seriously questioned.

Of secondary but still quite important consideration is the use of the term "sacrament" for ordination. The pre-eminence of baptism and eucharist needs to be maintained in any theology of sacraments. The discussion on a two-sacrament/seven-sacrament theology raises the question of sacramentality in general. Contemporary Roman Catholic theology on the Church as a basic sacrament and Jesus, in his human nature, as the most fundamental of all sacraments may quite possibly be the key to surmount the difficulties in these diverse sacramental theologies.

The second major issue, it would seem, which needs to be addressed more fully is, once more, the theology of episcopacy. Many of the issues which separate the Eastern and Western Churches, alluded to above, on this matter of episcopacy are equally central to the Anglican/Roman Catholic dialogues. In many areas the Anglican community is called the Episcopal Church, and Anglicans are referred to as Episcopalians. This is done not without cause, since the role of the bishop is central to the ecclesiology of the Anglican/Episcopalian Church. The role of bishop in the Anglican community from the sixteenth century down to the present has been essential to the Anglican tradition of ecclesiology. Vatican II has clarified the Roman position on episcopacy in a most important way, and this clarification can serve well as a base for dialogue. The caveats, which were expressed above, on the East/West dialogue apply as well to the Anglican/Roman Catholic dialogue, and their resolution must be seen as essential to furthering the ever-deepening unity between these two Churches of the Christian faith.

The Anglican/Roman Catholic statements also mention another issue: namely, the clarification of the priestliness of all believers, stemming from the sacrament of initiation, and the special priestliness of the ordained minister. Vatican II, as we saw, strongly affirmed the priestliness of all believers based on baptism, through which all share in the threefold ministry and mission of Jesus. Vatican II did not fully resolve the interrelationship of this threefold ministry and mission of all with the threefold ministry and mission of the ordained. Clearly, the Roman Catholic resolution of this theological interrelationship will benefit by the input of the Anglican scholars; indeed, it will not be resolved except through ecumenical discussion.

3. CHRISTIAN MINISTRY AND THE DIALOGUE WITH THE MAINLINE PROTESTANT CHURCHES

It is difficult, at times, to identify specific Protestant Church sectors, and the use of "mainline" is not meant to exclude any of the Protestant Churches, but only to stress the fact that the dialogue between those Protestant Churches which have historically emphasized episcopacy and sacramentality are the focus of these remarks. Clearly the Lutheran Church is part of this focus, and the Lutheran/Roman Catholic dialogues in the United States have been sponsored by the highest regional levels: the National Conference of Catholic Bishops on the one hand, and the USA National Committee of the Lutheran World Ministries, on the other. These dialogues began in Baltimore in July 1965 and continue to the present time. The topics which have been discussed are as follows:

1. The Status of the Nicene Creed as Dogma of the Church
2. One Baptism for the Remission of Sins
3. The Eucharist as Sacrifice

4. Eucharist and Ministry
5. Papal Primacy and the Universal Church
6. Teaching Authority and Infallibility in the Church
7. Justification by Faith

As one can readily see the issue of ministry has played a major role in these dialogues. Nonetheless, it is precisely dialogue number seven which holds the key to ministerial discussions. The issue of the adequate, complete and perfect expiatory sacrifice of Jesus, as the very basis of justification, lies at the heart of the divergence on ministerial theology. This complete and perfect expiatory sacrifice of Jesus affects the theological relationship of grace and good work. This grace/good work issue likewise lies at the heart of the divergence in ministerial theology. Convergence on these two issues is fundamental, and such convergence is necessary prior to any theological convergence on the meaning of ordained ministry in the Christian Church.

The pre-eminent role of the Word of God in Christian life and theology is equally important and fundamental, since the Word of God indicates the supremacy of grace in all that Christians do as well as the complete perfection of Jesus' sacrifice. All else is good work, and therefore totally subservient to the pre-eminence of the Word.

For the Roman Catholic theologian the way in which the causality of the sacraments is theologically proposed has, in the past, at times seemed to compromise either the completeness of Jesus' own expiatory sacrifice or the pre-eminence of grace. In the theory of instrumental causality of the sacraments, the instrumental cause has, on occasion, been so construed as to question the adequacy of the sacrifice of Jesus and therefore the gratuity of grace. For the Roman Catholic theologian, this issue is not a chimera. The Council of Trent wrestled with it in a major way throughout its sessions, and the counter-Reformation theologians proposed a variety of responses to harmonize the sacrifice of Jesus, which was once and for all, with the sacrifice of the mass.[7] In the Lutheran/Roman Catholic dialogues the theme of the sacrificiality of the eucharist was indeed discussed and statements were drawn up to present this theme, but underlying the problems were the two issues: justification by faith and the grace/good work relationship.

A theology of priestly ministry is intricately connected to one's understanding of sacramental causality. A theology of ordained ministry raises such questions as: What does the ordained minister "do"?

In what way is this "doing" associated with the work of Christ himself? What do such formulae as: "I baptize you," "I absolve you," "This is my body," "This is my blood" express as far as priestly activity (doing) is concerned? Sacramental causality, however, is not the precise place to begin in an effort to answer these questions; rather, the theological issue of the relationship of grace and good work is indeed the place to start. It is noteworthy that the Roman Catholic/Southern Baptist dialogues, from 1982–1984, have addressed forthrightly the topic of grace.[8]

When one considers the threefold ministry and mission of the ordained minister, which Vatican II uses so extensively, the following questions might be asked:

1. In the ministry of teaching, is the Word of God pre-eminent and in what way? The answer must include not only the fact of a teaching ministry, but the content of the teaching as well. This basic content was discussed in chapter one, in which the message of Jesus himself was delineated.
2. In the ministry of sanctifying, is the supremacy of grace over good work maintained? The answer must deal with the question of sacramental causality.
3. In the ministry of leadership, is the lordship of Jesus maintained? The answer must include the issue of the authority of the Word of God above all other magisterial, primatial, jurisdictional authority.

Since the scholastic period the question of presbyteral ordinations has at least been mentioned in Roman Catholic theology, and because of some papal bulls, the historicity of such presbyteral ordinations, i.e., priest ordaining to priesthood, is at least possible. Given the ecumenical situation, this issue needs a deeper study by Roman Catholic theologians today.

Even though the dialogues officially between the Lutheran Church and the Roman Catholic Church have been, perhaps, the most developed dialogues in which a Protestant Church has been involved with the Roman Catholic Church, the issues mentioned above apply equally to the Presbyterian and Reformed/Roman Catholic dialogues, which also have been taking place in the United States, under the auspices of the National Catholic Conference of Bishops on the one hand, and the North American Area of the World Alliance of Reformed Churches on the other. The same is true for the Southern Baptist/Roman Catholic dialogues, sponsored again by the NCCB and the Department of Interfaith Witness of the Home Mission Board of the Southern Baptist Convention. Other dialogues could also be mentioned, but these three series of dialogues have focused in a special way on the topic of sacramental, ordained ministry.

Of major importance for the ecumenical world is the so-called Lima Document of the World Council of Churches. Originally this document was entitled: *One Baptism—One Eucharist—and a Mutually Recognized Ministry.* The 1982 Lima statement of this working document was entitled simply: *Baptism, Eucharist and Ministry.* Ecclesiology plays a major role in this document, since it is with christology and ecclesiology that the very document begins (1–5). Only against this christological and ecclesiological base is the issue of ordained ministry considered (7 onward). In *Lumen Gentium* and *Presbyterorum Ordinis,* Vatican II treated in a respectful way the historical data on the development of Church ministry. The Lima Document, in a brief way, indicates its own respect for historical data (8–14). The document proceeds to discuss some of the difficult issues in Christian ministry, which separate the various Churches:

1. authority (15–16);
2. the very term "priest" and its connection with Jesus (17);
3. the ministry of women in the Christian Church (18);
4. the role of bishop, presbyter and deacon (19–25);
5. the fact that ordained ministry must be personal, collegial and communal (26–27); these three aspects are then applied to bishop, presbyter and deacon. In the various Christian communities there exist episcopal, presbyteral and congregational structures or systems and these need to be appreciated and to some degree be interrelated;
6. the meaning of apostolic succession (34–38), although historical data does not play a significant role in this section;
7. ordination (39–50);
8. finally, concluding remarks about the mutual recognition of ordained ministries (51–55).

Since the World Council of Churches represents so many parts of the Christian faith, the issues which this document highlights are significant for any ecumenical discussion on ministry. However, the document does not delve into any of the underlying areas such as ecclesiology, justification by faith, the relationship of grace to good works, etc. Nonetheless, the document clearly outlines the major specifically ministerial issues of disagreement, pointing the way toward possible areas of agreement.

4. THE ISSUE OF THE ORDINATION OF WOMEN

Early on in this volume, at the end of the sub-apostolic period, a summation of some of the issues on early indications of women in ministry was made. The Sacred Congregation for the Doctrine of the Faith issued on October 15, 1976 the *Declaration on the Question of the Admission to the Ministerial Priesthood.* The primary argument in this document against the ordination of women to the priesthood was the tradition of the Church, and in reviewing all the material from history, it does not seem that there have been any occasions in the Roman Catholic Church in which women were "ordained" to the priesthood. Prior to 200, as mentioned above, the word "ordination" is itself problematical, since there are no uncontested historical allusions to men being "ordained" in that period, much less women. In the patristic period women were deaconesses, and there are solid reasons to speak of this diaconal status as one which was consecrated by an ordination. Such a judgment is, of course, contested by a few scholars, so that even the diaconal ordination of women is not clearly accepted. In the report of the Catholic Theological Society of America on *Women in Church and Society,*[9] a listing was made of reasons in favor of the ordination of women to the priesthood, followed by a listing of reasons which oppose such ordinations. This listing was established on the basis of a review of some of the then current literature on the subject. In the listing of reasons in favor of such ordinations, n. 11 states: "The ancient tradition of the church provided a liturgy of ordination to the order of deaconess for women, and this gives precedent for their ordination to the priesthood."[10] This data on the ordination of women to the diaconate seems to be the strongest argument, *from an historical standpoint,* on the possibility of ordination of women to the priesthood, since diaconal ordination and priestly ordination are theologically so interconnected.

However, Vatican II has raised, inadvertently perhaps, other factors which must be taken into account on the issue of the priestly ordination of women. The following stress in the documents of Vatican II is consistently maintained: the call to ministry is ultimately not from a Church official but from the Lord himself. The Church officials must, of course, discern in faith whether the Lord is actually calling an individual or not, but the call and the commission is in the last analysis from the Lord. In today's world, it would seem, the Lord might indeed be calling a woman to priestly ordination. In other words, if the call is not directly from the bishop or some other Church official, but from the Lord himself, and even the commissioning is from the sacrament, not from delegation, and therefore, again, from the Lord himself, then great care must be exercised by all Church officials in their discernment of Christ's call and commissioning. This is not to downplay the role of the Church in the selection and ordination of ministers, but it is rather a caution, based on the very theology of Vatican II, not to absolutize historical data. As we have seen, the very history of ordained ministry in the Roman Church has itself not been totally absolute.

Sensitivity to this issue of women in ministry was mentioned in a special way by the United States bishops in their statement, *As One Who Serves* (C. III, b, 1, a), a statement which appeared after the declaration from the sacred congregation. The bishops in no way run counter to the declaration, but they do express a strong pastoral concern.

The Protestant approach to the ordination of women must also be considered in a very serious way by Roman Catholic scholars and leaders. Protestant Churches have allowed the ordination of women in their communities only after serious consideration of the gospel itself. Issues which these Churches have already confronted and to some degree resolved offer the Roman Church many paradigms for its own deliberations on this matter of women's ordination to the priesthood.

Admittedly, these observations merely touch the surface of some very profound issues, each of which needs a volume of its own for adequate discussion. These observations are made here only to indicate that the future history of theological discussion on ministry in the Roman Catholic Church cannot proceed in any enduring way without serious consideration of the ecumenical world, nor without serious deliberation on the position of women both in the Church and in society. The United States bishops began their serious investigation of the priest in our time with the following statement:

Priestly ministry is not a finished reality, fully achieved, like a work of art. Neither is it something frail, a fragile object unable to withstand the taxing passage through change and time. Rather, what the sources of faith and theology reveal is a priestly ministry as a living reality, grounded securely through a threefold dynamic relationship. Its roots are in the mystery of the risen Lord and the Church. Its nature involves a mission of service to Christ and to the community. Its exercise occurs within the Church and its structures (c. 2).

It is hoped that this volume contributes to the unfinished reality; that the tracing of priestly ministry through history indicates a taxing passage through change and time; that the rootage in Jesus the only priest and in the priestly community of the Church will make ordained ministry much more a mission of service both to Christ and to the community of both Church and world.

Notes

1. The Ministry of Jesus

1. Cf. R. Pesch, *Das Markusevangelium,* v. 1 (Freiburg: Herder, 1980) pp. 89–94. On p. 90, Pesch writes: "Die messianische Ausrüstung Jesu stammt nicht aus dem Taufwasser des Johannes, sondern vom Himmel." J. Gnilka, *Das Evangelium nach Markus* (Einsiedeln: Benziger 1978) pp. 49–55, 60–64, 167–170.

2. J. Fitzmyer, *The Gospel according to Luke* (Garden City, N.Y.: Doubleday and Co., 1981) p. 162.

3. Cf. E. Haenchen, *Commentary on the Gospel of John* (Philadelphia: Fortress Press, 1984) trans. R. W. Funk, p. 168: "Jesus is not one for himself, but exists for the Father." Cf. esp. pp. 249–252 for a lengthy description of this "from the Father" approach to Jesus' ministry in the gospel of John. Also, cf. R. Schnackenburg, *The Gospel according to St. John* (N.Y.: Seabury, 1980) trans. Cecily Hastings *et al.,* pp. 102–108. Also, J. Comblin, *Sent from the Father* (N.Y.: Orbis, 1979) trans. by C. Kabat, pp. 1–19. J. Kuhl, *Die Sendung Jesu und der Kirche nach dem Johannes-Evangelium* (Kaldenkirchen: Styler Verlag, 1967) pp. 58–192.

4. Cf. V.P. Furnish, *The Love Command in the New Testament* (N.Y.: Abington, 1972); P. Perkins, *Love Commands in the New Testament* (N.Y.: Paulist, 1982); R. Schnackenburg, *The Moral Teaching of the New Testament* (N.Y.: Herder and Herder, 1965) trans. J. Holland-Smith and W. J. O'Hara, pp. 90–109.

5. Cf. D. Senior, *The Passion of Jesus in the Gospel of Matthew* (Wilmington, Del.: Michael Glazier, 1985) p. 32; also pp. 41–42.

6. Cf. Fitzmyer, *op. cit.,* p. 1418. Cf. also K. H. Schelke, "Il ministro sacerdotale negli scritti e nelle chiese del Nuovo Testamento," *Il Prete per*

gli Uomini d'Oggi (Rome: An. Veritas Ediatrice, 1975) ed. G. Concetti, pp. 53–54.

7. Cf. R. Brown, *The Gospel according to John* (Garden City, N.Y.: Doubleday and Co., 1970) v. II, pp. 558–562.

8. N. Mitchell, *Mission and Ministry: History and Theology in the Sacrament of Order* (Wilmington, Del.: Michael Glazier, 1982) p. 61; cf. also A. Lemainre, "I presbiteri alle origini della chiesa," *Il Prete per gli Uomini d'Oggi*, pp. 81–82; Schelkle, *op. cit.*, p. 48: "Nel tempo del Nuovo Testamento un'aristocratica classe superiore ebbe a Gerusalemme una notevole importanza religiosa, politica e sociale." This political aspect cannot be set to one side.

9. Cf. O. Cullmann, *Jesus and the Revolutionaries* (N.Y.: Harper & Row, 1970) trans. by Gareth Putnam.

10. On the issue of Jesus and the title "messiah" cf. G. Bornkamm, *Jesus of Nazareth* (N.Y. Harper & Row, 1960) 3rd. ed., pp. 168–178. This is an early work on the subject, but inciteful as to his situating of the theme of messiah in a biblical study of Jesus. Also, Fitzmyer, *op. cit.*, pp. 197–200. F. Hahn, *Christologische Hoheitstitel* (Göttingen: Vandenhoeck & Ruprecht, 1966) pp. 133–225. This is a major source for the subject of Jesus' messiahship.

11. Many others could be cited; these are selected since they represent a spectrum of theologians. J. Bonnefoy, *Christ and the Cosmos* (Patterson, N.J.: St. Anthony Guild Press, 1965) trans. M. D. Meilach; O. Cullmann, *The Christology of the New Testament* (London, SCM Press, 1963); G. Bornkamm, *op. cit.;* J. Jeremias, *New Testament Theology* (N.Y.: Charles Scribner's Sons, 1971) trans. J. Bowden; L. Boff, *Jesucristo y la Liberación del Hombre* (Madrid: Ediciones Cristiandad, 1981) trans. F. Cantalapiedra; J. Sobrino, *Christology at the Crossroads* (N.Y.: Orbis, 1978) trans. J. Drury. Others could also be mentioned: D. Abernathy, *Understanding the Teaching of Jesus* (N.Y.: Seabury, 1983); J. Jeremias, *The Central Message of the New Testament* (N.Y.: Scribner's, 1965); R. Fuller, *The Foundations of New Testament Christology* (N.Y.: Scribner's, 1969; W. Kasper, *Jesus the Christ* (N.Y.: Paulist, 1976) trans. V. Green.

12. For the following, cf. J. Jeremias, *New Testament Theology,* pp. 76–121.

13. *Ibid.,* pp. 80–81; for opposing views, cf. E. P. Sanders, *Jesus and Judaism* (Philadelphia: Fortress, 1985) p. 271.

14. Cf. Kasper, *op. cit.,* pp. 89–99. Kasper includes in his notes an extensive bibliography on the issue of miracles in contemporary theology.

15. Jeremias, *op. cit.,* pp. 93–96.

16. Cf. the overviews of contemporary Catholic theology on the theme of original sin: H. Haag, "The Original Sin Discussion," *Journal of Ecu-*

menical Studies, v. 10 (1973) pp. 51–81; J. L. O'Connor, "Original Sin: Contemporary Approaches," *Theological Studies,* v. 29 (1968) pp. 215–240; B. McDermott, "The Theology of Original Sin: Recent Developments," *Theological Studies,* v. 38 (1977) pp. 478–512.

17. E. Schillebeeckx, *Jesus* (N.Y.: Seabury, 1979) trans. H. Hoskins, p. 141.

18. W. Kasper, *op. cit.,* pp. 73–74.

19. *Ibid.,* pp. 74–87.

20. L. Boff, *Jesus Christ Liberator* (N.Y., Orbis, 1978) trans. P. Hughes, p. 55. This volume is a translation of only the first section of Boff's study of Jesus. The Spanish volume cited above is a complete translation.

21. On the issue of the anawim and Jesus' connection with the poor, cf. G. Lohfink, *Jesus and the Community: The Social Dimension of the Christian Faith* (N.Y.: Paulist, 1984) trans. J. P. Galvin; W. E. Pilgrim, *Good News to the Poor* (Minneapolis: Augsburg, 1981); a lengthy and favorable discussion of this issue is in Sanders, *op. cit.,* pp. 270–293.

22. Cf. Jeremias, *The Parables of Jesus* (N.Y.: Charles Scribner's Sons, 1963) trans. S. H. Hooke, pp. 33–42, 124–146.

23. On this issue, cf. B. Kloppenburg, *The Ecclesiology of Vatican II* (Chicago: Franciscan Herald Press, 1974) trans. M. J. O'Connell, pp. 19ff.

24. For specific issues connected with this New Testament writing, cf. among others: O. Kuss, *Der Brief an Die Hebraer* (Regensburg: Friedrich Pustet, 1966).

25. The question of "priestly people" in 1 Pet as well as the use of "presbyteros" and "neoteros" is connected with Church ministry as presented by the New Testament. For technical considerations, cf. J. Elliott, "Ministry and Church Order in the NT: A Traditio-Historical Analysis (1 Pt 5, 1–5 & plls.)," *Catholic Biblical Quarterly,* v. 32, no. 3 (1970) pp. 367–391.

2. An Ecclesiological Presupposition

1. A. Michel, "Ordre, Ordination," *Dictionnaire de Théologie Catholique* (Paris: Letouzey et Ane, 1932) 1193. Michel also notes: "L'institution du sacerdoce est renfermée dans l'institution même de l'Église. C'est donc parallèlement à l'enseignement de Jésus sur l'Église qu'il faut découvrir, dans l'Évangile, son enseignement sur le nouveau sacerdoce, par lui institué" (*ibid.*).

2. A. Tanquerey, *A Manual of Dogmatic Theology* (N.Y.: Desclee, 1959) trans. J. Byrnes, p. 107.

3. *Ibid.,* p. 108.

4. *Ibid.,* p. 109.

5. *Ibid.,* p. 110. A similar presentation can be found in J. Salaverri, *Tractatus de Ecclesia Christi, Sacrae Theologiae Summa* (Madrid: Biblioteca de Autores Cristianos, 1962) pp. 518ff. Many of the other manuals of theology follow the same lines as those expressed by Tanquerey.

6. Cf. H. Küng, *The Church* (N.Y.: Sheed and Ward, 1967) trans. by Ray and Rosaleen Ockenden, pp. 72–79. Cf. also Y. Congar, "Quelques problèmes touchant les ministères," *Nouvelle Revue Théologique,* 93 (1971) pp. 785–800; D. Olivier, "Les deux visages du prêtre. Les chances d'une crise, *Points Chauds* (Paris: 1971); J. Coppens, "Le Caractère sacerdotal des ministères selon les écrits du nouveau testament," *Teología del Sacerdocio,* v. 4 (Burgos: Aldecoa, 1972) 11–39, responds to Küng, Olivier and Congar.

7. Küng, *op. cit.,* p. 72.

8. *Ibid.,* p. 73.

9. *Ibid.,* p. 75. Küng cites W. G. Kümmel, "Jesus und die Anfänge der Kirche," *Studia Theologica,* v. 7 (1953) pp. 1–27, esp. 26.

10. *Ibid.,* pp. 75–76.

11. *Ibid.,* pp. 76–79. Küng uses Kümmel and Vögtle as representative New Testament exegetes to substantiate his position.

12. J. Galot, *Theology of the Priesthood* (San Francisco: Ignatius Press, 1984) trans. by R. Balducelli, p. 86. I will cite Galot frequently, but Galot merely represents a large number of Catholic theologians who stress the institution of the Church by Jesus during his own lifetime. In these citations, it must be remembered that Galot merely stands for a wider current of Catholic thought. His volume is a thorough and comprehensive statement on the priesthood, but clearly one in which the ecclesiological presuppositon plays a role in the author's interpretation.

13. Cf. R. Brown, *Jesus: God and Man* (Milwaukee: Bruce, 1967).

14. In recent times, J. E. Bifel has developed helpful bibliographical data on contemporary discussion of the ordained ministry. His bibliographical material is arranged topically. Cf. "Boletin bibliográfico de teología sobre el sacerdocio," *Teología del Sacerdocio* (Burgos: Aldecoa); v. I (1969) pp. 279–337 covers the more important material from 1920 to 1968; v. II (1970) pp. 374–441 covers 1968 and part of 1969; v. III (1971) pp. 243–319 covers 1969 and part of 1970; v. IV (1972) covers 1970 and part of 1971.

3. Ministry: 27 to 110 A.D.

1. Cf. any of the introductions to the New Testament for the dating of the various New Testament writings, e.g.: Feine-Behm-Kümmel, *Einleitung in das Neue Testament,* 14th ed. (Heidelberg: Quelle & Meyer, 1965); N. Perrin, *The New Testament: An Introduction* (N.Y.: Harcourt Brace Jovan-

ovich, 1974); R. F. Collins, *Introduction to the New Testament* (Garden City, N.Y.: Doubleday & Co, 1983).

2. R. Brown, *The Churches the Apostles Left Behind* (N.Y.: Paulist, 1984). I have not followed the same order of these Churches as one finds in Brown's volume.

3. These titles have been gathered from the computerization of New Testament words: cf. *Computer-Konkordanz zum Novum Testamentum Graece* (Berlin: Walter de Gruyer, 1985) ed. H. Bachmann and W. A. Slaby.

4. L. Ott, *Das Weihesakrament,* (Freiburg: Herder, 1969) p. 5, n. 12. Cf. also A. Lemaire, "I presbiteri alle origini della chiesa," *Il Prete per gli Uomini d'Oggi,* p. 80 for a description of the use of the term "presbyteros" in the Greek world at the beginning of the Christian era. Inscriptions from Asia Minor (first to third centuries A.D.) refer more to "clubs" than to groups with overt political power. On the other hand papiri from Egypt (third century) witness to a political institution of presbyters. *Ibid.,* pp. 81–82, describes in detail the long history of presbyter (*zaquen*) in Jewish history. Lemaire adds, p. 82: "In un simile contesto si comprende con facilitá come i cristiani di origine giudica si siano anch'essi organizzazioni seguendo il modello dell'instituzione presbiterale."

5. Ott, *op. cit.,* p. 5; cf. also K. H. Schelkle, *Theology of the New Testament,* v. 4, *The Rule of God: Church and Eschatology* (Collegeville, Minn.: Liturgical Press, 1978) trans. W. Jurgens, pp. 75–77.

6. G. Bornkamm, "Presbyteros," *Theologisches Wörterbuch zum Neuen Testament, Theological Dictionary of the New Testament* (Grand Rapids: Eerdmans, 1968) p. 655, trans. G. Bromiley.

7. F. Moriarty, "Isaiah 1–39," *Jerome Biblical Commentary* (Englewood Cliffs, N.J.: Prentice-Hall, 1968) p. 268.

8. G. Wood, "Joel, Obadiah," *Jerome Biblical Commentary,* p. 440.

9. J. Fitzmyer, *op. cit.,* p. 253.

10. Cf. R. Brown, "Episkopos and Episkope," *Theological Studies,* v. 41 (1980) pp. 322–338; Schelkle, *op. cit.,* p. 81, discusses the first appearance of the term episkopos in the New Testament, Phil. 1, 1, and comments: "Bishops are mentioned in the plural; they, therefore, form a college." However, nothing in Philippians allows such a "therefore." Schelkle goes on to say that Paul in mentioning episkopos is speaking of an office which has "taken shape, an office which was not mentioned in the earlier Epistles, apparently for obvious reasons that it did not yet exist" (p. 81). This is revealing: Schelkle is saying that sometime in 50 A.D. the office of "episkopos" did not exist. He brings out the characteristic of a wandering missionary episkopos, when he notes that in 1 Tim and Titus episkopoi seem to need shelter from time to time (p. 82).

11. Galot, *op. cit.*, pp. 160–172.

12. E. Schillebeeckx, *Ministry: Leadership in the Community of Jesus Christ* (N.Y.: Crossroad, 1981) trans. J. Bowden.

13. *Ibid.*, p. 36.

14. R. Dillon and J. Fitzmyer, "Acts of the Apostles," *Jerome Biblical Commentary*, p. 204. Cf. also P.-R. Tragan, "Les 'Destinaires' du Discours de Milet," *A Cause de l'Évangile: Mélanges offerts a Dom Jacques Dupont* (Paris: Les Éditions du Cerf, 1985) pp. 779–798.

15. G. Denzer, "The Pastoral Letters," *Jerome Biblical Commentary*, p. 351.

16. *Ibid.* Cf. O. Barlea, "Dai presbiteri ai sacerdoti," *Il Prete per gli Uomini d'Oggi*, pp. 159–192. Barlea offers a new hypothesis, rejecting an East/West approach for a North/South approach to the differing forms of Church organization. In the northern part of the Mediterranean area monarchical leadership was dominant; in the southern part of the area (Egypt, North Africa, etc.) a presbyteral or communal leadership dominated. To verify this intriguing hypothesis, much more analysis of the documents is needed.

17. Cf. W. Schmithals, *The Office of Apostle in the Early Church* (Nashville, Tenn.: Abdington, 1969) trans. J. E. Steely, pp. 67–87; 231–278. Cf. also Schelkle, *op. cit*, pp. 61–67.

18. H. von Campenhausen, *Ecclesiastical Authority and Spiritual Power in the Church of the First Three Centuries* (Stanford: Stanford University Press, 1969) trans. J. Baker, p. 15.

19. Fitzmyer, *op. cit.*, p. 253.

20. Cf. R. Brown, *op. cit.*, p. 334.

21. Galot, *op. cit.*, p. 72.

22. K. H. Schelkle, *Discipleship and Priesthood* (N.Y.: Herder and Herder, 1965) trans. J. Disselhorst, pp. 30–31.

23. Fitzmyer, *op. cit.*, pp. 751–755.

24. K. Aland, *Synopsis Quattuor Evangeliorum* (Stuttgart: Wurttembergische Biblelanstalt, 1969) p. 141.

25. Fitzmyer, *op. cit.*, p. 845.

26. Galot, *op. cit.*, p. 77.

27. Cf. D. Stanley and R. Brown, "Aspects of New Testament Thought," *Jerome Biblical Commentary*, p. 798.

28. Schelkle, *op. cit.*, pp. 75–77.

29. Cf. Tragan, *op. cit.*, pp. 783–784.

30. N. Flanagan, *Friend Paul* (Wilmington, Del.: Michael Glazier, 1986) p. 102.

31. Mitchell, *op. cit.*, pp. 155–156.

32. *Ibid.*, p. 162.

33. Cf., R. Karris, *The Pastoral Epistles* (Wilmington, Del.: Michael Glazier, 1979) p. xiii.

34. R. Brown, "Episkopos and Episkope," *op. cit.*, pp. 331–333.

35. Ott, *op. cit.*, p. 7.

36. L. Hoffman, "L'Ordination juive a la veille du Christianisme," *La Maison Dieu*, v. 138 (1979) pp. 7–47. This volume of *La Maison Dieu* carries other articles on the question of ordination in the early Church.

37. Mitchell, *op. cit.*, p. 165.

38. R. Brown, K. Donfried, J. Reumann (eds), *Peter in the New Testament* (N.Y.: Paulist, 1973).

39. *Ibid.*, pp. 159–160.

40. *Ibid.*, pp. 161–162.

41. P. C. Empie and T. Austin Murphy, *Papal Primacy and the Universal Church* (Minneapolis, Minn.: Augsburg, 1974).

42. *Ibid.*, p. 15.

43. *Ibid.*, pp. 15–16.

44. *Ibid.*, p. 16.

45. Galot, *op. cit.*, p. 76.

46. *Ibid.*, p. 77.

47. Cf. H.-M. Legrand, "The Presidency of the Eucharist according to the Ancient Tradition," *Living Bread, Saving Cup* (Collegeville, Minn.: Liturgical Press, 1982) ed. K. Seasoltz, pp. 196–221.

48. Cf. F. Chenderlin, *Do This As My Memorial* (Rome: Biblical Institute Press, 1982).

49. *Ibid.*, pp. 231–237.

50. Cf. Fitzmyer, *op. cit.*, pp. 1387ff. for the textual difficulties in these few words. On p. 1402 he simply notes in a parenthesis: "Later Christian tradition understood the directive in still another way, in terms of the Sacrament of Orders." It is obvious that this biblical expert, on the basis of his research, does not find ordination in the text and context.

51. D. Dupuy, "Theologie der kirchlichen Ämter," *Mysterium Salutis,* 4/2 (Einsiedeln: Benziger, 1973), p. 507.

52. Cf. R. Brown, *op. cit.*, pp. 330–337.

Excursus on the Question
of the New Testament
and the Ordination of Women

1. English translation of this Report can be found in *Origins,* v. 6 (July 1, 1976) pp. 92–96.

2. Ibid., p. II, n. 3.

3. R. Karris, "The Role of Women according to Jesus and the Early Church," *Women and the Priesthood,* ed. C. Stuhlmueller (Collegeville, Minn.: Liturgical Press, 1978) p. 50.

4. Report, *op. cit.,* p. IV, n. 2.

4. Ministry in the Second Christian Century: 90 to 210 A.D.

1. B. D. Dupuy, *op. cit.,* p. 505.

2. Cf. J. P. Audet, *La Didache: Instructions des Apôtres* (Paris: J. Gabalda, 1958) pp. 187–210.

3. *Didache,* 15, 1–2; trans. is from J. Quasten, *Patrology,* v. 1 (Westminster, Md.: Newman, 1951) pp. 33–34.

4. Quasten, *op. cit.,* p. 33.

5. H. Legrand, *op. cit.,* p. 200.

6. R. M. Grant, *The Apostolic Fathers,* v. 1 (N.Y.: Thomas Nelson & Sons, 1964) p. 161.

7. R. A. Kraft, *The Apostolic Fathers: Barnabas and the Didache,* v. 3 (N.Y.: Thomas Nelson & Sons, 1965) p. 174.

8. *Letter of Clement,* 42; trans. by J. A. Kleist, *Ancient Christian Writers,* v. 1 (Westminster, Md.: Newman, 1948). Cf. also J. Colson, "Il ministero sacerdotale nei padri dei primi secoli," *Il Prete per gli Uomini d'Oggi,* p. 61: "Che questo insediamento degli episkopos e dei diaconi de parte degli apostoli e le loro disposizioni in vista della continuazione di questi ministeri non è presentata come una disposizione *formalmente e direttamente* espressa da Dio e da Cristo." Rather, it was the apostles who, according to Clement, established these ministries (42, 1); only in this sense, then, can we see them as possibly *iure divino.*

9. *Ibid.,* 44, 1–3.

10. R. M. Grant and H. H. Graham, *The Apostolic Fathers: First and Second Clement* (N.Y.: Thomas Nelson & Sons, 1965) p. 74; cf. also Mitchell, *op. cit.,* p. 179.

11. *Letter to Clement,* 40.

12. Legrand, *op. cit.,* p. 201.

13. Grant, *op. cit.,* v. 1, pp. 163–164; Mitchell, *op. cit.,* p. 180: "In 1 Clement, therefore, church order, status and ministry are not merely practical conveniences but divinely willed realities that form part of the tradition transmitted by Christ's apostles." This is the basis of their authority: not the stance of a Levitical high priesthood.

14. Grant, *op. cit.,* pp. 162–166.

15. H. Lietzmann, *A History of the Early Church,* v. 1, p. 248, cited by Bauer, *Orthodoxy and Heresy in Earliest Christianity,* ed. by R. Kraft and G. Krodel (Philadelphia: Fortress, 1971) p. 61.

16. The addition of "to some degree" is made because of the thesis of W. Bauer, *op. cit.*

17. *Letter to the Magnesians,* n. 7; trans. by R. M. Grant, *The Apostolic Fathers: Ignatius of Antioch,* v. 4 (N.J.: Thomas Nelson & Sons, 1966) p. 61.

18. *Ibid.,* n. 6, p. 60.

19. *Letter to the Trallians,* n. 2, *ibid.,* p. 72.

20. *Ibid.,* n. 3, p. 73.

21. *Letter to the Ephesians,* n. 4, *ibid.,* pp. 35–36.

22. Bauer, *op. cit.,* p. 61.

23. Grant, *op. cit.,* v. 1, p. 169.

24. Cf. E. P. Echlin, *The Deacon in the Church: Past and Future* (N.Y.: Alba House, 1971) pp. 18ff.

25. Mitchell, *op. cit.,* pp. 181ff. Cf. Colson, op. cit., pp. 68–71 for an analysis of Hermas. According to Colson we see that the Roman Church was still in flux as regards the naming and function of various ministries.

26. Grant, *op. cit.,* v. 1, p. 173.

27. *Letter of Polycarp,* 6, trans. from Quasten, *op. cit.,* p. 81.

28. W. R. Schoedel, *The Apostolic Fathers: Polycarp, Martyrdom of Polycarp, Fragments of Papias* (N.J.: Thomas Nelson & Sons, 1967) p. 20.

29. Quasten, *op. cit.,* p. 81.

30. Schoedel, *op. cit.,* p. 19.

31. Kraft, *op. cit.,* p. 38.

32. Quasten, *op. cit.,* p. 101.

33. Grant, *op. cit.,* v. 1, p. 165.

34. *Adv. Haer.* 3, 3, 1; trans. from F. R. Montgomery Hitchcock, *The Treatise of Irenaeus of Lugdunum Against the Heresies* (London: SPCK, 1916). Texts can be found in H. Vogels, *Textus Antenicaeni ad Primatum Romanum spectantes* (Bonn: P. Hanstein, 1937).

35. *Adv. Haer.* 3, 3, 2.

36. *Ibid.*

37. Quasten, *op cit.,* p. 302; he refers to Van den Eynde and Bardy.

38. *Ibid.,* p. 302.

39. *Ibid.,* p. 303. J. A. Aldama, "El Sacerdocio ministerial en San Ireneo," *Teología del Sacerdocio* (Burgos: Aldecoa, 1972) pp. 111–142, concludes one of his sections as follows: "El análisis que hemos hecho de todos los pasajes en que utiliza san Ireneo los términos sinónimos *presbyter* y *senior,* parece dar como resultado, si no absolutamente cierto al menos muy prob-

able, que para el obispo de Lyon, *presbyter* es equivalente de *episcopos*" (p. 122).

40. *Adv. Haer.* 4, 2, 6.

41. Ott, *op. cit.,* p. 12.

42. Cf. Vogels, *op. cit.,* p. 12–13.

43. Cf. Clement of Alexandria, *Stromata,* 6, 13, 107.

44. Cf. J. M. Hanssens, *La Liturgie d'Hippolyte* (Rome: Institutum Orientalium Studiorum, 1959) pp. 372ff.

45. Cf. Eusebius, *Hist. Eccl.* 6, 8, 5.

46. von Campenhausen, *op. cit.,* pp. 248–250.

47. *Ibid.,* pp. 252–253.

48. Cf. J. Pelikan, *The Emergence of the Catholic Tradition* (Chicago: University of Chicago Press, 1971) p. 59.

49. *De Praescript.* 41, 6; *De Monagamia,* 12, 2.

50. P. M. Gy, "Notes on the Early Terminology of Christian Priesthood," *The Sacrament of Holy Orders* (Collegeville, Minn.: Liturgical Press, 1962) p. 99.

51. Dupuy, *op. cit.,* p. 511. Cf. also M. G. Gómez, "La 'Plebs' y los 'Ordines' de la sociedad Romana y su traspaso al pueblo cristiano," *Teología del Sacerdocio,* pp. 251–293. Gómez utilizes Roman sources throughout and he diagrams in a very helpful way the interrelationships of the Roman and Christian systems on pp. 292–293.

52. *Ibid.,* p. 512.

53. *De Pudicitia,* 21, 17.

54. *De Praescript.* 20, 7.

55. Cf. H. Marot, "Conciles antenicéens et conciles oecuméniques," *Le Concile et les Conciles* (Paris: Éditions du Cerf, 1960) pp. 19–43.

56. Cf. Hanssens, *op. cit.,* pp. 283–340.

57. R. H. Connolly, *Didascalia Apostolorum* (Oxford: Clarendon Press, 1929) p. xxvi.

58. *Ibid.,* pp. xxxviii–xxxix.

59. *Ibid.*

60. *Ibid.,* pp. 87–88.

61. *Ibid.,* pp. xxxix–xi.

62. Dupuy, *op. cit.,* p. 500; cf. also, B. Botte, "Collegiate Character of the Presbyterate and Episcopate," *The Sacrament of Orders,* pp. 75–97.

63. Dupuy, *op. cit.,* p. 503.

64. *Traditio Apostolica,* 1, 2–4; trans. from B. S. Easton, *The Apostolic Tradition of Hippolytus* (N.Y.: Macmillan, 1934) pp. 33–34.

65. *Ibid.,* 1, 8; *ibid.,* pp. 37–38.

66. *Ibid.,* 1, 9; *ibid.,* pp. 38–39.

67. Galot, *op. cit.*, pp. 171–172.

68. Cf. von Campenhausen, pp. 178–212; for the "ordination of women" question, cf. C. Osiek, "The Ministry and Ordination of Women according to the Early Church Fathers," *Women and Priesthood*, pp. 59–68.

5. Ministry in the High Patristic Church: 210 to 600 A.D.

1. Connolly, *op. cit.*, p. xxxviii.

2. Cf. Pelikan, *op. cit.*, p. 332: "During the fifth and sixth centuries, christology and mystagogy in the East and anthropology and ecclesiology in the West, brought together much of the dogmatic development of the preceding centuries and laid the foundations for later constructions of Christian doctrine. . . . The sixth century was also a time when, each in its own way, the East and the West articulated an orthodox consensus about what was to be regarded as normative."

3. Cf. Tertullian, *De Praesc.* 20, 4–7; *De Virg. vel.* 2.

4. Cf. Y. Congar, "Die Wesenseigenschaften der Kirche," *Mysterium Salutis*, 4/1, p. 541.

5. Cf. von Campenhausen, *op. cit.*, p. 158.

6. J. N. D. Kelly, *Early Christian Doctrines*, 3rd ed. (London: Adam & Charles Black, 1965) p. 408.

7. Cf. Y. Congar, *Die Lehre von der Kirche: Von Augustinus bis zum Abendländischen Schisma* (Freiburg: Herder, 1971) trans. H. Sayer, pp. 13ff.

8. Ignacio Ortíz de Urbina, "Das Glaubenssymbol von Chalkedon: sein Text, sein Werden, seine dogmatische Bedeutung," *Das Konzil von Chalkedon* (Würzburg: Echter, 1959) v. 1, p. 398.

9. *Ibid.*, p. 402.

10. Pelikan, *op. cit.*, pp. 109–110.

11. 1 Clem. 42, 2.

12. Pelikan, *op. cit.*, p. 112.

13. J. Knox, *Criticism and Faith* (N.Y.: 1952) pp. 66–67.

14. Pelikan, *op. cit.*, p. 115.

15. Origen, *Princ.* 2.

16. Pelikan, *op. cit.*, p. 116.

17. B. Botte, "Holy Orders in the Ordination Prayers," *The Sacrament of Orders*, p. 8.

18. Cf. J. Bligh, *Ordination to the Priesthood* (N.Y.: Sheed and Ward, 1956) pp. 24–26.

19. B. Botte, "Collegiate Character of the Presbyterate and Episcopate, *The Sacrament of Orders*, p. 83.

20. J. Gaudemet, "Holy Orders in Early Conciliar Legislation," *The Sacrament of Orders*, p. 182.

21. S. Cyprian, *Ep.* 3, 3; *Ep.* 66, 4; *Ep.* 69, 5.

22. Cited by Congar, "Die Wesenseigenschaften der Kirche," p. 545.

23. *Ibid.,* n. 29.

24. *Ibid.,* pp. 545–546.

25. *Ibid.,* p. 547.

26. *Ibid.*

27. Botte, *op. cit.,* p. 84.

28. Cf. H. Küng, *The Church,* p. 436; also E. Kammermeier, "Klerikale Kleidung," *Lexikon für Theologie und Kirche,* v. 6, p. 326.

29. Cf. A. G. Martimort, *L'Église en Priére: Introduction à la Liturgie* (Tournai: Desclée & Cie, 1961) pp. 502–503.

30. Cf. E. Vacandard, "Célibat ecclésiastique," *Dictionnaire de Théologie Catholique* (Paris: Letouzy, 1910) pp. 2068ff; D. O'Neill, *Priestly Celibacy and Maturity* (N.Y.: Sheed and Ward, 1965) pp. 12ff.

31. O. Rousseau, "Priesthood and Monasticism," *The Sacrament of Orders,* p. 169.

32. *Ibid.,* pp. 170ff.

33. Gaudemet, *op. cit.,* pp. 198ff.

34. B. Cooke, *Ministry to Word and Sacraments* (Philadelphia: Fortress, 1976) p. 559.

35. Cf. G. Reilly, *Imperium and Sacerdotium according to St. Basil the Great* (Washington, D.C.: The Catholic University of America Press, 1945).

36. Quasten, *Patrology,* v. 3, p. 459.

37. St. John Chrysostom, *On The Priesthood,* 3, 4–6; trans. in Quasten, Patrology, v. 3, p. 460.

38. *Ibid.,* p. 460.

39. Botte, *op. cit.,* p. 26.

40. *Ibid.*

41. Martimort, *ibid.,* p. 26.

42. Daniélou, "The Priestly Ministry in the Greek Fathers," *The Sacrament of Orders,* p. 127.

43. Botte, *op. cit.,* p. 14.

44. *Euchologium sive Rituale Graecorum,* cited by Botte, *op. cit.,* p. 14.

45. *Ibid.,* p. 14.

46. *Ibid.,* p. 13.

47. *Ibid.,* p. 8. Cf. also A. G. Martimort, "La testimonianza della liturgia," *Il Prete per gli Uomini d'Oggi,* pp. 193–221.

48. Cooke, *op. cit.,* p. 364.

49. Jerome, *Ad Evangelum, The Principal Works of St. Jerome* (N.Y.: NPNF, 1893) pp. 288–289. Quoted in Echlin, *op. cit.,* p. 65.

50. *Ibid.,* pp. 65–66.

51. *Ibid.,* p. 66.

52. Echlin, *op. cit.*, p. 52.

53. Osiek, *op. cit.*, pp. 66–67.

54. P. M. Gy, "Notes on the Early Terminology of Christian Priesthood," *The Sacrament of Orders,* pp. 114–115.

6. Ministry in the Early Medieval Church: 600 to 1000 A.D.

1. J. Pelikan, *The Emergence of the Catholic Tradition* (100–600) (Chicago: The University of Chicago Press, 1971) p. 332.

2. *Ibid.,* p. 333.

3. *Ibid.,* p. 334.

4. *Ibid.*

5. Y. Congar, *Tradition and Traditions* (New York: Macmillan, 1967) trans. M. Naseby and T. Rainborough, p. 24.

6. *Ibid.,* p. 46.

7. Y. Congar, "La Primautè des quatre prémiers conciles oecuméniques," *Le Concile et Les Conciles,* ed. B. Botte (Paris: Editions du Cerf, 1960) pp. 101–109.

8. *Ibid.,* p. 108.

9. O. M. Dalton, *The History of the Franks* (Oxford: Clarendon Press, 1927) v. 1, p. 269.

10. Pelikan, *op. cit.,* p. 339.

11. Cf. *ibid.,* pp. 334–349.

12. H. Marot, "Conciles antenicéens et conciles oecuméniques," *Le Concile et Les Conciles,* p. 42.

13. T.-P. Camelot, "Les Conciles oecuméniques des IVe et Ve siècles," *Le Concil et Les Conciles,* pp. 71–72.

14. Cf. F. Beck, "The Byzantine Church in the Age of Photius," *The Church in the Age of Feudalism,* by F. Kempf, H. G. Beck, E. Ewig, J. Jungmann (N.Y.: Herder and Herder, 1969) trans. by A. Biggs, pp. 174ff. This volume will be cited as *HCH* III.

15. E. Ewig, "Climax and Turning Point of the Carolingian Age, 814–840," *HCH* III, p. 109.

16. F. Kempf, "Constitution of the Church, Worship, Pastoral Care, and Piety: 700 to 1050," *HCH* III, p. 260.

17. *Ibid.*

18. Dalton, *op. cit.,* p. 276.

19. J. Jungmann, "Constitution of the Church, Worship, Pastoral Care, and Piety: 700 to 1050," *HCH* III, p. 309.

20. Kempf, *op. cit.,* p. 264.

21. *Ibid.,* p. 268.

22. *Ibid.,* p. 288.

23. Dalton, *op. cit.,* p. 272. Cf. also I. Onatibia, "Presbiterio, colegio apostólico y apostolidad del ministério presbiteral," *Teología del Sacerdocio,* pp. 71–109. Onatibia argues that in the first five centuries one finds that the presbyterium is the successor of the apostolic college. By the end of the fifth century this approach has become quite muted. The importance of the episkopoi is certainly one reason for this muting of the presbyteral college, but the development of the individual priest in the rural communities, with few collegial ties to other priests or bishops, played a role; Onatibibia describes this as "la pulveración del presbitério, siendo en adelante rarísimas las ocasiones en que los fieles podían contemplar reunidos en un mismo lugar a todos los elementos que constituían la Iglésia local" (p. 107).

24. E. Ewig, "The Western Church from the Death of Louis the Pious to the End of the Carolingian Period," *HCH* III, p. 127.

25. Kempf, "Renewal and Reform from 900 to 1050," *HCH* III, p. 320.

26. Kempf, "The Gregorian Reform," *HCH* III, p. 368.

27. Gregory the Great, Ep. 5, 37, cited in Pelikan, *op. cit.,* p. 352.

28. Pelikan, *op. cit.,* p. 358.

29. E. Ewig, "The Papacy's Alienation from Byzantium and Rapprochement with the Franks," *HCH* III, pp. 3ff.

30. Kempf, "Constitution of the Church, etc." p. 286.

31. Cf. *ibid.,* pp. 288–290.

32. Cf. E. E. Reynolds, *The Roman Catholic Church in England and Wales* (Wheathampstead-Hertfordshire: Anthony Clarke Books, 1973) p. 21.

33. Reynolds, *op. cit.,* p. 29.

34. Cf. Ewig, *op. cit.,* pp. 20ff.

35. Cf. Ewig, "Climax and Turning Point of the Carolingian Age, 814–840," *HCH* III, pp. 120ff.

36. Kempf, "The Church and the Western Kingdoms from 900 to 1046," *HCH* III, p. 216.

37. Jungmann, *op. cit.,* p. 313.

Excursus on Minor Orders

The data for this brief excursus is heavily dependent on L. Ott, *Das Weihesakrament.* Other sources have, of course, been taken into consideration also.

7. Ministry in the Scholastic Period: 1000 to 1400 A.D.

1. F. Kempf, "Changes within the Christian West during the Gregorian Reform," *HCH* III, p. 472.

2. Cf. M.D. Chenu, *S. Thomas et la théologie* (Paris, 1959).

3. Cf. J. Gilchrist, "Simoniaca haeresis and the Problem of Orders from Leo IX to Gratian," *Proceedings of the Second International Congress of Medieval Canon Law*, ed. S. Kuttner and J. Ryan (Vatican City, 1965) pp. 209–235.

4. P. Lombard, *Libri IV Sententiarum* (Quarrachi: Typ. Colegii St. Bonaventure, 1916) v. 2: L. IV, D.XXIV, C. v.

5. *Ibid.*, C. xiii.

6. Cf. Ott, *op. cit.*, p. 47.

7. Hugh of St. Victor, *De sacramentis christianae fidei*, II, 2, 5; 3, 5.

8. P. Lombard, *op. cit.*, cc. xiv–xvi.

9. *Ibid.*, c. xiii.

10. Ott, *op. cit.*, p. 48.

11. Alexander Hales, *Comm. in Sent.*, IV, d. 24, q. a, a. 1 sol. 2 ad 1.

12. Ott, *op. cit.*, p. 76.

13. St. Thomas, *Summa Theologica*, L. III, q. 38, a. 4, Respond.

14. *Ibid.*, q. 37, a. 2, Respond.

15. *Ibid.*, q. xi, a. 4, Respond.

16. Trans. from E. Lewis, *Medieval Political Ideas* (London: Routledge & Kegan Paul, 1954), v. 2, pp. 380–381.

17. Cf. Botte, *Le Concile et Les Conciles.*

18. Cf. *Concilia Galliae*, 314–506, ed. C. Munier (Brepols: CSEL) v. 148; there are twenty-five local councils during these two hundred years.

19. St. Thomas, *op. cit.*, 1. xxxiv, a. 1, Respond.

20. St. Bonaventure, *Comm. in Sent.*, L. IV, D. xxiv, p. 1, a. 1, q. 1.

21. *Ibid.*, d. xxiv, p. 1, a. 2, q. 2, Concl.

22. J. D. Scotus, *Comm. in Sent.*, L. IV, d. xxiv, q. unica.

23. *Ibid.*

24. *Ibid.*

25. *Ibid.*

26. For a discussion of Scotus' use of "De congruo," cf. A. Wolter, *Duns Scotus on the Will and Morality* (Washington, D.C.: The Catholic University of America Press, 1986) pp. 3–123.

27. St. Thomas, *op. cit.*, q. XL, a. 4.

8. Ministry in the Theology of the Reformers

1. S. Harrison Thomson, *Europe in Renaissance and Reformation* (N.Y.: Harcourt, Brace & World, 1963) p. 459.

2. *Die Bekenntnisschriften der evangelisch-lutherischen Kirche* (Göttingen: Vandenhoeck & Ruprecht, 1959).

3. *The Book of Concord* (Philadelphia: Muhlenberg Press, 1959) ed. T. G. Tappert.

4. J. Reumann, "Ordained Minister and Layman in Lutheranism," *Eucharist and Ministry* (N.Y.: USA National Committee of the Lutheran World Federation, 1970) p. 228; Reumann cites E. M. Carlson, "The Doctrine of the Ministry in the Confessions," *The Lutheran Quarterly,* 15 (1963), pp. 118ff.

5. P. Manns, "Amt und Eucharistie in der Theologie Martin Luthers," *Amt und Eucharistie* (Paderborn: Bonifacius-Druckerei, 1973) p. 105.

6. Ibid., pp. 105–106.

7. G. Lindbeck, "The Lutheran Doctrine of the Ministry: Catholic and Reformed," *Theological Studies,* 30 (1969) p. 588.

8. A. C. Piepkorn, "The Sacred Ministry and Holy Ordination in the Symbolical Books of the Lutheran Church," *Eucharist and Ministry,* p. 102.

9. *Ibid.,* p. 105.

10. *Ibid.,* p. 107.

11. M. Luther, *The Babylonian Captivity of the Church, WA* 6, 564, 11–12. [WA = Weimarer Ausgabe of Luther's Works.]

12. M. Luther, Exposition of Ps. 82, WA 31, 1, p. 211, 17–19.

13. M. Luther, *Von den Schleichern und Winkelpredigern, WA* 30, 3, p. 525, 24.

14. B. Gerrish, "Luther on Priesthood and Ministry, *Church History,* 34 (1965) pp. 416.

15. L. Green, "Change in Luther's Doctrine of the Ministry," *The Lutheran Quarterly,* 18 (1966) pp. 174ff.

16. R. Fisher, "Another Look at Luther's Doctrine of the Ministry," *The Lutheran Quarterly,* 18 (1966) pp. 260–271.

17. Manns, *op. cit.,* p. 87; in his footnote to this passage he lists in detail each of these writings by Luther.

18. *WA,* 6, 493, 33.

19. Manns, *op. cit.,* p. 71.

20. *WA,* 5, 16; cf. also ibid., 25.

21. Manns, *op. cit.,* p. 75.

22. *WA,* 7, 339, 18.

23. Manns, *op. cit.,* pp. 129–130.

24. *Ibid.,* p. 99.

25. *Justification by Faith,* ed. H. G. Anderson, T. A. Murphy, J. Burgess (Minneapolis: Augsburg, 1985) p. 17.

26. Ibid., pp. 17–39.

27. H. Obermann, *The Harvest of Medieval Theology* (Cambridge: Harvard University Press, 1963).

28. *Justification by Faith,* p. 22.

29. G. Ebeling, Luther: *Einführung in sein Denken* (Tübingen: J. C. B. Mohr, 1965) p. 189.

30. *Ibid.,* p. 190.

31. *Confessio Augustana* in *Creeds of the Churches,* ed. J. H. Leith (Richmond: John Knox Press, 1963) p. 69.

32. J. Danielou, "The Priestly Ministry in the Greek Fathers," *The Sacrament of Holy Orders,* p. 127.

33. St. John Chrysostom, cited by Daniélou, *op. cit.,* p. 118.

34. *Ibid.,* p. 122.

35. G. Lindbeck, "Papacy and *Ius Divinum:* A Lutheran View," *Papal Primacy and the Universal Church,* ed. P. C. Empie and T. A. Murphy, (Minneapolis: Augsburg, 1974), pp. 193–208.

36. "Eucharist and Ministry: A Lutheran-Roman Catholic Statement," *Eucharist and Ministry,* n. 16, p. 12.

37. John Calvin, *Institutes of the Christian Religion,* (Philadelphia: The Westminster Press, 1960) ed. J. T. McNeill, trans. F. L. Battles.

38. *Ibid.,* Book IV, c. 3, n. 1, p. 1053.

39. *Ibid.,* n. 1.

40. *Ibid.,* n. 2.

41. *Ibid.,* n. 3.

42. *Ibid.,* n. 4.

43. *Ibid.*

44. *Ibid.*

45. *Ibid.*

46. *Ibid.,* n. 5.

47. *Ibid.,* n. 6.

48. *Ibid.,* n. 7.

49. *Ibid.,* n. 8.

50. *Ibid.*

51. *Ibid.,* n. 9.

52. *Ibid.,* n. 12.

53. *Ibid.,* n. 14.

54. *Ibid.,* n. 15.

55. *Ibid.,* n. 16.

56. *Ibid.*

57. *Ibid.,* c. IV, nn. 1–4.

58. *Ibid.,* n. 9.

59. *Ibid.,* c. V.

60. *Ibid.,* n. 3.

61. *Ibid.,* n. 13.

62. *Ibid.,* c. XIX.

63. *Ibid.,* nn. 22–27.

64. *Ibid.,* n. 28.

65. *Ibid.*

66. *Ibid.,* n. 31.

67. Ott, *op. cit.,* pp. 118–119.

9. The Sacrament of Order and The Council of Trent

1. *Concilium Tridentinum,* edited by Gorresgesellschaft (Freiburg: Herder, 1919 ff) vol. VII/1, 363, 30–33. Hereafter abbreviated as *CT.*

2. *CT, ibid.,* 438, 6; 440, 16.

3. The writings of the Reformers used as a basis for these articles were: Luther, *The Babylonian Captivity of the Church;* Calvin, *Institutes of the Christian Religion;* Bucer, *Liber reformationis* and his commentary on St. John; Melanchton, *Loci communes.*

4. *CT,* IX, 3, 37.

5. *CT,* IX, 38–41.

6. *CT,* IX, 48–51; in this discussion the theologians and the bishops were divided on whether it was simply the election itself or the ritual of episcopal consecration which was the moment of conferral of jurisdiction.

7. *CT,* IX, 53–55.

8. For a lengthier description of these debates, cf. L. Ott, *Das Weihesakrament,* pp. 122ff; A. Michel, "Ordre: Concile de Trente," *Dictionnaire de Théologie Catholique* (Paris: Letouzey et Ane, 1932) v. XI/2, 1349–1365.

9. *CT,* IX, 621–30 to 622–15.

10. Translation is from: *The Church Teaches: Documents of the Church in English Translation,* trans. by J. F. Clarkson, J. H. Edwards, W. J. Kelly, J. J. Welch (St. Louis, Mo.: B. Herder Book Co., 1955) pp. 329–332.

11. Michel, *op. cit.,* 1355.

12. Calvin, *Institutes of the Christian Religion,* v. 2, pp. 1471–1475; also 1072–1077.

13. Michel, *op. cit.,* 1356–1357.

14. J. Galot, *La Nature du Caractère Sacramentel* (Paris: Desclée de Brouwer, 1958) p. 231.

15. *Ibid.,* p. 224.

16. L. Kosters, "Priester," *Lexikon für Theologie und Kirche* (Freiburg im B.: Herder & Co., 1936) v. 8, 470.

17. J. Blinzler and Y. M.-J. Congar, "Allgemeines Priestertum," *Lexikon für Theologie und Kirche* (Freiburg: Herder, 1963) v. 8, 753–756.

18. F. Solá, "De Sacramento Ordinis," *Sacrae Theologiae Summa,* v. 4, p. 596.

19. *Ibid.,* p. 599.

20. *Ibid.,* p. 599, n. 16.

21. L. Lercher, *Institutiones Theologiae Dogmaticae,* v. IV/2, p. 286.

22. Galot, *Theology of the Priesthood,* p. 179.

23. *Ibid.,* p. 180.

24. The English translation is taken from *The Church Teaches,* pp. 331–332.

25. Paul VI, *Motu Proprio,* English trans. in *The Roman Pontifical* (Vatican City: The Vatican Polyglot Press, 1978) pp. 113–118.

26. H. Jedin, *A History of the Council of Trent,* v. 2, p. 381.

27. For a detailed account of Trent's discussion on the relationship of the sacrifice of the mass to the sacrifice of the cross, cf. Osborne, "Ecumenical Eucharist," *Journal of Ecumenical Studies,* v. 6, (1960), pp. 598–619.

28. Calvin, *op. cit.,* p. 1477.

29. Calvin, *op. cit.,* pp. 1478–1479.

30. Calvin, *op. cit.,* p. 1478.

31. Calvin, *op. cit.,* p. 1477.

32. Galot, *Theology of the Priesthood,* p. 179.

33. Ott, *op. cit.,* p. 123.

34. Calvin, *op. cit.,* p. 1084.

35. Ott, *op. cit.,* p. 127.

36. A. Duval, "The Council of Trent and Holy Orders," *The Sacrament of Holy Orders,* p. 220.

37. *Ibid.,* p. 221.

38. Galot, *op. cit.,* p. 180.

10. The Sacrament of Order in Counter-Reformation Theology

1. Michel, *op. cit.,* pp. 1365–1391.

2. Ott, *op. cit.,* pp. 128–168.

3. R. Bellarmine, *De Controversiis christianae fidei adversus huius temporis haereticos* (Rome: Giunchi et Menicanti, 1838) v. 3.

4. *Ibid.,* "De Sacramento Ordinis, Liber Unicus," pp. 1075–1091.

5. *Ibid.,* p. 1075.

6. *Ibid.,* p. 1082.

7. *Ibid.,* p. 1084.

8. *Ibid.,* p. 1087.

9. *Ibid.,* p. 1089.

10. *Ibid.,* p. 1087; 1089 (bis).

11. *Ibid.,* p. 1077.

12. *Ibid.,* p. 1082.

13. *Ibid.,* p. 1083.

14. *Ibid.,* p. 1082.

15. *Ibid.,* p. 1084.

16. *Ibid.*

17. *Traité des Saints Ordres (1676) compare aux Ecrits Authentiques de Jean-Jacques Olier (1657),* ed. by G. Chaillot, P. Cochois, and I. Noye (Paris: Procure de la Compagnie de Saint-Sulpice, 1984).

18. C. Bouchaud, *ibid., Preface,* p. vii.

19. Cf. G. Chaillot, "Les Enjeux de la Présente Édition Critique," in Introduction, *ibid.,* pp. xxiii–xxvii. Chaillot refers directly to many passages in the *Traité* itself and to dissimilar passages in Olier's own writings. In reading these introductory remarks of Chaillot one must continually refer to the passages in the critical text itself.

20. *Ibid.,* pp. xxvii–xxxvi. Again, Chaillot refers to sections in the *Traité* and to dissimilar passages in Olier's own writings.

21. *Ibid.,* p. xxxvii.

22. *Ibid.,* pp. xxxxix–xiviii. Again references are made to both the *Traité* and Olier's own writings, which are found in the body of the text.

23. Michel, *op. cit.,* pp. 1365ff.

24. *Ibid.,* p. 1368.

25. *Ibid.,* p. 1378.

26. For some background on this period, cf. T. M. Schoof, *A Survey of Catholic Theology, 1800–1970* (N.Y.: Paulist, 1970) trans. by N. D. Smith.

27. R. Aubert, "Light and Shadows of Catholic Vitality," *The Church in the Age of Liberalism* (N.Y.: Crossroad, 1981) ed. by R. Aubert, J. Beckmann, P. Corish, R. Lill, trans. by P. Becker, pp. 208ff.

28. *Ibid.,* p. 213.

29. *Ibid.*

30. *Ibid.*

31. *Ibid.,* p. 214.

32. The reference to Martina is in Aubert, *op. cit.,* p. 215.

33. The reference to Daniel-Rops is in Aubert, *op. cit.,* p. 215.

34. *Denzinger,* 2653. Cf. also C. A. Bolton, *Church Reform in 18th Century Italy (The Synod of Pistoia),* 1786 (The Hague: Martinus Nijhoff, 1969) pp. 79ff.

35. Cf. Bolton, *op. cit.,* p. 97 for the citation from Ricci.

36. Cf. R. Aubert, *The Church in a Secularized Society* (N.Y.: Paulist, 1978) trans. by J. Sondheimer, p. 213.

37. Cf. J. J. Hughes, *Absolutely Null and Utterly Void* (London: 1968).

38. Cf. Aubert, *op. cit.,* p. 218.

39. *Denzinger,* 3319.

40. *Denzinger,* 3316.

41. *Denzinger,* 3317.

42. *Denzinger,* 3317.

43. Cf. H. Chadwick, "The Discussion about Anglican Orders in Modern Anglican Theology," *Concilium: Apostolic Succession, Rethinking a Barrier to Unity* (N.Y.: Paulist, 1968) v. 34, ed. H. Küng, pp. 141–149. Chadwick indicates clearly the various changes made in the ordinal, some due to Presbyterian influences and the intention of the Anglican Church to continue to do what the Church throughout the centuries had intended.

44. Cf. Hughes, *op. cit.*

45. *Denzinger,* 3450.

46. *AAS* 41 (1908) pp. 555–577.

47. Pius XI, "Ad Catholici Sacerdotii," Eng. trans. authorized by NCWC (Washington, D.C.: NCWC, 1936); cf. *Sixteen Encyclicals of Pius XI,* NCWC.

48. Pius XII, "Mediator Dei," *Denzinger,* 3849–3853.

49. Pius XII, "Sacramentum Ordinis," *Denzinger,* 3857–3861.

50. *Ibid.,* trans. from *The Teaching of the Catholic Church,* ed. by K. Rahner, p. 350.

51. AAS 42 (1950) pp. 657–702.

52. AAS 51 (1959) pp. 545–579.

11. Ministry in the Documents of Vatican II

1. Cf. J. Lecuyer, "Decree on the Ministry and Life of Priests: History of the Decree," *Commentary on the Documents of Vatican II* (N.Y.: Herder and Herder, 1969) v. 4, pp. 183–209; B. Kloppenburg, *The Ecclesiology of Vatican II,* pp. 263–293; A. Ancel, *Il sacerdote secondo el Concilio Vaticano II* (Vicenza: Ed. Favero, 1966); A. de Bovis, "Le Presbyterat, sa nature et sa mission d'après le Concile Vatican II," *Nouvelle Revue Théologique,* 89 (1967) pp. 1009–1042; P. de Haes, "Le sacerdoce a la lumiere de Vatican II," *Collec. Mechlin.* 51 (1966) pp. 353–382; F. Marty, "Decret sur le ministère et la vie des prêtres," *Documents Conciliaires* (Paris: Centurion) v. 4, pp. 159–182; E. V. Tarancon, *El Sacerdocio a la luz del Concilio Vaticano II* (Salamanca: Sigueme, 1966); F. Vandenbroucke, "Le Sacerdoce selon Vatican II," *Questions Liturgiques et Paroissiales* 48 (1966) pp. 107–122; F.M. Thuraisamy, *The Image of Priest: A Study of the Image of the Priest according to the Second Vatican Council as compared to the Pre-Conciliar Image* (Rome: Gregorianum, 1969). One must also use the *Acta Synodalia Sacrosancti Concilii Oecumenici Vaticani Secundi* (Vatican: Typis Polyglottis Vaticanis, 1974) vv. 3 and 4 (abbreviated CV). The decree on the pastoral office of bishops in the Church, *Christus Dominus,* provides some insight into the theology of the ordained minister, i.e., the bishop, but this decree basically repeats the material which had been treated in greater detail in *Lumen Gentium.* Therefore, the history of *Lumen Gentium,* particularly those sections which deal with the ordained minister, but above all the

bishop, is necessary for a full understanding of Vatican II theology on priesthood. Cf. the study by G. Philips *et al.,* "Dogmatic Constitution on the Church," *Commentary on the Documents of Vatican II* (N.Y.: Herder and Herder, 1966) pp. 105–305. It should also be noted that *Presbyterorum Ordinis* improves on and clarifies many passages in *Lumen Gentium,* particularly on the history of the special ministry in the early Church.

2. Cf. Lecuyer, *op. cit.,* p. 183.

3. *Ibid.,* p. 183. It was only during the course of discussion that the bishops moved away from the juridical and obligational aspects of priestly life to a theology of ordained ministry. It was not the initial intent of the council to develop such a theology.

4. Cf. the brief overview on this matter by M. Schmaus, "Ämter Christi," *LThK,* v. 1, 457–459. Schmaus has added a small bibliography of this topic. F. Wulf, "Decree on Priestly Ministry: Commentary on the Decree," *Commentary on the Documents of Vatican II,* pp. 215–217, provides some background material on this threefold structure. For Roman Catholics, it was Pius XII, in *Mystici Corporis* and in other writings, who employed this threefold structure in an official way.

5. Schmaus, *op. cit.,* 458; cf. Didymus the Blind, *Commentary on 1 Peter,* 2, 9.

6. Schmaus, *ibid.;* cf. St. Augustine, *City of God,* 17, 4, 9.

7. Schmaus, *ibid.;* cf. St. Augustine, *Sermon on Psalm 26,* 2.

8. Cf. St. Bonaventure, *Lignum Vitae,* 39, 40, 42, 45.

9. Calvin, *Institutes of the Christian Religion,* bk. 2, c. 15, 2, p. 496.

10. *Ibid.,* bk. 2, c. 15, 3, p. 498.

11. *Ibid.,* bk, 2, c. 15, 6, p. 502.

12. *Ibid.,* p. 503. In this section one sees that the basic issue is not the priestliness either of Jesus or of the minister, but the interpretation given to the eucharist as a "re-sacrificing." The efficacy of Christ's propitiatory act and the relationship of grace and good work lie at the base of Calvin's objections to the Roman position.

13. Cf. W. Pannenberg, *Grundzuge der Christologie* (Gutersloh: Gerd Mohn, 1966) pp. 218ff; Pannenburg approaches the Protestant use of this threefold office of Jesus in a theological way, stressing the issue of the full expiatory value of Jesus and the total gratuity of salvation, as opposed to good works. Andreas Osiander in 1530 seems to have been the first to have utilized this threefold structure.

14. Cf. Schmaus, *op. cit.,* 458; Petau, *De Incarnatione,* 11, 9.

15. Schmaus, *op. cit.,* 459.

16. Cf. Lecuyer, *op. cit.,* pp. 191ff; *CV,* v. 3, p. iv, pp. 225–243 for the emendated text presented to the plenary session in October 1964; pp. 244–272 presents the oral responses to this schema.

17. Cf. Lecuyer, *op. cit.,* p. 200. Paul VI informed the bishops: "Public

debate is not opportune on this subject which is so important and which demands such profound prudence." Bishops who wished to convey their concerns on this matter were advised to do so and submit them directly to the pope. The papal intervention was applauded by the bishops.

18. Wulf, *op. cit.*, p. 214.

19. The translation is from Kloppenburg, *op. cit.*, p. 268. Cf. *CV*, v. 4, p. vii, p. 107. The wording is clear: the decree does not utilize the "definitio scholastica" on priesthood. Unless this change is fully appreciated, the teaching of Vatican II on the theology of the priesthood cannot be understood.

20. Schmaus, *op. cit.*, 457–458.

21. Kloppenburg, *op. cit.*, p. 19.

22. *Ibid.*, p. 21.

23. Wulf, *op. cit.*, p. 220.

24. Kloppenburg, *op. cit.*, p. 263.

25. *Ibid.*, pp. 263–264. What is valuable about Kloppenburg's approach, not only in this section but throughout his volume, is his systematic cataloguing of Vatican II statements. The amassing of statements leaves no doubt about the position of Vatican II on such issues as this one.

26. F. Klostermann, "Dogmatic Constitution on the Church," *Commentary on the Documents of Vatican II*, v. 1, p. 241.

27. *Ibid.*, p. 240.

28. Ibid. This emphasis on the mission and ministry of the baptized *qua* baptized in the evangelization of the world raises the entire issue of the "political" dimension of the Christian call. Lay participation in the political arena is encouraged precisely because of this theological, baptismal base. Since a cleric also has this mission and ministry from his baptism as well, it is difficult to see how such involvement is curtailed by ordination.

29. The statement in art. 2 of the decree must be considered not only in view of the context of the decree, but also in view of the conciliar background. Cf. the statement of Marty referred to in footnote 19.

30. Wulf, *op. cit.*, p. 224.

31. This is a summation of Wulf's four points, listed *op. cit.*, pp. 224–225.

32. F. Sola, "De Sacramentis vitae socialis christianae seu de Sacramentis Ordinis et Matrimonii," *Sacrae Theologiae Summa* (Madrid: BAC, 1962) v. 4, p. 599.

33. Wulf, *op. cit.*, p. 224.

34. G. Philips, *op. cit.*, p. 116.

35. J.-P. Torrell, *La Théologie de l'Episcopat au Premier Concile du Vatican* (Paris: Les Éditions du Cerf, 1961) pp. 135–160.

36. Philips, *op. cit.*, p. 129.

37. Cf. Wulf, *op. cit.,* pp. 233–236; K. Rahner, "The Dogmatic Constitution on the Church," *Commentary on the Documents of Vatican II,* pp. 188–195.

38. Kloppenburg, *op. cit.,* p. 222.

39. *Ibid.,* pp. 222–223. In this section of his book, Kloppenburg cites in full passage after passage from the documents of Vatican II regarding the mission and ministry of a bishop. He clearly concludes that there is a "new conception" of a bishop; cf. pp. 224–225 for the citations. At issue, of course, is the relationship between the power of the pope and the power of bishops.

40. Cf. Rahner, *op. cit.,* p. 193.

41. By October 30, 1963, the bishops at Vatican II had decided to teach that episcopacy was part of the sacrament of order; in elucidating what this meant, the threefold office structure was used. It is clear, then, that Vatican II taught that by ordination (not by any delegation) a bishop has from Christ himself the *tria munera:* teaching, sanctifying and leading.

42. J. Dearden, "Universality and Collegiality," *The Ministry of Bishops: Papers from the Collegeville Assembly* (Washington, D.C.: NCCB, 1982) p. 8.

43. Cf. Wulf, *op. cit.,* pp. 233ff; cf. Kloppenburg, *op. cit.,* pp. 276ff. In the discussion held in the forty-third general meeting (October 1963 onward) the bishops debated this issue; some held that the bishops shared their power with the presbyters, while others maintained that the presbyteral power came from ordination itself. The second position was adopted by the council, so that it was even said in the clarifying remarks that "the sole source of presbyteral priesthood is located in the priesthood of Christ." Cf. Kloppenburg, p. 277.

44. Kloppenburg, *op. cit.,* p. 276.

45. *Ibid.*

46. H. Crouzel, "The Ministry in the Church: Reflections on a Recent Publication," *The Clergy Review* v. 68, n. 5, May 1983, p. 166.

47. Wulf, *op. cit.,* p. 267.

48. It is well known that a minority of bishops at Vatican II wanted to retain the scholastic definition of priesthood. Their desire was rejected; nonetheless, from time to time, some indications of this scholastic definition perdure. However, the few times this occurs in no way offsets the overwhelming use of the new definition of priesthood, based on the threefold structure of Christ's own mission and ministry. Wulf's interpretation, *op. cit.,* p. 271, is that the eucharistic service of the priest is merely the most important in the priestly role of sanctifier, which does not indicate that it is overall the most important role of the total priestly activity.

49. *The Decree of the Ministry and Life of Priests* indicates very clearly

that celibacy is not an essential element of priestly life: "It is true it [celibacy] is not demanded of the priesthood by its nature" ("non exigitur quidem a sacerdotio suapte natura, uti apparet ex praxi Ecclesiae primaevae et ex traditione Ecclesiarum orientalium") (n. 16). This passage is cited by Paul VI in his encyclical (n. 17). This non-essential relationship constitutes the basis for any and all discussion on the meaning and value of priestly celibacy. If this is not understood as the beginning of the entire dialogue, then the arguments put forward for priestly celibacy often begin to take on the intent of "proving" an essential relationship, which is theologically false.

12. Christian Ministry in an Ecumenical Perspective

1. W. de Vries, "Die Enstehung der Patriarchate des Ostens und ihr Verhaltnis zur papstlichen Vollgewalt," *Scholastik,* v. 37 (1962) p. 359.

2. *Called to Full Unity* (Washington, D.C.: USCC, 1986).

3. *Ibid.,* pp. 187–213.

4. *Ibid.,* pp. 243–253.

5. *Ibid.,* p. 249.

6. *Ibid.,* p. 252.

7. Cf. K. Osborne, "Ecumenical Eucharist," *op. cit.,* pp. 598–619.

8. Cf. *Southwestern Journal of Theology,* v. 28 (1986) n. 2; the entire issue resumes the dialogical statements on the topic of grace.

9. S. Butler, ed., *Women in the Church* (Mahwah, N.J.: The Catholic Theological Society of America, 1978).

10. *Ibid.,* p. 17.

Index of Authors

Biblical authors are not included.
A few anonymous authors are cited by volume, e.g., *Didache.*